I0763594

Forget Me Not

Series in Victorian Studies

JOSEPH MCLAUGHLIN, SERIES EDITOR

Katherine D. Harris, *Forget Me Not: The Rise of the British Literary Annual, 1823–1835*

Rebecca Rainof, *Fictions of Maturity: Plot, Purgatory, and the Victorian Novel of Adulthood*

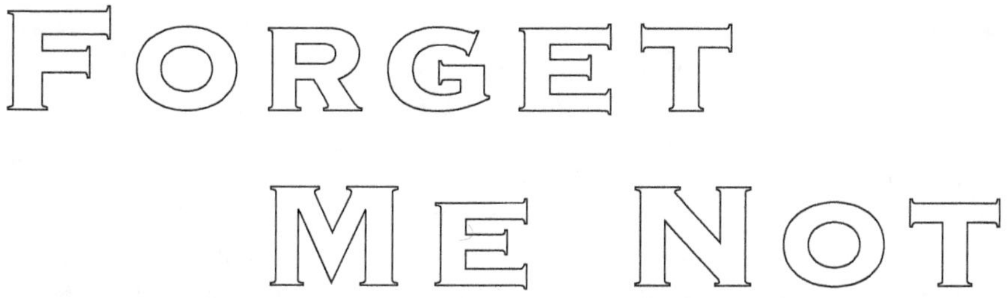

Forget Me Not

The Rise of the British Literary Annual, 1823–1835

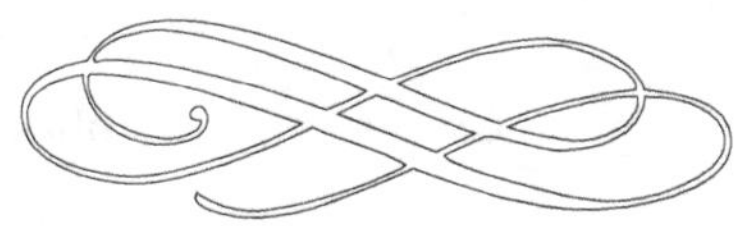

KATHERINE D. HARRIS

Ohio University Press Athens

Ohio University Press, Athens, Ohio 45701
ohioswallow.com
© 2015 by Ohio University Press
All rights reserved

To obtain permission to quote, reprint, or otherwise reproduce or distribute material from Ohio University Press publications, please contact our rights and permissions department at (740) 593-1154 or (740) 593-4536 (fax).

Printed in the United States of America
Ohio University Press books are printed on acid-free paper ∞ ™
25 24 23 22 21 20 19 18 17 16 15 5 4 3 2 1

Library of Congress Cataloging-in-Publication Data

Harris, Katherine D.
Forget me not : the rise of the British literary annual, 1823–1835 / Katherine D. Harris.
pages cm. — (Series in Victorian studies)
Includes bibliographical references and index.
ISBN 978-0-8214-2136-9 (hardback) — ISBN 978-0-8214-4520-4 (pdf)
1. English literature—19th century. 2. Gift books—Great Britain. 3. Femininity in literature. 4. Art, Victorian. 5. Women and literature—England—History—19th century. I. Title. II. Title: Rise of the British literary annual, 1823–1835.
PR1143.H27 2015
820.8'007—dc23

2015001037

CONTENTS

ILLUSTRATIONS

FIGURES

TABLES

Acknowledgments

After discovering a fascinating footnote on the origin of some Romantic-era women's poems, I became ensconced in a search for this text called a literary annual. Then–New York University faculty member Carolyn Dever introduced me to Marvin Taylor, of Fales Library at New York University, who allowed me to handle Fales's collection of a dozen literary annuals, including the rare 1829 *Friendship's Offering*. They were fascinating and exactly what every graduate student desires: something undiscovered! At a later point, David Greetham, of the Graduate Center of the City University of New York, gave me the freedom to turn my small collection of literary annuals into a nascent digital archive with the proviso that the project adopt the strict protocols of a scholarly edition. The Wertheim Study at the New York Public Library Central Research branch, now renamed the Schwarzman Building, offered a quiet space to inspect the NYPL's disparate collection of literary annuals in the general research collection during my years at the Graduate Center. Elizabeth Denlinger, curator of the Carl H. Pforzheimer Collection of Shelley and His Circle, allowed me to inspect my first paperbound *Forget Me Not* literary annual volumes and then engaged me in invigorating conversations about the material artifact and rare book libraries. David Greetham continued to encourage my explorations into the history of literary annuals and has never wavered in his support of my work.

Since the day I began this project, both the digital and the traditional version, Paula Feldman has offered guidance and advice about the study of literary annuals. Marilyn Gaull taught me how to write literary history just before she pushed me to study at the Graduate Center with David Greetham. A variety of faculty, including Gerhard Joseph, Patricia Clough, Anne Humphreys, Rachel Brownstein, and John Bowen (from the Dickens Universe), all inspired me to investigate the "so what" of these little books.

Susan Wolfson, who led the seminar "Figures on the Margin: The Language of Gender in British Romanticism" for the Summer Seminar in Literary and Cultural Studies at West Virginia University in June 2003, provided a larger historical context to Romantic-era women poets and became an example and mentor for pushing the boundaries of literary criticism. Laura Mandell, Margaret Linley, and Martha Nell Smith have offered valuable advice throughout the years after generously reading through early versions of many chapters.

The New Scholars award from the Bibliographical Society of America offered an early opportunity for me to give a talk at the annual meeting and then have a very lengthy version of the talk published in *Papers of the Bibliographical Society of America,* an article that launched my career. I offer many thanks to the Digital Humanists and Alan Liu at the First Annual Nebraska Digital Workshop, Center for Digital Research in the Humanities, University of Nebraska–Lincoln, September 2006 for helping to shape the digital side of this project, the Forget Me Not Hypertextual Archive. For my first of several trips to London, my thanks go to the Bibliographical Society (England) Research Grant, which funded further research at the British Library and other surrounding London archives in 2007. The Scholarship for Tuition to the University of Virginia's Rare Book School to take the seminar "The Printed Book in the West since 1800," held at the Grolier Club in New York City in January 2008, provided the opportunity to enhance my understanding of the evolution of printed works.

My deepest gratitude is extended to Stephen Behrendt, who invited me to the National Endowment for the Humanities Summer Seminar "The Aesthetics of British Romanticism, Then and Today" in 2010 to work alongside a stellar group of Romantic-era scholars, especially Mercy Cannon, Soledad Caballero, and Kathleen Beres Rogers, all of whom (including Steve) read several drafts of the same chapters simultaneously and repeatedly and restored my faith in this project, academic publishing, and colleagues. Thank you to the many intrepid research assistants who helped along the way: Amy Leonard, Robyn McCreight, Maria Judnick, Jennifer Cairns, and Hai Nguyen. Their curiosity about the project sparked many interesting conversations. To the Society for Textual Scholarship and the Society for the History of Authorship, Reading, and Publishing, great thanks are owed for the willing and gleeful exchanges about all things bibliographic and textual at many of their annual conferences—often the only conferences where my interests converged in an incredibly fruitful and exciting series of meetings. Wayne Storey offered guidance and urged me to complete the project, to get it out there—a sentiment echoed by Matt Kirschenbaum, who once told me that if the book was running long, footnote everything. Lorraine Kooistra's interesting work on the Victorian side of literary annuals provided the impetus for soliciting Ohio University Press to publish this manuscript. Thank you to San Jose State University and the Department of English and Comparative Literature for the semester-long sabbatical in early 2012 for one last trip to the British Library and the time to clean up the manuscript before submission, as well as the award of several internal grants to work on parts of this project from 2006 through 2009. During that sabbatical, audiences at the University of Victoria, University of Birmingham, and King's College offered intriguing perspectives on various aspects of this project. Conference attendees at the Studies in Gothic Fiction conference during this same sabbatical encouraged the pursuit of the Gothic theme in literary annuals. Thank you to Ray Siemens, James Mussell, Willard McCarty, and Franz Potter for those invitations.

Thank you to those who have buoyed me since the beginning, from thoughtful e-mails on focusing chapters to clapping in celebration after a talk: Kathi Inman Berens, Jamie Skye Bianco, Roberto Herrera, Jeff Drouin, and Steve Ramsay. Heather, Dave, and Ogden have watched over my soul all these years, even from across the country. Tom Davis, a Silicon Valley original, is to thank for the gorgeous photos of these little books and has more than once collaborated on projects from interesting literary reads to blog posts on algorithms. An unlikely source of inspiration comes from my running and cycling partners, who demonstrate resilience, patience, generosity, and luminescence.

I saved writing the acknowledgments until the very last moment and then wrote a lengthy draft thanking everyone for the past fifteen years of support. Somewhat anxious that I had left out some grant sponsor or archive, I erased the entire document. In the end, there is truly only one person to thank for this long-overdue but incredibly satisfying submission:

Thank you, David Greetham

The concluding discussion about Gothic short stories in the annuals appeared as an earlier version in *The Forgotten Gothic: Short Stories from*

British Literary Annuals, 1823–1831 (xvi–xxxvii), a print edition of nineteenth-century Gothic short stories that includes a critical introduction on the impact of 1820s British literary annual and Gothicism and relevant appendixes (Zittaw Press, 2012). An earlier version of the biography of Rudolph Ackermann appeared in *The Encyclopedia of Romantic Literature,* edited by Frederick Burwick, Nancy M. Goslee, and Diane Long Hoeveler (Blackwell Publishers, 2012). Chapter 2 is a revised version of the article "Borrowing, Altering and Perfecting the Literary Annual Form—or What It Is Not: Emblems, Almanacs, Pocket-Books, Albums, Scrapbooks and Gifts Books," *Poetess Archive Journal* 1, no. 1 (2007). Chapter 7 appeared as an earlier version in the article "Feminizing the Textual Body: Women and Their Literary Annuals in Nineteenth-Century Britain," *Papers of the Bibliographical Society of America* 99, no. 4 (December 2005): 573–622.

INTRODUCTION

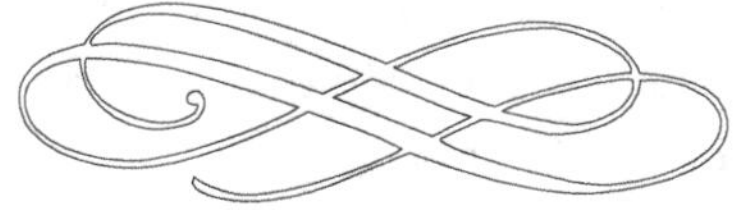

The Sociology of the Literary Annual

"The Annuals," wrote Southey in 1828, "are now the only books bought for presents to young ladies, in which way poems formerly had their chief vent." And the young ladies found them much more to their liking than the manuals of conduct.

—Anne Renier, *Friendship's Offering*[1]

WITH THE RISE OF THE MIDDLE CLASS, THE IMPOSITION of the Industrial Revolution, and the voluminous production of reading materials, early nineteenth-century England was drowning in a literary legacy that had become muddied with scribblers and poetasters. But the economy relied on consumption of this literary legacy. In fact, the publishing industry had become so powerful that the collapse of over-ambitious, check-writing publishers in 1826 caused the scandalous ruin of reputable publishers, printers, booksellers, and authors and influenced the export of Englishness. The literary annual—with its poetry, short stories, dramatic scenes, sheet music, travel accounts, political statements, historical renderings, classical references, descriptions of Europe, war accounts, art-work, portraits, lavish bindings, and bevy of famous authors—introduced a literary and visual genre that would be both scorned and embraced by England and beyond. Literary annuals are early nineteenth-century British texts published yearly in England from 1822 to 1860, intended primarily for a middle-class audience and therefore moderately priced (between twelve shillings and three pounds). Initially published in duodecimo or octavo sizes, the decoratively bound volumes exuded a feminine delicacy that attracted a primarily female readership that participated in the production and evolution of the Poetess Tradition.[2]

The Poetess Tradition was originally defined in 1820s England with the publication of Alexander Dyce's *Specimens of British Poetesses* (1825) to represent poetry written by women and published in the popular press. Laura Mandell, Anne Mellor, Virginia Jackson, and Yopie Prins eschew this essentialist idea that femininity, and therefore bad poetry, was the result of biological determinism. Instead, as Paula Feldman, Susan Wolfson, and Stuart Curran have argued, the Poetess Tradition resulted from a newly formed aesthetic that catered to the mass forms of media. Rather than representing a lesser form of poetry, the Poetess Tradition altered the cultural value of poetry in a time when most literary historians posit that none of the canonical authors were producing anything of much quality.

Lorraine Janzen Kooistra, in a more recent study of the literary aesthetics of gift book poetry, focuses on women poets and the development or furthering of the poetess aesthetic as it was explicitly demarcated by the poetry and careers of Eliza Cook, Adelaide Anne Procter, and Jean Ingelow. Though Kooistra does not identify the Poetess Tradition, it is apparent in her description of the poetry, especially in relation to Laura Mandell's and Yopie Prins's work on the poetess: "Although individually distinct in style, their poetry tended to be narrative in nature, direct in expression, musical in appeal, and affective or sentimental in content, dilating on losses familiar to all. . . . They also celebrated the resilience of the human spirit; the various joys of domestic work and social life; the love of everyday objects and animals; and the beauty of nature" (131).

Portraits of women, bucolic scenes, and nationally recognizable paintings were converted to steel-plate engravings and included in these portable, hardbound volumes. With a liberal reinterpretation of artwork and reliance on ekphrastic poetry, the annuals continued the tradition of a mixed-media form that is reminiscent of fifteenth-century emblems. During the first decade of success, the literary annuals with their gilt edges and silk covers became valuable tokens of love or friendship and were consigned to the drawing room.

Generally, eighty to one hundred entries of prose and poetry were compiled for each annual, with over fifty different authors included in any one volume. Well-published but "minor" poets (both men and women) earned a comfortable income by contributing to literary annuals. Even members of the Romantic and Victorian British literati were coaxed into contributing by lucrative financial remuneration, including William Wordsworth,[3] Samuel T. Coleridge, Mary Shelley, Walter Scott,[4] Robert Southey, Alfred Lord Tennyson, John Ruskin, Elizabeth Barrett Browning, Robert Browning, and William Thackeray. Lord Byron's and Percy Bysshe Shelley's writings were wildly successful in the annuals, though published posthumously (see appendix B). Sir Walter Scott was paid five hundred pounds for two contributions to the 1829 *Keepsake*. More commonly, well-known authors were paid fifty pounds for a forty-line poem. Popular women poets, including Felicia Hemans and Letitia Elizabeth Landon, were in demand for their domestic and sentimental contributions to annuals and were officially, yet begrudgingly, accepted into the professionalized world of authorship despite their poetess poetry.

Rudolph Ackermann introduced the literary annual to the British public in November 1822 with the publication of the 1823 *Forget Me Not*, a title continued well past Ackermann's lifetime by Frederic Shoberl until 1847. This popular and successful experiment in literary miscellany, described as an "epidemic" of literary annual titles by one reviewer, began a trend that would rise to an all-time high in 1828 with 100,000 copies of fifteen separate annuals earning an aggregate retail value of over £70,000, *Forget Me Not, The Literary Souvenir, Friendship's Offering, The Keepsake*, and *The Comic Annual* the leaders among them, both in technological innovations and in literary quality (see appendix C). By November 1829, the number had climbed to forty-three separate titles published in Britain alone (see appendix A). Inspired by the sentiment to be remembered, other annuals requested memorializing (*Remember Me*), suggested gift giving (*Friendship's Offering*), recommended domestic archiving (*The Keepsake*), or paid homage to femininity (*Hommage aux Dames*).

By 1831, even men had become targets with the publication of *A Father's Present to His Son* and, later, the *Young Gentleman's Annual*. Literary annuals fed a popular frenzy that drove authors, publishers, and editors alike. Not until 1840 did the number of titles fall below forty, lingering in derivative forms until the early twentieth century in both the United States and Europe. Annuals were not forgotten, though; they appear in British and American nineteenth-century novels alike, among them George Eliot's

1872 *Middlemarch* (set in 1820s England), Mark Twain's *Adventures of Huckleberry Finn* (set in 1830s America), and William Thackeray's 1847 *Vanity Fair.*

Though the history of literary annuals becomes convoluted with gift books, Christmas books, and poetry volumes, the first ten years offer insight into the phenomenal rise of a popular genre, its bibliographic genesis from other literary forms, its attempted social control of women, and its redefinition of the feminine. Within the first decade of the annual's success, male editors, authors, and publishers presented readers with an idealized femininity that approximated the propriety, education, and social instruction offered by earlier and more narrowly didactic conduct manuals. However, readers and consumers of the annual privileged its feminine aspects—not those promoted as such by patriarchal annual producers but those aspects that were best suited to female writers and readers.

SOCIOLOGY OF THE LITERARY ANNUAL

> Forget Me Not!—how universal and how deep-rooted the feeling which this name expresses! In every corner of the world, at last wherever the dwelling of civilized man is to be found, this sentiment has a home. . . .
>
> From the commencement of this work, it has been my ambition to make its tendency correspond with its expressive title, to procure for it an intrinsic merit that may preserve it from being forgotten, and to exclude from its pages whatever is unworthy of being remembered.
>
> —Preface, Frederic Shoberl, editor, 1844 *Forget Me Not*

> [T]he Proprietor is induced to hope that his book will not be a mere fleeting production, to *die* with the season of its birth, but *live,* a reputed and standard work in every well-selected library.
>
> —Preface, Frederic Mansel Reynolds, editor, 1829 *The Keepsake*

These editors created literary materials that invited readers to enjoy moments of visual and literary stimulation. Entire volumes were devoted to decadent markings and creating a valuable object to be treasured in multiple instantiations of family gatherings. Reading an annual, according to these editors, imbues the audience with a sense of culture. With each passing generation of ownership, the annuals gain and remake meaning from both their contents and their materiality. Editors of the annuals were not haphazard in the visual and aesthetic beauty of their work. Instead, they offered the literary annuals as a living moment. For this reason, my study of these early annuals analyzes annuals through multiple lenses concerning textuality and the sociology of the text.

My arguments align with Jerome McGann in his *Critique of Modern Textual Criticism,* in which he defines a "work" as a series of specific "texts," a series of specific acts of production, and the entire process that both of these series constitute. The "text" is a component in the production of a "work." This distinction and debate highlight the sociological aspects of producing writing and places responsibility for production beyond the singular author's creative imagination, that is, beyond the traditional or ideal Romantic-era author's creative genius.[5] A work gains meaning not only from its reader but also from the multiple levels of meaning involved in every mode of physical and creative production, and then again from each consumer's or reader's individual engagement with the work and its collective memory—in essence, palimpsest-like traces similar to Freud's mystic writing pad.

In "A Note upon the 'Mystic Writing Pad,'" Freud describes memories as permanent traces of an original act. To avoid distorting that memory, people use writing as a mnemonic apparatus, a simulated memory. Freud points out that memories lose their importance over time and are occasionally jettisoned from the perceptual apparatus of the mind, meaning that we voluntarily forget. The physical manifestation of a memory through writing allows us to replicate the mind's attempt to preserve original acts. However, the simultaneous permanence of writing and the limitation of the medium (such as a sheet of paper) do not allow us to forget. Conversely, if written upon a chalkboard, which is ephemeral, the memory will become completely lost upon erasing the chalkboard. Freud is searching for a model that allows "an unlimited receptive capacity for new perceptions and [an apparatus that] lays down permanent—even though not unalterable—memory-traces of them" (176). He finds a model to proximate memory in a child's toy, the "Mystic Writing Pad": "an ever-ready receptive surface and permanent traces of notes that have been made upon it" (177). Emotion, creativity, and humanity are expressed through written language and deposited as symbolic codes on a sheet. When that sheet is lifted, the writing disappears, much like the child's toy. Though the markings—the visual manifestation of language and all its symbolic content—have been erased, the impression or indentation of the writing remains. More writing is then composed on the same sheet, entangling what was written and its impressions with what is being written and its symbolic meaning.

The mystic writing pad represents symbolic negotiation between impression and expression, in much the same way that memory and life coexist in a book. This relationship allows a work to contain a memory of its original birth, including authorship, creative imagination, literary value, printing, binding, selling, material value, readers, ownership—everything in its contemporary performance. Unlike the mystic writing pad, a book consists of not only writing but also relationships necessary to the creation and survival of the book itself, a community of influences that continues to acquire meaning. Each entity that imbues meaning is like a permanent trace on the writing pad but is not necessarily used. Freud points out that "it is enough that they are present" (179). In another sense, each literary work is an event rather than an object, according to McGann.[6]

Before we proceed further into discussions about textuality, the differences among *codex, book, text,* and *work* need to be defined to highlight this intersection between material object and culture. *Codex* is an exact (scientific) bibliographic term used to describe a format for organizing written material. Essentially, the codex is a bound and stitched form of the "book," which became the standard book format that we know today. Before the invention of the codex, written material was produced on rolls or single sheets (usually made from papyrus)[7]—a medium that allowed writing only on one side. With this limited space for use, the numbers of sheets and/or rolls became cumbersome to store and preserve because dedicated space was required for each roll. For reference purposes, this medium proves impossible to cite from because long written records span many sheets and lack paragraph references. The practice of stitching (essentially binding) parchment or papyrus into one cohesive container that was flat with an articulated seam essentially bound information into a singular referential source that was easy to access. The codex became common practice by the third century and, though it has evolved, remains the preferred format today—a testament to the practicality of this form. Accordingly, I use the term *codex* to describe physical form.

The second term, *book,* refers to a manuscript or printed record "issued as an individual unit between its own covers" (as defined by John

Carter in *ABC for Book Collectors,* 48). The term *codex* actually refers to the stitched form. The term *book,* however, refers to the form and function of the information contained within. According to David Greetham, a "book" can "refer to almost any portable material with handwriting on it: metal, stone, wax, clay, potsherds, or official articles like coins and seals" (*Textual Scholarship,* 47). However, here, I refer to a "book" as a literary object in codex format.[8]

The book contains both "bibliographic codes" and "linguistic codes." The *bibliographic code* is distinguished from the content or the semantic construction of language within a text (linguistic code) by the following elements, as George Bornstein describes: "[F]eatures of a page layout, book design, ink and paper, and typeface . . . publisher, print run, price or audience. . . . [Bibliographic codes] might also include the other contents of the book or periodical in which the work appears, as well as prefaces, notes, or dedications that affect the reception and interpretation of the work" (30, 31). *Linguistic codes* are specifically the words. Also within the book are paratextual elements that do not necessarily fall under the bibliographic or linguistic codes. In *Paratexts,* Gerard Genette defines these as extraneous "liminal devices and conventions, both within and outside the book, that form the complex mediation between book, author, publisher and reader" (i). Paratexts are not generally the linguistic codes embedded within a work but constitute title pages, dedications, inscriptions, adverts, forewords, and so on that implicate "a book's private and public history" (i).[9]

To integrate the physical description of a book with its sociological meaning, I turn to an integrated theoretical stance of bibliography (the science of books) and textual criticism (the theory of books). I meld bibliography with textual criticism to account for the variables that created the literary annuals' phenomenal, yet ephemeral, place in both literary history and social memory/history—for neither discipline fully accounts for the success of the book and its "cultural capital."

Bibliography, "the discipline that studies texts as recorded forms, and the processes of their transmission, including their production and reception" (McKenzie, 12), attempts to logically order the information presented by the actual material book form. The literary annual, with its specific visual presentation, requires a scientific evaluation of its form using the elements of bibliography. However, a study of the codex itself will not render an adequate living history of the literary annual genre; its "textuality" must also be studied. In *Theories of the Text,* Greetham offers a definition of textuality that integrates economic, psychological, and political theoretical styles with literary criticism:

> It is, on the one hand, a place of fixed, determinable, concrete signs, a material artefact, and yet, on the other, an ineffable location of immaterial concepts, not dependent at all on performance transmission. It is, on the one hand, a weighty authority with direct access to originary meaning, and, on the other, a slowly accumulating, socially derived series of meanings, each at war with the other for prominence and acceptance. It is a place inhabited only by a sole, creative author who unwillingly releases control to social transmission, and it is also a place constructed wholly out of social negotiations over transmission and reception. (63)

Studying the social, cultural, economic, theoretical, and physical elements of a text/work necessitates, according to D. F. McKenzie in *Bibliography and the Sociology of Texts,* showing "that forms effect meanings" (13). This methodology insists that the content of any given literary work is influenced by its packaging. In addition, the theoretical apparatus allows "us to describe not only the technical but [also] the social processes of [a literary work's] transmission. . . . [I]t accounts for non-book texts, their physical forms, textual versions, technical transmission, institutional control, their perceived meanings, and social effects. It accounts for a history of the book and, indeed, of all printed forms including all textual ephemera as a record of cultural change, whether in mass civilization or [in] minority culture" (McKenzie, 13). McKenzie refers to a "sociology of the texts," which discards bibliography's restrictive scientific study of the book—a study that "worked only from the physical evidence of books themselves" (15). Instead, McKenzie works from "textual criticism," which is concerned with "getting the right words in the right order; on the semiotics of print and the role of typography in forming meaning; on the critical theories of authorial intention and reader response; on the relation between the past meanings and present uses of verbal texts. It offers an illustration of the transmission of texts as the creation of the new versions which form, in turn, the new books, the products of later printers, and the stuff of subsequent bibliographical control" (21).

Textual criticism considers the material object in conjunction with the creativity in its production. Accordingly, institutions as well as individuals create meaning in forms and create forms from meaning. Neither the reader nor the publisher is solely responsible for textuality; nor is the author the sole agent in creative production. Robert Darnton visualizes the sociology of the text in his "Communications Circuit" diagram (68), which highlights the institutions involved in textual exchange. With each individual and each institution, the text/work accumulates information, communications, and meanings. Darnton diagrams that flow as unidirectional, which is not necessarily the case with textuality. Deirdre Phelps points out that Darnton's model does not contain the most important element, the book itself, and cannot account for relationships between the object and the institutions: "Darnton's formulation does not account for the reader's response to the binding, which he or she will certainly always see, nor even to the binder as supplier (to whom the reader could presumably appeal for a different style of binding), but only to the binder as bookseller, theoretically allowing consideration of the reader's response to whether a book could or could not be bought from that binder but not whether it could be different in style" (84). She proposes, instead, using an "Interactive Socio-Textual Model," which can establish "a place for the interaction of the object and its parts with other agents" (76).

McKenzie proposes a system of evaluation that links all elements of a text's life and allows a work to remain "open" to new meanings instead of closed at the point of printing. Whereas bibliographers view a text (the writing produced by an author) as a closed object, denied further meaning, textual critics like McGann and Greetham allow the text to remain open to accumulate meaning—essentially becoming a "work" (form and content as these are defined and redefined in the processes of production, dissemination, reception, and reproduction). The work is a form of cultural and social meaning as well as a marker of cultural and political capital and social history/memory.

Because this system of evaluation calls for an open work that continues to provide meaning, the evaluations "are themselves contingent, and contingent upon their proponent's opportunity and ability to articulate and defend them, an opportunity derived directly from the social matrix in which the theories are embedded," as is pointed out by Greetham in *Theories of the Text* (402). Though the system of evaluation can be contaminated by the evaluator, this introduces new meaning to an already-layered work. The evaluator's commentary adds to the "archive."

The material object is traditionally defined as closed once it is produced. But I contend (and in this I am aligned with Jacques Derrida) that the textual object, the physical book, is also an archive of creation, memories, and moments—especially the literary annual, which was intended to represent memories. In *Archive Fever,* Derrida suggests that the moments of archivization are infinite throughout the life of the artifact: "The archivization produces as much as it records the event" (17). Archiving occurs at the moment that the previous representation is overwritten by a new "saved" document. Traces of the old document exist but cannot be differentiated from the new. At the moment an archivist sits down to actively preserve and store and catalogue the objects, the archiving is once again contaminated with a process. This, according to Derrida, "produces more archive, and that is why the archive is never closed. It opens out of the future" (68). Literary works become archives not only in their bibliographic and linguistic codes but also in their social interactions yet to occur. The reengagement with the work is what adds to an archive and continues the archiving itself beyond the physical object.[10]

For instance, the narrator of *Middlemarch* creates a conflated temporal moment with the gift-giving scene between Ned Plymdale and Rosamund Vincy. The "publication which marked modern progress *at that time*" (emphasis added) differentiates the narratorial moment (mid-Victorian era) from the moment of the literary annuals' popularity (late-Romantic era before the ascension of Queen Victoria). George Eliot refers to the literary annual *The Keepsake* in her 1871 novel, fifteen years after the popularity of the genre had completely disintegrated. Eliot recapitulates the history of the reception of annuals as well as the conflicting desires surrounding their popularity. The conversation among Plymdale, Rosamund, and Lydgate reflects the importance of consumer exchange in the form of gift giving and the material object's (the annual's) importance in the negotiation between popular and intellectual culture. Eliot thought the exchange important enough to include in her historically based novel and uses the instance to demonstrate a piece of culture as well as to assign humanistic roles to her characters.

Plymdale, being "one of the good matches in Middlemarch, though not one of its leading minds" (263)—a critique not only of Ned Plymdale and Rosamund Vincy but also of the intellectual quality of his gift—follows the fashions closely. Plymdale is the nonintellectual fop because of his fascination with the annuals; Lydgate is the scientific man of self-professed high morals who disdains the sentimentality of *The Keepsake*'s contents; and Rosamund is the leisure-class woman who secretly cherishes the fashionable object but fears accusations of being influenced by fashion and popular culture.

The genre's detractor in the novel, Dr. Lydgate, represents social responsibility and critiques the genre as filled with "sugared inventions." However, he will eventually become a copperplated man—a caricature of his former self. The literary annuals, their contents, reception, success, and eventual ridicule represent the success and eventual failure of Lydgate's career and character. Eliot seems to tease her readers for desiring this sentimental piece of popular culture. However, Eliot's realism points to the annuals as a more complicated and perhaps genuine art form than early nineteenth-century critics recognized. With this scene in *Middlemarch,* Eliot records the distorted social memory of the annuals and comments on their essential role in the literary world, that is, she allows the annuals to reappear in a different social Victorian moment. Because of Eliot's reference and the narrator's temporal discernment, the meaning of the literary annual becomes conflated with its reappearance in fictional literature. The physical occurrence of the annual within the narration and its ideological representation in the Victorian-period novel adds to the genre's "textuality." The literary annual, as a work, is a marker of a particular nineteenth-century moment at the same time that it becomes written over with meaning from later cultural, social, and historical moments.

Indeed, across the ocean, American authors add to the ideological archive associated with the British literary annuals: Mark Twain lets Huck Finn fondle a copy of *Friendship's Offering* literally displayed on a coffee table along with *Pilgrim's Progress,* the family Bible, hymn books, and other politely religious, beautifully bound literature "piled up perfectly exact on each corner of the table" (104). Huck notes that the annual is full of "beautiful stuff and poetry" but does not read any of the poetry—a commentary on the initial superior quality of the engravings in American literary annuals versus their poetic contents. Published in 1884, *The Adventures of Huckleberry Finn* reflects the social and cultural temperature of the American 1830s, including a time rife with literary annual volumes, both British and American. The British-published *Friendship's Offering* enjoyed success in the United States, as did the later 1840s American-published *Friendship's*

Offering. Twain might be referring to either publication in his novel. However, American literary annuals moved away from the literary miscellany format to include political essays on temperance, slavery, women's rights, and so on, thinly veiled by the literary annual's binding.[11]

When all of these elements of textuality and the archive are considered in conjunction with the literary annual as a genre that bloomed as a result of early nineteenth-century popular culture, a study of the genre must conclude that neither the material object nor its literary contents are wholly responsible for its popularity and success. In fact, Jerome McGann emphasizes that we need to study the "object" and the concrete bibliographic codes that are rehistoricized with every generation. According to McGann, texts are not messengers of culture, which would indicate that they are merely channels of transmission (fixed and empty), but instead "represent—are in themselves—certain kinds of human acts" (*Textual Condition,* 4). McGann, here, moves away from the authority of the singular author and denies that the creative impulse is the sole initiator of the work. For McGann, that authorial creative imagination is merely a part of the entire sociological process of creating a work; the work is not rooted in the author, nor does it wither as soon as it is communicated (or written), as Percy Bysshe Shelley argues in "A Defense of Poetry": "[W]hen composition begins, inspiration is already on the decline, and the most glorious poetry that has ever been communicated to the world is probably a feeble shadow of the original conception of the poet" (504). By thinking about texts as organisms, McGann intertwines textuality with the human condition: "Both the practice and the study of human culture comprise a network of symbolic exchanges. Because human beings are not angels, these exchanges always involve material negotiations. Even in their most complex and advanced forms—when the negotiations are carried out as textual events—the intercourse that is being human is materially executed: as spoken texts or scripted forms. To participate in these exchanges is to have entered what I wish to call here 'the textual condition'" (*Textual Condition,* 3).

Textuality is a holistic study of the codex, book, text, and work, which is not limited by bifurcating form from content, bibliographic code from linguistic code. The text/work is a body that is not exclusively bibliographic or linguistic, much like the physical, emotional, and mental form of a human being, and textuality is the social condition of various times, places, and persons. The entire "work" (that is, each literary annual) functions like a human body: each part contributes to the survival of the individual. If extremities are lost, the body, the person is altered. *The book itself is like this body.* For instance, the cover contributes to the sociocultural meaning of the content, in a similar fashion as the publisher or author.[12] Without the cover, the initial presentation of the work is altered, hence its meaning is re-constructed. And with the annuals, each volume is unique, much like a body, with each variant binding or owner's inscriptions.

Each "body" is influenced by several "literary institutions," roles that contribute to the production of texts/works: author, editor, illustrator, publisher, printer, and distributor. Each contributes to the meaning: "[L]iterary works are only material things to [the] degree that they are social projects which seek to adapt and modify themselves circumstantially"; "In cultural products like literary works the location of authority necessarily becomes dispersed beyond the author" (McGann, *Critique,* 102, 84). And each institution is influenced by its sociocultural surroundings—a process that allows a book to be a constantly evolving "work."

Editors and publishers of literary annuals consciously marketed their works as completed memories and thereby imbued the physical object with a humanity or intellect. With this in mind, we can see the literary annual as a particular form of transmissive interaction and not merely a channel of transmission (McGann, *Critique,* 3, 16). Even after printing and binding, each volume acquires meaning with each reader, reading, literary movement, critical reception, or resurrection. In each literary annual's preface, the editors state that they desired this type of longevity and encouraged constantly shifting meanings.

In the context of this study, the literary annual is not merely an object or an artifact. Instead, I move beyond the linguistic and bibliographic codes of annuals to consider the entire production of meaning caused by each literary annual, each interaction with a reader, each translation, each subsequent reinterpretation. As I discuss throughout these chapters, annuals were reinterpreted, translated, and revised so many times that they gathered meaning beyond what Ackermann intended in the original 1823 volume. For these reasons, venturing into the debate surrounding form and genre is inappropriate. The literary annual borrowed a certain physical format from European and historical influences, but the combination of contents and the physicality qualifies the literary annual as a genre. To equate the annual with a form is to ignore the richness of these volumes and their impact on literary history.

In his "Preface," editor Frederic Shoberl personifies the 1835 *Forget Me Not,* presenting a human body instead of a textual object:

> This year, Reader, the Forget Me Not presents itself to thee as "an old friend with a new face;" but, though somewhat altered in external appearance, its spirit remains unchanged. Thou wilt find that, though increased in size, and clothed in a different garb from that which it has been accustomed to wear, it is governed by the same earnest desire as ever to minister to thine amusement and information; to touch thy kindly sympathies and affections; and, while it conveys good-humoured reproof of the vices, the follies and the frailties of mankind, to encourage the higher and nobler feelings of our nature. Wouldst thou have stronger evidence of this than our assertion—turn to its pages. (3–4)

Shoberl portrays his latest volume as an intimate figure in a fragmented body. The public face is refreshing because of its amended presentation, but its clothing hides a body from public view and suggests an atmosphere of individuality, secrecy, and intimacy. This body, like a female body, is sequestered beneath appropriate coverings. However, the sentimental and moral guidance still exists underneath the improved clothing. For both the giver and the receiver of an annual, that guidance existed beyond the immediate fashionable experience of receiving a volume. A reader, drawing some new morsel of meaning with every reading, was expected to reengage with the work throughout her *and the annual's* lifetime.

REVISING THE ANNUAL'S CRITICAL TRADITION

> The Annuals created a *craze,* the craze denoted some *insanity* in the public mind of the period; and much of this insanity is apparent within the curious circle of prolific writers, from which the general contributions were obtained. . . .
>
> This Annual was ephemeral not because it was effeminate; but because it was *unequal,* with a bias towards the trivial. It was one

> of the "*cakes*" of literature, not the bread. And even cakes become distasteful, when they provide only two or three currants each, notwithstanding that the surface is liberally endowed with *sugar.*
>
> —Chas Tallent-Bateman, "The 'Forget Me Not'" (1902; emphasis added)

Despite their phenomenal popularity, literary annuals enjoyed little critical acclaim until very recently. In the late 1970s, literary scholars began to reassess the annuals, their literature, authors, and textual form in terms of a literary aesthetic that considers the annuals as an alternative representation of nineteenth-century culture. The annuals have been called "toy-books" (iv) by Andrew Boyle, an often-cited historian and indexer of British annual contributors, and the literature they contain has been dismissed as the "left-handed work of great authors" (Erickson, 31) and "the sweepings of their desks—the worst poems of the best authors" (Boyle, iv). In the past twenty years, however, scholars including Jerome McGann, Paula Feldman, Judith Thompson, Susan Wolfson, Morton Paley, Anne Mellor, Sonia Hofkosh, Judith Pascoe, Margaret Linley, Bill Bell, Kathryn Ledbetter, Harriet Jump Devine, Laura Mandell, and Ann Hawkins have ignored this narrow view and published more than seventy articles and book chapters that discuss the role of literary annuals in nineteenth-century literature and culture.

In an 1837 article for *Fraser's Magazine,* Thackeray anonymously lambasted the annuals, though the genre was still too close for him to adequately evaluate its use. *The Bookseller* published an article, "The Annuals of Former Days," in 1858 that signals the death, and hence historicity, of the annuals. 1902 brought Tallent-Bateman's misguided chronicle of the *Forget Me Not,* with Frederick Faxon's indispensable bibliographical index being published shortly thereafter, in 1912; both of these works signal a resistant acceptance of the genre.[13] In 1929, Frédéric Lachèvre indexed the French versions of annuals (1823–48) in *Bibliographie sommaire,* while in the United States, Ralph Thompson published a concise analysis of the antislavery American annual *The Liberty Bell* in 1934. Shortly thereafter, he introduced his bibliographical index of American annuals (complete with the table of contents from each volume) in 1936, which was republished in 1967 along with Andrew Boyle's index of British annual contributors, both publications coinciding with Earl Hutchison's *Journalism Quarterly* article, which questions the communicative effect of the literary annual. Prior to these, and because of surprising widespread interest in annuals, the publisher Cobden-Sanderson published and re-presented (in 1929, 1930, and 1931) three annuals based on the form, contents, and purpose of the original *Forget Me Not*. During the same general time period, Amy Cruse contemplated gendered space and literary annuals in her 1930 monograph, *The Englishman and His Books in the Early Nineteenth Century*. Bradford Booth's *Cabinet of Gems* appeared in 1938, dedicated to anthologizing contributions from nineteenth-century annuals. A. Bose's 1953 article, "The Verse of the English 'Annuals,'" bridges scholars who published their studies prior to the feminist liberation of literature and before the Thompson and Boyle indexes appeared. Anne Renier published her often-cited *Friendship's Offering: An Essay on the Annuals . . .* in 1964 and began a trend to produce illuminating examination of the annuals. Faxon's index of British contributors was reprinted in 1973, followed shortly by E. Bruce Kirkham and colleagues' index of American contributors, published in 1975.

Through the first half of the twentieth century, these contributions in the British annual's critical history mimicked the disdain expressed by the nineteenth-century British critical press. In the 1902 *Papers of the Manchester Literary Club* (quoted in the epigraph at the outset of this chapter), Charles Tallent-Bateman suggests, "The history of the 'Forget-me-Not' Annual has never been written," and he asks, "May I be her historian and commentator?" (78). He follows this earnest request with an immediate evaluation of the British annual's literary aesthetic: "My subject is not a section of 'high literature'" (78). The historicizing continues throughout the article, crediting Rudolph Ackermann with the overwhelming success of the first British-published literary annual and chronicling Ackermann's contributions to the genre. However, Tallent-Bateman spends much of the article critiquing the literary annuals, as quoted in the epigraph above, with domestic and diseased images—conflicting metaphors that associate this genre with nurturing and destruction.

In the 1973 reprint of Frederick W. Faxon's 1912 *Literary Annuals and Gift Books: A Bibliography,* Eleanore Jamieson and Ian Bain prefaced the volume by anticipating a renewed interest in literary annuals and gift books. They appended insightful and textually accurate studies of the annuals while retaining Faxon's original mixed assessment of the genre. This reprint supposedly signals a burgeoning scholarly interest in these early nineteenth-century British texts (5), which were deemed "nothing else but a craze" (84) by Tallent-Bateman. Faxon's editors suggest that the scholarly interest is tied to the antiquarian market for literary annuals, a suggestion that reflects Faxon's original motives: Faxon, interested in his father's library of annuals, began keeping a list of literary annuals and the various national library holdings. Out of interest for collectors, Faxon published his bibliography in 1912 shortly after several critical articles on the annuals appeared in print.

Other than these early scholarly inquiries prior to the reprint of Faxon's work, the annual lived in textual and literary obscurity until the 1970s, when scholarly interest emerged in earnest, though no complete monograph on the genre has ever been published. Studies of these works, their female audience, and women authors fell under the newly enfranchised women's studies discipline as recovery projects. Even within this developing scholarly field, most investigations and mentions of the annuals still centered on canonical male authors.

Current studies in publishing, book history, and annuals have elided the annual's significance. Lee Erickson, in *The Economy of Literary Form* (1996), proclaims that annuals were the downfall of poetic standards and the economic success of single-volume poetry: the genre provided a public space for the "left-handed work of great authors" and the not-so-Great Authors (31). The most cited historian of the annuals, Andrew Boyle, suggests that well-known authors "offered the sweepings of their desks—the worst poems of the best authors" and were ashamed of their involvement with the sentimental object (iv). Boyle calls the annuals saccharine "toy-books" and claims that their novelty relied on the steel-plate engravings (iv). In the monumental *Reading Nation in the Romantic Period,* William St. Clair dedicates only three pages (229–32) to annuals and makes a short mention in the appendix, contributing only what had routinely been circulated by Faxon and Boyle, without correcting any misconceptions. *Poetry, Pictures, and Popular Publishing* (2011), Lorraine Kooistra's ambitious study of illustrated gift books between 1855 and 1875, offers a starting point for understanding the overwhelming volume of these materials during the Victorian period. By working through poetry and illustrations using D. F. McKenzie's sociology of the text, Kooistra argues that "at the moment the text becomes embodied in form and enters the material world, the 'eye' of the reader replaces the 'I' of the poet, affirming the book's human uses and social destinations" (1). By invoking McKenzie, Gerard Genette, Jerome

McGann, George Bornstein, and others involved in bibliography, history of the book, and textual scholarship, Kooistra associates the importance of the reader with making meaning as it is disseminated in a particular work. She begins with 1855, asserting that the twenty years following that date represent the long 1860s of the "golden age of wood-engraved illustrations," the periodical press, and Christmas gift books (2).

Because the literary annual as a genre combines elements of various forms as well as solidifying another, the gift book, scholars and libraries have misnamed the annual, cataloging it inconsistently as "annual," "gift book," "gift-book," "gift books—19th Century," "miscellany," and "anthology," the keywords used by the New York Public Library for its 375 literary annuals. The University of South Carolina's extensive collection of over 300 British and American holdings is found only under "gift books" but is searchable by individual authors; the Library of Congress's American holdings similarly categorize annuals as "gift books," the same term that is applied to Miami University's collection of over 200 American and British annuals and Brown University's collection of over 400 British and American annuals. In contrast, the American Antiquarian Society's category is appropriately labeled "annuals." In England, the University of Liverpool's collection of 200 British volumes (searchable as "spec annuals") is rivaled only by the British Library's massive collection (searchable only by individual volume title). The University of Edinburgh has a moderate number of literary annual holdings, but the catalog is not organized with subject headings and is therefore searchable only by individual volume title. This frustrating and confusing dilemma will be difficult to rectify because the phrase *gift book* has been institutionalized, primarily by the Library of Congress's subject keyword. Creating a uniform category will not rectify the problem—too many institutions hold only partial runs of literary annual titles. Though scholarly interest in annuals fluctuates, many special collections curators still accept the prevailing attitude that literary annuals are second-rate literature and hence not valuable.

Microfilmed volumes, a single volume's facsimile, and two digital editions are the only resources for a scholar who seeks full-text runs of even the most popular titles. A selection of 20 British literary annual titles is currently available only in an expensive and incomplete, nonsearchable microfilm collection published by Chadwyck-Healey. Chadwyck-Healey provides no rationale for their selection of 20 British titles and 162 volumes and ignores the other 280 titles and 1,838 British volumes published between 1822 and 1860 (see Faxon, *Literary Annuals*). Kathryn Ledbetter and Terence Hoagwood began rectifying this access problem by publishing a digital annotated edition of the volume with *Romantic Circles,*[14] a project that briefly discusses the publishing and cultural impact of annuals but focuses more specifically on *The Keepsake.*[15] My digital archive of the *Forget Me Not* provides not only some full text but also a sense of each volume's physicality as well as the nineteenth-century reception. The full text of this archive has also been included in the Poetess Archive Database, which offers searchable TEI-encoded texts of the *Forget Me Not* volumes along with other nineteenth-century literary annuals and poetry. Zachary Leader and Ian Haywood edited a collection, titled *Romantic Period Writings, 1798–1832,* that includes some poems from literary annuals. In 2006, Paula Feldman published a print facsimile of *The Keepsake for 1829*. And in 2012, I published *The Forgotten Gothic,* an edited collection of Gothic short stories from the most popular early literary annuals. However, these are the annuals' only facsimile and full-text print representations.

Despite this resource deprivation, both British and American literary annuals have been mined for their poetry and their unique relationship to women readers. Judith Pascoe, one of the literary annual's excavators, suggested in "Poetry as Souvenir" that Mary Shelley's contributions to the 1831 *Keepsake* were not "aesthetically indifferent" (178), as is argued by Judith Pike; Shelley copied her *Keepsake* poem, "The Dirge," into a letter, "calling it 'the best thing [she] ever wrote'" (179), and identified the annuals as "suitable sites of publication" (180). Stephen Colclough proposed that John Clare used the annuals to create an authorial existence during a time in which "without access to these texts his work would not have been available to a national audience" (468).[16] So, too, Lord Tennyson's contributions to the annuals "provided much needed exposure to a burgeoning new middle-class readership which included a growing number of female readers" (Ledbetter, "BeGemmed," 236). Even James Hogg, the Ettrick Shepherd, acquired a devoted audience that gave him "the opportunity of extending his periodical range while taking his literary reputation to a wider audience" (Currie, 89). The Brontës, according to Christine Alexander, had access to the 1829 *Friendship's Offering,* 1830 *The Literary Souvenir,* and 1831 *Forget Me Not,* as is evidenced by "painstakingly executed copies of eight engravings . . . made by Charlotte, Branwell and Emily . . . from these three volumes" (414). Indeed, Christine Alexander finds indisputable similarities between the children's juvenilia and writings published in these annuals, especially with Sir Walter Scott's Gothic writings, and she notes that references and engravings that imitate these annuals' contents pop up in Charlotte Brontë's later novel, *Jane Eyre* (421).

Between 1825 and 1835, Hogg produced forty-five prose and poetry pieces for a variety of British annuals, including *Forget Me Not, Friendship's Offering,* and *The Literary Souvenir,* three of the genre's best sellers. *The Anniversary*'s editor, Allan Cunningham, gushed at Hogg's contributions: "Your poem is excellent—your tales capital. . . . I hardly think you ever wrote aught better than some of what you sent me" (quoted in Currie, 89). Nevertheless, none of these studies addresses the sociology, textuality, and literary history of the genre as a whole, most likely because access to the physical object is so limited.

Because literary annuals were sites of women's writing, they were largely dismissed as intellectually inferior, popular, sentimental publications during the nineteenth century. In the twentieth century, as is the fate of popular literature, the genre suffered a dismissal from literary studies primarily because the poetry was considered aesthetically inferior when compared to canonical Romantic and Victorian poets. In his 1953 article, A. Bose applauds the annuals for their range but criticizes them for their "sentimental piety" and the fact that they supposedly provided " 'relief with a pleasurable excitement, without any great expense of thought.' The stuff of their poetry is feeling, feeling that never presumes to well up from disturbing depths of the soul. They are just what the 'generality of men may read—the millions' " (40, 50). According to Bose, the range of contributions exists, but their "expression is in a minor key" (51). In the late twentieth century, Isobel Armstrong associated these women poets with heightened domesticity and claimed that they accepted and reflected "the dominant views concerning how, what and why a woman wrote" (quoted in Jump, 16). In fact, these authors, including Letitia Landon and Felicia Hemans, subvert this domesticity "to problematize both her own self-presentation and the conventional demands of readers" (Jump, 16).

Digital versions of some poetry, fiction, and essays from literary annuals are scattered among several digital archives, including Victorian Women Writers Project, the Internet Archive, The Poetess Archive Database, and several of the Networked Infrastructure for Nineteenth-Century

Electronic Scholarship (NINES) federated projects on both canonical and noncanonical authors. Of late, Digital Humanists have been employing data mining in addition to TEI markup to allow for a distant reading of nineteenth-century materials. However, we have yet to reach a critical mass of noncanonical materials that would permit us to sufficiently study the literary annuals and their contents. The latest digital editions of literary annuals, including my own, allow researchers to search and discover various relationships between and among literary annual authors that are otherwise lost to inadequate facsimiles or incomplete anthologies.[17]

For those interested in canonical male authors, the literary annuals offer an opportunity to study their interaction with popular culture and/or the female poetic voice: Tennyson's "St. Agnes," published in *The Keepsake* for 1837, treats the same topic as John Keats's "Eve of St. Agnes," published in 1820; an 1825 *Forget Me Not* poem has the same title as Wordsworth's partially published "Ruined Cottage" (1814); Maria Abdy's poem "The Aeolian Harp" (in the 1838 *Friendship's Offering*) treats a topic similar to that of Coleridge's "Æolian Harp" (composed in 1797 and published in many versions throughout Coleridge's life). However, Abdy's poem does not appear even in the newly institutionalized anthologies.

Scholarship in Romantic and Victorian women poets has propelled the publication of several anthologies that collect only the writings of women poets, usually organized by the poet's name or chronological order of birth. Many of these anthologies—including Duncan Wu's *Romantic Women Poets: An Anthology*—have been well received and institutionally adopted for courses. Susan J. Wolfson published a definitive volume of Felicia Hemans's poetry,[18] which, for the first time, includes explicit annotations pointing to literary annuals as the source of much of Hemans's work. Even with these important anthologies, scholars do not have an opportunity to witness the accompanying engravings, the ornate boards (covers), the gilt pages, or the surrounding texts.[19]

The British literary annual is a site of publication exploding with scholarly possibilities, some of which have been explored and many of which have not: thematic artwork (engravings of women, classical scenes, natural scenes, and violent destructive scenes, from oil paintings); various poetry; various prose (fiction and nonfiction); relationship of writing to engraving; editorial decisions (construction of tone in ordering the writing and engravings); political writings; comic writings; anonymous authors. When

I first envisioned this book project, it included chapters on the annual's authors from several vantage points, including the canonical author, the Romantic poet, the woman author/poet, and the relationship among and between these authors.[20]

I originally began my work on the annuals so long ago with the thought that the women authors were being dismissed because of their association with literary annuals. I wanted to save them, or at least bring them and their writing to the attention of other scholars, by addressing the anonymity of their names, authorizing the public name, the burden of woman, and literary fame and women authors outside the Romantic ideal. I briefly address some of these topics in the textuality and femininity chapter, but not to any devoted length. I wanted to ruminate on Wordsworth's "Ruined Cottage" (published only partially in 1814) as it compares to a poem included in an annual that deals with the same topic and was written by a woman. Wordsworth began composing his poem in 1797 and continued revising it throughout his lifetime. However, this poem, in its completed version, was never published. These interrelationships become important in discovering the literary relationships among works—much in the same way that Percy Bysshe Shelley's and Horace Smith's "Ozymandias" (1818) poems can be compared. Though published at the same time and with each author's knowledge of the other's poem, only one poem made it into our canon. The other can be obtained only through an online source or from Smith's collected works, now out of print.

Working on the annuals has sparked many other debates surrounding institutionalization, authentication, and canonization of their contributors. The phrase *literary canon* has become the subject of numerous books, talks, and conferences in recent years, especially with respect to women's poetry of the long nineteenth century. Should we consider works by women solely based on gender? Or should we consider these works by an aesthetic valuation? Both questions create more questions than answers. For instance, does eliding gender difference discriminate against poetry written by women or enhance it?

Canonization or anthologizing women's poetry from the nineteenth century may also perform the same aesthetic discrimination against men, solely based on gender. Grouping poetry based on gender would seem to still marginalize that poetry, extracting it from the standard "canonical" texts because the aesthetic valuation is rigidly based on a patriarchal value system. How do we integrate this "rediscovered" poetry that was lost because women did not have an easily available outlet to publish their works?

In the chapter on reviews and puffery and again in the chapter on feminine and textuality, I very briefly address the aesthetic evaluation of the annual's literary contents, but it is merely a report of the contemporary reviewer's evaluation. I never answer that question: Is the writing or poetry any good? Why answer this question? In those planned but unexecuted chapters, I worked against this idea of a normative aesthetic—both in an attempt to alter it and to evaluate it, asking these questions: How does the poem on a ruined cottage compare to Wordsworth's composition, a poem that has been institutionalized into our canon by anthologies, collections, and curricula? How much revision did Wordsworth commit to his final version? How much did the annual poet revise? And should the relationship between the poems become part of their analysis?

Before any of the annual's poetry or prose can be explicated, compared, or associated, the literary history and the material object itself need to be inserted into the scholarly discussion. The literary annual, in both its bibliographic and its linguistic codes, affects the meaning of the literary text. In this project, I have taken that moment to incorporate all of the literary institutions with the object itself to create a sociology of the literary annual. My project offers a starting point, an invitation or call to action, for other scholars to work in the area. In many of the endnotes, I invite scholars to pick up a thread that I am able to address only briefly in the context of this project. This study recuperates the bibliographical reputation of literary annuals before getting into these feminist issues in the final chapter—and in this way marries the materiality of the text to the literary—a bibliographical study that sets the table for further analysis of the feminine, empire, and nationalism.

CORPUS OF STUDY

For the purposes of this project, I have limited my scholarly investigations to British literary annuals that achieved economic success in the heyday of the annual, 1823–32: *Forget Me Not, The Keepsake, The Comic Annual, Friendship's Offering, The Literary Souvenir, The Gem,* and so forth. Though Ackermann's *Forget Me Not* sparked the entire phenomenon, most scholars study Alaric Watts's *The Literary Souvenir* (for its genre-altering format) or

Charles Heath's *The Keepsake* (for the canonical authors/contributors). My research begins with the first literary annual, the *Forget Me Not,* introduced by Rudolf Ackermann in November 1822, and focuses on the first decade of the annual's popularity, with brief forays into the late 1830s and 1840s to provide evidence of the public's desire and fascination with the phenomenon. After 1830, the annual's format altered, its purpose became much more complicated, and the themes became multifaceted. Femininity became the sole selling point for some annuals, but for others (for example, religious annuals) it did not; in addition, women became the dominant contributors (according to Harry Hootman's research) and would soon become the editors of annuals. For these reasons, it is very difficult to generalize about the genre after 1830 and is therefore a necessary cessation point for this literary history.

The literary annuals that have been studied for their popularity are primarily those produced in 1828 and 1829, particularly *The Keepsake,* because of its more famous (that is, canonical) contributors. Much work has already been done in scholarly articles on Victorian literary annuals and gift books of the 1830s. My study addresses the first decade of the literary annuals as a liminal space when Romantic-era literary production was thought to be stagnant. The literary annuals published in these seven to eight years highlight that literature was becoming something beyond the single-author volume of poetry, that authorship itself was no longer the realm of an elite set. Also, because *The Keepsake* is the primary focus of study for most scholars of literary annuals, it has become the de facto representative of this genre. However, my study questions this assumption and refocuses on Rudolph Ackermann's annual, *Forget Me Not*. Because of his innovations in the mechanization of print and the production of engravings between 1800 and 1822, *The Keepsake*'s publishers were able to enter the market with great success. Though Ackermann's contributions are elided in current studies of literary annuals, he is most certainly a central figure in this literary history. My study begins with this first literary annual and its influences and traverses the rise in popularity to the heyday of the genre in 1830—the moment when other scholars (especially Paula Feldman, Kathryn Ledbetter, and Margaret Linley) take up studies of *The Keepsake* for 1828–35. Lorraine Kooistra's study of gift books and literary annuals begins in 1855 to complete the scholarship on this genre.

The overwhelming evidence of Rudolph Ackermann's ingenuity as a publisher in early nineteenth-century London culminates in the development and execution of the first literary annual. Chapter 1 focuses on the international publishing legacy created by this German immigrant and eventually naturalized British citizen. Well-known and well liked in the publishing industry, Ackermann created a publishing house that would exist in some form until the 1980s, when the family name was finally removed from the American version of the publisher's legacy. In this chapter there is also a study of nineteenth-century print culture as it pertains to the literary annuals and their German influences.

Chapter 2 dives into the literary forms that haunt Ackermann's popular and successful annual. Meditative practices through reading/gazing upon emblems, constructing anthologies, mimicking almanacs and their publishing cycles, and sentimentalizing printed albums all contributed to the eventual form of the literary annual. With an abundance of illustrations, this chapter defines and studies the surrounding literary forms that built up to the moment when Ackermann published the first literary annual.

Chapter 3 moves through the exciting first years (1822–30) of the publishing industry surrounding the literary annuals and chronicles the revisions to the literary annual based on French, German, and Spanish influences. Ackermann and other editors/publishers focused on inculcating a sense of nationalism into the literary annual—only to export the volumes to Europe, South America, America, and eventually India.

The brief chapter 4 captures the degradation of Ackermann's original plans for the literary annual and highlights the decline into volumes of beauty. This chapter also focuses on the parody volume, which eventually came to satirize the complex sentiments and lack of politicizing inherent to the original literary annuals, signaling that the literary annual had become too popular.

Chapter 5 focuses on the role of engravings and the business of engraving. Woodcut and steel-plate engravings determined the success of some annuals—until woodcut engravings became more refined because of inventions by literary annual publishers. This chapter highlights the translation from artist's creation to engraver's illustration copy. The engravings included in most literary annuals offered a portable gallery of images to readers all over England and abroad. Some annuals eventually took on the moniker of a scrapbook and collected primarily engravings to create a personalized viewing space.

Chapter 6 takes on the complicated relationship between editor and reviewer during the early nineteenth century—a collusion that resulted in rampant puffery. This chapter historicizes the profits and losses afforded to literary annual editors and publishers and dispels the common belief that these popular volumes were also financially successful. While editors struggled to earn a profit, they grappled with defining a sense of taste for their reading public. Reviewers often praised and condemned the contents of an annual in a single review, all the while claiming their role as the guardians of literary taste.

As often happens with textual studies and publishing histories, the literary analysis becomes obscured in favor of representing a history. Chapter 7 grapples with the Poetess Tradition and the conflicting standards of femininity in early nineteenth-century England. Through my analysis of eighteenth-century conduct manuals and poetry from the literary annuals, this chapter establishes that the femininity that Ackermann, Shoberl, and the other male publishers and editors attempted to establish was, in the end, incongruous. When women poets and authors began dominating the pages of the literary annuals, the tone altered from that of a proposed and standardized femininity to one that questioned patriarchy.

The conclusion to this book begins the work of studying a particular type of literature in the literary annuals: the Gothic short story. With an analysis of the numerical data of Gothic short story contents, the conclusion highlights that Ackermann and Shoberl focused the *Forget Me Not* on popular types of literature, and perhaps literature that was not as appropriate for their women readers as these two originally proposed. This final chapter also demonstrates a continuing fascination with the literary annual, given the republication and homage paid to Ackermann and his *Forget Me Not* by Modernist-era editors and publishers. Though seemingly disparate in the study of literary annuals, the conclusion briefly demonstrates the wealth of scholarly potential in studying the literary annuals.

Appendixes include reference material and full text of some literature that cannot be otherwise included in the body of these chapters. Portions of the appendix material have been gleaned from Faxon's and Boyle's extensive work but with updates, revisions, and amendments based on my research and that of other scholars, such as Harry Hootman, Paula Feldman, and Laura Mandell. At some point, all of this material should become part of a digital archive of literary annuals.

ONE

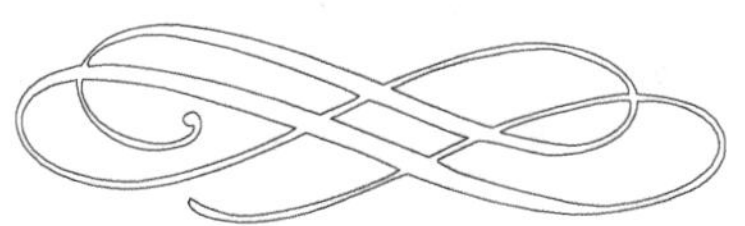

British Ingenuity from German Invention

The Legacy of Rudolph Ackermann

> [M]ay all mothers, who would so be shocked, be dom'd! As if mothers were such sort of logicians as to infer the future hanging of *their* child from the theoretical hangibility . . . of every infant. . . . [M]y whole heart is faint, and my whole head is sick (how is it?) at this damned, canting *unmasculine unbawdy* (I had almost said) age!
>
> —Charles Lamb, Letter 474 (1829; emphasis added)

RUDOLPH ACKERMANN (1764–1834), A PRINTSELLER, BOOKseller, publisher, inventor, and businessman, popularized aquatint, lithography, and illustrated books from his vast London publishing house, R. Ackermann, and the Repository of Arts shop. Ackermann's shop preceded the opening of the National Gallery in 1824, but his idea was that his shop, commercial as it was, would essentially exhibit artwork by those who were not admitted into the Royal Academy, especially the work by his engravers, draftsmen, and colormen. His shop and publications had a reciprocal relationship that catered to the idea of consumerism. An industrious inventor, he built a successful business on innovative printing technology and capitalized on current movements in politics and culture but never seemed to personally subscribe to political views himself. By maintaining some distance from British politics, Ackermann adeptly negotiated the conflict between his German heritage and the growing sense of British nationalism: "To the end of his days he retained a strongly marked German pronunciation of the English language, which gave additional flavour to the banters and jests uttered in his fine bass voice; but he wrote in English with great purity on matters of affection and of business long before middle life" (*Notes and Queries* [1869], quoted in Samuels, 130).

Many publishers, artists, and authors, including Alaric A. Watts, John Clare, J. B. Papworth, John Murray, James Hogg, William Jerdan, Sir Walter Scott, J. M. W. Turner, William Combe, Thomas Rowlandson, and Thomas Hood, refer to Ackermann in their memoirs and letters with a certain fondness.[1] He patented a process for creating waterproof paper, cloth, and other substances in 1801 (Patent no. 2491); he was among the first businessmen to use gas to light his workshop; in 1818–20, he worked on a patent for movable carriage axles (Patent no. 4212); and he created Lord Nelson's funeral car in 1805 ("Ackermann," *DNB,* 58; Maxted, "London").

In 1796, Ackermann began laying the foundation for creating his public/private salon at the Repository of Arts: he moved from No. 96 Strand to a spacious multilevel building at No. 101 Strand by taking over the lease from political lecturer John Thelwall (J. Thompson, 182). Prior to Thelwall's occupation of No. 101 Strand, William Shipley ran an art school in the Beaufort Buildings—Shipley being the founder of the Royal Society of Arts (J. Thompson, 177). Ackermann also ran a drawing school at No. 101 until 1806, when he closed it to make room for his now-famous Repository of Arts shop (Jervis, 101), which he advertised in the first number of his premiere magazine, *Ackermann's Repository of Arts:* "[W]hen the interposition of government put a stop to [Thelwall's] exhibition, Mr. Ackermann purchased the leace [*sic*], and it became once more the peaceful academy of drawing" (quoted in J. Thompson, 182). Upstairs were the gallery, tea room, circulating library, and evening talks or *conversazione* for invited guests (ibid.). Judith Thompson describes it as a "multilevel cultural emporium . . . with a spacious Library and tea-room, decorated with classic busts, draperies and urns, where he also held the evening 'conversations' of

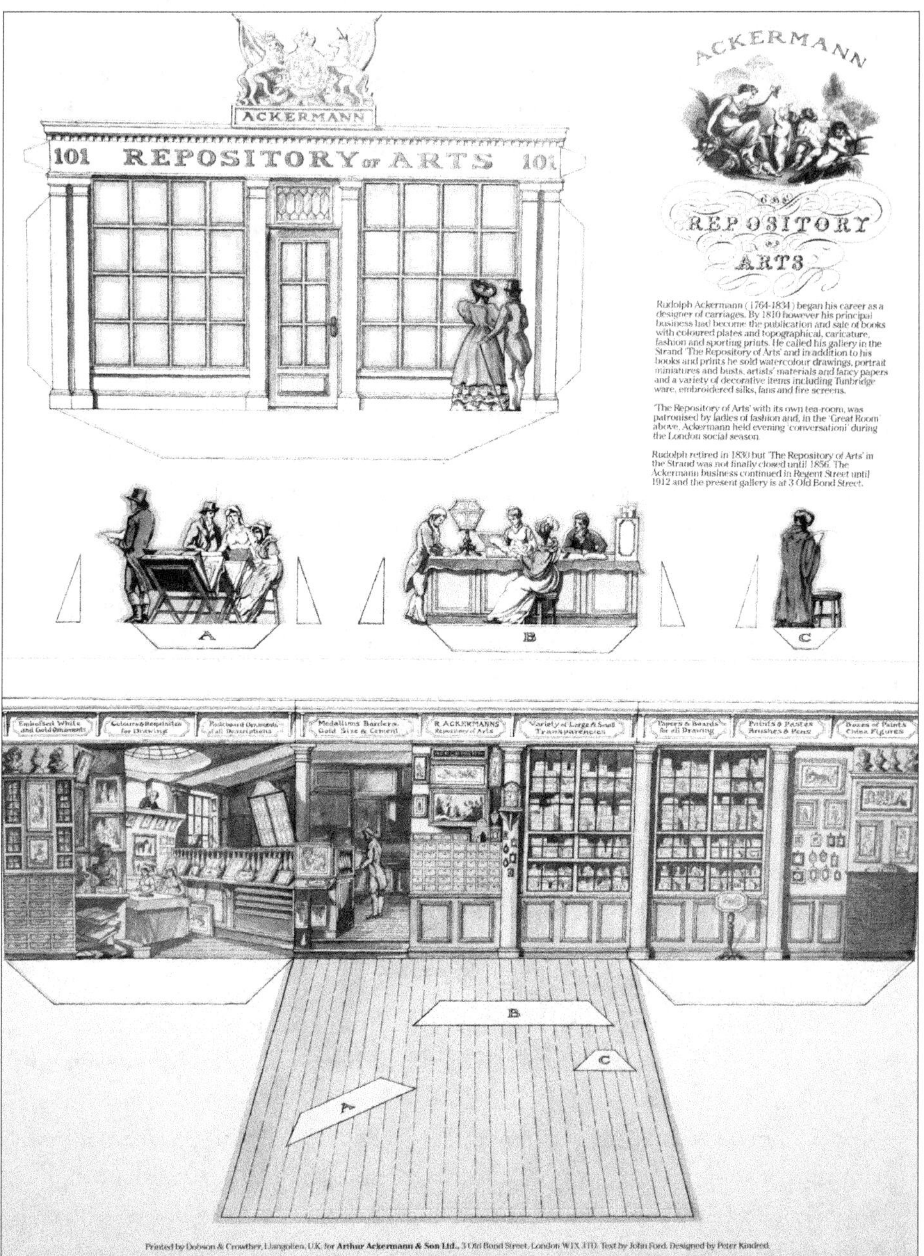

Figure 1.1 Cutout model of Ackermann's Repository of Arts shop, 1809 *Repository of Arts* (from the Katherine D. Harris Collection; photo credit, Tom Davis)

his dilettanti society, intended 'for a select number of gentlemen, professors and lovers of literature and the fine arts'" (ibid.) (fig. 1.1).

According to Thompson, with this segregated design Ackermann set up a hierarchy whereby the affluent and elite were invited upstairs, while the common consumer was allowed to browse the endless supply of artwork and art supplies downstairs. Ackermann sold subscriptions to the third-floor circulating library where patrons could borrow books as well as prints, watercolors, and drawings (Bermingham, *Learning,* 138). The ground floor was the Repository—a large, and very successful, shop that sold furniture in addition to prints.

Ackermann's shop was not the only one on the Strand to mix art and commerce. Ann Bermingham notes that the Strand also housed Lackington Allen & Co.'s Temple of the Muses and S. & J. Fuller's Temple of Fancy, both of which sold art supplies and artwork to an elite clientele to mingle "art, education, and commerce [in the production of] a hybrid social institutional environment. These shops were places of social intercourse, commercial exchange, and aesthetic instruction . . . [and] invested both commerce and art with an aura of domestic comfort" (*Learning,* 127).

Ackermann printed and bound his publications in his building and employed a bevy of craftsmen, artisans, and artists to produce his popular publications: letterpress printers, bookbinders, leather suppliers, ink suppliers, fancy papiers, colormen, and more, as chronicled by Bermingham and by Ackermann's principal biographer, John Ford (*Ackermann,* 46). After successfully establishing a business based on hand-colored aquatint plates, in 1818 Ackermann became one of the first British publishers to operate and own a lithography press.[2]

When the thirty-year lease on No. 101 Strand expired, in 1827 Ackermann removed to No. 96 Strand, which had been completely redesigned by his friend, the architect J. B. Papworth (Jervis, 108),[3] with a massive warehouse, a private residence, showrooms, a library, ware rooms, printing presses, gilders' rooms, and framers' quarters spread over eight floors (Ford and Fraser, 50). This new location also had the bonus of easy access: "The facility of access for Carriages to his New Premises, and the convenience for their waiting in Beaufort Buildings, are advantages to which he cannot refrain from directing their attention" (publisher's insert, *Edinburgh Review* 41 [June 1827]: n.p.).

With more than 450 volumes (Ford, *Ackermann,* 220–32) attributed to his publishing house and a yearly income of £30,000, Ackermann succeeded in building a recognizable brand, especially with colored plates. His most important contributions to the publishing culture of early nineteenth-century England were the result of various friendships and networks that he established, the successful and productive relationship between Thomas Rowlandson and William Combe among them (see later discussion of *The Tours of Dr. Syntax*).[4] As a publisher, Ackermann continued printing manuals on drawing by various authors even after the drawing school closed (Jervis, 101): *Ackermann's New Drawing Book of Light and Shadow, in Imitation of Indian Ink* (1809–12); *Rudiments of Landscape: In Progressive Studies* (1813); *The First Principles of Landscape Drawing* (1829); *Groups of Figures for Decorating Landscapes* (1798); *Grammar of Flower Painting* (1826); *Six Progressive Lessons for Flower Painting* (1810); *Letters upon the Art of Miniature Painting* (1822); *Fifteen Academical Studies of the Passions; Principles of Practical Perspective* (1815); *An Essay on Mechanical Drawing* (1811); *A Treatise on Ackermann's Superfine Watercolours* (1801).[5]

Ackermann also found a way to make architecture accessible and artistic to his clientele by displaying architecture in 372,000 aquatint engravings for his topographical books published from 1811 through 1816: *The History of the Abbey Church of St. Peter's Westminster, A History of the University of Oxford, A History of the University of Cambridge,* and *The History of the Colleges of Winchester, Eton and Westminster* (Jervis, 103). With the publication of the *Microcosm of London* (1808–11),[6] Ackermann "elevated the commercial building to the status of the major public landmarks featured in his famous and popular aquatints, equivalent to a church [or] a parliament building" (Bermingham, *Learning,* 184). Ann Bermingham suggests that this multi-volume work is a sign of a culture of commerce rather than a focus on art. In other words, Ackermann's publication "is on the social and cultural institutions of London, the theaters, the shops, and the markets; the things that made the city an exciting and interesting place" (*Learning,* 135). By focusing its engravings and articles on commercial buildings instead of historical landmarks, the *Microcosm* buoyed this idea of civic pride. Ackermann, like other shop owners, converted this pride into national pride with his monthly magazine, *The Repository of Arts* (published 1809–28). Ackermann eventually realized that the primary audience for the *Repository* should be women and shifted the tone and content of articles toward women, including fashion and cultural events as the primary topics. His shift, along with that of other publishers, encouraged "female consumption by characterizing it as a patriotic and virtuous exhibition of taste in the home" (Bermingham, *Learning,* 140).

Ackermann is credited with establishing lithography as a fine art in England (*DNB,* 58),[7] earning a reputation for the beautiful color plates and aquatints that he produced in *The Repository of Arts,* an "elegant and fashionable periodical Work contain[ing] upwards of 500 coloured Engravings, and form a Library of itself; it presents entertainment and information to every taste, and will serve as a mirror of the times, and a work of reference to future ages" (advert in 1824 *Forget Me Not*). Mimicking the very popular *Lady's Magazine,* which began in 1770 and ceased publication in 1837, Ackermann's magazine contained plates of the latest fashionable dresses and hats, descriptions of the fabrics and design, and the occasional fabric sample. At a price of three shillings, sixpence, this magazine accumulated three thousand subscribers in its first year, 1809, and appeared regularly until 1828.[8] By its conclusion, the magazine had seen forty volumes produced in monthly parts (*DNB,* 59)—quite a success, considering the reading public's fickle tastes (fig. 1.2).

The Poetical Magazine (1809–10) began the very successful relationship between author William Combe and artist Thomas Rowlandson, which eventually resulted in several volumes of *The Tours of Dr. Syntax* (1812, 1816, 1820–21). Allen Samuels notes that publishers during Ackermann's time were responsible for throwing focus on either the engravings or the writing, judging which was to be most profitable. Ackermann readily employed this technique with many of his works, including, most notably, the *Forget Me Not* (Samuels, 379). However, his practice of employing artists to first render images and then writers to explicate the visual was practiced even before he turned to the literary annuals. Rosemary Hill notes that Auguste Pugin, illustrator of Gothic architecture for *The Microcosm of London* and frequent contributor to Ackermann's *Repository of Arts,* drew images for which his daughter, Catherine, often wrote text to accompany ("A. C. Pugin," 16).[9]

With this established printing house and consumer base, Ackermann created a system of printing that yielded a higher production rate. Because of this, consumers of the *Forget Me Not* and later annuals did not subscribe to the publication. Instead, in some years, Ackermann printed upwards

Figure 1.2 “Evening Dresses,” plate 3, vol. 5, 1811 *Repository of Arts* (from Internet Archive, http://archive.org/details/repositoryofarts511acke [accessed June 26, 2013])

of 20,000 copies in a year from a quarter of a million plates per edition (Ford, *Ackermann,* 64–65).[10]

Ackermann understood the value of a beautiful volume and committed his business to producing works that married print culture to visual and verbal beauty. More importantly, he understood the business of producing and re-producing literary and artistic culture. His goal, in the end, was to produce commodified and exportable representations of England's best works in a time when readers were overwhelmed with reading materials.

REMAKING EUROPEAN INVENTION WITH BRITISH INGENUITY

Many other publishers produced annuals that outsold Rudolph Ackermann's *Forget Me Not* (1823–47), but this inventor, who established the literary annual as an extremely marketable model, came to represent Englishness, femininity, and popular artistry because he believed in elevating all aspects of printing to the form of art rather than relegating publishing work to craftsmanship. Andrew Boyle and Ralph Thompson trace the literary annual's lineage to the Parisian *Almanach des Muses* (1765–1833) and its German imitation *Musenalmanach* (1770) (R. Thompson, *American,* 3). But Charles T. Tallent-Bateman, in a 1902 article, cites the German *Minerva* (1809–33, published in Leipzig by Ernst Fleischer) as the annual's precursor. British influences include the Stationers' Company almanacs; Southey's *Annual Anthology,* published in two volumes (1799 and 1780); *The Poetical Register and Repository of Fugitive Poetry,* published 1801–11; and *Angelica's Ladies Library, or Parents and Guardians Present,* published in 1794 (R. Thompson, *American,* 165). But the British literary annual tradition begun by Rudolph Ackermann carved out a niche and format that were unique and separate from those of the almanac and poetry anthologies.[11] Given his goals for the annuals, Ackermann, as a threshold figure between market and aesthetics, created a product for early nineteenth-century readers that represented the highest form of British ingenuity coupled with taste, that indefatigable marker of class boundaries in early nineteenth-century England.

In advertisements for and the preface to the first *Forget Me Not* volume, published in November 1822, Ackermann's publication solidified the literary annual genre—a genre that was protected by editors and vociferously defended by reviewers until 1828:

- *Purpose*: Annuals are "expressly designed to serve as annual tokens of friendship or affection" (advert in 1823 *Forget Me Not*).

- *Publication time frame*: "It is intended that the Forget-Me-Not shall be ready for delivery every year, early in November" (Preface to 1823 *Forget Me Not,* vii).

- *Continual evolution*: "[T]he Publisher has no doubt that, in the prosecution of his plan, he shall be enabled, by experience, to introduce improvements into the succeeding volumes" (ibid.).

- *Authorship*: "[H]e shall neglect no means to secure the contributions of the most eminent writers, both at home and abroad" (ibid.).

- *Originality*: "To convey an idea of the nature of the pieces which compose the bulk of this volume, it will be sufficient to state that they will consist chiefly of original and interesting Tales and Poetry" (advert in 1823 *Forget Me Not*).

- *Engravings*: "[W]hile his long and extensive connexion with the Arts, and the credit with which he has acquitted himself in his various undertakings in that line, will, he trusts, be a satisfactory pledge that his best exertions shall not be wanting to give to this Work in a decided superiority in regard to its embellishments, over every other existing publication of the kind" (Preface to 1823 *Forget Me Not,* viii).

- *Useful information*: "The third portion comprises a Chronicle of Remarkable Events during the past year: a Genealogy of the Reigning Sovereigns of Europe and their Families; a List of Ambassadors resident at the different Courts; and a variety of other particulars extremely useful for reference to persons of all classes" (advert in 1823 *Forget Me Not*).

- *Exterior format*: "The Forget Me Not is done up in a case for the pocket, and its external decorations display corresponding elegance and taste with the general execution of the interior" (advert in 1823 *Forget Me Not*).

With each criterion, Ackermann creates a sense of propriety, education, and social grace that would mark the literary annual for the next decade. He not only establishes the purpose of the volume by highlighting its physical features and editorial practices but also offers instructions to consumers to purchase the volume with the intent of distributing it further. By locating the publication date in the following year but releasing the volume in November, Ackermann ensured that annuals would become part of, if not the cause for, widespread holiday exchanges of literary materials that mimicked the long-standing practice of Almanac Day. Reviewers staunchly condemned any pretender annual that was published outside the holiday time frame, November through January, yet still claimed to be of the literary annual family.[12] In one promise, Ackermann assured consumers that costly volumes would be guided by an experienced publisher who would respond to consumer requests for a better product each year. In turn, each editor would use the preface to proclaim improvements to his (or her) title for each succeeding year.

This promise of originally authored material establishes the literary annual as more than an anthology; the authors are generally contemporary British figures instead of writers of classic literature. And as is discussed later, literature from abroad would not overwhelm the annual's contents. Presenting original works by contemporary authors requires consideration of authorial ownership, but by promising originality, Ackermann committed to commodifying a representation of fresh, current national literature. However, this claim of originality would plague the editors of the annuals through the 1830s.

Though the declaration of including superior engravings is standard, Ackermann meant to use his experience and established audience to create a personal, portable exhibit of text and image, thereby merging the latest vogue for visualizing literature and turning readers into spectators. An annual had to contain both literature and engravings to be considered within the family.

With the useful information, Ackermann attempted to establish the literary annual as referential and useful across class boundaries, similar to the almanac. However, because of the cost (twelve shillings), the working classes were presumably not included in this declaration. A list of coach fares was included to aid a lady in ensuring that she was treated fairly; but confronting a coachman about overcharging the fare would belie the purpose of the annual—to instruct in morality, feeling, and taste. Because it is mere information, this element was eventually discarded for the 1825 volume, in favor of additional creative contributions.

The neoclassical embellishments adorning early annuals' covers and slipcases remind readers of the three graces: charm, beauty, and literature. Ackermann, with this final marker of the literary annual, focused on establishing the literary annual in association with *taste,* a slippery term that denotes pleasure, desire, appetite, imagination, and shared feelings, according to the philosophers Thomas Hobbes, Edmund Burke, and Immanuel Kant. Carolyn Korsmeyer, in "Tastes and Pleasures," notes that "[t]aste requires intimate, first-hand acquaintance with its objects" (para. 12) and "also provides the guiding metaphor used to describe the ability to discern beauty in nature and art" (para. 11).

For Charles Lamb, writing to B. W. Procter in January 1829, the annuals represented women readers' lack of rationalism. After having his sonnet rejected by Thomas Hood because "it would shock all mothers," Lamb lashed out against the entire genre for eliding appreciation of literary aesthetics: "and may all mothers, who would so be shocked, be dom'd!" (Letter 474 [see chapter epigraph]). Though this letter reeks of Lamb's frustration, the "unmasculine unbawdy . . . age" comment reflects the debate between base pleasures and aesthetic taste—a debate that was directed toward the annuals only after the genre became successful. In fact, Ackermann promised taste and propriety in the annuals but often used that promise only to sell annuals.

The association with pleasure and beauty was problematic for women readers during the early nineteenth century. Ackermann and various annual editors would continually defend the genre as tasteful while printing literary materials that were perhaps more scintillating and aligned with the idea that aesthetic taste is rooted in physical sensation (as is discussed by Denise Gigante in *Taste: A Literary History*). The diminutive size—duodecimo, 3.5 x 5.5 in.—represents a particular form of femininity by being portable in the pocket or in the hand. Though the size eventually grew to quarto editions without slipcases and instead wrapped in silk covers, the annual's embellished boards marked the extravagance of the entire genre and were continued through its lifetime, even in rebindings.

Why Ackermann's *Forget Me Not* succeeded where other earlier experiments had failed is still somewhat of a mystery. Numerous conduct manuals flooded the market during the 1790s. Some ladies' magazines were beginning to flourish, but they were not as permanent a material object as the annuals. The mystery lies in the combination of German publishing history and literary culture, as well as in Ackermann's business savvy in the London publishing industry. Ackermann's willingness to invent new forms and demonstrate shifts in taste making stemmed from his ability to eschew the traditions of British publishing and literary culture. As a German émigré, he was the right man to capitalize on these middle-class reading audiences.

NINETEENTH-CENTURY PRINT CULTURE

Middle-class merchants, bankers, professional men, and manufacturers "could spend full evenings with their families and their books" (Altick, 86). The twelve-shilling annual fell between the sensational cheap reading materials and the expensive "corrupting" novels. *Forget Me Not, The Keepsake,* and *The Literary Souvenir* avoided contents that celebrated indoctrinating evangelical preachings, though the *Friendship's Offering* seemed to focus more in this area. Like many printed materials in the early nineteenth century, annuals were marketed as "wholesome literature" for the entire family that moved beyond the quick entertainment of a broadside or a daily. The contents of the annuals appealed to that small class of readers and book buyers with limited leisure—a class growing exponentially in British society.

Competing serial publications at the annual's advent were predominantly periodicals, journals, and cheap twopenny newspapers. Annuals were something new, different, and substantial. Their contents and physical appearance communicated a different standard of propriety and morality than even the ubiquitous temperance pamphlets. The literary annual made its British debut at a moment in print culture when innovative technological advances, literacy rates, demand for reading materials, and publishing and book-selling practices increased the production of printed materials.

Stereotype (introduced in 1802),[13] machine printing (by steam press, introduced in 1814),[14] and paper tenacity (through use of the Fourdrinier machine, introduced in 1807) were new technologies that increased the production rates and numbers of reading materials available to the increasingly literate British population. Allan C. Dooley, in *Author and Printer in Victorian England,* suggests that stereotyping influenced the canon by offering authors the opportunity to reprint their works. However, authors were hesitant to commit to stereotyping, because the plates would effectively seal the text from future revisions though "the author's profits on later impressions would be greater, and a book need never be unavailable as long as the plates or paper matrices were kept" (78).

Frederick Kilgour reports that "[t]he population in England and Wales doubled, from approximately nine million in 1801 to eighteen million in 1851. . . . From 1750 to 1840 in England and Wales the literacy rate of men went from 63 to 68 percent, and that of women from 36 to 52 percent" (99). Evangelicalism, according to Richard Altick in *The English Common Reader,* contributed to this increase in literacy, because the movement inspired the mass production of Bibles all over England and encouraged the "working class" to become literate:[15] "[P]roselytizing religion, the distribution of Bibles and didactic literature became a large industry" (100). Printing technology improved just as substantial book orders were submitted, and the British working classes were ready to become more literate through reading these free pamphlets (103–4). Altick also attributes the increase in literacy to inventions in reading apparatus, including low-cost spectacles, oil and paraffin lamps, low-cost candles, and peaceful locales outside the home (91–94).

Consumers and readers had a choice, and the expense of the material marked the class of the consumer. A majority of the contents in the most prolific materials, periodicals, consisted of sensational news and hurriedly written fiction—definitely not the literary and aesthetic qualities espoused by the literary annuals. Editors and publishers, Ackermann especially, marketed the annual as a lovingly assembled mass of thoughtful literary and visual renderings for quiet contemplation or studious conversation.

To compete with the litany of literary materials (both salacious and didactic), Ackermann relied on his shop's first- and second-floor clientele to recognize the annual as worthy of their time and money. The variety of burgeoning genres of reading material during the early nineteenth century included fiction (as exemplified by Ann Radcliffe's *The Mysteries of Udolpho* [1794] and Sir Walter Scott's *Waverley* [1814]), serialized fiction (Charles Dickens's *Pickwick Papers* [1836] and *Master Humphrey's Clock* [1840]), silver fork novels (Thomas Henry Lister's *Granby* [1826]),[16] poetry volumes (by such authors as Charlotte Smith, Hannah More, Sir Walter Scott, George Gordon Byron, Letitia Elizabeth Landon, and Felicia Hemans), nonfiction personal accounts (such as Olaudah Equiano's *Interesting Narrative* [1789] and Mary Wollstonecraft's and Helen Maria Williams's *Letters*), juvenile literature (by authors such as Anna Letitia Barbauld and Wollstonecraft), conduct manuals (such as those by Wollstonecraft), textbooks and reference works (including Cobbett's *Grammar of the English Language* [1818]), twopenny and threepenny weekly and daily newspapers (Limbird's *Mirror of Literature* [established in 1822],[17] *Penny Magazine* [established in 1832], *Nic Nacs, Diorama, Freebooters, Batatelles,* and sixty others), monthly and quarterly magazines (such as *Town and Country Magazine* and *Fraser's Magazine*), review periodicals (*Quarterly Review, Analytical Review, The Literary Gazette, Monthly Review,* and *The Gentleman's Magazine*), art periodicals (as exemplified by Ackermann's *Repository of Arts*), women's periodicals (*The Ladies Diary, Lady's Monthly Museum,* and *The Lady's Magazine*), literary annuals (such as *Forget Me Not* [established in 1823]), juvenile literature, comics, classic reprints (such as the expurgated *The Family Shakespeare* [1818] and Shakespeare's plays [1825]), theatrical journalism, and temperance periodicals.[18]

Book production alone, excluding periodicals and newspapers, "in the nineteenth century exceeded that of the eighteenth by 440 percent," which Kilgour attributes to printed materials becoming less labor intensive in setting type, creating paper, or printing multiple copies and the division of bookselling from printing (112). In "On Cheap Periodical Literature," published in *The Gentleman's Magazine* in June 1825, the anonymous author observes the quantity and quality of the voluminous amounts of publications: "This is the golden age of literary and commercial enterprise. Never was the press more actively employed, or ampler scope allowed for the diffusion of every species of information, than at the present period. . . . Never were publications so numerous, or of such varied character" (483).

Annuals were priced out of the range of a working-class, and even a moderate-income middle-class, family. Altick's research concludes that a middle-class family—an economic stratum slightly higher than that of the industrial worker—earned a modest weekly income of "48*s.* [shillings], or roughly £125 a year; a beneficed clergyman lived well, if hardly in splendor, on £300 to £400; an officer of the line could marry on £200 to £400" (276). Both the working and middle classes could afford only a few books a year. However, the increased availability and cheap price of newspapers afforded an opportunity for the unskilled laborers in the working class to access reading materials—whether as the original consumer or as the tenth reader (table 1.1).

The more esteemed reading materials began at two shillings with critical periodicals, but the annuals were not the most expensive materials available—and Ackermann ensured that his *Forget Me Not* was priced at the

TABLE 1.1 RETAIL PRICES OF READING MATERIALS, 1814–35

Type of publication	*Price*[a]
Cheap weekly magazines (e.g., *Mirror of Literature*, 1822)	1.5*d.*–6*d.*
Political tracts	2*d.*
Cheap nonfiction	6*d.* per part 4*s.*6*d.* per complete volume in 1827
Weekly magazines	6*d.*–1*s.*
Daily newspapers	7*d.*
Recycled (i.e., illegally hired/lent to multiple readers)	1*d.*–3*d.*
Reprints (literature) (e.g., Shakespeare's plays)	1*s.*–12*s.*
Critical periodicals (e.g., *Fraser's Magazine*)	2*s.*
Monthly magazines	2*s.*6*d.*–4*s.*
Numbered series (fiction)	2*s.*–5*s.* per weekly installment[a]
Poetry volumes	5*s.*
Review periodicals (e.g., *Quarterly Review*, *Edinburgh Review*	6*s.*
Literary annuals	8*s.*–£3
Three-volume novels	15*s.*–21*s.* in 1814–23
Serialized novels	20*s.* total for parts 21*s.* per complete volume (e.g., *Pickwick Papers*, 1836)
Scott novels	31*s.*6*d.* in 1820
Circulating library	35*s.* per year with unlimited access

Source: Altick, *English Common Reader,* 260–93, 318–47.

[a] Abbreviations for currency: £ = pounds, *s.* = shillings; *d.* = pence.

[b] However, as Altick points out, the total cost by the conclusion of the numbered series was not as cheap as the consumer could have wished. For instance, a Bible issued in 173 numbers cost in total £5.15*s.*: "We can assume that few of the purchasers who endured to the end of a serial issue counted up what they had spent; or, if they did, they failed to reflect that by determinedly saving sixpence or a shilling a week, rather than giving it to the canvasser, they might have had their completed book sooner and much more cheaply" (265).

lower end of the scale. Between 1814 and 1823, a three-volume novel, the more expensive reading, was sold at a retail price of between fifteen and twenty-one shillings (a guinea). Sir Walter Scott's novels sold at the higher end and eventually reached a retail price of thirty-one shillings, sixpence by 1820). As a result of this exorbitant price caused by the booksellers' collusion, the high price of paper, and the cost of hand labor (Altick, 262), fiction readers accessed the circulating libraries for a shared copy of popular novels; there, readers could leisurely pore over all of the latest fiction at thirty-five shillings per year (Altick, 263). Between 1827 and 1832, the remainders or reprint business also thrived in competition with the expensive novels; noncopyrighted works were available as "number publications and classic reprint series" (Altick, 264). In numbered publications, the subscribers paid weekly for the installment of fiction or nonfiction literature. Ackermann, aware of his audience, increased the price only slightly from year to year, as opposed to pressing consumers to expend three pounds.

The working class typically did not enjoy the benefits of the circulating library. The high cost of living and low wages during the early nineteenth century precluded them from obtaining a spare five shillings, which would buy five pounds of butter or ten pounds of meat (Altick, 276). These reprints and numbered publications were, in effect, still priced out of the range of the average factory worker regardless of the materials intended to be the "economy book" for them. The middle and lower middle classes enjoyed these economy books and benefited from the cheap form of entertainment more than any other literate class. However, the cheaper reading materials suffered from sensationalism, which left this set of people without "wholesome literature" with which to educate themselves. As a result, a relatively small number of consumers enjoyed literature of the higher quality that was produced by publishers such as Ackermann.

FROM GERMANY TO LATIN AMERICA: ACKERMANN NATIONALIZES THE ANNUAL

Relying on the various debates surrounding aesthetic and literary taste and the turn from rational thought, Ackermann constructed his literary annual business venture around beauty. The resultant product, the *Forget Me Not,* encapsulated elements from already successful genres, including the French literary "almanach," the German "Taschenbuch" (pocket-book), and the "album" and traditional "almanac." Ackermann and Shoberl acknowledge these predecessors in the preface to the first *Forget Me Not:*

> The British Public is here presented with the *first attempt to rival the numerous and elegant publications of the Continent,* expressly designed to serve as tokens of remembrance, friendship, or affection, at that season of the year which ancient custom has particularly consecrated to the interchange of such memorials. The Publisher flatters himself that as well from the nature of the literary department, in which *it has been his aim to unite the agreeable with the useful,* as from the execution of the graphic embellishments, this first volume of the Forget-Me-Not will be deemed not unworthy of the purpose for which it is intended. . . .
>
> . . . [A]mong the documents introduced into the concluding sheets, the Publisher begs leave to direct the Reader's attention to the important Tables exhibiting the results of the late Census, compiled from the returns of the Population of Great Britain, just printed by order of the House of Commons. For some of the other useful articles of reference in this part of the volume, he professes his obligations to the *Gotha Almanac,* a work of acknowledged accuracy and of high reputation on the Continent. (v, vii; emphasis added)

Focusing on the utility of the first *Forget Me Not* and pointing to the tables and charts, Ackermann authorizes the information with the stamp of the British government and European information. Mention of the "Continent" lends the annual a cosmopolitan reputation, which is intended to draw in an audience interested in European and British information while simultaneously erasing those same boundaries: "In submitting to the Public that plan of the work here announced, the Projector candidly acknowledges that he is influenced by the honest ambition of rivalling at least, if not surpassing[,] the many elegant and tasteful productions of the Continent, expressly designed to serve as annual tokens of friendship or affection" (1823 advert). Having evolved into a very savvy businessman, Ackermann was constantly attuned to the changes in nationalism ever-present in London and used a rhetoric in his publishing that unmistakably built upon patriotism, as Ann Bermingham notes in *Learning to Draw*: "Commerce, in

Ackermann's mind, was a nationalistic, public-spirited labor and during the wars he made every effort to mix business with patriotism by producing endless caricatures of the French and by publishing books like *Loyal Volunteers of London* in 1809. . . . More ambitious schemes ranged from a proposal to leaflet Paris by balloon with anti-Bonaparte literature to a successful fund-raising effort for the relief of war-torn Germany" (142). Because of Leipzig's importance to British trade on the Continent, John Ford supposes that Ackermann's patriotism and benevolence toward the citizens of Leipzig were buoyed by the British government, and his reward was naturalization in 1809, an act that would reap trade benefits seven years later (*Ackermann,* 32, 33).[19]

Ackermann admittedly borrowed from the German tradition of the *Taschenbuch,*[20] or pocket-book, "a small book, adapted to be conveniently carried in the pocket" (*OED*), which focuses less on "useful information" and more on literature. Roger Chartier, Lydia Cochrane, and Guglielmo Cavallo claim in *A History of Reading in the West* that the size of the book impacted the place and space intended for reading: "Because the codex was not bound to fixed conventions of manufacture and make-up, but could instead take on different formats and sizes ranging from a handy pocket size to a weighty tome, it changed the way the book was correlated to the physiology of reading. The physical structure of certain books dictated, hindered or at least suggested certain postures, gestures and ways of reading" (87). With an intentional portability in the smaller duodecimo size and comfort that serial form offers to readers, the early annuals were meant for transportation and entertainment rather than serious study. This association of book size with leisurely reading is perhaps the reason that editors were so adamantly vociferous in their prefaces about the literary merit and visual pleasure to be derived from the contents of their annuals.

However much Ackermann attributes his *Forget Me Not* and the literary annual form to this German production, the reviewers and editors began at this moment to praise Ackermann's literary emulation and to colonize the German form in the name of England. In December 1823, a review in *Blackwood's Edinburgh Magazine* historicized the success of the Taschenbuch and its German authors:

> However, all things go on in *melius,* and this year has produced some very pretty and ingenious attempts at turning the epidemic

> curiosity of Christmas into channels of instruction and intellectual amusement. Among those in the natural progress of improvement, the last is to be presumed the best; and the work, whose title stands at the head of this article, strikes us as not merely the best in point of invention and decoration, but to be, from its original composition, the subjects of its poetry, and the tendency of its spirit, as strikingly deserving of a place in the library, as on the table of the drawing-room of fashion.
>
> The Germans, of all men the wisest in their literary generation, have led the way in this species of performance, and some of the greatest names that ever figured in German literature, have indulged their taste, and enhanced their reputation, by contributing to the Yearly Literary Pocket Books, and Souvenirs. Schiller's most vivid poems first found their way to popular applause through this avenue; Goethe, the idol of his countrymen, and undoubtedly a poet of singular genius, sent out some of his most beautiful tales and scattered conceptions on what he quaintly calls, the "Papillon Wings" of the "*Taschenbuch.*" Kotzebue, a writer of more dubious fame, though at the height of the lighter drama, often floated his lesser plays into the world on those wings; and, perhaps, on the whole, there is no portion of German authorship more popular, than those yearly records of its happy thoughts, and slighter sketches of vigorous design;—those memorials of past beauty and promises of future attraction. Their productiveness as a mere speculation is evident from their number, their eager rivalry, and their increasing excellence; *and our English neglect of so interesting a mode of authorship, is among the more striking instances of the tardiness with which sometimes crosses the seas.* (669; emphasis added)

With the publication of several literary annual titles by November 1823, the reviewer finds that that month in particular presented a "carnival" of literary fun—a transformation of the dowdy, domestic German tone inherent in Taschenbücher. The review effectively erases the German influence only to replace it with a celebration of British nationalism. This is a case of importing a foreign form and then successfully translating it into a British commodity as part of the Christmas gift-giving phenomenon. The reviewer continues,

> The majority, however, of these German *Souvenirs,* have the stamp of their country rather too heavily laid upon them for our taste. Wisdom out of season, and prolixity that disdains an aid, solemn catalogues of names important to none but their possessors, and unwieldy labour of a reluctant and cloudy imagination, make the majority the weightiest performances that ever augmented the weight of a winter, between the Rhine and the Danube. But, unquestionably, all the good may be accessible without its counterpoise; and it might be difficult to limit the interest capable of being brought within the pages of an annual publication, expressly devoted to mingling the graceful and the useful; the attractive tale, the animated poetry, the dignity of moral thought, and the elegance of high life, and its captivating and brilliant recollections. (669)

Though celebratory at first, the reviewer draws boundaries in comparing the literary quality and taste of the British and German productions because of tone and useful information—perhaps not very useful to the English. But the Germans, who populated a significant number of London's printing houses, defended their national heritage while working toward British patriotism. Frederic Shoberl, one such German living abroad, defends German literature in the preface to his translation of *Parables by D. F. A. Krummacher: Translated from the German* (1824 [priced at six shillings]): "The Translator, therefore, will detain the reader no longer than to express a confident hope that the appearance of a volume of such unexceptionable tendency will contribute to shake the national prejudice against foreign literature in general entertained by some of his countrymen, whose minds ought to be superior to that sentiment" (iv).

Shoberl's defense of German literature may not have necessarily been warranted by 1828; the *Foreign Quarterly Review* was regularly critiquing twenty-eight to thirty German Taschenbücher each year—and commending them on their literariness in comparison to the British versions:

> We still remember, with what gladness and avidity, when resident in Germany, we seized on the *first Taschenbuch* of the season, bringing home with us two copies, one to lie on the drawing-room table, (for we would not be too selfish,) and the other to be indeed *our pocket-book* and companion, in our walks through the dark autumnal

> forests, till every page had been carefully read, and we had formed our own unbiassed opinion of its merits. In two or three days we had a second volume to be welcomed in like manner,—then another—and another,—till towards the end of November, when they were all out, and even the "Aglaia," latest and coyest of beauties, had made her appearance, we rejoiced to find ourselves in arrears as to our duties of reader and critic, and would perhaps for a month or two afterwards, purposely reserve half a dozen volumes, in order to have the comfortable reflection that our amusement was not exhausted, that the Christmas roses were not all blown and withered, and that the virgin lustre of the Minerva's, Cornelia's, Aurora's, Orphea's, &c. &c. &c. had not yet on too familiar acquaintance "faded into the light of common day."—Nor need this feeling seem overstrained and capricious, when it is taken into consideration that these annuals, though now very inferior to our own in point of graphic embellishment, are yet in literary merit, especially in their prose essays, greatly superior,—the *best* writers in Germany having frequently exerted themselves *in good earnest,* to render these publications important and interesting, while in our country, a short hasty fragment from a *highly* distinguished author has been in most instances as much as any Souvenir-editor could hope to obtain. ("Article 15," 642)

According to Frederick Burwick, in the foreword to William Taylor's biography by Georg Herzfeld, German literature had already influenced British culture by 1790 specifically because of Taylor's translations of German literature (2–3). Kurt Mueller-Vollmer attributes the early nineteenth-century British appropriation of German works to the publication of Germaine de Staël's *On Germany,* published in England in 1813 (152), and the numerous translations of *De l'Allemagne*. Taylor's *Historic Survey of German Poetry,* published in 1830, fostered an English affinity for German poetry because Taylor included translations that were accessible to English speakers. With the Hanoverian kings on the British throne during the 1790s, a mutual cultural exchange between the countries seems plausible, including the exchange of printing techniques and reading materials (Burwick, 3).[21]

Ackermann never publicly admitted to "borrowing" more than the format of this German tradition, but many clues point toward the *Forget Me*

Not as the translated British version of a German pocket-book, the *Vergissmeinnicht,* a title that translates to "forget me not." Ackermann would have seen copies of this German pocket-book. Todd Kontje, in "Male Fantasies," suggests that 1770 marks the establishment of a German culture, including a national literature, distinct from any other nations' influence and just five years before Ackermann set up shop in London's printing district (131). In an analysis of correspondence between two German-Jewish authors, Donovan Anderson found that the 1813 publication of Germaine de Staël's novel, *De l'Allemagne,* "contested an exclusive and inward looking German identity and took Staël's book as an opportunity to reflect on questions of authorship" (559) (fig. 1.3).

Though we do not have explicit evidence of Ackermann's knowledge of the *Vergissmeinnicht,* tangible links exist between the two titles, the least of which is Ackermann's abridged publication of an English translation of *Mimili,* a novel that was overwhelmingly successful in 1815 Germany and had been translated into several languages by 1824.[22] *Mimili,* originally

Figure 1.3 1818 *Vergissmeinnicht* title page and frontispiece (from the Katherine D. Harris Collection; photo credit, Tom Davis)

written by German author Heinrich Clauren (aka Karl Gottlieb Samuel Heun), tells the story of a Swiss woman's naïve, inadvertent sexuality and conflicted love. A foreign traveler, a young man, approaches the young shepherdess's bucolic home and is welcomed by her father. The young man falls in love with Mimili but is often tempted by her beauty. He makes several sexual advances but is rebuffed. By the time he must leave, he begs Mimili's father for permission to marry her. Her father, not wanting to be hasty and acknowledging that this young man is the first that Mimili has encountered, asks him to return in a year to see whether the passion still burns between them. During this year, the patriotic young man joins the military and disappears after the 1815 Battle of Waterloo. When Mimili receives a friend's letter informing her of her young man's fate, she mourns endlessly until the moment when the young man miraculously appears, having been only wounded in the battle. They are married as evidence of their fortitude and genuine love.

Originally published in the German magazine *Der Freimüthige* (*The Free Speaker*) from 1815 through 1819, Clauren's novel *Mimili* sold nine thousand copies in three years (Saul, *Cambridge History of German Literature,* 265) and inspired a genre of sentimental prose that capped the German Enlightenment and was typically referred to pejoratively as part of Biedermeier literature, a "derisive statement about the earlier period's unsophisticated aesthetics [as well as] a nostalgia for what was perceived to be an uncomplicated idyll of domestic comfort and family values that were lost with the arrival of the industrial revolution."[23] This style of writing also signals a shift toward family and relationships as opposed to concern for the self or individual experience.

In 1839, German literary critic Herman Marggraff reflected on *Mimili* as "a threat to German culture" and described Clauren's work as almost pornographic and certainly erotically charged for an audience of men:

> The reader is warned that we are now in the period in which the authors of almanacs and the late Clauren are leading the dance of literature. Mediocrity, naked, unadorned, wanton, with its paunch, wallowed on the slovenly couch of literature and on the boards of the stage. There it stretched itself and blinked its eyes, and molded, with the very soft wax of language, delicate little fingers with kissable lips and velvety cheeks, with dainty calves and lovely legs that could be seen as far as the garters, for Mimili's frock was rather

> short; and quite a good deal of the bosom could be seen for the bodice was cut low. (quoted in Löwenthal, *Literature,* 36–37)

Based on the success of *Mimili,* Clauren began publishing an annual pocket-book entitled *Vergissmeinnicht* (*Forget Me Not*), named after the flower given to the young man by our heroine, Mimili. This successful German publication ran from 1818 to 1834 and was published in duodecimo with a few engravings and long prose pieces by Clauren that totaled approximately five hundred pages per volume. The 1818 and 1821–23 volumes include only a sonnet at the outset of each volume and perhaps one other poem afterwards. The *Foreign Quarterly Review* in 1828 was lukewarm in its reception of the German pocket-book, described as

> edited, indeed hitherto exclusively written by H. Clauren, an author who has never been a special favourite with us, though his works are highly popular in Germany, and some translated specimens have been well received in England. His Annual seldom exhibits poetry, and now consists of two novels, entitled "The Three Orphans," and "Love in the Mail Coach." Prefaced by a laudatory sonnet of Hofrath Winkler, this volume seems to be as lively and well adapted, *ad captandum* [to please or arouse the rabble], as its predecessors. ("Article 15," 645)

Ignoring this type of negative reception that had been consistent since Clauren's publication of *Mimili* in 1815 and the *Vergissmeinnicht* in 1818—or perhaps because of it—Ackermann borrowed the title to create his *Forget Me Not.* Ackermann and his editor, Frederic Shoberl—also German—translated, condensed, and published an English version of Clauren's *Mimili* in the 1824 *Forget Me Not.* Ackermann's translation follows the seemingly didactic path of the German original, including the more lascivious tests of Mimili's chastity. With this type of ladies' publication, one would expect that *Mimili* would become expurgated or even bowdlerized, but not so. The battle scenes and Mimili's fashions are expunged, perhaps in the interest of space. After all, Ackermann condensed the novel from 150 pages to 62 duodecimo pages. The engravings of Mimili herself do not necessarily represent the heaving bosoms of either version. In fact, these are in the tradition of the bucolic landscape scenes that would come to dominate the

Figure 1.4 (*left*) "Mimili" from "Mimili" in the 1824 *Forget Me Not,* drawn by F. F. Burney and engraved by W. I. Fry (from the Katherine D. Harris Collection)

Figure 1.5 (*below*) "Mimili Feeding Poultry" from "Mimili" in the 1824 *Forget Me Not,* drawn by F. F. Burney and engraved by W. I. Fry (from the Katherine D. Harris Collection)

literary annuals, scenes engraved by those craftsmen whom Ackermann advocated for entry into the Royal Academy as "artists" (figs. 1.4 and 1.5).

As was the tradition of the day, much literature and many engravings were plucked from more expensive hardbound publications and republished in periodicals, such as the weekly *Mirror of Literature,* for consumption by the lower classes. Ackermann's version of *Mimili* apparently was revised without attribution to Clauren and published in *The Flowers of Literature,* a four-volume anthology published in 1824 as a hardbound edition that professed to collect the finest literature from several years. With a similar mission, *The Portfolio for 1824,* a twopence sixteen-page weekly periodical, borrowed an even further abbreviated and defiantly expurgated version of Clauren's novel from *The Flowers of Literature,* reduced the tale to five pages of double-column text spread over two weeks, and retitled it "The Soldier's Reward: A Tale of the Mountains." The new title removes Mimili as the main character, while the revised story refocuses the reader on patriotism, war, and the domestic role of women—a true Biedermeier account. Gone are the "pornographic" references to Mimili's heaving bosom and her shapely calves, with the exception of the soldier's initial description:

> She indeed seemed to the romantic fancy of our youthful traveller, no less than a beautiful though frail vision. She appeared not to have passed her 16th year, and, joined to a form the most exquisite, possessed the most beautiful countenance imagination can conceive. Youth and health revelled in her dimpled cheek, in her coral lips, and the plumpness of her whole love-inspiring figure. The silent mirrors of her soul were of an azure blue, and protected from your admiring gaze by long and silken lashes, which tempered the fire of her own passion-fraught glances. She was drest in a simple though elegant dress; she wore a corset of velvet, with muslin sleeves; a habit-shirt of the finest cambric, modestly, though to our traveller's mind, enviously concealing her neck and bosom, and yet not so much as to deprive you of an idea of its beautiful whiteness, which sight was sufficient to remind you of the "glance that some saint has of heaven in his dreams." Her petticoat would be, to our English notions, rather too short, and yet he would not have it half an inch less for the world; inasmuch as it gave sufficient testimony of an exquisitely shaped leg, and a well turned ancle [*sic*]. (no. 74, 217)

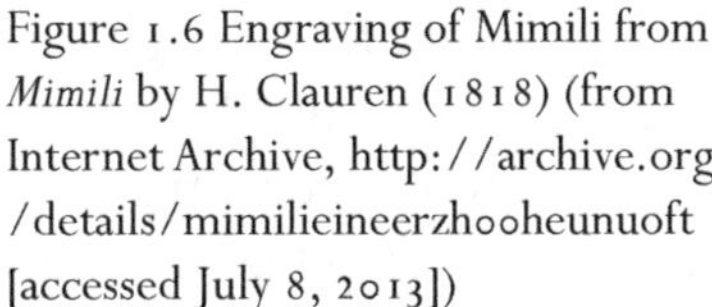
Figure 1.6 Engraving of Mimili from *Mimili* by H. Clauren (1818) (from Internet Archive, http://archive.org/details/mimilieineerzhooheunuoft [accessed July 8, 2013])

The engravings of Mimili in the *Forget Me Not* do not necessarily represent either Clauren's or Ackermann's version.[24] Nor do they seem to represent the pornographic references made by Margraff (fig. 1.6).

This alteration to the translated and then continued revisions to British versions of *Mimili* is important for two reasons: first, the contents of literary annuals were marketed as respectable literature intended to counteract the titillation of novels and periodical readings; and second, they were supposed to represent the best of British literary culture and publishing. Ackermann's version of *Mimili* would certainly draw reviewers' disdain, similar to that received from German critics, in addition to the negative British and German reviews of the *Vergissmeinnicht*. Why would Ackermann include a piece that was essentially considered a contamination of literary culture? Did he not then anticipate the eventual disdain for his literary annual in England? Or did he foresee the continued transmission of this tale to the weekly periodicals and an inherently larger, less-educated reading public?

If we consider that Ackermann had participated in restitution efforts for German victims of Napoleon's 1813 and 1814 campaigns, then perhaps anglicizing *Mimili* and offering up a reconstituted *Vergissmeinnicht* was a response to the German critics and an effort to preserve German culture while celebrating British innovation. Or perhaps Ackermann and Shoberl were actively engaging in nationalizing German literature for the British. Andrew Piper suggests that "translations in the early nineteenth century played a key role in importing and domesticating the foreign, in smoothing over such linguistic differences. In responding to the increasingly mass, and monolingual, reading public, romantic translations contributed to the standardization of European cultures. . . . Translations drew attention to the foreign as much as they made such foreignness intelligible to domestic audiences" (155). Piper also suggests that translations allowed British publishers to avoid authorial control and copyright issues with translations, all the while supplying the public with new content (155). Translators, then, Piper continues, "came to stand in the romantic age for a new industrializing world of letters" (155). Shoberl, an experienced and successful translator of German and French texts,[25] would have most likely committed the German prose to an appropriate English translation.

The story of *Mimili* was more than a tale of morality and sentimentality—it represents a patriotic triumph over war and an enemy that had plagued the British throughout the Romantic era. For his women readers, Ackermann failed to be wholly didactic in publishing *Mimili,* but perhaps he was not completely loyal to the idea of representing femininity in another repressive literary representation. Instead, he offered women an eroticism without overindulging in celebrations of warfare as originally portrayed in Clauren's version. Or was he attempting to transport the Biedermeier literary culture into England to encourage moving away from British High Romanticism and into a cosmopolitan representation of Britishness?

Because of Clauren's international success and an extremely public plagiarism lawsuit, Londonites would have been familiar with Clauren's name. After all, he was the epitome of the literary annual writer: prolific, popular, and profitable (Kontje, 136). By condensing Clauren's best-selling novel into a short story in his 1824 *Forget Me Not,* Ackermann tied himself to a German tradition of literature and print culture that he only mildly acknowledged in print. The title and Clauren are not the only connections, though.

The *Vergissmeinnicht* format evolved to include a series of unpaginated poems that are accompanied by engravings interspersed among the first twenty-five pages; the more significant number of remaining pages contains only prose pieces. The 1821 volume opens with an emblematic sonnet,[26] similar in topic, tone, and poetic focus to that of the 1823 *Forget Me Not* (fig. 1.7).

Sonnet

Modestly, I bloom along the streams
Whose little ripples refresh me
What glares from out my eye, however,
Will speak to you in confident timbre.

"Do you wish to tear me from the little stem?
Am I simply to be plucked for the lady-love?
[or] For the boyfriend, who, constantly clasps hands with you?
At all events, on account of fragile weakness of the heart?"

So the little flower—An emblem of its image
Is found in this little book, and it [book] echoes its [flower's] words.
Ah! A heart rich only in feelings:
May it reach its kindred heart.
Then every leaf will proclaim it widely/openly,
That—Forget-me-not—should be its motto.

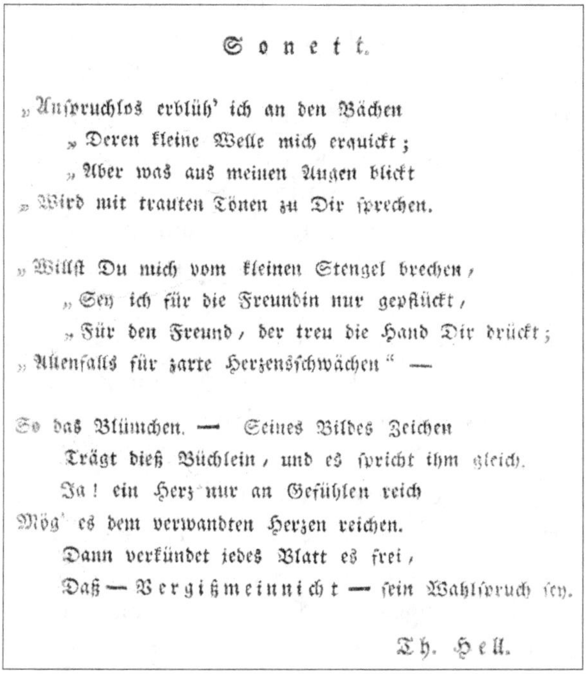

S o n e t t.

„Anspruchlos erblüh' ich an den Bächen
„Deren kleine Welle mich erquickt;
„Aber was aus meinen Augen blickt
„Wird mit trauten Tönen zu Dir sprechen.

„Willst Du mich vom kleinen Stengel brechen,
„Sey ich für die Freundin nur gepflückt,
„Für den Freund, der treu die Hand Dir drückt;
„Allenfalls für zarte Herzensschwächen" —

So das Blümchen. — Seines Bildes Zeichen
Trägt dieß Büchlein, und es spricht ihm gleich.
Ja! ein Herz nur an Gefühlen reich
Mög' es dem verwandten Herzen reichen.
Dann verkündet jedes Blatt es frei,
Daß — V e r g i ß m e i n n i c h t — sein Wahlspruch sey.

T h. H e l l.

Figure 1.7 Opening "Sonett" in German, 1821 *Vergissmeinnicht* (from the Katherine D. Harris Collection)

In the last stanza of the *Vergissmeinnicht*'s opening sonnet, the flower encourages an invisible listener (and potential flower picker) to equate the sentimental flower with its namesake book and "pluck" from the book instead of the flower from the stream's bank. With this book, the sentimental feelings inspired by the flower will be transmitted to the recipient of the book. This person will then "forget me not"—"me" being the listener, the book, and the flower—a motto echoed in Ackermann's *Forget Me Not* and many other literary annuals.

Clauren's were not the only German translations slipped into the *Forget Me Not:* Ackermann also relied on the fiction of Augustus von Kotzebue, a prolific German novelist and playwright who was violently murdered in 1819 and whose autobiography was offered by a London publisher in 1827. According to Matthew Scott, more than thirty of Kotzebue's plays were either translated or adapted for the British stage in the 1790s ("Circulation," para. 13). The translations of his work represent a moment of prolific production for England—one that Ackermann capitalized on when it came time to produce a literary annual with recognizable, popular authors. Kotzebue's prose appears three times in Ackermann's literary annuals, but after 1824, no prominent German author appeared in Ackermann's annual again.[27]

Often, a translated piece of prose or poetry in a literary annual heralds the "translated by/of/from" in the subtitle to signal the appropriation of foreign literature into the British tradition. In a review of titles listed in Harry E. Hootman's database of British annuals and gift books (table 1.2), the rough estimates of foreign literature translated or adapted for British literary annuals (1823–50) suggest that translations and adaptations did not overwhelm the annuals' contents. However, these numbers indicate the predilection of publishers and editors for endorsing poetry and prose that focused on matters external to England.[28]

Not satisfied with remaining a London business and importing literature with translations, Ackermann ventured into exporting the *Repository of Arts* magazine to New York, Halifax, Quebec, the West Indies, Hamburg, Lisbon, Cadiz, Gibraltar, Malta, the Mediterranean, the Cape of Good Hope, and the East Indies (Jervis, 105). Eventually, he would export his *Forget Me Not* to Latin American countries, translated as *No Me Olvides,* beginning in 1824.

In 1825, Ackermann sent his youngest son, George, to Mexico to inquire about setting up bookselling enterprises. After drafting a seemingly

TABLE 1.2 SEARCH TERMS

Search term	*Category*	*Poetry*	*Prose*	*Years appeared*
Translation	Title[a]	17	3	1825–38
Translated	Title	1	1	1835 and 1836
German[b]	Title[c]	13	5	1825–43
Schiller	Title	6	2	1826–49
Schiller	Author	1	0	1830
Kotzebue	Author	0	3	1823–24
Goethe	Title	4	3	1825–38
Goethe	Author	1	0	1830
French[d]	Title	10	13	1825–49
Spanish[e]	Title	21	8	1825–46
Italian[f]	Title	21	7	1825–46
India (variations)[g]	Title	41	24	1825–47
Persia (variations)[h]	Title	18	4	1825–47

[a] Typically followed by "of" or "from."

[b] A search for "Germany" revealed in a single prose work, "Jacob, Tales of Jews in Germany," published in the 1843 *Friendship's Offering*.

[c] Typically followed by "of" or "from."

[d] Four (3 prose and 1 poetry) of these refer to the French Revolution. A search for "France" in the title revealed literature mostly about the country rather than translations of literary works.

[e] For this search term, the use of "Spanish" in the title does not necessarily indicate a translation. A search for "Spain" in the title revealed mostly literature about the country rather than translations of literary works.

[f] Not all of these are necessarily translations.

[g] This search uncovered references to the continent of India, North American Indians, East India Company, and as a qualifier of nationality. Without physically reviewing all of the literary annuals poetry and prose, I could not identify all of the materials specifically relating to India. For instance, 3 poems and 3 prose works include "Benares" (a city in India) in the title; 2 poems and 1 prose work were found for "Hindu"; 13 poems and 5 prose works were found for "Hindo" and its variations; and 1 poem resulted in a search for "East Indies."

[h] This search includes "Persian" in the results.

reluctant Spaniard, Joseph Blanco White,[29] as author and editor, Ackermann ventured into the Catholic, Spanish-speaking industry of Mexico, Guatemala, Caracas, Colombia, and Argentina with *No Me Olvides*. Evidence from the *Literary Gazette* and the *Foreign Review* indicates that Pablo de Mendibil continued editorial duties between 1827 and 1829: "*No Me Olvides.—Collection de Producciones en Prosa i Verso Originales, Imitidas i Traduzidas para* MDCCCXXIX. Por D. Pablo de Mendibil, Ackermann, Mejico: asimismo en Colombia, Buenos Aires, Chile, Peru, i Guatemala." A review in the *Literary Gazette* in 1829 states, "The 'No Me Olvides' is a partial translation of the 'Forget me not,' but in great part composed of original articles, among which we should wish to particularize several of peculiar merit. Suffice it to remark, that the lover of a well-drawn picture of Spanish manners will be highly gratified with 'El Remolon de la Escuela,' one of the most charming sketches which we remember to have read" (262). Playing on the original didactic and moralistic qualities of the early annuals, this reviewer notes the impact these ideals of Britishness were expected to have on the already-elite society of Latin America.[30]

An earlier review in the *London Literary Gazette* of December 22, 1827, provides details about the translation of British authors but neglects to reflect upon the second editor's original contributions:

> The sweetly embellished volume, *No me Olvides,* or Spanish *Forget me Not,* published annually by Mr. Ackermann, has this year issued from the press under the auspices of a new editor, Don Pablo de Mendibil. It is adorned with graphic illustrations similar to those in the *Forget me Not,* the publication of which we recently noticed; but in its literary contents it differs materially from the English work, of which this Spanish *librillo* must be regarded not merely as an imitation, but as a very successful rival. We find in it several clever original pieces in prose and verse. With regard to the translations, the editor, after referring in his preface to the humorous pictures which form an agreeable part of the embellishments, says,—"In the articles which refer to these and the other plates, I have not only departed from the English as far as the genius of Castilian literature, and the taste of the readers for whom the *No me Olvides* is destined, seemed to require,—but in some I have abandoned the original altogether, and worked upon a different plan." The manner in which this part of the work is executed really deserves our best commendation. The pieces are, as the editor intimates, sometimes re-cast. In changing their language they also change their costume, and assume that variation of form which the German writers call a *bearbeitung.* It would be fortunate were the commendable example thus set, to have some influence on many English translators, whose slavish labours to reproduce foreign phrases and idioms—as if the English language wanted power of expression!—must disgust the

better informed, who can divine what is meant and often render the jargon unintelligible to the unlearned. The translations of the *No me Olvides,* both the prose and the poetical, are distinguished by great spirit and freedom. It is interesting to peruse the pathetic "Sister's Dream," of Mrs. Hemans; the "Bridal Morning," by L.E.L.; the "Wedding Ring," by Miss Mitford; and mark how the English ideas are re-produced or modified in the easy, flowing, Spanish assonantes, or in other kinds of verse and rhyme, totally different from those in which the originals are clothed. The first of the prose pieces is the "Vision of Las Casas," originally written in German by Engel, which well deserved to appear in a Spanish dress, on account of the nature of the Subject, and the useful lesson it is calculated to convey to the people among whom the *No me Olvides* will chiefly circulate. This is followed by the "Booroom Slave" of Mrs. Bowditch, and the "Magician's Visiter" of Mr. Neele; the latter of which was given in the *Literary Gazette,* from the English *Forget me Not.* Mrs. Holland's "Sketch," Mr. Roby's "Mab's Cross," one of the Legends of Lancashire, and all the other stories, are ably rendered into Castilian. We wish we had found Miss Mitford's genial and well-drawn picture of the "Country Apothecary" among the number. Mr. Hood's "Death in the Kitchen" is happily re-modelled, under the title of *"El Sermon del Cabo de Escuadra, 6 la Predicacion en la Cocina;"* and the "Logicians," another humorous piece by the same writer, is extremely well given. Spanish readers will find much gratification in the perusal of this interesting work. (anonymous review, 824)

The review carefully remarks upon the Castilian translations and applauds the German translation of appropriate lessons for these Spanish-speaking readers. It is as if the reviewer himself is selling an ideal British identity through Ackermann's publications.[31] Because of the volatile economic and political climate and the frequent pirating and selling of his books by the French, Ackermann withdrew his business from South America by the end of 1828.

In 1825, Ackermann installed his oldest son, Rudolph Jr., in a Regent Street print shop, where he operated for the next forty years, eventually dropping "Jr." and renaming his shop The Eclipse Sporting and Military Gallery. After Ackermann's stroke in 1830, the three younger sons took over R. Ackermann, briefly adding "& Co." to title pages but renaming the entire business Ackermann & Co. in 1832. The 1834 *Forget Me Not* volume indicates a discrepancy in business titles and possibly signals piracy in the printing world. The 1834 volume that I inspected lists the publisher on the title page as "Ackerman & Co.," leaving off the second *n* in Ackermann's name. This volume, published and distributed in November 1833, continues the trend of Ackermann's vacillating public name, but it may also signal one or more of several significant reasons, including the following: illegal printed editions of the 1834 volume, which would not have been uncommon; the further evolution of Ackermann's business; his loss of control (he died in 1834 and had turned over the business to his sons in 1830); or a serious mistake by printers that was not caught by the detail-oriented Ackermann, perhaps because of his imminent death. Ackermann's family would continue to lead the publishing industry in illustration books and decorative prints for the next twenty years.

After a successful career in the publishing industry, Ackermann made his last venture, the *Forget Me Not*, one of his most successful because he anticipated his readers' desires for a collection of literary and artistic materials that could become a valuable family heirloom, a literary work that would influence aesthetic taste and empower a female readership well beyond his death.

TWO

A Family History of Albums, Anthologies, Almanacs, and Emblems

With Ackermann's experience and business savvy, by 1822 he had found a middle-class audience that was primed for a literary object both beautiful and entertaining but not overtly didactic like conduct manuals. The annual's proper separation from other genres came from its preparation, production, and packaging of the literary, artistic, and beautiful in such a way that it transported and translated its readers away from the daily life represented in the periodicals and newspapers of the day. An annual—produced as a small, portable volume with paper, silk, or leather boards and gilt edges—was marketed as a luxury object because of its rigid boards and material stability. Its eventual moral degradation combined with its beauty would lead it to become one of the most popular literary genres of the early nineteenth century.

Lee Erickson, in *The Economy of Literary Form,* argues that literature is "the art of writing something that will be read twice" and journalism is "what will be grasped at once" (10). Because the daily, weekly, or even monthly production schedule of newspapers, magazines, and journals requires, even invokes, a hasty printing, the materials used to produce these periodicals were meant to withstand only enough handling until the next issue was produced. In addition, the materials used in the production of magazines, periodicals, and newspapers were not sturdy enough to withstand multiple rereadings; the content was filled with consumable material that was expended after it had been read once. Erickson concludes that early nineteenth-century audiences of annuals were the sort of readers who could pay for "a work in a literary form which will provide the most pleasure upon rereading and has the most satisfying verbal texture. . . . [W]hen the cost . . . is low, readers will care less about the pleasure of prospective rereadings and prefer a work in a genre that gives the most immediate pleasure" (10). This pleasure, the basest form of enjoyment, was rooted in the physical during the early nineteenth century and was frowned upon by aesthetes and literati. But the immediacy of such pleasure was buoyed by the materiality of some of these texts—something Ackermann and many other editors balanced in the production of the annuals. The annual descended from a long line of literary forms that vacillate between privileging the author and the reader, the visual and the literary, the content and the material object. The most prominent feature, it turns out, was the desire of the readers. Albums, gift books, almanacs, anthologies, scrapbooks, and even emblems contributed to the successes and failures in the literary annual business.

MISIDENTIFYING GIFT BOOKS AS LITERARY ANNUALS

The "gift book" was a traditional category that succeeded and incorporated the literary annual phenomenon. In "Creating a World of Books," Cindy Dickinson corrects a misconception regarding gift books and literary annuals: "The distinction between annuals and gift books is a technical one. Unlike annuals, true 'gift books,' which developed out of the annuals genre, were published only once. However, these two genres seem to have been indistinguishable for gift-giving purposes, and the two terms were usually used interchangeably" (54). Some literary annuals were published only once and are mistakenly categorized as a "gift book." However, as with most serial publications, conforming to established standards comforts an audience and guides their expectations from year to year. Not all gift books are literary annuals, then. If the original intention was to publish the title the following year and the volume conforms to the genre standards defined by Ackermann, the gift book can be called a literary annual.

REACHING BACK TO THE FIFTEENTH CENTURY FOR EMBLEMS

The first *Forget Me Not* demands in its very motto-like title that its readers remember, savor, and appreciate the poetry, prose, and "useful information" between its covers, an act that reminds readers that the phrase is a consumable and the book is economically valuable. It also reminds readers of the sentimental value of this phrase. Ackermann's editor, Frederic Shoberl, acquaints readers with the versatility of this phrase in his 1844 preface:

> Forget Me Not! whispers the lover, when obliged to quit the object of his heart's fondest adoration. Forget Me Not! exclaims the friend, at parting, to the friend who has been to him as another self. Forget Me Not! murmurs the expiring father to the agonized partner of his life and their sobbing children. Forget Me Not stimulates the efforts of the patriot and the hero, the poet and the philosopher, the man of science and the projector, who are each cheered in their labours by the confident hope that they shall live in their glorious deeds, in the creations of their minds, in their beneficent inventions, in their splendid discoveries, and not be forgotten when they "go hence and are no more seen." FORGET ME NOT, in short, is a desire implanted by the God of Nature himself in the human breast, and, if I mistake not, of kindred origin to that "longing after immortality," which is the parent of the sublimest virtues, of the highest and holiest emotions. Obdurate, indeed, and thoroughly depraved must be that heart, which is sensible of no claim and conceives no wish to be remembered in absence or in death by those who are left behind! (3–4)

In each of these vignettes of expiration, Shoberl admonishes his readers to celebrate a person's request to be remembered and commends the departing individual's desire to be preserved. Memory resonates throughout these requests to be immortalized and applies not only to the book and its contents but also to the literary and material value of the annual itself. In a sense, Shoberl vindicates his own request for readers to remember the annual, *Forget Me Not*. And because the annual is an object, the most beneficial method of remembering it is to *own* it so that it may be preserved and saved from "being forgotten" (1844 preface, 4).

The literary annual, though unique to the nineteenth century in its particular form, developed from a long tradition of both European and British literary works, including the sixteenth-century emblem: a popular form that combined a picture, a motto, and a poetic epigram to illustrate a moral lesson or meditation (*OED*). Italian Andrea Alciato's *Emblematum Liber* (*Book of Emblems*) "had enormous popularity and influence in the sixteenth and seventeenth centuries. It is a collection of 212 Latin emblem poems, each consisting of a motto (a proverb or other short enigmatic expression), a picture, and an epigrammatic text."[1] First published in 1531, Alciato's emblems primarily consisted of translations of lyrics and epigrammatic poems from the *Greek Anthology*. Alciato's work evolved into pseudo-ekphrastic poems when editors and publishers of the first printed edition added crude, unauthorized illustrations to accompany each poem. The author improved on the illustrations for the 1534 Paris edition, arranging each emblem into a more cohesive representation of the verse and adding a motto to each page. Though this is not the traditional definition of ekphrasis, Alciato's emblems soon came to be known for their illustrations and accompanying mottos rather than the original literature.

As Bernhard F. Scholz points outs, the typographical arrangement, at first unauthorized by the author, became tied to the composition of the text. Scholz suggests that the emblem form was really an "emergent rather than an ideally distinct form," emergent because it is a "continuing movement toward form kept in check by the constraints of the poetics of *imitatio*" ("Illustrated," 157). In other words, the ekphrastic quality of Alciato's emblems was acquired through print technologies rather than being a traditional poetic rendering of the images.

Emblematum Liber was published in 171 editions from 1531 through the late seventeenth century. The book's popularity waned in the eighteenth century, with only five editions printed. The genre, however, had caught the British public's attention in the sixteenth and seventeenth centuries: two other emblem volumes, George Wither's *Collection of Emblemes* and Francis Quarles's *Emblems, Divine and Moral*,[2] also won favor with the public. However, Wither's and Quarles's volumes were religiously oriented and have been described by David Greetham as "collections of quotations from Scripture or other 'improving' literature with accompanying woodcuts and doggerel verses as moral" (*Textual*, 109). In addition, Wither's and

Quarles's popular emblem books, though influenced by the Dutch, contained longer metrical meditations than did Alciato's volume. Linda Phyllis Austern notes that "[e]mblematic reference is a central element of the era's portraiture, pageantry, masque, drama, and all other creative junctures between the arcane world of the symbol and mundane life. As such, it may underlie the semiotics of virtually any late sixteenth- or seventeenth-century text, image, or building" (102). And Johann Hasler proposes that emblems, specifically *Atalanta Fugiens* (1687), represent a multimedia experience because the author (Michael Maier) tells us that "the work is 'to be looked at, read, mediated, understood, weighed, sung and listened to,' all at the same time in order to get a deep and true understanding of the cryptic meditative messages found in the apparently bizarre engravings, with their textual descriptions and accompanying music" (Hasler, 139).

Though these Dutch and English emblem books were continually republished throughout the eighteenth and nineteenth centuries, we see evidence of this return to moralizing, specifically in an 1860 volume published by Longman, Green, Longman and Roberts in London: *Moral Emblems with Aphorisms, Adages, and Proverbs, of all Ages and Nations, from Jacob Cats and Robert Farlie:*

> Would the limit allotted to this Introduction permit of a more detailed account of the life and works of this highly gifted, good man, numerous incidents and passages in both might be adduced, which would awaken in the breasts of Englishmen and women (for he was especially the poetic champion of the worth and virtues of the fair sex) an appreciation and esteem of his genius and character, as great almost as that felt for him by his own countrymen and women: among whom Father Cats, as he is affectionately called, is honoured as the bard of Home and of the Domestic hearth, the still popular and revered instruction of his countrymen in the Virtues of Social life, and in the Maxims of purest world-wisdom. (xi)

The second edition of this 1860 reproduction of Cats's *Proteus* confirms the revaluing of domesticity, philosophy, and moral instruction from these visual and textual renderings:

> The Plan of the present Volume, as a selection from several works, not only precluded an adherence to the original order of

> the pieces selected, but tended in some degree to conceal the unity of purpose that underlies the whole series. The Emblematic Writings of Jacob Cats form no mere collection of Fables or Parables strung together at random: they are the result of wide observation and mature thought, and embody a whole system of Moral Philosophy. Few writings more completely bring before us a man who has striven to act up to a high standard of Christian duty, and whom the memory of his own struggles has impelled to warn, instruct, and encourage others. With this design, he has not merely made use of familiar facts or incidence in the physical world to enforce a lesson in morals; he has not merely, like older writers, exposed the follies or the vices of men under fables and allegories, but he has carefully analysed the several stages in human life, and adapted his teaching to the needs and the dangers of each. But, living in an age in which the profession of a moral purpose sufficed generally to deter readers from opening a book, he felt that he must draw attention to his work by something like a stratagem. If, however, he prefixed to his "Sinne en Minne Beelden" the title of "Proteus," he did so not merely to suit the fashion of his time, but to express the general view he had taken of human life. To him that life appeared to be divided into three distinct stages, in the first of which the natural affections and sentiments predominate, while in the second, the man feels himself concerned in the wider interests of his fellow-citizens; and in the third turns his thoughts to that unseen world which he is so soon to enter. The first stage is the season of love and marriage; the second is taken up with discharge of civil duties; while the third is the period of devout meditation, in which the man is drawn away from the world into more immediate communion with God.

Making a study of emblematic images was encouraged, especially with the 1830 textbook publication of *Iconology; or, Emblematic Figures Explained, in Original Essays on Moral and Instructive Subjects* by W. Pinnock. The author believed that iconography and allegory offered children the best kind of moral education "since by ocular impression it firmly imprints ideas on the memory, and strongly calls those ideas into action by the mere sight or recollection of the symbol" (3). Pinnock warns the student against vulgar representations in emblems, that complaint made by eighteenth-century poets and philosophers that mottoes, pictures, and doggerel verse represent the most base and reductive sentiments stimulated by the visual. Allegorical education and concentration on a symbol will "enable children of tender years to acquire information on subjects of which ancient sages were ignorant, and make them better geographers, astronomers, and natural philosophers" (4).

Similar to J. Cats's and Alciato's emblems, the literary annual reproduces the format but divides the emblematic elements and process: the motto is included on the title page and represents the tenor of the entire volume; and the illustration is first engraved and then verbally rendered in truly ekphrastic style. Initially, the annual was intended to offer instruction in morality and propriety, allowing readers to meditate on the visual and literary. And like the *Emblematum Liber,* the early annual's pocket-sized delicacy allowed the book to be a portable reference of morality and propriety as well as an indicator of education, wealth, friendship, or leisure. The beautiful binding found a home in the lady's drawing room and on her bookshelf once the year had expired or the volume had been read—intended as a permanent object that enhanced a collection or represented a memory.[3]

The emblematic poems in the first three volumes of the *Forget Me Not* resonate with this act of remembering and expand its sentimental value: (1) a request to "keep my gift, though the gift be small" (line 37, "Poetical Address" [1823]), referring to the actual size of the book as well as a self-deprecating comment about the sentimental value of the gift; (2) a spiritual "forget me not" to remember "Our Lord" (line 56, Barton, "The Heart's Motto" [1824]); (3) a memorializing of the dead with the forget-me-not flower "entwind [r]ound Friendship's or Affection's shrine" (lines 46–47, Barton, "To the Flower Forget Me Not" [1825]); and (4) declarations of romantic love, jubilant or sobbing, the most frequent use of the "forget me not" motto:

> Forget not, oh! Forget not me,
> I ne'er shall cease to think of thee,
> Oh, never, never!
>
> . . . .
>
> Forget not love—forget not truth—
> And plighted vows of earliest youth—
> Oh, never, never!

A heart that fondly trusted thee,
Blessings breathed oft and fervently,
Thoughts ever studious thine to please,
And folded hands, and bended knees,
Forget not, oh! Forget not these,
No! never—never!

(lines 1–3 and 19–27, Neele, "Forget Me Not" [1825])

Indeed, even the engravings began to express this sentiment: The 1827 and 1831 *Forget Me Nots* include engravings that highlight people literally engraving mottos onto extremely hard surfaces—an engraving within an engraving. A free hand writing an inscription in tree bark can also be found in J. Cats's *Proteus* (1618) and then again in emblems published in 1627, 1629, and 1703 by various authors.[4] The 1618 motto accompanying this bodiless act of inscription offers a meditation on love and loss. In the 1827 *Forget Me Not,* "Love's Motto" replicates this act of inscribing onto a tree a brief motto. In this case, the motto, "forget me not," is being authored by a young man with Cupid on his shoulder. The untitled poem offered by Letitia Elizabeth Landon to accompany the engraving (1–2) meditates on a lover's thoughts about his beloved and ends by requesting to be memorialized in her heart and on the bark of this tree (figs. 2.1 and 2.2).

In the 1860 *Moral Emblems,* this tree inscription again appears as a translation of *Proteus* but is absent the free-floating hand. The motto at the head of the image, suggesting that gradually love occupies the senses ("sensim amor sensu occupat"), is accompanied by mottoes flanking either side of the page: "time is the herald of truth," "perfection is not reached at once," and "slow and sure" (21). The accompanying motto and verse meditate on love:

[*Motto*] Love takes possession of the mind insensibly.
[*Verse*] Though scarce at first apparent to the fight,
The words which on the tender bark we write;
Yet how distinct, 'ere long, the letters shew
In size increased, as with the rind they grow!
So by degrees, as on that lettered bark,
Doth Time expand to flame, Love's slightest spark:
So to the germ of Vice in early youth,
Time gives the increase with the body's growth;

Figure 2.1 Frontispiece, 1824 *Forget Me Not*, drawn by E. F. Burney and engraved by J. S. Agar (from the Katherine D. Harris Collection)

Figure 2.2 "Love's Motto," 1827 *Forget Me Not,* drawn by R. Westall and engraved by E. Finden (from the Katherine D. Harris Collection)

And errors deem'd at first too slight to trace,
Spread to a depth no efforts can efface.
From small beginnings rise the fiercest strife;
Nor Love, nor Vice, at once leap into life:
The breeze at first so zephyr-like and warm,
Is but too oft the prelude of the storm.
That so it is; how many have to grieve!—
The mischief when full grown we can perceive;
But how it grew—we scarcely can believe.

(21–22)

Cats's original Latin verses are printed on the next page along with biblical verse and more recent references, including Sidney Godolphin and Robert Wilmont. Ideally, this is a meditation on the virtues of true love instead of sentimentality and lust (fig. 2.3).

Bernhard Scholz suggests that this editing of the image indicates that the original copperplate engravings, by Adriaan van de Venne, were replaced with contemporary steel-plate engravings, a modernization of the pictura that incorporates the nineteenth-century contemporary reader into the image rather than having the image as a distant point of meditation ("Re-editing," 204). In the 1827 *Forget Me Not,* both the image and the accompanying poem place the reader inside the situation of memorializing a lover and thereby incorporate that contemporary reader into a modernized version of an emblem. The 1860 modernization of Cats's emblems, though, removes that reader from the act of inscription and memorialization, only to return the reader to a meditation distant from amorous explication.

Ackermann was familiar with the emblem form: in 1809, he sold to 175 subscribers an emblem volume, *Religious Emblems, Being a Series of Engravings on Wood, Executed by the First Artists in That Line, from Designs Drawn on the Blocks Themselves by J. Thurston, Esq.[, . . . and] Descriptions Written by the Rev. J. Thomas, A.M.*[5] Unlike the emblem engraving, these literary annual subjects are always in the act of writing it out, never completing the phrase. The idea is that the viewer must see the person performing the supposed labor of writing in order to perceive the sentiment behind engraved sentiment—a sentiment similar to the purpose of literary annuals themselves: they must be given openly with a presentation plate "engraven" by presenter/giver.

Figure 2.3 Sensim Amor emblem and Plutarchus emblem in *Proteus* (1618) (from Internet Archive, http://www.archive.org/stream/moralemblemswithoocats [accessed July 26, 2011])

Frequently, lines were requested from literati to characterize a particular annual's purpose. In one instance, the motto was the result of a contest. By 1827, Ackermann and other publishers began declaring this sentiment on the title pages of their annuals in the form of mottos, such as

> Appealing, by the magic of its name,
> To gentle feelings and affections, kept
> Within the heart like gold.

This motto, written by the popular nineteenth-century poet Letitia Elizabeth Landon ("L.E.L."), became the permanent entreaty on the title page of all the *Forget Me Not* volumes until its demise in 1847 and provides a consistency missing in most other annuals.

Publisher George Murray Smith offered five pounds, five shillings in 1828 "for some lines to serve as a motto for the title page. The prize was won by Mr. Thompson, who pursued the unpoetical trade of a seedsman in Fenchurch Street" (*Recollections,* 9). Mr. Thompson's four lines first appeared on the 1829 title page of *Friendship's Offering:*

> This is affection's tribute, friendship's offering.
> Whose silent eloquence, more rich than words,
> Tells of the giver's faith, and truth in absence,
> And says—forget me not.

Editor Alaric A. Watts bought a few lines from Sir Walter Scott for his annual, *Literary Souvenir:*

> I have song of war for knight;
> Lay of love for lady bright;
> Fairy tale to lull the heir;
> Goblin grim the maids to scare.
>
> (1826 title page)

The motto represents the miscellaneous collection of poetry, fiction, nonfiction, and travel accounts that Watts accumulated to present in the *Literary Souvenir.* The *Literary Souvenir* motto seems less sentimental than the *Forget Me Not*'s, perhaps indicating that each volume's contents will match these sentiments. This does not prove true, however.

As the literary annual phenomenon progressed, this idea of ekphrastic renderings in the emblematic style would come to plague authors. In the 1832 *Fisher's Drawing Room Scrap Book,* Letitia Elizabeth Landon offers a collection of engravings (landscape scenes, portraits, and events), their poetic illustrations, and any thoughts or historical facts that inspired the poems. For instance, the engraving entitled "Lismore Castle" is accompanied by a four-stanza poem of the same title as well as explanatory notes, a practice not common to annuals. In these particular notes, Landon introduces the inspiration for the poem, citing *O'Driscol's History of Ireland,* Edmund Spenser's *Faerie Queene,* and Henry II's rule over Ireland. To verbally illustrate another engraving, "Blarney Castle," she declines to offer a poetic illustration and instead tells her readers that "it is impossible better to illustrate Blarney Castle, than by compositions which embody its very spirit" (45). She includes brief verse from Voltaire, Jean-François Marmontel, and Marie Antoinette and a few paragraphs of reflections on the same.

By inserting notes, Landon subscribes to "a local detour or a momentary fork in the text," as Gerard Genette points out in *Paratexts* (328). These "original notes" are undefinable as either text or paratext, according to Genette. The notes, sometimes thought to "disorder the text," in fact do not interrupt the text's effect. Instead, they act as an extension of the text, allowing the author a "second level of discourse" (328). With this, Landon provides another level of information for her readers—essentially an insight into the creative process as well as the work's historical impetus. She creates a printed, as opposed to handwritten, layering of information much the same as a scrapbook.

ACCUMULATING MEMORIES IN SCRAPBOOKS

A scrapbook, much like an album, is intended as an informal receptacle of unassociated and impromptu clumps of words and images. Each scrapbook, pocket-book, or album represents an importance that is conflated with public and private, and a scrapbook may entertain different moments or memories or may be a snapshot of a life. The annuals adopted many elements of the scrapbook, including an accumulation of seemingly disparate information that formed an intellectual moment.

In his article for the inaugural volume of *The Keepsake* (1828), Leigh Hunt interchanges the terms *almanac* and *pocket-book* but defines their use synonymously with *scrapbook:*

> We remember a series of pocket-books in a great drawer, that, in addition to their natural size, seemed all to have grown corpulent in consequence of being fed with receipts, and copies of verses, and cuttings out of newspapers. The hook on the clasp had got from eyelet to eyelet, till it could unbuckle no further. These books, in the printed part, contained acrostics and rebuses, household

> receipts for various purposes, and a list of public events. There was love, politics and eating. It is a pity the readers could not grow as corpulent as their pocket-books, with as little harm. (7)

A scrapbook captured the printed press's daily influence on this grandmotherly figure of whom Hunt writes. Hunt imbues this book object with a responsibility for retaining memories, privacy, home, and such other domesticities that normally are not printed.

A BLANK ALBUM FOR EVERY GIRL

The next category represents a type of work that was not completed at the printers. Instead, these books invited owners to author and collect memories. The album, a miscellany generated by others but motivated by its owner, is simply a beautifully bound book of blank pages that invites, even entices, its owner to reveal and publicize admiration and desire—albeit a desire for ownership of writing, but nonetheless a desire. With women as the dominant owners of these blank spaces, the fulfilled album becomes a feminized space that represents her identity—a process that is mimicked intellectually instead of physically in the literary annual

Albums, also referred to as commonplace books, pocket-books, and diaries, were nothing but blank pages bound decoratively and used to collect autographs and writings. Albums were the less-formal cousin to the literary annual and were filled up in emulation of annuals' contents. Patrizia Di Bello notes that "[u]nlike museums, galleries, histories or encyclopedias, which could also be defined as containers of miscellaneous items, albums impose little taxonomic order or value on their contents" (7). The album's owner could then display those materials to reinforce class boundaries or demonstrate taste. Di Bello continues that an album represents the owner's participation "based on individual encounters and across personal exchanges. . . . However personal, and unlike diaries, albums have no particular connotations of secrecy" (23).

Technically, in the nineteenth century, the term *pocket-book* referred to the size of a book, a literary genre, *and* a bound book with a pocket for collecting ephemera. Typically for the latter, a leather binding continued with a flap that fit snugly into a latch to close the pocket-book. A sleeve for a thin pencil and a pocket made from the front board and an accordion-style folder encouraged readers to fill up their pocket-books with annotations and receipts (fig. 2.4). *The Country and Town Ladies' Memorandum Book, or Polite Pocket Museum* of 1822 also includes a pull-out engraving of Rushbrook Hall in Suffolk, the latest fashions, cash accounts for each month, blank memorandum pages, engagement pages for each month, descriptions of quadrilles and country dances, a table of expenses, coach fares to theater districts, a marketing table, a table of stamp prices, and forty pages of enigmas to be answered in the following year (figs. 2.5 and 2.6). The title page indicates that this hybrid pocket-book and almanac had been published since 1800 and was to be continued annually. At 32mo and according to the inscription written on the first verso page, this particular pocket-book was intended to be given to a young lady by her mother. The owner used the last two blank pages to record a literary passage in ink but used pencil to record cash accounts and engagements. The enigmas, however, remain without annotation in this volume. Clearly, this pocket-book was intended for a woman of means, someone who had the leisure time to attend the theater and dances, and also a practical woman who kept track of her expenses.

Figure 2.4 1770 *Vergissmeinnicht* pocket-book clasp and pocket (from the Katherine D. Harris Collection; photo credit, Tom Davis)

Figure 2.5 Pullout engraving, "Rushbrook Hall, Suffolk," from 1822 *Country and Town Ladies' Memorandum Book, or Polite Pocket Museum,* engraved by T. Higham (from the Katherine D. Harris Collection; photo credit, Tom Davis)

The general assumption is that album owners were young women who carried the albums with them in hopes of receiving a line or two from admirers or local literati. The more well-established authors, including Hemans, Wordsworth, Tennyson, and Lamb, complained vociferously about this practice.

Felicia Hemans, while visiting William Wordsworth at Dove Cottage in 1830, wrote to John Lodge that her privacy and seclusion were interrupted by American tourists who had discovered that she was visiting the area. Because of their association with a colleague of Hemans's, she could not refuse seeing them. She became annoyed not only with the intrusion but also with their requests: "The young ladies, as I feared, brought an Album concealed in their shawls, and it was levelled at me like a pocket-pistol before all was over" (Wolfson, *Felicia Hemans,* 510). Hemans described the encounter with violent images, as if she were being robbed and her authorship were the coveted prize. She was doubly annoyed by the duplicitous hidden agenda concealed by their clothing. However, for the

Figure 2.6 "Walking Dress" from 1822 *Country and Town Ladies' Memorandum Book, or Polite Pocket Museum* (from the Katherine D. Harris Collection; photo credit, Tom Davis)

remainder of her visit, she was bothered with these requests only twice and was able to shirk "the dust of celebrity" (Wolfson, *Felicia Hemans,* 511). Being asked to contribute to an album was a sign of fame and marker of credibility. Authors who grumbled also recognized their own fame and grudgingly contributed a few lines to savor this fact.

Though authors complained of the deluge of requests to pen a verse for some young lady's album, they not only contributed but also requested verses from other literati as favors for family and friends. In his letters, Charles Lamb frequently called an album request an intrusion. However, in the same letter he would ask friends, including Wordsworth, Bernard Barton, B. W. Procter, Hazlitt, and Southey, to contribute something to a friend's album.[6] In a January 19, 1829, letter, he gives explicit instructions to B. W. Procter for this task:

> I had another favour to beg, which is the beggarliest of beggings. . . .
>
> A few lines of verse for a young friend's album (six will be enough). M. Burney will tell you who she is I want 'em for. A girl of gold. Six lines—make 'em eight—signed Barry C———. They need not be very good, as I chiefly want 'em as a foil to mine. But I shall be seriously obliged by any *refuse scrap.* . . . M.B. will tell you the sort of girl I request the ten lines for. Somewhat of a pensive cast, what you admire. (*Letters,* 5:152–53; emphasis added)

In a January 22, 1829, letter, Lamb offers further description of the young lady to guide Procter in creating her personalized poem:

> Don't trouble yourself about the verses. Take 'em cooly as they come. Any day between this and midsummer will do. Ten lines the extreme. There is no mystery in my incognita. She has often seen you, though you may not have observed a silent brown girl, who for the last twelve years has run wild about our house in her Christmas holidays. She is Italian by name and extraction. Ten lines about the blue sky of her country will do, as it's her foible to be proud of it. But they must not be over-courtly or lady-fied, as she is with a lady who says to her "go and she goeth; come and she cometh." Item, I have made her a tolerable Latinist. The verses should be moral too, as for a clergyman's family. She is called Emma Isola. (5:154–55)

Lamb's resistance is marked in his sarcasm throughout these instructions. In addition, his request is filled with thinly veiled comments regarding the girl's mental acumen and nationality (and Lamb's prejudice toward it)—she is "dark," "wild," obedient, proud, and intellectually simple.[7] In directing Procter's creativity, Lamb offers Emma a record of her character flaws in the form of Latin and morality instruction.

Despite the request and in-between these instructions, Lamb laments the "albumean persecution":

> We are in the last ages of the world, when St. Paul prophesied that women should be "headstrong, lovers of their own wills, having albums." I fled hither to escape the albumean persecution, and had not been in my new house twenty-four hours, when the daughter of the next house came in with a friend's album to beg a contribution, and the following day intimated she had one of her own. Two more have sprung up since. If I take the wings of the morning and fly until the uttermost parts of the earth, there will albums be. . . . Why, by dabbling in those accursed albums, I have become a byword of infamy all over the kingdom. I have sicken'd decent women for asking me to write in albums. There be "dark jests" abroad, Master Cornwall; and some riddles may live to be clear'd up. (5:153–54)

Lamb, a master of punning verses, apparently contributed to several albums with sarcasm that was not recognized by the album's owner. By writing these scandalous verses, Lamb tinged his own legacy with indelicate memories recorded in random albums that, once they left his hands, were beyond his control. Lamb's sarcasm in the letter *hints* at mild regret for writings that would survive him and could influence a future public's opinion of him.

Despite his resistance, Lamb conceded that "the age is to be complied with" (5:153)—a fact that William Wordsworth also believed. When he was inundated with these types of requests, Wordsworth turned to another author, Felicia Hemans, who wrote that he told her "that when he was more troubled with those importunities than he is at present, he found it convenient to administer the same line to all patients. The one he selected for the purpose, and adhered to [for] a considerable time, was 'The proper study of mankind, is *man.*' Think of this in the midst of the butterfly-winged cupids and roses of a young lady's Album!" (Wolfson, *Felicia Hemans,* 511). Wordsworth borrowed the quotation from Pope's *Essay on Man: Epistle II* (1733)

(Wolfson, *Felicia Hemans,* 511n2). Hemans passingly referred to the fewer requests suffered by Wordsworth, but these diminished requests signaled an author's decreasing popularity—not necessarily a desired effect. Hemans also couched her rhetoric in medicinal language, as if Wordsworth's album tidbits provided a poetic salve that was more like a mild enema or diuretic intended to purge the debilitating and cloying sentiments.

The daily deluge of requests was foisted onto everyone, including those who were not so poetically inclined: in an early treatment of drawing-room books, Amy Cruse notes that Lord Chesterton in T. H. Lister's *Granby* (1827) cannot escape Lady Harriet Duncan's request for a few lines. This character refuses not because of indignation but because he is fearful of suffering the "agonies of inspiration" (Cruse, 285).

In essence, these album-toting young women, with the help of authors, created a highly personalized literary miscellany. The authors, though, sometimes contributed verses based on their views of appropriate femininity. For instance, Lamb's description of Emma both castigates her wild self and observes her burgeoning intellectual self. The blank album required its owner to create a pastiche of memories and memorable writing that did not necessarily originate from its owner.

The blank pages offered in the 1823 and 1824 literary annuals were used as "albums" with owners creating notations, writing poems, and requesting autographs to fill the space. During the height of popularity, Leigh Hunt identified the literary annual format as part of the new category of pocket-books that are "books for the pocket, without implying that they are to be written in. . . . The bindings are seldom very costly, but they are more so than ordinary, sufficient to render the present graceful; and they are generally in good taste. . . . [A]nd omitting the barren or blank part, and being entirely original, produce such a pocket-book as had not been yet seen" (10, 11). Writing in 1827, Hunt had already seen the disappearance of the blank apparatus in the annual form, and he described the successful format that was to become the standard. When this feature disappeared from the annual's format, owners would request autographs on the one or two blank pages at the beginning of the volume. The remainder of the volume was usually left pristine without any marginalia or annotations—most likely because the literary annual was a valuable object.[8]

The impromptu writing in albums soon became the printed materials in literary annuals, almost as if the albums provided an intermediary space in which authors could practice their poetry before submitting it to editors. Alternatively, poetry spontaneously produced for an album perhaps was surreptitiously borrowed without the author's permission and submitted to the annuals anonymously. In the 1829 *Forget Me Not,* for example, James Montgomery contributed the poem "Epitaph on a Gnat, found crushed on the leaf of a Lady's Album, and written (with a different reading in the last line) in lead pencil beneath it"

Lie there, embalm'd from age to age!
This is the album's noblest page,
Though every glowing leaf be fraught
With painting, poesy, and thought;
Where tracks of mortal hands are seen,
A hand invisible hath been,
And left this autograph behind,
This image from th' eternal mind;
A work of skill surpassing sense,
A labour of Omnipotence!

Though frail as dust it meet the eye,
He form'd this gnat who built the sky;
Stop—lest it vanish at thy breath—
This speck had life, and suffer'd death.

(67)

In this poem, the author speculates on the circumstances of the gnat's demise as well as its place in a book of memories. Another poem pilfered from an album and published in the 1829 *Keepsake* addresses more serious topics:

Lines

Written in the Album of Elliot Cresson of Philadelphia.
By the Author of Lorenzo De' Medici [William Roscoe]

From distant climes the stranger came
With friendly view and social aim,

The various tribes of earth to scan
As friend to friend—as man to man.

No glittering stones the stranger brought;
No arts profess'd, no wealth he sought;
His every wish one view confined,
The interchange of mind with mind.

What he the richest prize would deem,
Was friendship, kindness, and esteem;
What he could in return impart—
The same warm feelings of the heart.

Not his with selfish views alone
To trace his course from zone to zone;
His hope—to stretch affection's chain
From land to land—from main to main,

The various powers and virtues tell
In human heads and hearts that dwell;
In bounds of love, the race to bind,
And make one people of mankind.

(312)

The inclusion of these poems in the literary annual serves to differentiate albums from annuals: by lifting a poem from veritable obscurity in a personal album and printing it in the public space of a literary annual, the poem is removed from the private and offered for public consumption. Albums were not normally published and distributed for a mass audience; they were distinct remembrances for a single audience member. "Borrowing" a poem from an album creates a palimpsest of authorial identity and removes authority from the original writer.

Authors could not wholly control their writings. Instead, the owner of a piece became the person who possessed it. With this conviction, benefactors often gifted items not of their own pen to annuals' editors. Many editors admitted this gift in the preface, a footnote, or a postscript, essentially excusing themselves of responsibility for the poem's originality (as occurred with Alaric Watts's 1826 postscript to *The Literary Souvenir*).

In the 1829 *Keepsake,* editor Frederic Mansel Reynolds notes just such a gift: "Neither is it necessary to particularize any of their contributions except two; one of which, as posthumous, and the other, as the gift of an individual, not its author: allusion is made to an Essay and Fragments by Percy Bysshe Shelley, for the possession of which, the Editor is indebted to the kindness of the Author of Frankenstein [Mary Shelley]" (iv). The gifts extended to private letters as well: The editor of the *Forget Me Not,* Frederic Shoberl, included a private letter from Lord Byron to James Hogg in the 1844 volume. The letter was offered for publication by D. L. Moir, a frequent contributor to the annuals under the pseudonym Delta, with an appropriate footnote establishing ownership: "This letter, with two other letters of the Noble Bard's to Hogg, was lost at the time of the publication of Mr. Moore's Journals and Correspondence of Lord Byron. The original is now in my possession, and was last year presented to me by a lady, who had found it among the papers of her brother, the late Major A____n, an intimate acquaintance of the Shepherd [James Hogg]" (353n1). The footnote not only claims valid ownership by Delta but also impresses the volume with an intellectual quality not expected of annuals: by publishing the lost correspondence of a national hero, Delta attempts to help complete the picture of Byron. However, the letter seems unimportant in its content and was published to fan the ever-present Byron-mania:

> 13, Terrace, Piccadilly,
> March 1st, 1816.
>
> Dear Sir,
>
> I never was offended with you, and never had cause. At the time I received your last letters, I was "marrying, and being given in marriage," and since that period have been occupied or indolent; and am at best a very ungracious or ungrateful correspondent—hardly ever writing letters but by fits and starts.
>
> At this moment my conscience smites me with an unanswered letter of Mr. W. Scott's, on a subject which may seem to him to require an answer—as it was on something relative to a friend of his, for whose talents I have a sincere admiration.
>
> My family, about three months ago, was increased by a little girl, who is reckoned a fine child, I believe, though I feel loth to trust to my own partialities. She is now in the country.

I will mention your wishes on the score of collection and publication to Murray, but I have not much weight with him; what I have I will use. As far as my approval of your intention may please you, you have it; and I should think Mr. Scott's liking to your plan very ominous if it's successful.

The objections you mention to the two things of mine lately published are very just and true; not only with regard to them, but to all their predecessors, some more and some less. With regard to the quarter from which you anticipate a probably and public censure, on such points I can only say, that I am very sure there will be no severity but what is deserved: and, were there ever so much, it could not obliterate a particle of the obligation which I am already too much under to that journal and its conductors, (as the grocer says to his customers) "for past favours."

And so you want to come to London? It is a d—d place, to be sure, but the only one in the world, (at least in the English world,) for fun. Though I have seen parts of the globe that I like better, still, upon the whole, it is the completest either to help one in the feeling one's self alive—or forgetting that one is so.

I am interrupted, but will write you again soon.

Yours very truly,
Byron

P.S. I forgot to thank you for liking, &c. &c.—but am much obliged to you, as well as for a former compliment in the inscription of your "Pilgrims of the Sun." (353–54)

Publishing a private letter signifies that the intention/purpose of annuals as repositories of memories had expanded to somewhere between an album collection of autographs and a scholarly exercise in editing.

One of the alterations popularized by the *Literary Souvenir* mimicked elements of the "album" genre. The *Literary Souvenir* included printed facsimiles of authors' signatures in the last three to six pages of the book (figs. 2.7 and 2.8). Though the autographs are intended to "authorize" the annual's literary contents with the imprimatur of its famous contributors, in effect the tactic closes the owner's written influence on the work. With the exception of an inscription or presentation plate, no blank pages or calendars

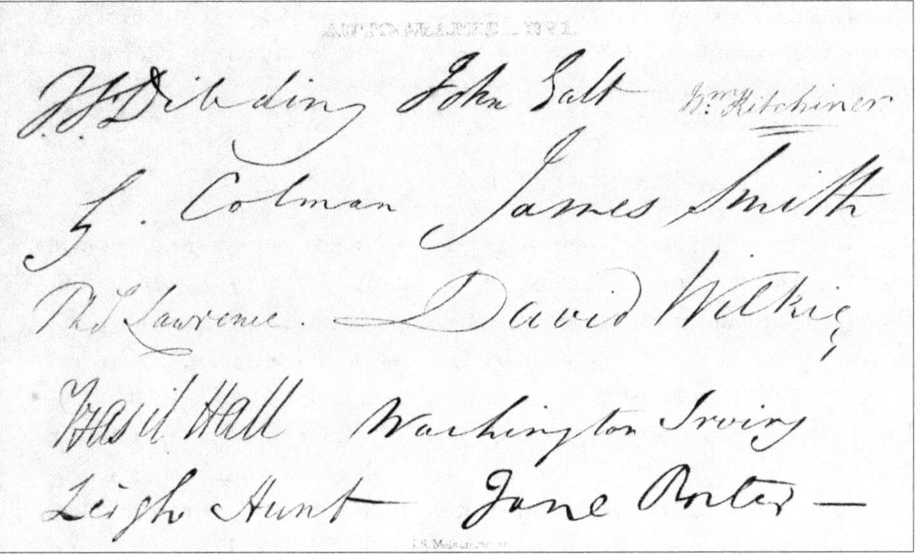

Figure 2.7 "Autographs No. 1" from 1826 *Literary Souvenir* (from the Katherine D. Harris Collection; photo credit, Tom Davis)

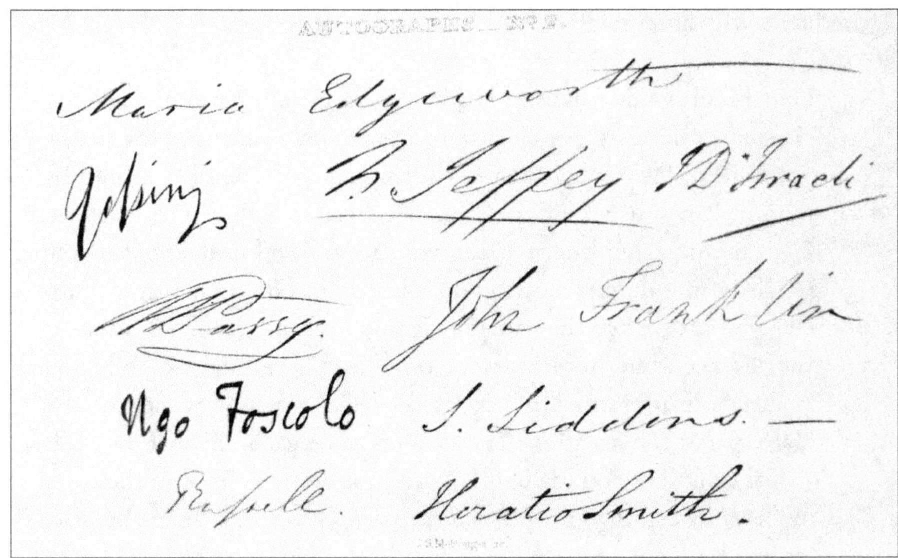

Figure 2.8 "Autographs No. 2" from 1826 *Literary Souvenir* (from the Katherine D. Harris Collection; photo credit, Tom Davis)

or memos are provided for scribbling as in an album. The success of *The Literary Souvenir* suggests that consumers apparently wanted a completed product, a souvenir of the moment, in which the reader or owner never ventured into "authorship."

A LONG TRADITION OF ALMANACS

The differentiation among genres of pocket-books, memorandum books, and almanacs was forced because of the Stamp Act in 1712, which continued in England even on imported almanacs until 1828. By 1775, all British almanacs were produced by the Stationers' Company, were released/published in November on Almanac Day, and continued their popularity even into the nineteenth century, with 605,000 copies printed in 1801 (Perkins, 14) (fig. 2.9).[10] During the eighteenth century, the Stationers' Company had difficulty controlling their rights to print calendars and almanacs. Pretenders popped up as soon as Almanac Day arrived and caused a flooded, saturated market by November 22.[11]

Similar to the literary annual, the almanac form and contents, as defined by Maureen Perkins, required several elements to avoid being castigated by critics and reviews:

> First of all would be an introductory page with chronological cycles and eclipses, the major items of reference affecting the whole year ahead. Then would come twelve pages of calendar, month by month. It was usual for the calendar pages to follow a set pattern. Each month would have at the very top a section devoted to the phases of the moon, showing on what days and at what times they changed. . . . After the calendar would be other items of interest, varying according to editor or compiler. There might be hints on health, interpretations of ingress charts, stores of wonders, and blank pages for notation. These items gave each almanac its individual character and made it a work of literature. Even in the early nineteenth century, people did not simply consult their almanac, but read it. . . .
>
> [However,] [t]he almanac contained no fiction, poetry, or puzzles, but it was replete with tables of statistics. (15–16, 55)

Figure 2.9 "'Almanac Day' at Stationers' Hall" from *Book of Days* (1869), p. 715.

By 1826, almanacs had deviated from their original construction. The 1826 *Janus, or the Edinburgh Literary Almanack* was pilloried for pretending to be the precursor to the literary annual, and it leans more toward Ackermann's original 1823 *Forget Me Not* with its literary contents: "A 'literary almanack' has, in title at least, the semblance of family-commodities for all ages and conditions: poetry and sentiment for the young ladies; astrological predictions of political wonder and national woe, set into marvellous proper verse, for their grandams; and for the travelling, agricultural, and professional animals of our own sex [men], sure prognostics of foul and fair weather, of terms and returns, of full moons and eclipses" (anonymous review, 169).

Unlike the annuals, almanacs were primarily intended for the lower classes because they contained astrology, which was likened to prediction rather than rational thought. In *The Year Book* for 1841, author William Hone reflects on, even satirizes, the prognostications of one famous almanac author, Henry Andrews of the *Vox Stellarum:* "His prophecies, under the name of 'Francis Moore, Physician,' were as much laughed at by himself, as by the worshipful company of stationers for whom he annually manufactured them, in order to render their almanac saleable among the ignorant, in whose eyes a lucky *hit* covered a multitude of blunders" (117). Hone irreverently gestures toward the inevitability of a confused (and highly ignorant) readership when the *Vox Stellarum* moved to publishing political vignettes rather than Andrews's prophecies in 1821. Mortimer Collins, in an 1876 survey of several decades of almanacs, notes that the owner, the reader of all of these eighteenth- and nineteenth-century almanacs, was not the reader intended for the more sophisticated *Imperial Almanac* printed for 1826:

> The Imperial Almanac for 1826 was quite enough to finish the old collector. It began with a splendid preface, in which the editor "confidently hoped" that it would be equally interesting to the Man of Science, the Man of Taste, and the Man of Business." The collector was neither. He had no business at all; he was so unscientific as to prefer alchemy to chemistry, and astrology to astronomy; and as to taste! well, he liked old pictures without knowing why, and old friends and old port for reasons he was always ready to give, but he was not a man of taste. He was an unclassifiable man; and, when he opened that Imperial Almanac for 1826, and found in it the Astronomer Royal's Catalogue of Stars, all the Eclipses till 1900, a Synchronatic Table of European Monarchs from 1066, his head began to whirl. "Jessy, my dear," he said to his niece, "get me *Poor Robin* and the port wine from the corner cupboard." (424–25)

Collins concludes that the almanac "served for a year's reading and guidance, and ranked next to the Bible in value" (430). Each copy acted as a predictor of more than weather; it held a certain promise of future memories.[12]

In addition to the lower classes, women, although "not specifically criticized as almanac users," were often considered as such, because of the "belief that almanacs were generally the literature of the easily influenced and the undiscriminating, who accepted written authority no matter how suspect. Women, it was felt, could be included in such a category" (Perkins, 44).

Almanacs were maligned as engendering class differentiation and were thought to suppress the proper education of the lower classes. Charles

Knight recognized an opportunity to use almanacs as a form of education and not simply recreation or heretical prediction.[13] He led the attack on early nineteenth-century almanacs as being "vulgar and saw them as being alien to his own culture" (Perkins, 9). He claimed that the Society for the Diffusion of Useful Knowledge was created to combat the "lesser" reading materials being circulated to people who had no access to education: "The reform to almanacs was an attempt to minimize social divisions and to promote social harmony, to encourage the absorption of disparate readers into a unified audience" (Perkins, 9). As the champion for reform, Knight fostered the belief that

> the *British Almanac, Penny Magazine,* and *Penny Cyclopaedia* all encouraged readers to equate knowledge and understanding, suggesting that the result would be to increase the owner's worth and self-respect. . . . However, the radical press interpreted "useful knowledge" as an awareness of corruption in state and church, an awareness that would alter the deference of the working man towards his social "superiors." . . .
>
> "Useful knowledge" was intended to replace a faulty perception of society and the natural world, and one of the areas in which its proponents hoped it would fulfill this function was the popular understanding of the time." (Perkins, 65, 89)[14]

But he praised the *Ladies' Diary,* probably because he approved of the mathematics contributor, Olinthus Gregory.[15]

During the nineteenth century, some publishers moved from the traditional almanac—prognosticator, astronomical, and astrological information—to a calendar "to signal a move away from astronomical and astrological content" in the nineteenth century (Perkins, 23):

> In both England and Australia, even those who tried to repudiate the astrological tradition maintained the format and some of the terminology, and it was often this terminology which angered reformers when the content of the almanac seemed innocent enough. The imitation of the layout may have been simply a market technique, to persuade those used to the older astrological almanac to make the change to the rational versions. In the nineteenth century,

> when lunar phases were dethroned from their position of prominence at the top of each calendar page, the space left was often filled with a morally uplifting or educational verse, so that the page looked very similar. (Perkins, 17)

The 1768, 1821, and 1822 *Ladies' Diary; or, Woman's Almanack* retain the lunar phases printed at the top of each month; however, the 1800 *Vox Stellarum* replaces this section on the first page of each month with verses such as this one for January:

> Behold, good Reader, what I here shall Shew;
> A Month like this, I think, I never knew:
> O strange! Six Aspects and Three Oppositions;
> These will affect Men of no mean Conditions.—
> What'er the Heavens in their secret Doom
> Ordained have, must needs to Issue come.
>
> (2)

The Ladies' Diary, published from 1704 to 1840, eschewed astrology and prediction for mathematical problems, typically including enigmas, queries, and the answers to the previous year's questions (fig. 2.10).[16] On the final pages of the 1768, 1821, and 1822 *Diary,* the listed prize winners for many of the enigmas were men, though the intended audience for this particular almanac was women.

In contrast, *Simpson's Gentleman's Almanack and Pocket Journal* for 1816, another Stationers' Company publication, acted as a reference for its business-minded male readers, not a workbook of mathematical problems, as is indicated by its contents page. With its charts, tables, and diary features, this invited annotation (as opposed to *The Ladies Diary,* which afforded no blank space for calendaring or diaries) and also contains 112 ruled pages for memorandums, appointments, and cash accounts. The 1816 duodecimo volume's softcover binding allows for portability and heavy use (because a soft binding will not crack from daily openings) (figs. 2.11–2.14).

The 1823 *Forget Me Not,* with its stiff paper-covered boards, delicate binding, and charts, including British consuls abroad, a genealogy of European sovereigns, and a detailed population of England, could not withstand more than ten to fifteen openings—a limited use at best. The ruled pages

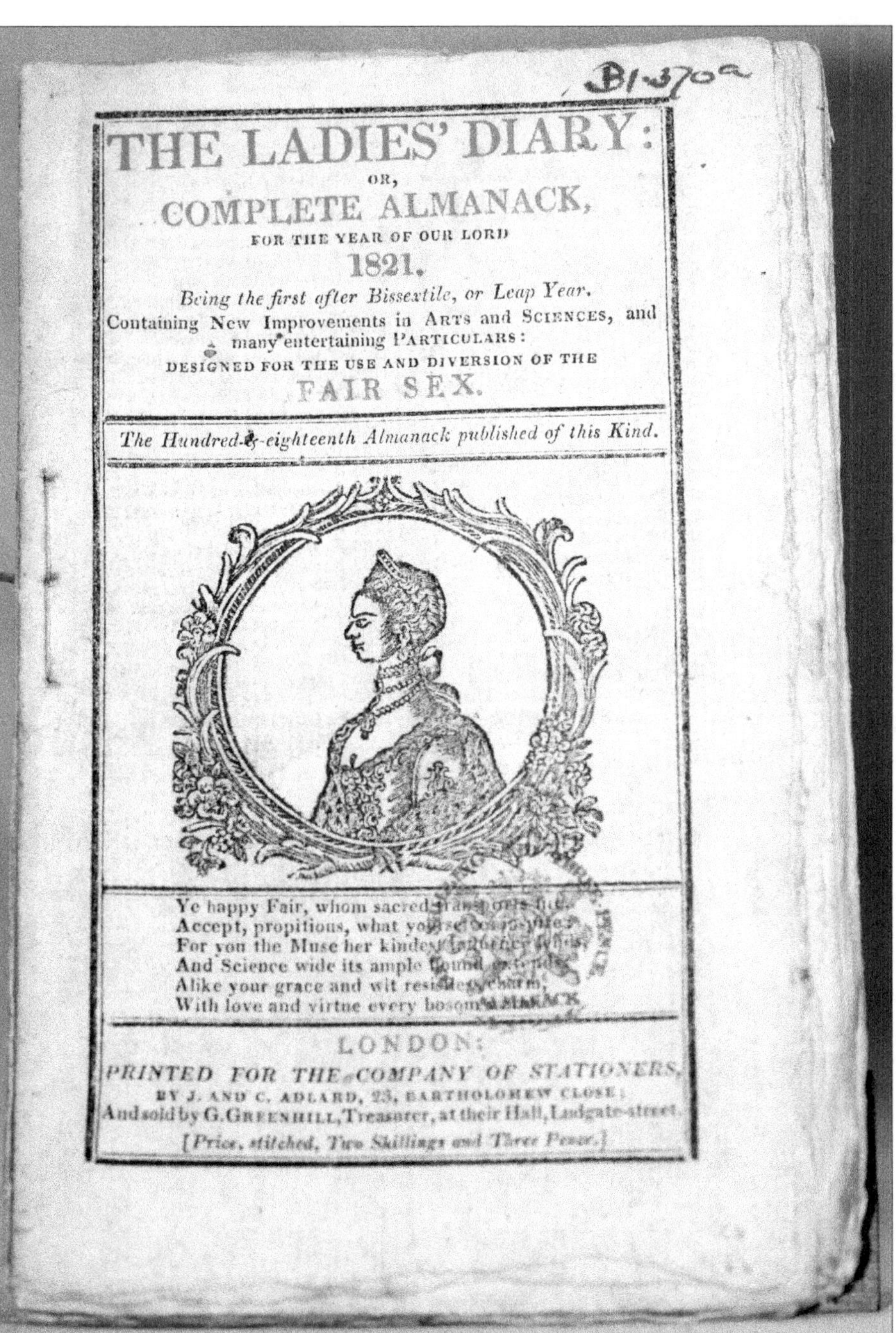

THE LADIES' DIARY:
OR,
COMPLETE ALMANACK,
FOR THE YEAR OF OUR LORD
1821.
Being the first after Bissextile, or Leap Year.
Containing New Improvements in ARTS and SCIENCES, and many entertaining PARTICULARS:
DESIGNED FOR THE USE AND DIVERSION OF THE
FAIR SEX.

The Hundred-&-eighteenth Almanack published of this Kind.

Ye happy Fair, whom sacred [illegible]
Accept, propitious, what yo[illegible]
For you the Muse her kinde[illegible]
And Science wide its ample [illegible]
Alike your grace and wit resi[illegible]
With love and virtue every bo[illegible]

LONDON:
PRINTED FOR THE COMPANY OF STATIONERS,
BY J. AND C. ADLARD, 23, BARTHOLOMEW CLOSE;
And sold by G. GREENHILL, Treasurer, at their Hall, Ludgate-street.
[*Price, stitched, Two Shillings and Three Pence.*]

Figure 2.10 Title page, *Ladies' Diary . . . for 1821* (from the Katherine D. Harris Collection; photo credit, Tom Davis)

CONTENTS.

Figure 2.11 (*left*) Table of contents, 1816 *Simpson's Gentleman's Almanac* (from the Katherine D. Harris Collection)

Figure 2.12 (*below*) Information tables, 1816 *Simpson's Gentleman's Almanac* (from the Katherine D. Harris Collection)

26

DUTIES ON MALE SERVANTS.

No.	At per Servant. [illegible]	Total per Year.	No.	Bachelors. At per Servant	Bachelors. Total per Year.
	l. *s.*	*l.* *s.*		*l.* *s.*	*l.* *s.*
1	2 8	2 8	1	4 4	4 4
2	3 2	6 4	2	5 2	10 4
3	3 16	11 8	3	5 19	17 17
4	4 7	17 8	4	6 16	27 4
5	4 18	24 10	5	7 13	38 5
6	5 3	30 18	6	8 4	49 4
7	5 5	36 15	7	8 12	60 4
8	5 12	44 16	8	9 5	74 0
9	6 2	54 18	9	10 0	90 0
10	6 13	66 10	10	10 17	108 10
11	7 13	84 3	11	12 1	132 11
12	——	91 16	12	——	144 12
13	——	99 9	13	——	156 13
14	——	107 2	14	——	168 14
15	——	114 15	15	——	180 15
16	——	122 8	16	——	192 16
17	——	130 1	17	——	204 17
18	——	137 14	18	——	216 18
19	——	145 7	19	——	228 19
20	——	153 0	20	——	241 0

And so on at the same Rate for any number of Servants.

DUTIES ON CARRIAGES WITH FOUR WHEELS.

No.	At per Carriage with 4 Wheels for private Use.	Total per Year.	No.	Stage Coaches & Post Chaises with 4 Wheels, at 10*l.* 10*s.* each.
	l. *s.* *d.*	*l.* *s.* *d.*		*l.* *d.*
1	12 0 0	12 0 0	1	10 10
2	13 0 0	26 0 0	2	19 19
3	14 0 0	42 0 0	3	29 8
4	15 0 0	60 0 0	4	38 17
5	15 15 0	78 15 0	5	48 6
6	16 8 0	98 8 0	6	57 15
7	17 0 0	119 0 0	7	67 4
8	17 12 0	140 16 0	8	76 13
9	18 3 0	163 7 0	9	86 1

And for every additional body on the same wheels, the further sum of 6l. 6s.

Carriages with two wheels, drawn by one horse .... 6*l.* 10*s.* each.
Ditto, drawn by two or more horses .... 9*l.* 0*s.*
And for every additional body used on the same wheels.... 3*l.* 3*s.*
Taxed Carts .... 1*l.* 9*s.*

27

HORSE-DEALERS' DUTY.

	£. *s.* *d.*
Every person exercising the business of a horse-dealer, within London, Westminster and Liberties, the parishes of St. Mary-le-Bone, and St. Pancras in Middlesex, the Weekly Bills of Mortality, or the Borough of Southwark	25 0 0
Every person in any other part of Great Britain	12 10 0

DUTIES ON HORSES.

Duties on Horses for riding, or drawing Carriages. No.	At per Horse.	Total per Year.	Duties on other Horses and on Mules. No.	At per Horse.	Total per Year.
	l. *s.* *d.*	*l.* *s.* *d.*		*s.* *d.*	*l.* *s.* *d.*
1	2 17 6	2 17 6	1	17 6	0 17 6
2	4 14 6	9 9 0	2	——	1 15 0
3	5 4 0	15 12 0	3	——	2 12 6
4	5 10 0	22 0 0	4	——	3 10 0
5	5 11 6	27 17 6	5	——	4 7 6
6	5 16 0	34 16 0	6	——	5 5 0
7	5 19 6	41 16 6	7	——	6 2 6
8	5 19 6	47 16 0	8	——	7 0 0
9	6 1 6	54 13 6	9	——	7 17 6
10	6 7 0	63 10 0	10	——	8 15 0
11	6 7 0	69 17 0	11	——	9 12 6
12	6 7 0	76 4 0	12	——	10 10 0
13	6 7 6	82 17 6	13	——	11 7 6
14	6 7 6	89 5 0	14	——	12 5 0
15	6 7 6	95 12 6	15	——	13 2 6
16	6 7 6	102 0 0	16	——	14 0 0
17	6 8 0	108 16 0	17	——	14 17 6
18	6 9 0	116 2 0	18	——	15 15 0
19	6 10 0	123 10 0	19	——	16 12 6
20	6 12 0	132 0 0	20	——	17 10 0

And so on at the same rate for any number of horses, or horses and mules.

DUTIES ON DOGS.

	l. *s.* *d.*
For every greyhound kept by any person, whether his property or not	1 0 0
For every hound, pointer, setting dog, spaniel, lurcher, or terrier, or where two or more are kept	0 14 0
One dog not of the above description	0 8 0
Persons compounding for their hounds	36 0 0

APRIL, 30 Days.] *Almanack,* 1816. [Week 15.

	Bills due, Appointments, &c. Monday 8.
8 Monday	John, King of France, died in the Savoy, Strand, 1364.
9 Tuesday	Lord Bacon died, 1626. ☉ rises, 5h. 18m.
10 Wednesday	☉ sets, 6h. 44m.
11 Thursday	*Maunday Thursday.* Lord Wellington defeats Soult before Toulouse, 1814.
12 Friday	Good Friday. Holiday at all the Public Offices. Full Moon, at 7 morn. Lord Rodney's Victory over Count de Grasse, 1782.
13 Saturday	☉ rises, 5h. 10m.
14 Sunday	Easter Sunday. ☉ sets, 6h. 52m.

APRIL, 30 Days.] *Cash Account.* [Week 15.

RECEIVED. £.	s.	d.	Monday 8.	PAID. £.	s.	d.
			Brought forward...			
			Carried over....			

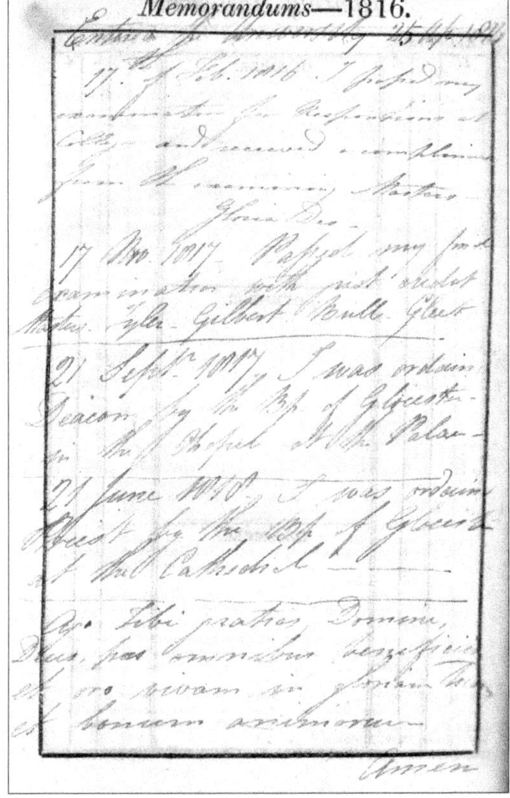
Memorandums—1816.

Figure 2.13 (*above*) Ruled pages, 1816 *Simpson's Gentleman's Almanac* (from the Katherine D. Harris Collection)

Figure 2.14 (*left*) Memorandum page, 1816 *Simpson's Gentleman's Almanac* (from the Katherine D. Harris Collection)

of *Simpson's* almanac invite the user not only to reference the information but also to record data, much like the 1824 and 1825 volumes of *Friendship's Offering,* another very successful literary annual. The ruled pages are not an invitation, however, to include creative writings—simply because of lack of space and the interference of astrological data, holidays, and important dates on the page. In this volume, readers are allowed the luxury of only one completely blank leaf (recto and verso) on which to write.[17] This particular almanac, costing one shilling, three pence, was published by Longman, Hurst, a publishing house that would later split into two different entities and publish some of the most significant and popular literary annuals, including *The Literary Souvenir* and *Heath's Book of Beauty.*

Ackermann borrowed various elements of the British almanac described above for his first *Forget Me Not* and declared it to be full of "useful knowledge" and educational literature. In that first 1823 volume, he employed William Combe to write poems for each month and then appended statistics about British population, the genealogy of European sovereigns, British consul agents abroad, and finally a historical chronicle for 1822. Another popular almanac, *Old Poor Robin: An Almanack,* includes a similar "Chronological Account of Remarkable Occurrences" for 1800 and adds a preface and a lengthy motto to its pages, similar to Ackermann's first experiment with annuals.[18] Leigh Hunt sarcastically refers to the original almanac style of literary annuals when mentioning their portability and useful information in his article included in the first *Keepsake* (1828): "[A]nd lastly, the hackney-coach fares, so very useful, that every body resolved to lug them out and convict the coachman on the spot; which he never does, because he knows it will be to no purpose" ("Pocket-Books and Keepsakes," 9). With *Friendship's Offering* incorporating statistics, blanks, and a calendar in its initial years, it is obvious that the annual as a polite remembrancer and tasteful literary genre would not be cemented until 1826, regardless of Ackermann's savvy jettisoning of the almanac style with the publication of the 1824 *Forget Me Not.* By removing the useful information, Ackermann abandoned the almanac and succumbed to the public's pressure for more literary luxury.

Ackermann promised his literary annual each November in time for the gift-giving season. However, he would have been aware of the ritual release on Almanac Day in London and most likely capitalized on this already-established schedule. Publishing literary annuals in November became a standard for editors, publishers, and booksellers. Some prefaces in annuals attempt to excuse their late publication date, perhaps in January or February. This late release also signaled an oversaturation of the annuals market; in other words, the latecomers suffered slow sales because the other annuals had all been bought and distributed. The most popular annuals (*Forget Me Not, Literary Souvenir, Friendship's Offering,* and *The Keepsake*) generally maintained a consistent November release, at least during the 1820s, the heyday of the annuals' production.

By adopting the British almanac style and distributing the annual on or around Almanac Day, Ackermann demonstrated how thoroughly he understood the readership. His publications using aquatint and an established readership would have doubled by incorporating the already-known almanac style into the literary annual. The annuals excluded astrological or astronomical information even in their early years. With a significantly increased price (see table 2.1) and being marketed as a sign of luxury, the annual was priced out of reach of the working class.

Though these British almanacs represent much of the format of Ackermann's and other publishers' initial forays into the literary annual, Ackermann and his editor, Frederic Shoberl, credited the French for the development of the annual. In the 1823 *Forget Me Not* Preface, "he professes his obligations to the *Almanac de Gotha,* a work of acknowledged accuracy and of high reputation on the Continent . . . [for] useful articles of reference" (v, vii). Ackermann also attributed his literary annual form to an earlier almanac, *Almanach des Muses,* published in France from 1765 through 1833.[19]

TABLE 2.1 THE PRICE OF ALMANACS

Almanac	*Price*	*Date*
Ladies' Diary	9 pence (stitched)	1768
Simpson's	1 shilling, 3 pence	1812
Vox Stellarum	1 shilling, 10 pence	1815
	2 shillings, 3 pence	1816
Ladies' Diary	2 shillings (stitched)	1822
Forget Me Not	12 shillings (paper boards/slipcase, gilt edges)	1823
Imperial Almanac	1 shilling, 3 pence	1823

The 1781 volume of the *Almanach des Muses* opens with a calendar, lunar phases, and important dates, and then begins paginating 300 pages of fugitive verses. The table of contents, housed at the conclusion, is organized by author's name and is followed by sheet music and publisher's adverts, both included in the pagination. The 1767 volume is much more brief, at 170 pages, and titles its preface as "Avertissement," similar to the 1823 *Forget Me Not*'s original preface (figs. 2.15, 2.16, and 2.17).

This publication does not rival the *Forget Me Not,* because it does not present its literary and informational data as a beautiful object: the original covers are flimsy paper with no board for support; the 1767 and 1781 volumes contain only one engraving, a frontispiece, with a head engraving on the first page of poetry; the inferior paper and pressed printing allow the type to interrupt text; and no gilt edges or stamped binding provide a sense of delicacy. While *The Ladies' Diary* is but a thin pamphlet of stitched folds and the *Almanach des Muses* lacks illustrated boards, the *Almanac de Gotha* is wrapped in gilt edges and housed in a slipcase.

Figure 2.15 Frontispiece, 1767 *Almanach des Muses*, drawn and engraved by M. Poisson (from the Katherine D. Harris Collection; photo credit, Tom Davis)

ALMANACH
DES
MUSES.
1781.

Poisson inv. et Sculp.

A PARIS.
Chez DELALAIN l'Aîné, Libraire rue S.t Jacques,
vis-à-vis la rue du Plastre.

Figure 2.16 Frontispiece, 1781 *Almanach des Muses*, drawn and engraved by M. Poisson (from the Katherine D. Harris Collection; photo credit, Tom Davis)

ALMANACH
DES MUSES,
Ou choix des Poéſies fugitives de 1780.

VERS A ADÉLAÏDE,
Le premier jour de l'An.

SALUT à nos beautés nouvelles,
à qui ce jour donne quinze ans !
L'avenir, qui s'ouvre pour elles,
n'eſt tiſſu que de jours brillans :
mais hélas ! le tems a des ailes,
& tout s'envole avec le tems.
Toi ſeule, aimable Adélaïde,

Année 1781. A

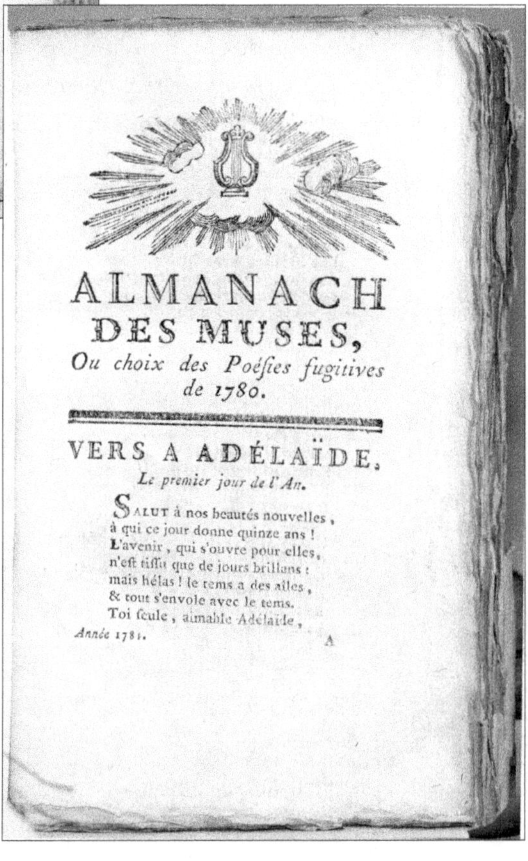

Figure 2.17 Head engraving, 1781 *Almanach des Muses* (from the Katherine D. Harris Collection; photo credit, Tom Davis)

At 48mo, the 1812 *Almanac de Gotha* contains tightly printed and difficult-to-read text, accompanied by a calendar and interspersed with eleven portraits and landscape scenes throughout the calendar. A pullout page provides a genealogical chart of the House of Saxon, which leads into paginated reference materials, including a table of contents at the conclusion (fig. 2.18). This French almanac adds the engraving as a point of visual entertainment to complement the useful information, but it lacks any literary materials. The recto-printed engravings are set off by their blank verso pages, indicating that the engravings could be excised from the volume and mounted by the owner. The *Almanac de Gotha,* though, is not a luxury item despite the slipcase signaling a sense of preservation; it is a step closer to the beauty of an annual, but the contents are still geared toward information rather than entertainment.

Frederick W. Faxon, Andrew Boyle, Ralph Thompson, and other bibliographers of literary annual contents suggest that only these German and French titles could have influenced Ackermann's original decisions. However, the closest older sibling to Ackermann's literary annual format is Charles Malo's *Hommage aux Dames,* published from 1813 through 1830 by Chez Janet in Paris—this is a traditional almanac as defined by Perkins.

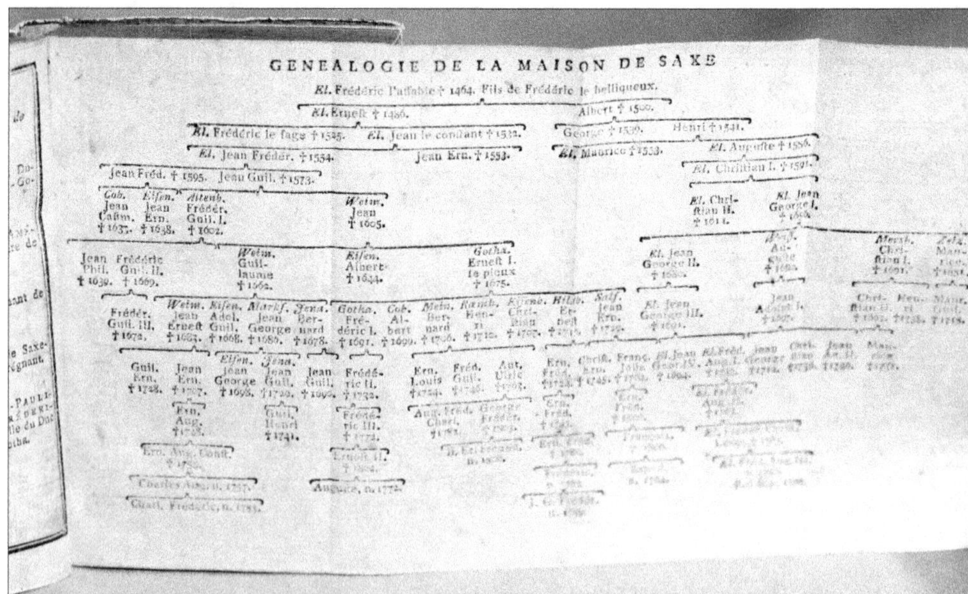

Figure 2.18 Pullout genealogical chart of the House of Saxe 1812 *Almanac de Gotha* (from the Katherine D. Harris Collection; photo credit, Tom Davis)

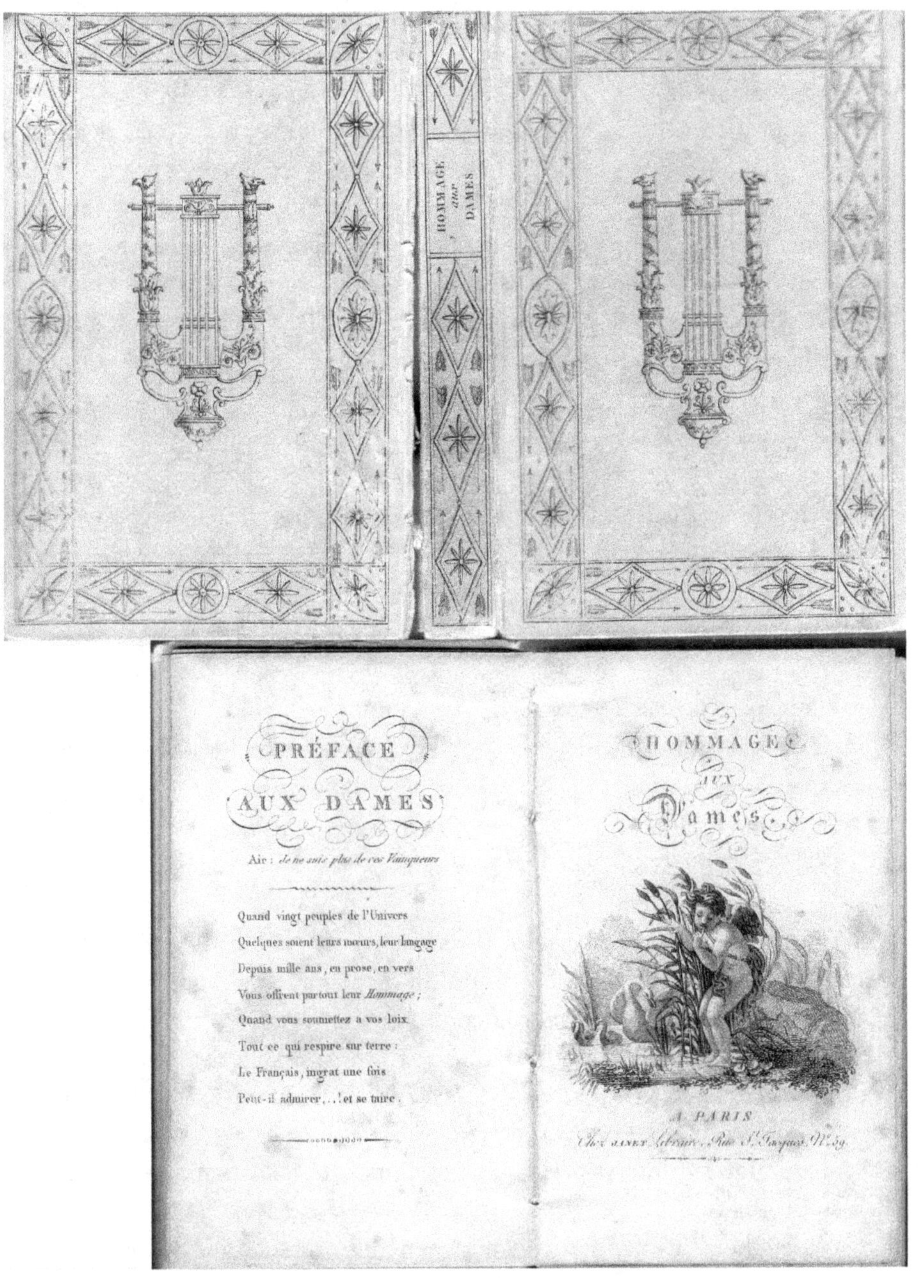

HOMMAGE
aux
DAMES

PRÉFACE
AUX DAMES

Air : *Je ne suis plus de ces Vainqueurs*

Quand vingt peuples de l'Univers
Quelques soient leurs mœurs, leur langage
Depuis mille ans, en prose, en vers
Vous offrent partout leur *Hommage* ;
Quand vous soumettez à vos loix
Tout ce qui respire sur terre :
Le Français, ingrat une fois
Peut-il admirer, . . ! et se taire.

HOMMAGE
AUX
Dames

A PARIS
Chez JANET Libraire, Rue S.t Jacques, N.o 59.

Figure 2.19 Boards, title page, and preface for the French almanac *Hommage aux Dames*, c. 1815 (from the Katherine D. Harris Collection)

The French 1815 *Hommage aux Dames* is filled with the traditional factual information expected of an almanac, including monthly astrological data in the first pages after the title page and blank pages for monthly entries in its last few pages (fig. 2.19).

This French volume, though, extends beyond the traditional almanac style to include 148 pages of poetry, prose, and a dramatic scene, as well as 44 unpaginated pages to open the volume, which pages include all six engravings of the volume and their accompanying pieces. Here, the useful information of an almanac has been paired with the aesthetic tastes of its women consumers, as is demonstrated in the preface to the 1815 volume, reproduced here with English translation.

Préface aux Dames

Air: Je ne suis plus de ces Vainqueurs
Quand vingt peuples de l'Univers
Quelques soient leurs mœurs,
  leur langage
Depuis mille ans, en prose, en vers
Vous offrent partout leur *Hommage*;
Quand vous soumettez a vos loix
Tout ce qui respire sur terre:
Le Français, ingrat une fois
Peut-il admirer . . . ! Et se taire.

Preface to Women

Melody: I am no longer of these Victors
When twenty nations of the universe,
Whatever their customs, their
  language,
For one thousand years in prose, in verse,
Pay their tribute to you;
When everything that breathes on earth
Submits to your laws:
Can the French, ungrateful,
Admire, for once! . . . and remain silent.

Though this poem concludes with a reprimand of the French, its complete message refers to the tradition of worshiping women and their femininity. *Hommage aux Dames* encourages the tradition: its literature is dedicated to women; its diminutive size (3.5 × 4.75 in.) and delicate presence are contrasted against the universal laws of femininity; and its engravings and glazed paper boards reflect a leisure class who will appreciate the rich attire of the volume's presentation, similar to Ackermann's impending British production.

While there are similarities between this almanac form and Ackermann's literary annual form, their differences distinguish the annual genre as a unique phenomenon. Internally, the arrangement and pagination differ from Ackermann's final product: In the *Hommage aux Dames,* the six engravings with their accompanying prose and poetry pieces are included in the unpaginated first forty pages of the volume; the pagination begins with a poem entitled "Hommage aux Dames"; and the table of contents, alphabetically arranged by author, appears after the last piece of writing and is followed by blank monthly pages. Many of these features do not seem to follow a logical progression of information. The table of contents privileges the authors rather than the content, and the unpaginated engravings, poems, and prose could be excised in the rebinding of the volume. And, obviously, the engravings are not privileged in this volume as they are in the literary annuals; instead, the writing, both by the contributors and by the owners/audience, holds the attention of the readers.

The blank pages are preceded by a "Souvenir" title page, which allows readers to incorporate their memories into the volume. Because the almanac was meant to be kept throughout the year, as is intimated by the monthly astrological data and the monthly diary pages, the *Hommage aux Dames* served as a souvenir of a particular moment, "a remembrance, a memory" (*OED*). By incorporating herself into the volume, the reader becomes part of the work, ownership to be read alongside the printed material.

In a tradition adopted by editors of British literary annuals, on a prefatory page, Charles Malo invites contributors to submit prose and poetry for publication in his *Hommage aux Dames.* In essence, Malo creates fuzzy boundaries between author and audience—a marketing tactic that encourages the purchase of volumes not just for their aesthetic beauty but also for authorial vanity. This practice of including the reader in the creation of a volume both as author and as diarist encourages continued consumption through memory, reading, poetic/prose contributions, diary entries, and factual/referential information. Accordingly, this almanac, *Hommage aux Dames,* is not a complete product; it waits for its readers to complete it.

The 1819, 1823, and 1829 *Hommage* volumes were sold with half and three-quarter slipcases that were completely covered with the same paper boards as the volume itself, as opposed to Ackermann's practice of covering only the front and back of his slipcases. The boards for these volumes of the *Hommage,* however, are consistently the same throughout the years: blue-green paper boards with a lyre on both front and back boards. With the *Forget Me Not,* Ackermann varied the designs on his paper boards from year to year and never produced a volume with the same image on both the front and back boards. However, Ackermann's green paper boards

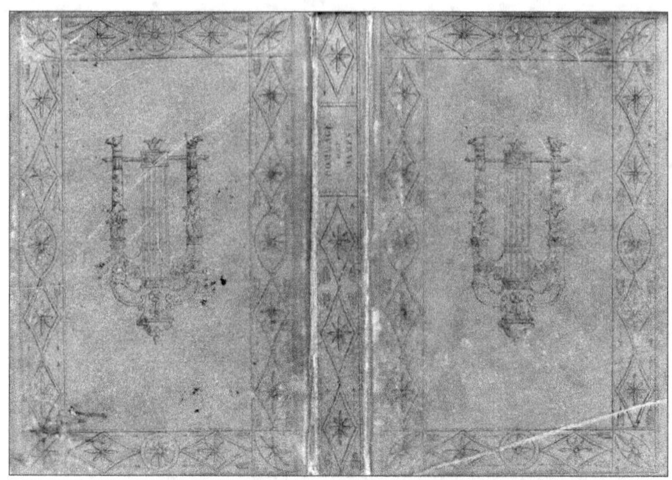

Figure 2.20 Boards for 1819 *Hommage aux Dames* (*top*), 1830 *Forget Me Not* (*middle*), and 1828 *Hommage aux Dames* (*bottom*) (from the Katherine D. Harris Collection)

are similar in tone and hue—perhaps an indication that Ackermann borrowed more than the style from the French *Hommage.* In Ackermann's defense, though, a lyre did not appear on his boards until the 1830 volume (fig. 2.20).[20]

True to its almanac style, the *Hommage* calendar introduces each volume. But the publisher improved upon the format in subsequent years by limiting the number of engravings to three to five interspersed throughout each volume and paginating the prose and poetry. The author's name is still privileged in the table of contents, which remains at the conclusion of each volume. The 1823 volume encourages "pensees" (thought) as well as souvenirs to be inscribed onto the final blank pages, but the 1828 volume discourages this inscription by excising the blank pages altogether, perhaps in a move to mimic the British literary annuals' successful style.

These two titles, *Forget Me Not* and *Hommage aux Dames,* seem to have been in communication, jumping geographical boundaries with mimicked format and more. For example, in a move that unites the nationality of each country under the literary annual style, the 1828 *Hommage* volume opens with the engraving "La Contemplation," a painting by Richard Westall rendered into engraving by Lecomte. This engraving was published two years after Ackermann had already introduced Westall's painting as the frontispiece to his 1826 *Forget Me Not,* engraved by Edward Finden (fig. 2.21). As was common practice, the *Forget Me Not*'s steel plate of "The Contemplation" could have been sold to and reproduced by these Parisian publishers. However, minor details around the setting sun in each engraving demonstrate that the plates were interpreted by two separate engravers. Though Westall was popular during the 1820s, this replication of his work—with both images situated at the beginning of each volume—implies a conversation, a community, between textual objects that was not predicated on representations of national community.

Hoping to capitalize on Ackermann's stylized almanac and in a dedication to the earlier *Hommage aux Dames,* John Setts Jr. published an 1825 British *Hommage aux Dames.* Completely independent of the Parisian publication (Faxon, 98), Setts paid his own homage to the French volume by mimicking its layout: the British *Hommage aux Dames* contains several blank pages for notes and some music—similar to the almanac style. However, this title suffered the fate of many other titles and failed to appear the following year.

Figure 2.21 "The Contemplation," engravings from the 1826 *Forget Me Not* (*above*) and 1828 *Hommage aux Dames* (*below*) (from the Katherine D. Harris Collection)

ESCHEWING THE ANTHOLOGY

With flowers referenced in British literary annual titles (such as *Iris, Blossoms at Christmas, First Flowers,* and *Amaranth*), poetry that meditates on flowers, and engravings that reproduce bouquets of flowers (fig. 2.22), the literary annual represents a metaphorical bouquet of poetry and prose—an "anthology" of sorts, which is traditionally defined as "a collection of the flowers of verse,

Figure 2.22 "Forget Me Not" bouquet engraving, 1825 *Forget Me Not* (from the Katherine D. Harris Collection)

i.e., small choice poems, especially epigrams, by various authors; originally applied to the Greek collections so called" and, alternatively, "with some reference to the original meaning (in Greek) of a flower-gathering" (*OED*). While the literary annuals are collections of metaphorical flowers, the genre differs from a traditional anthology because of its intended audience, engravings, annual publication, and purpose.

Ina Ferris, in discussing Isaac D'Israeli's antiquarian miscellany, *Curiosities of Literature,* qualifies miscellanies and anthologies as secondary genres to original literature:

> Such genres and their authors have generally fared poorly in critical discourse, both then and now, typically seen as parasitical, secondary, dim of mind and vision, as in the proverbial book-worm scorned by William Hazlitt in one of his more platonic moments as someone who sees "on the glimmering shadows of things reflected from the minds of others." . . . Genres of collection, compilation, and republication, they were typically gathered under the suspect sign of "book-making," regarded less as literary forms than as adjuncts of the book trade. Frequently initiated by booksellers rather than authors, they were understood as contingent and ramshackle collections rather than compositions, modes of lazy and opportunistic publication that exploited the technological power of the press to transfer and reproduce text rather than the mental powers proper to authorship and literary genres. (523–24)

In *Dreaming in Books,* Andrew Piper discusses the miscellany—a catchall term he uses for almanacs, taschenbuchs, and gift books—in terms of anthologies and other printed literary texts. In essence, he suggests that the miscellany "served a crucial ordering function in an age of too much writing. . . . Where the collected edition [that is, a single-author poetry volume] aimed to canonize its author and in the process create a literary canon, the miscellany was far more a document of the carnivalesque impulse to undo such rules, standards, or means. With the absence of any obvious organizing principle and the simultaneous presence of high, low, and outright weird texts, the romantic miscellany authorized the reader to create linkages between such cultural strata" (121–22). Though Piper continues into a discussion of literary annuals and readership, this comment elides the heavy-handed editorial control displayed by many literary annual editors—a control typically reinforced in the preface. Piper focuses on the production of meaning through the bibliographic interaction between reader and miscellany but ignores the cultural history of literary annuals.

Poetic anthologies aimed at middle-class women, also known as beauties, were didactic in nature and therefore useful, claims Ferris. Miscellanies such as the *Mirror of Literature,* though, were republications. However, the excerpts provided in that periodical afforded less-affluent readers access to literary publications such as the annuals.[21]

Leah Price, in *The Anthology and the Rise of the Novel,* suggests that the anthology produced a contrast "between two paces of reading—a leisured appreciation of beauties and an impatient, or efficient, rush through the plot" (5). With the annuals already incorporating the useful knowledge of the almanacs and the meditative contemplation of the emblem, this start-stop reading pace encouraged by anthologies belies an annual's value. For example, Ackermann and Shoberl at first included some abridged material but elide the anthology qualification by offering only Clauren's translated and expurgated *Mimili* (discussed in the previous chapter). After this brief foray into offering an abridged novel, Ackermann, Shoberl, and other annual editors abandoned republication and excerpting novels and instead opted for publishing original materials using the short story as their primary prose selections. Though the editors of literary annuals took great care in arranging and organizing the materials into a fluid theme intended to be read in a linear fashion to obtain the most relevant use of the volume similar to an emblem, the annual's array of contents encourages fragmented and fractured looking by its readers—paging between the various engravings, skipping over poems or longer stories in favor of a particular author's contribution as could be deciphered from the table of contents, or interrupting the reading experience to gaze upon an engraving inserted midway through a short story. As several critics have noted, the annuals' place in the drawing room meant that contemplation of any particular contribution was not solitary but was instead intended to be shared and experienced with another or several others simultaneously. In this way, annuals emulate the anthology and move away from the solitary didacticism of the emblem.

Ralph Thompson claims that the literary annual phenomenon took its cue from *The Poetical Register and Repository of Fugitive Poetry* (published 1801–11) and *Angelica's Ladies Library, or Parents and Guardians Present* (published in 1794):

> There cannot be a doubt that a book like this, purposely adapted for the use of the female sex, by writers, whose characters are established without controversy, abounding with entertainment, and inculcating the purest principles of morality and religion, will not fail to contribute to the improvement of the rising generation, by infusing virtuous and liberal ideas into the minds of a class of readers, which must add inestimable happiness to thousands of worthy families, by forming and training the most beautiful part of the creation in the paths of virtue and true felicity; in filling up the various stations of this transitory life in that rank of society, which Providence in his infinite wisdom allots them, with credit to themselves, and satisfaction to those, who are interested in their present and future welfare. (Advertisement in *Angelica's Ladies Library*, iii)

By comparison, in the *Forget Me Not* prefaces, Ackermann and Shoberl appear to espouse the same idea about didactic contents and a conduct manual of sorts for young ladies. But as discussed above, those two did not necessarily follow through. While Thompson may claim that *Angelica's* is a precursor in form, it certainly is not in its 470 pages of content, especially in the first piece, "Dr. Gregory's Legacy to His Daughters," which pronounces social expectations of femininity.

Similar to the annuals, *The Poetical Register and Repository of Fugitive Poetry* professed a particular time period for publication: the 1805 volume appeared on time in June; in the 1803 volume, the decided moment for publication was March; and the 1802 publication professed that February was the target.[22] None of these moments marks the gift-giving season or Almanac Day that Ackermann originally relied on to distribute and publicize his annuals. In *The Poetical Register's* five hundred pages, original poetry is separated from fugitive poetry. And the editor's preface indicates that he will collect every fugitive verse that is worthy of publication to happily display it for his readers. This volume focuses on using print to preserve poetry instead of self-consciously placating the reading audience. However, the editor does profess and provide a critique of the *Almanach des Muses,* cites it as an influence for this title, and then claims improvement over its German and French predecessors:

> Since the first publication of works something similar in plan to the present, nearly half a century has now elapsed. Whatever merit may

be due to the first idea of such a repository, undoubtedly belongs to France. It was not, however, till the year 1765, that a volume of the kind appeared, worthy of preservation. In that year, the *Almanach des Muses* was first established; and it has been continued, sometimes with more, sometimes with less merit, down to the present period. For many years it was adorned by the names of Voltaire, Cresset, Dorat, Bernard, Colardeau, Leonard, De Lille, and other authors scarcely less distinguished, whose productions, though often morally reprehensible, always bore the stamp of genius. When the epoch of the Revolution arrived, it was prostituted to the purposes of those who had a leading share in that Revolution, and became a collection of miserable verses in praise of the most abandoned principles, and their abandoned propagators. To what a state of degradation it was fallen, may be easily guessed, from the circumstance of its containing several inscriptions and poems in honour of Marat! For the last two or three years, it has been gradually recovering its antient [*sic*] credit.

The plan was next adopted in Germany, but in what year is unknown to the editor of the Poetical Register. Two volumes are still annually published in that country: they are edited by Schiller and Voss. That which is under the care of Schiller is devoted principally, if not entirely, to the compositions of young authors, which receive the corrections of the editor.

It has long been a subject of surprize to the editor, that no collection similar to that of our Gallic neighbours was formed in England. Two volumes have, indeed, been published within the last three years, professedly in imitation of the French work, but, in reality, differing from it very considerably. The volume, which is now submitted to the public, is an enlargement, and, it is hoped, an improvement of the plan on which the *Alamanach des Muses* is conducted. That work includes only poetry and criticism; the first nearly, if not all, original, and the latter to a very limited extent. (iii–iv)

Andrew Boyle claims that Robert Southey's *Annual Anthology,* printed in 1799 and 1800, is a precursor to the literary annuals (preface to *Index,* iii). Interestingly, Southey understood the draw of emblematic literature, since he owned and studied a copy of Jacob Cats's book of emblems, *Proteus,* during the 1790s.[23] Southey put together the *Annual Anthology* at the urging of William Taylor, who sang the praises of the *Almanach des Muses* later in the 1830s.[24] Taylor actually stated that someone should produce an almanac very similar to the German and French form and urged Southey to do it:[25]

> I wonder some one of our poets does not undertake what the French and Germans so long supported in great popularity—an Almanack of the Muses—an annual Anthology of minor poems—too unimportant to subsist apart, and too neat to be sacrificed with the ephemeral victims of oblivion. Schiller is the editor of one, and Voss of another such poetical calendar in Germany; their names operate as a pledge that no sheer trash shall be admitted. What say you to the following eclogue of Voss's? it is not a bucolic, but a diabolic idyll. (letter to Southey, September 26, 1798, *Memoir,* 228)[26]

On December 30, 1798, Taylor proposes to fill just such an almanac with his own works:

> What you said respecting the foreign Almanacks of the Muses has served me as a hint, and I think of speedily editing such a volume. For this I have more motives than one. Among others, that there are some half a hundred pieces of my own, too good to perish with the newspapers in which they are printed. I have also among my more intimate friends some who will willingly contribute, and if I should find all my stores deficient by a sheet or two for the due size of a volume, why it is but turning to and filling it myself. Can you assist me with a title? Pratt has damned the word Gleanings, which I thought of: and will you assist me with anything else? I have some tolerable balladlings, and some tolerable stories for more. (239)[27]

Laura Mandell, in "Putting Contents on the Table: The Disciplinary Anthology and the Field of Literary Criticism," argues that Southey's anthology began to "separate works of historical interest, antiquarian 'curiosities,' from canonical works of earlier periods by confining each to their own kind of book" (2). Mandell continues on to differentiate miscellanies from anthologies based on the inclusion of original writings or historical literature. Anthologies create canonicity by validating authorship; miscellanies reprint. And beauties, those poetic compilations meant to educate, fall somewhere in between.

While Southey's volumes, deemed miscellanies by Mandell ("Putting Contents," 17), contain original poetry from authors of the British Romantic period, the volumes do not rival the beauty of the annuals, nor do they include any engravings. In addition, anthologies collect both previously published and unpublished works for printing. Even in Ackermann's initial forays, the literary annual format was heralded to contain previously unpublished, original works—a claim vociferously defended by its editors but apparently elided when it came to translations.

In some instances, editors include a note either in the preface or at the conclusion of the story, poem, or song stating that a particular work had recently mistakenly been printed in a periodical and newspaper and was beyond the author's control or knowledge. Alaric A. Watts, editor of the *Literary Souvenir* for its entire run, used this strategy most often in his prefaces and some footnotes about editorial control being inadvertently undermined.[28]

Robert Southey's two-volume *Annual Anthology* presents a collection of poetry by authors who were expected to soon represent canonical English literature. However, Southey's experiment was intended as high literary art, not accessible for the middle class, and certainly not a beautifully bound cultural object.

An anthologia, typically a collection of fugitive verses, is very similar to the often uneven collection of writings in literary annuals. Anne Ferry, in studying the history of poetry anthologies, proposes that the anthologist, similar to an editor, works diligently to produce a certain type of literary experience. Promise of a complete anthology is encoded in the larger volume; however, the smaller anthologies require brief poems, with the anthologist convincing readers that "what is most *poetical* is experienced in small proportions" (Ferry, 85). A smaller page also means that the poetry takes less time to read. According to Ferry, the "folio was used for serious subjects because a book of that size . . . could be laid flat for sustained study" (85). The annuals, though starting out as diminutive duodecimos, were soon pumped up to quarto but not to accommodate more or longer poetic selections. Instead, the engravings dictated the size of the page.

In its alternative meaning as a gathering of flowers, an anthology has significance in that many of the literary annual titles were named for flowers. Richard Sha offers that the publication of *A Botanical Dictionary* in 1778 caused a shift in the understandings about perversity, sexuality, and monogamy (*Perverse,* 43). Sha contends that this perversity caused Lord

Byron and his circle to encode their homosexuality in botanical terms, not to hide their sexuality but to signal a perversity or a revolution in sexuality. The publishers and editors of the annuals, though mostly men during the first ten years, unknowingly supported a subversive femininity in the annuals that was domestic yet sexual and undisciplined. Perhaps in naming the annuals after flowers in their poetry, the editors and publishers were also subscribing to this type of perverse and revolutionary Romanticism.

The literary annuals, as a genre, were predominantly filled with sentimental poems. But as the genre grew in popularity, its contents evolved to include some politically driven poetry and prose. Like Alciato's emblems, the literary annual became more than its creators intended—more than a symbol of British propriety and education. It came to represent a conflation of past, present, and greatly anticipated Victorian future.

THREE

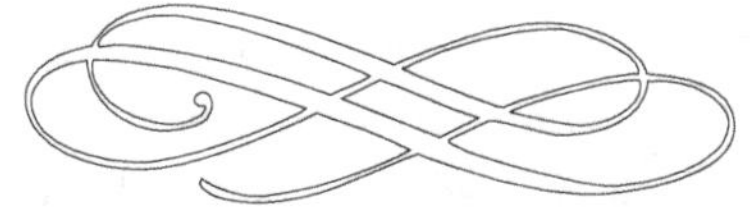

The First Generation's Success

Forget Me Not, Friendship's Offering, *and* The Literary Souvenir

THOUGH PUMMELED IN THE BRITISH CRITICAL PRESS TO the point that a "modern literary lady's maid [would] . . . sneer at the Annuals," the genre nevertheless served the larger purpose of exposing a burgeoning audience of women and girls to "very many of the best lyrical poems of nearly all our most popular contemporary writers which appeared in the first instance in their pages," as is noted in the 1858 *Bookseller* article "The Annuals of Former Days" (494). Even after Rudolph Ackermann's initial foray into the *Forget Me Not,* the genre continued to evolve based on demand and readers' desires. Each year, he and Shoberl offered a better version of the *Forget Me Not* until the genre settled on a definitive tradition. But the first few years for all literary annual titles were tenuous, as if publishers and editors were still experimenting with the contents and the annual's materiality. By the conclusion of 1825, most of the popular and best-selling titles had settled on British nationalism to inspire a loyal set of readers. This chapter focuses on the materiality and bibliographical codes of early British literary annuals as a way to explain the development of a particular voice in this unique medium. Though other publishers had discussed this particular genre, it was Ackermann who moved forward quickly enough to launch an entire movement in the publishing industry.

LAUNCHING A GENRE: *FORGET ME NOT, THE GRACES,* AND *FRIENDSHIP'S OFFERING*

Already possessing John Samuel Agar's engravings of Edward Burney's emblematic designs (*Twelve Months*) and accompanying verses by William Combe,[1] Ackermann engaged Frederick Shoberl, his editor for the *Repository of Arts,* to craft a volume that mimicked almanacs, emblems, and diaries to embrace the progress of seasons in a monthly calendar form (fig. 3.1). Though the first volume's pages contained tiny, smudged type that lacks the later decadence of blank margin space, this volume was meant to lightly entertain but demanded rapt attention to understand the mildly instructive sentiments and appreciate the volume's visually stimulating beauty.

Figure 3.1 "June" woodcut engraving, 1823 *Forget Me Not*, drawn by Burney and engraved by J. S. Agar (from the Katherine D. Harris Collection)

The opening pages of the first *Forget Me Not* invite reader participation and encourage gift giving with a presentation plate and tissue guard (fig. 3.2). The engraving includes the year and title of the annual as well as four lines to guide the writer's hand. Encircled in a wreath, the inscription space mimics a tapestry onto which the inscriber will position himself or herself to be woven into the text. If the placement and visual cues do not offer enough guidance, Shoberl calls attention to this presentation plate in the preface, titling the brief introductory statement "Advertisement":[2] "In addition to the above-mentioned Plates, there will be found at the beginning of the volume an engraved wreath of the flower, bearing the name selected for the title of this work, with a blank for the purpose of receiving a presentation inscription" (vi).

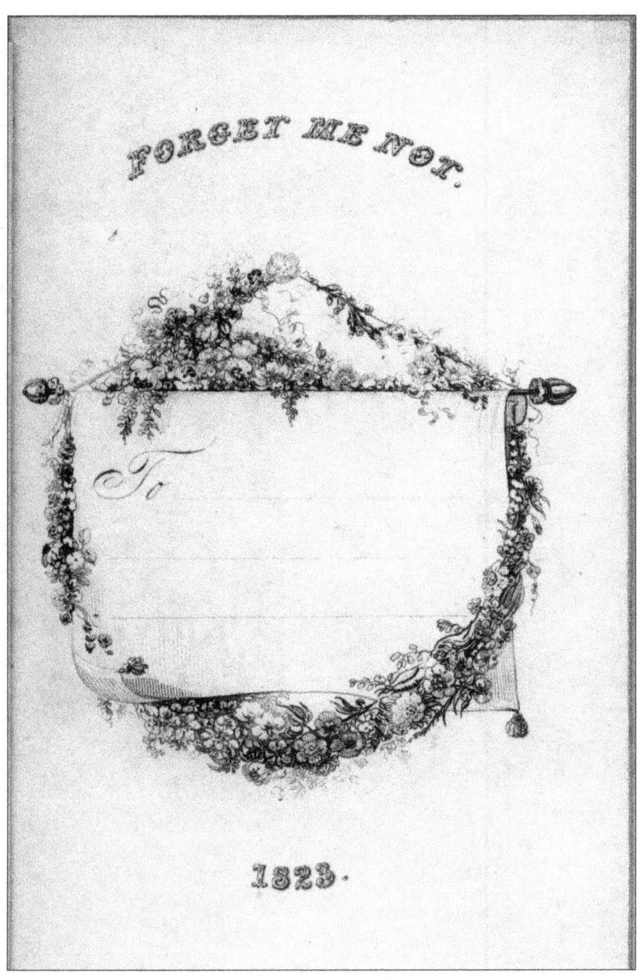

Figure 3.2 "Forget Me Not" presentation plate, 1823 *Forget Me Not* (from the Katherine D. Harris Collection)

Frederic Shoberl, aware of Ackermann's successful and popular publications, built on this well-known reputation to advertise the first *Forget Me Not* in such a way as to bolster sales of the next few years' volumes: "[W]hile his [Ackermann's] long and extensive connexion with the Arts, and the credit with which he has acquitted himself in his various undertakings in that line, will, he trusts, be a satisfactory pledge that his best exertions shall not be wanting to give to this Work a decided superiority in regard to its embellishments, over every other existing publication of the kind" ("Advertisement," vii–viii)

Before launching the volume into Agar's engravings of *Twelve Months,* this *Forget Me Not* introduces a steel-plate engraving, "Madonna," also engraved by John Samuel Agar (fig. 3.3). This frontispiece sets the tone for

Figure 3.3 "Madonna," frontispiece, 1823 *Forget Me Not*, from the original painting by Vincenzio de san Gimignan and engraved by J. S. Agar (from the Katherine D. Harris Collection)

Ackermann's experiment by presenting an image of the Madonna "from a painting by Vincenzio de san Gimignano, in the Dresden Gallery," a Tuscan painting hung in a German venue. The Anglo-German publisher borrowed an Italian painting from his homeland, re-presented it as an artistic rendering committed by well-known British engraver John Agar, and presented the overtly religious scene as an introduction to a volume that was proclaimed one that would "rival the numerous and elegant publications of the Continent" (v). Subtly, almost indistinctly, Ackermann and Shoberl created a multinational introduction that tenders British nationalism as its best feature. This highly religious scene suggests that the contents will not only offer purifying and contemplative education but also display artwork that is typically unavailable to the general public, held either by private owners or in distant venues.

Directly underneath the painting, the name of the printing shop, "R. Ackermann," is emphasized, along with a referential date, January 1, 1823, that marks the painting as exclusive to this publication. More pointedly, much like his own naturalization to England's soil, Ackermann claims the work product of a foreign national for England's own.

> Lithography, that delightful art, by means of which the genuine feeling and touches of the Painter are rendered with the utmost fidelity, so that each impression may justly be said to become an original of the Master, was transplanted but a few years since from a foreign soil to this country. Here it has not only taken root, but, from assiduous care bestowed on its cultivation, and the exercise of British ingenuity, it has acquired such vigour and perfection, that its productions rival and bid fair soon to surpass all those of exotic growth" (Advertisement in Publisher's Adverts, 1824 *Forget Me Not*).

Shoberl and Ackermann grappled with a sense of anonymity in their opening volume, but not at the request of authors. Reminiscent of the emblem genre, this first *Forget Me Not* incorporates an emblematic engraving and poem with each month of the year over the first 28 pages. The following 242 pages offer various works of prose before turning to a single poem, "Honest Little Paulo," which is not included in the table of contents (table 3.1). With the exception of Augustus von Kotzebue, no authors are mentioned in the table of contents, though their names are included on the first page of each prose selection. Authorial anonymity would be an issue only through the next year or two, after which authors would proudly claim their contributions to the annuals as part of the move toward forming British nationalism through authorial identification.

Ackermann was not the only publisher to invoke British nationalism in the pages of the annuals. In December 1823, *The Graces or Literary Souvenir* made its debut as one of three literary annual titles (see appendix A). This title was most likely inspired by the long-running French publication *Almanach des Muses.* Mimicking Ackermann's initial volume, *The Graces* also claims superiority over Continental literary production. However, this preface to the inaugural volume specifically references German literary

TABLE 3.1 TABLE OF CONTENTS, 1823 *FORGET ME NOT*

traditions but more pointedly denigrates them, and almanacs in general, for their simplicity and agrarian information. The lengthy preface, quoted in its entirety below, represents a lost piece of the literary annual contents, primarily because access to this volume is rare:

> The conception of this Volume was suggested by the German Literary Almanacks, an old and most popular species of publication on the Continent. But it has obvious improvements on their plan. Those Almanacks are generally loaded with a weight of genealogical lists, statistical tables, and catalogues of minor public functionaries, which could be endured by no taste but that singular one which makes the German mind at once the wildest and the most formal, the most metaphysical and the most material, to be found among nations.
>
> The present Work is the first of an annual series, intended to embrace, in succession, every topic of accomplishment, elegance, and polite information, that can interest the general reader.
>
> Tales, and Poetry, of the highest composition; the Principles of the Fine Arts; Engravings of the utmost skill and beauty that can be produced by the English artist; with other subjects of value and attraction, to be subsequently disclosed, will form the substance of these volumes.
>
> The Number now offered to the Public, contains the contributions of well known Writers, whose continued assistance the Publishers have hopes of being able to obtain. The most distinguished names in Continental Literature have been the regular contributors to the national Almanacks and Souvenirs; and the honours of Goethe, Schiller, Grillsparzer, and a host of other poets and philosophers, have found no degradation in the intercourse with those popular and interesting productions.
>
> The principal contents of the following pages are—
>
> The Months, in descriptive verse; with a Calendar of the Flower-Garden, and its cultivation, attached to each Month.
>
> A Diary for the brief record of remarkable dates, incidents, literary hours, &c.
>
> A Spanish Tale.
>
> Poems, by various contributors.
>
> The Deipnosophist, or Supper-conversation: A collection of remarkable thoughts and *jeux d'espirit* of the higher ranks;—in some instances derived from sources rarely accessible.

> An Obituary; a feature entirely new in those works, and comprehending all the more important biographical facts of the principal persons who have died during the year.
>
> Lists of Public Literary Bodies, &c.
>
> The Frontispiece is a copy of Titian's famous picture of the "Casket," or "Titian's Daughter." The original is considered to be the finest performance, in point of general animation, beauty of the head, natural elegance of the attitude, and power of colour, that ever came from the pencil of the master.
>
> The Publishers wish the present Volume to be looked on less as an example, than as an indication of what they may be able to produce in future. They pledge themselves, that neither diligence nor expenditure, the opportunities of their extensive correspondence with literature and the arts abroad, nor of their known resources in this country, will be spared, to place this work in the first rank of publications of its kind. (*The Graces*, vii–x)

Because almanacs are based on information specific to an agricultural economy, *The Graces* purposefully attenuates the German taste for rustic data in favor of lists that would provide polite but not necessarily useful information, very similar to Ackermann's original publication:

> Lists.—Of Foreign Ambassadors—Literary and Philosophic Institutions—Theatres—Private Collections of Pictures—Print Shops—Music Shops—Booksellers and Publishers—Circulating Libraries—Reading Rooms—Bankers in the Metropolis—Value of Foreign Money (*The Graces,* xii)

The Graces purposely moves toward polite literature to combat the radical press's invocation of the useful for the purposes of educating and uplifting the working class. This polite information is intended for a different consumer, even different from Ackermann's, though *The Graces* mimics Ackermann's 1823 selection of months in descriptive verses. The "Diary" contains blank spaces but none of the lunar phases, enigmas, or prognostications of the earlier almanac. The volume also includes forty-three pages of brief anecdotes and newsworthy information, all to be used for entertaining dinner conversation. "The Deipnosophist[,] . . . [a] collection of remarkable thoughts and *jeux d'espirit,*" is "attributed to a French statesman, remarkable for the depth and brilliancy of his expressions. Some have been said to belong to an Individual of still higher rank, celebrated for grace of manners and spirit of conversation" (204). Though a mixed collection of gossip and information, this piece no doubt allows ladies to appear informed about current events; some of it refers to Napoleon and the French Revolution, but the politics are not wholly apparent.

This implied reader engages in social and cultural affairs, seems to have leisure time, and is decidedly located in London, as can be surmised from the list of circulating libraries published in the volume:[3]

Andrews, New Bond Street
Bishop & Garrod, New Street, Baker Street
Booth, Duke Street, Portland Place
Capes, Fleet Street
Carpenter, Holborn
Cawthorn, Cockspur Street
Chapple, Pall Mall
Colburn, Conduit Street
Crew, Grenville Street, Brunswick Square
Ebers, Old Bond Street
Hebert, Cheapside
Hodgson, Upper Mar-le-bone Street
Hoitt, T&J, Upper Berkeley Street
Hookham, Old Bond Street
Horn, Queen Street, Cheapside
Ilberry, Tichfield Street
Iley, Duke Street, Manchester Square
Keys, Coleman Street
Moore, Store Street, Bedford Square
Newman & Co., Leadenhall Street
Rice, C., Mount Street, Berkeley Square
Sames, St. James's Street
West, Great Portland Street
Wilson, Gracechurch Street
Wilson & Swaile, Gt. Russell Street (322)

Conversely, Ackermann's lists in the 1823 *Forget Me Not* (see table 3.2) are more sobering, span the final 119 pages, and contain historical accounts, population indexes, and other lists that are a mix of both European and British data rather than entertainment guides. Though not indicative of an agricultural or working-class community, this series of lists implies an informed or educated reader, one who is concerned about both British and European issues. Judging by the prominence of Great Britain's information, though, the general tenor is continued economic, intellectual, and physical growth of England—an indicator of its dominance over those European nations addressed in the pages of the 1823 *Forget Me Not*.

Even with a diary, the months in verse similar to those in the 1823 *Forget Me Not,* poems, obituaries, and strict instruction to read the contents in order, *The Graces* seems misplaced among the original literary annuals. Instead, it anticipates the decadence, frivolity, and social agenda of the literary annuals published after 1828, and it encourages women's intellectual independence intertwined with beauty. Indeed, the front cover demonstrates female friendship with its rendering of the three graces: three women clothed loosely in wraps falling off their shoulders, arms around

TABLE 3.2. LISTS FROM 1823 *FORGET ME NOT*

Genealogy of the European Sovereigns and Living Members of their Families	273
Reigning Sovereigns of Europe with the Date of their Accession	340
Lists of the Diplomatic Agents of the Principal Courts of Europe	343
Population of Great Britain, according to the census of 1821.	
I. General Summary of Houses, Families, and Persons in Great Britain, in 1821	362
II. Comparative State of the Population of the Counties and Shires of Great Britain, in 1811 and 1821	363
III. Table, exhibiting the Population of the Metropolis at different Periods, since the Year 1700	366
IV. Population of the several Parishes of the Metropolis	367
V. Population of the Principal Towns and Boroughs of England, Wales, and Scotland, in 1821	370
VI. Summary of Baptisms, Burials, and Marriages in the Metropolis and in England and Wales, in the Years 1811 to 1821, inclusive	376
Population of upwards of Seven Hundred of the Principal Cities in the World, exclusively of Great Britain	377
Historical Chronicle for 1822	388

Figure 3.4 *The Graces* 1824 cover (from the Katherine D. Harris Collection; photo credit, Tom Davis)

and completely enclosed in one another, standing on a small, uneven platform, with one breast exposed to the reader (fig. 3.4). Always intertwined, dancing, and exposing only one breast, this neoclassical depiction of ancient goddesses represents the daughters of Zeus who are companions to the Muses and personify feminine charm. The singular exposed breast later became a motif in literary annual engravings, representing femininity and domesticity.

The State Hermitage Museum and the Victoria and Albert Museum both report that Antonio Canova was commissioned by John Russel, sixth Duke of Bedford, to re-create a marble figure group of the Three Graces that was originally done for Empress Josephine. Canova finished the sculpture in 1817 and saw its installation in Woburn in 1819. According to the Hermitage, the public eagerly awaited the presentation of this statue and the inevitable duplications that would have been cut during the early nineteenth century.[4] By invoking this group of women on the cover of *The Graces,* the publishers signal their text's femininity in conjunction with the intellectual acumen of this particular reading public. Even in the opening poem, the volume becomes a conflated image of beauty, wit, and wisdom. (See appendix D for full text of the opening poem.)

The third and final entrant in 1824, *Friendship's Offering,* went to market with a series of obfuscated claims about its literary form, calling itself a gift, an annual series, and a pocket-book (iii–iv) but directly marketing the volume to a British public with the same promises as Ackermann's original "Advertisement":

> To address a word to the British Public in favour of a little volume intended to compete with those elegant productions of continental taste, which are such established favourites in the countries where they originated, is perhaps needless. They have ever been highly esteemed as New Year's gifts and as Christmas present, although they are not confined to such purposes exclusively. While it is confidently trusted, that this attempt will bear comparison with the choicest foreign works alluded to, both with regard to splendour of embellishment, and an union of the agreeable with the useful, it is also presumed, that to be minutely particular in describing its claims to public notice, would be considered unnecessary. The volume must speak for itself.

> It may be sufficient to say, that this commencement of the *annual series* intended, contains, independently of its graphic decorations, original contributions from well known and popular pens, which need only to be read, in order to be justly appreciated.
>
> The description of "the most interesting European Cities, &c." are, in great measure, the results of the personal observation; and their fidelity, not less than that of the views accompanying them, may in consequence be depended upon. The beauty of the views themselves, will be apparent from the most cursory inspection.
>
> By the continuation of a work like the present, it is hoped that the mere *Pocket-book* of the year (the purposes of which it is partially intended to supply) will be elevated in character, and rendered more generally useful and interesting than hitherto. Should it meet the public approbation, every endeavour shall be made to render the Annual Remembrancer of each succeeding year more attractive, and deserving patronage, than its predecessor. (iii–iv)

Friendship's Offering suffered through many administrative and publishing changes until settling with the publisher Smith Elder. The first volume, published in 1824 immediately following the 1823 *Forget Me Not,* was more mimicry of the *Forget Me Not*'s form than an original work. It contains landscape descriptions with engravings, a lump of prose pieces, and a lump of poetry. The editor's preface does not declare anything rich or new but does state the hope that this work will prove better than a pocket-book, useful and only mildly literary. Editor Thomas K. Hervey declares in the 1825 preface that his annual is a "justice to the public" (iii), as if production serves the community. The 1824 volume contains fifty-three weekly calendar pages, five informational charts at its conclusion,[5] and five other information pieces between the poems, including a printed inscription, "Pauperism in Europe," "Compendious Weather Guide," General Observations on Weather," and "The Four Seasons." The authors' names are absent from their contributions in both the table of contents and on the pages themselves until the 1827 volume. This annual, like the early *Forget Me Not,* does not pay attention to organization and tonal flow of the entire volume and does not provide running heads, a textual apparatus that Gerard Genette describes in *Paratexts* as referential signals: "In theory they are only reminders, handy when one is reading and consulting the text, but sometimes running heads transcend this role and play their own part, by surreptitiously giving a title to a chapter that is in theory untitled, or by highlighting details that change from page to page . . . or by playing a tune that differs from that of the chapter's official intertitle" (316). Though Genette is here discussing running heads as markers of intertitles within a novel, the reference applies with the literary annuals as well. The running head reminds the reader of her place within the annual's three hundred or more pages by printing the title of the poem or prose piece flush to the right margin. The running head thus signals the change in literary pieces and creates a reference embedded with the text. Without these intertitles, the reader must inconveniently return to the starting point of the piece to be reminded of her reading point, a lack that seems to disregard the very act of reading contemplation. Not until the 1826 volume did *Friendship's Offering* alter its form to include authors' names, running heads, and a specific ordering of the volume's contributions. The informational charts and sheet music disappeared from the 1826 volume, never to return to *Friendship's Offering*. The *Forget Me Not* and *The Literary Souvenir* volumes always included these running titles and authors' names (with the exclusion of the 1823 *Forget Me Not*). *Friendship's Offering* seems to be a title that mimicked the literary annual genre, admitting this in the 1827 preface in stating that "ours is the rivalry of emulation, not of envy" (B.E.P., vii). Instead, this title really represents a diary and resource, not a leisure experience. Similar to *The Graces,* the volume provides ample space for notations or calendaring events, similar to an almanac. By incorporating the individual, these two annuals became even more localized in both their politics and geographic references—anticipating the annual's eventual fixed presence in a drawing room.

The invitation to owners to mark their volumes became severely truncated by 1825 with the disappearance of utility and information, two decidedly almanac-style qualities. The blank spaces—the space intended for notation and thought by its reader—were converted into printed poetry and prose in most literary annuals, a move that denied the reader's pen. The *Literary Souvenir,* edited by Alaric Watts, was the first to completely excise the reader-author from its pages. According to Alaric Watts's biography, the editor had dreamed of a literary miscellany that would appeal to the burgeoning reading class of women. In it, he wished to include engravings, poetry, and prose that would be educational in nature. However, Watts's publishers, Hurst Robinson and Co., were already committed to publishing *The Graces or Literary Souvenir,* with the Reverend George Croly as editor. Because Watts and Croly were friends, Watts withdrew his offer to produce a new literary annual that would compete directly with *The Graces* (Watts, *Alaric Watts,* 1:168–69). With the public failure of *The Graces,* Croly stepped down, and the publishers asked Watts to assume the position (1:170). Watts expanded the almanac-style literary annual and instituted a literary annual format absent the blank pages in the new title, *The Literary Souvenir.*

Watts adopted the same stance as Ackermann and debuted his annual in November 1824 for 1825, with a nod specifically toward the German almanacs in the preface. The Continental influence is passingly mentioned but only in reference to the artistic exchange of ideas between Britain and Europe: "[T]hey borrow so many useful hints from English literature, that we have an undoubted right to make reprisals whenever we meet with any suggestions of theirs *at all worthy of our adoption*" (iv; emphasis added). Watts, like Ackermann, defended the "borrowed" format, but Watts's defense invokes a right to retaliate against the Europeans' repeated thefts by incorporating an idea that barely meets the minimum standard of British artistry, a remark that draws decidedly nationalistic boundaries and reflects a contentious relationship between England and its neighbors. These are hardly the sentiments expected of an educational tool for women and young ladies. However, as we shall see, the literary annuals' contents, though proclaimed virtuous in the preface, generally incorporate moments of bawdy humor, mildly immoral behavior, and decidedly nondidactic tales.

With the demand to move away from almanacs and represent the literary annuals as the very best of British ingenuity and intellect, editors began their campaign to incorporate more literature, more representations of British intellectual commodities. In the preface to the 1825 *Forget Me Not,* the editor uses the space to attract prominent authors and at the same time entices readers for the following year: "[A]nd we trust, that the eminent and respectable names embraced in this volume . . . will enduce many more of the votaries of literature and the muse to lend their aid" (iv). And indeed they did: In the 1823 *Forget Me Not* volume, only author Augustus von Kotzebue is named in the table of contents' list of twenty-two literary contributors. In 1824, Bernard Barton, James Montgomery, H. Clauren, Kotzebue, J. H. Wiffen, J. B. Papworth, and Henry Neele are identified as twelve of the thirty-nine contributors to the *Forget Me Not.*

In the next volume, twenty-nine of the forty-seven contributions are attributed in the table of contents, with Letitia Landon and Mary Russell Mitford signing their initials in the text.

Ackermann and Shoberl relied on this growing reputation of literary annuals to attract even more popular authors: "the Publisher . . . confidently trusts, that, as the plan of the Forget Me Not becomes better known, many more of our eminent and popular writers will be induced to lend the powerful aid of their talents" (1824 preface, iv). Eventually, Ackermann would earn a reputation for generous payment of his more well-known authors, such as John Clare: "I am informed that Mr. Ackermann has a juvenile to come out with the 'Forget me not' this year—has the Editor written to you about it? I hope you will contribute in this work, for Mr. A, is punctual in his payment I believe" (Eliza Emmerson, February 26, 1829). Clare submitted the poem and was paid promptly one month later:

> I have to thank you for the promptness with which you have answered my call in behalf of my intended Juvenile Annual: The poem which you have sent & which is considered well suited to the work, is estimated at about six pages. For such articles I know not what others [have] given, but I have for my own part been paying at the rate of half a guinea per page. Should this meet your expectation, have the goodness to furnish me at your convenience with whatever you may think equivalent to the balance of £5 which I enclose. (Rudolph Ackermann, March 13, 1829)

Each year, not only are the authors' names revealed but also the quantity of literature increases by one-third. The 1823 *Forget Me Not* contains about 400 pages, 100 pages of which are charts and information. The 1824 volume also contains almost 400 pages, but only 2 of them are charts. The 1825 volume contains no information or charts in its approximately 400 pages. The 1827 *Forget Me Not* triples the number of poems to almost seventy in over 100 pages, compared to only twenty-eight poems in the 1826 volume. The number of pages does not increase but instead remains consistent around 360–420 pages in the 1823–31 volumes. Nor does the number of engravings increase, remaining consistently at twelve to fourteen throughout 1823–31. Of the seventy poems included in the 1827 volume, Letitia Elizabeth Landon, Reverend Croly, Mary Russell Mitford, Felicia Hemans, William Ainsworth, David Lyndsay (aka Mary Diana Dods), James

Bird, Richard Polwhele, Thomas Hood, John Bowring, and Bernard Barton all receive credit with full name attribution appended to their contributions, both in the table of contents and in the pages of the annual.

Though the *Forget Me Not* continued to publish large numbers of poems in its pages well into the 1830s, it seemed to excel at including more pages of short fiction than any other literary annual during this first decade of success. Nonetheless, Shoberl accounts for this increased valuing of poetry in the Preface to the 1827 *Forget Me Not*:

> It will likewise be obvious that this volume is much richer in poetical compositions than any of the preceding portions of the Forget Me Not; and many of those compositions are of so high an order that the Editor can assert, without fear of contradiction, that a miscellany possessing within so small a compass equal claims to public favour has rarely issued from the press. Some of these pieces are tributes of personal friendship; many more the spontaneous offerings of well-wishers, solicitous to aid by their talents in maintaining the Forget Me Not in that high station to which the public voice has elevated it. (iv)

The evolution of the contents follows a public desire for that polite literature that Ackermann, Watts, and Croly originally envisioned—but wrapped in a container of luxury that signals external validation of these titles.

THE BUSINESS OF BINDINGS AND THE PROMISE OF NEW TYPE

Literary annual editors and publishers understood the value of commodifying the beauty of a literary annual and offered bindings that represented a sense of luxury. The annuals, because they were so prolific in terms of the number of titles, offered a moment for publishers to experiment with coverings and other bibliographical details. The printing and binding business was booming during the early nineteenth century, especially in London. Affluent families often acquired leaves or unbound books in order to have them bound in a singular and unique leather binding, while others collected volumes to build personal libraries that would demonstrate their education and therefore social standing.

The first British literary annuals were originally published in small octavo and duodecimo sizes with glazed paper boards and a slipcase usually bearing the same image (figs. 3.5 and 3.6).[6] According to Philip Gaskell,

"[P]aper boards with lettering and typographic decoration printed on the spine and covers began to appear at the end of the eighteenth century, and became increasingly common during the succeeding decades" (248). Accordingly, "cloth as a covering material . . . was stronger and more durable than paper, cheaper and more abundant than leather, and . . . regular and predictable in quality" (Gaskell, 231).[7] In 1821, William Pickering, publisher of the annuals *The Bijou* (1828–30) and *The Carcanet* (1828, 1830), was among the few publishers who produced volumes in a dyed cotton cloth binding with a printed label on the spine (Keynes, 13). In *Bookcloth, 1823–1980,* William Tomlinson notes that "the series of experiments on which Archibald Leighton embarked with Pickering's

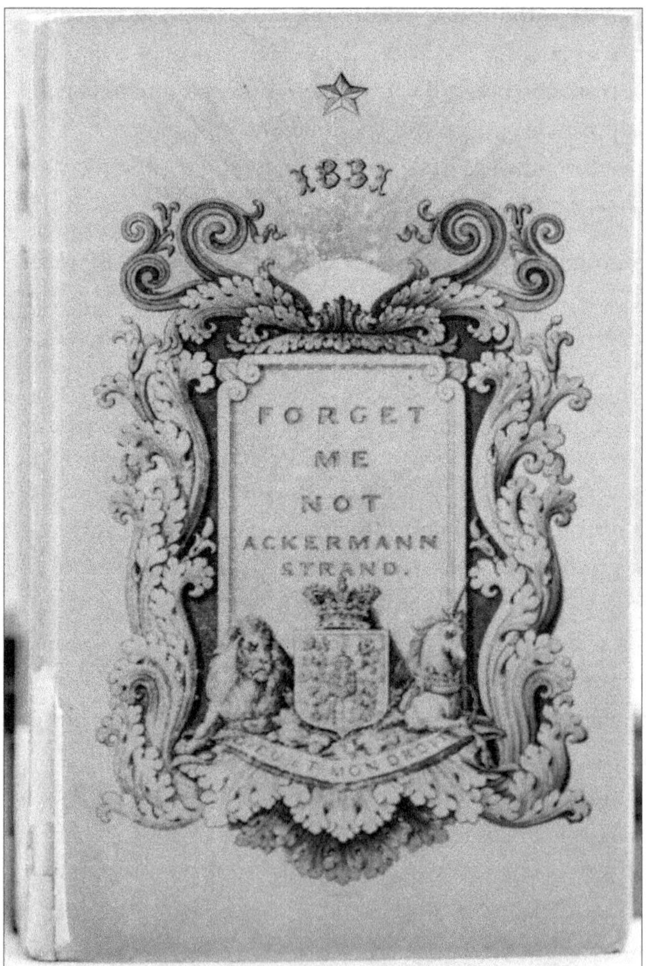

Figure 3.5 Front board, 1831 *Forget Me Not* (from the Katherine D. Harris Collection; photo credit, Tom Davis)

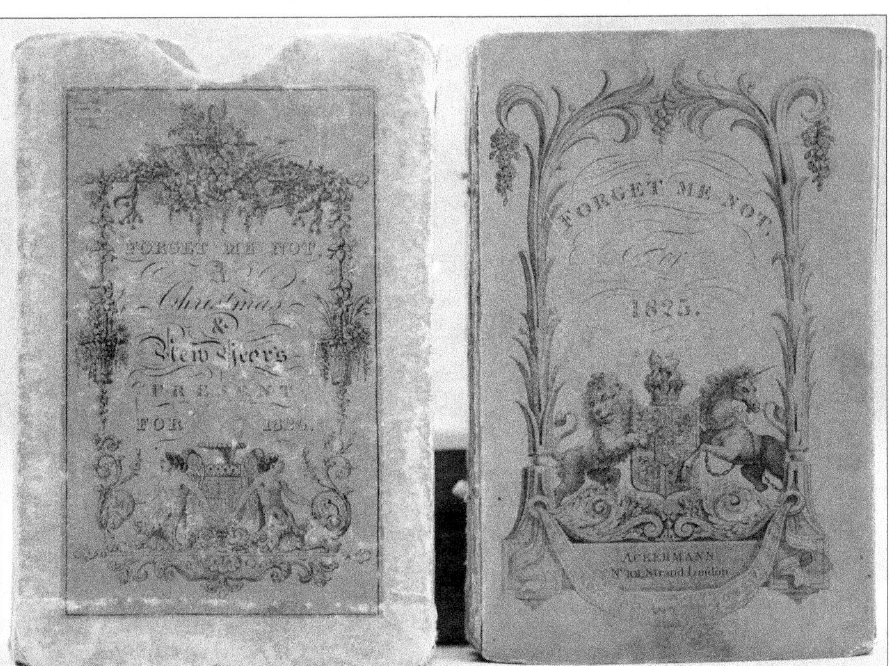

Figure 3.6 Slipcase, 1825 *Forget Me Not* (from the Katherine D. Harris Collection; photo credit, Tom Davis)

encouragement were aimed at the production of a thin fabric of sufficient stiffness and impermeability to enable the binder to work quickly and therefore cheaply and cleanly" (13).

At a price of twelve shillings to three pounds, the literary annual was a gift that suggested additional binding to complete its beauty—a cost shouldered by either the presenter, the recipient, or the bookseller—at first. Tomlinson notes that "the introduction of such a starch-filled book-cloth in the 1820s not only provided a new material for binding books but precipitated a revolution in publishing. With the almost simultaneous adoption of casing (the making-up of the covers separately from the book), it was to throw back on the publisher the responsibility for binding, which had previously been accepted by the retail bookseller or the purchaser of the book" (1). However, the annuals were bound in a variety of styles; eventually the bindings moved to the ever-popular leather. Watts's *Literary Souvenir* was one of the few to be delivered to the bookseller already bound in leather boards.

Figure 3.7 Rebindings in leather boards, 1824 (*bottom*) and 1827 (*top*) *Forget Me Not* (from the Katherine D. Harris Collection)

Friendship's Offering, begun just a year after the *Forget Me Not,* was originally published in glazed paper boards similar to those of the *Forget Me Not.* The *Forget Me Not* was published with paper boards through 1831, when Ackermann switched to silk covers to mimic *The Keepsake,* a later entry into the literary annual competition. Ackermann's move to silk, however, was a common phenomenon in the late 1820s, as is noted by Tomlinson: "There was nothing new in the idea of binding books in common fabrics. The use of velvets and embroidered materials had been common in the Tudor and Stuart periods. Silks and satins were being used in large quantities on the annuals and gift books that were fashionable at around the time that starch-filled bookcloth made its first appearance and some of these books continued to be bound in silk until 1845. But the aim here was elegance rather than durability" (3). Philip Gaskell notes, along the same lines, that "paper boards were neither very durable nor much cheaper than trade leather, and a considerable portion of books (whether or not they had first been put into paper boards by the publisher) were trade-bound in leather by the retailer as before; often the leather cover was simply stuck on top of the paper boards" (231). Gaskell also points out that marking the spine of a cloth book was initially problematic because printers typically used paper labels on the spine. In 1832, a method was introduced and popularized for impressing words onto the spine and then embossing them. Gaskell passingly refers to William Pickering's 1830 experiment in gold-blocking the cloth spine and emphasizes that it was an experiment that was not repeated (235n9a). However, *The Keepsake* volumes for both 1828 and 1829 are covered in silk (a type of cloth) and have their titles and other information marked on the spine. These two volumes, from separate private collections, may have been embossed after 1832, but the font, spacing, and style of the embossing are identical. Hence, Reynolds and his publishers and printers used embossed cloth spines earlier than 1832—an important development in printing history to which the literary annual may stake a claim.

The bindings of literary annuals are difficult to study, because their bindings exist in various forms today.[8] In *A List of London Bookbinders, 1648–1815,* Ellic Howe notes that with the growth of bookbinding in London a healthy trade in prayer books and Bibles in slipcases reached a pinnacle during the early nineteenth century. With their slipcases and embossed covers, literary annuals may have been replicated in these gospel-like bindings to convince the reading public of the wholesome value of the literature and engravings within. However, Howe notes that the business of bookbinding was predicated on curtailing retail costs:

> The retailer, then, was the substantial buyer of bookbinding. It was of two kinds: bespoke, and for retail stock. The bookseller sometimes acted as agent for his customers in bespeaking the binding of books in any special style which they favoured. "Two of my customers," says John Dunton (*Life and Errors,* 1818 ed., p. 258), "gave particular charge that no man in London should find the books they bought of me but Mr. Baker and Mr. Steel."
>
> A book cannot well be sold by retail in unbound sheets; and a retailer was therefore obliged to have the books for his shop folded, sewn, and bound. This was done for purely practical purposes, and as inexpensively as possible, without any labelling or gilt tooling. Plain forel, unlettered calf, sheep binding with volume numbers but no lettering on the back, "original boards with label, uncut"—all these are retailers' bindings. Cheaply bound because the retailer had to pay for it, but necessarily bound because otherwise the books could not be sold over the counter. The most expensively bound books normally stocked by a retailer were bibles and prayer books. Hence bookbinders regarded bible binding as "the cream of the trade." (xxiv)[9]

G. Thomas Tanselle has found that the annual's slipcase, also known as a sheath, offers the earliest form of the modern book jacket or dustwrapper.[10] Definitive evidence of anything but a slipcase had not been uncovered until Mark Godburn's April 2009 discovery of a book jacket encasing the 1830 *Friendship's Offering*, noted by Michael Lieberman on his blog, *Book Patrol*: "A librarian digging through the archives at the Bodleian Library, University of Oxford has found the earliest known example of a publisher's dust jacket. The dust jacket, which had been separated from the book it was created for, was found bound with other booktrade ephemera."[11] The next-earliest book jacket was found on the 1833 *Keepsake* (as reported by John Carter in *Publisher's Weekly,* September 22, 1934, on page 1121).

The literary annuals were typically produced on machine-made paper, which can be determined by the lack of watermarks or chain marks from the paper molds, hence reducing the overhead of producing such a volume and increasing—only slightly—the profit margin. Beginning in the 1820s, paper was mass-produced from linen by a paper-making machine, the

Fourdrinier (Gaskell, 221). From 1820 to 1850, many printers were experimenting with mechanizing their binding processes, including paper making, creating boards, and gathering, sewing, and binding the quires (Gaskell, 229). Ackermann changed printers for the *Forget Me Not* volumes but returned to some (such as Thomas in Whitefriars for 1824 and 1827). There is some speculation that he printed in-house. Apparently, J. B. Papworth produced plans for the new building at 96 Strand and left the basement for printers. Some engravings have a different printer appended, different from the printer who was responsible for the text of the volume. Perhaps Ackermann performed the assembly in-house. We know he owned a lithography printer, but business records are unclear on whether he made his own paper or printed some volumes in-house.

When the *Literary Souvenir* first appeared in 1825, the editor, Alaric Watts, had a larger octavo edition printed (4.75 × 7.75 in.), in contrast to the smaller octavo (3.5 × 5.5 in.). Though the *Literary Souvenir* was published in this larger size, only the margins increased, not the typeface or the font. The publisher recycled the already-set plates used for the primary smaller octavo edition. Consumers paid a higher retail price, usually a pound more than for the smaller octavo edition, for larger sheets of uncut paper and more blank space on each page, not more writing or a resetting of the type and recasting of the plates. The lavish two-inch margins of the larger paper afforded a white space not otherwise provided in cheaper reading materials, such as almanacs and miscellanies. Watts continued this dual printing until 1835, when the final volume of this title was published as a quarto.

In a continuing tradition of artistic printing, editors and publishers were aware of the value of external and internal presentation of their products. It was not enough that the boards were ornately decorated or covered in the finest materials. But the reading experience, influenced by the organization of the literary information, became indebted to these types of small bibliographical alterations.

In his 1826 preface, Alaric Watts emphasizes the importance of both the linguistic and the bibliographic elements of *The Literary Souvenir* and urges readers to consider the "mechanical part of the work" in addition to its contents: "I would not have the beautiful typography of the present volume escape notice altogether. In order that the mechanical part of the work should not be unworthy of the matter and illustrations, it has been printed from an entirely new font of type" (viii). Frederic Shoberl, too, moved beyond declarations of the finest literary and graphic embellishments to proclaim that "among other arrangements for improving the appearance of the Forget-Me-Not, a new and elegant type, cast expressly for the purpose, was procured" (1825 preface, ii). Both Shoberl and Watts point to marriage of form and content in this prefatory side note, well aware of the marketing of literary *and* visual aesthetics.

Reynolds in the 1829 *Keepsake* preface and Watts in the 1826 *Literary Souvenir* preface mention that the overflowing amount of engravings and writings that caused them to add sheets of letterpress to the volumes to accommodate the readers' demand for "more" created a literary miscellany that was "more" fulfilling in both literature and beauty than ever before. This alteration in size and increase in letterpress convinced consumers that they would receive "more" content, engravings, and value for the same price—as if the literary annual volume were an investment instead of an indulgence. At the behest of Alaric Watts, the octavo edition of the *Literary Souvenir* was sold for twelve shillings between 1825 and 1835 despite the increase in engraving quality and the number of written pieces—a fact that he points out in several of his prefaces, a move that positions him as a benefactor to his readers. These increases enhanced the value, both financially and emotionally, of the annuals and enabled beautiful typography intended to increase an owner's/reader's emotional attachment to the volume.

ALARIC WATTS, REVISING THE GENRE

The development of this genre, though begun by Ackermann and advanced by Shoberl, moved away from declarations of polite literature because of Alaric Watts. For Watts, annuals were for men of feeling and taste, an assumption that refers to aesthetics predicated on late eighteenth-century aesthetics in literary taste. More importantly, Watts used the *Literary Souvenir* to represent or argue with the publishing world, especially concerning issues of copyright, editorial control, and authorial ownership. His *Literary Souvenir* was less about highlighting the didactic at Christmastime and more about establishing literary legacies and displaying modern art. In the 1828 *Literary Souvenir* preface, Watts declares,

> In introducing to the public the fourth volume of the *Literary Souvenir,* I trust I shall be pardoned for referring to the state of annual publications, on its first appearance, as well as for vindicating to

> myself whatever merit may be my due, as the principal cause of the manifest improvements they now exhibit, both as regards their literary and graphic contents. At that time, the embellishments and literature of its rivals were avowedly of an order adapted rather for the meridian of the nursery, than for "children of a larger growth." The *Literary Souvenir* . . . has aimed at interesting a different order of readers; and the best proof of its success that can be adduced, will be found in the very large yearly increase of its sale, and the emulous efforts of the proprietors of other annual publications. . . . If, therefore, to Mr. Ackermann be due (as undoubtedly it is), the praise of having introduced books of this class into this country, I may fairly lay claim to the secondary merit of having contributed to render them what they now are. (v–vi)

And indeed, November 1827 saw the publication of Charles Heath's luxurious *Keepsake,* with canonical authors overflowing from its pages and ladies' portraits gracing the large octavo.[12]

In this 1828 preface, Watts continues a diatribe against some criticism of the *Literary Souvenir*'s engravings and literary merit; he accomplishes this by, at first, holding up the British annuals as superior to even Schiller's contributions to the German almanacs. He condemns the reviewers who offer approbations to ten or fifteen foreign pocket-books and almanacs by stating that these volumes are "out of reach of the ordinary reader. . . . A critic may expatiate with considerable security on the overwhelming merits of foreign pocket-books, because the probability is that nine out of ten, or even a still larger portion of the readers of English Annuals have never had an opportunity of weighing the correctness of his assertion" (vi–ix).

In this seeming defense of English readers' access to materials, Watts condemns the foreign materials as containing "compositions bombastic in style, as lax or lack-a-daisical in sentiment" (ix), and counters the critics' accusations that English annuals contain articles that are "too light and frivolous a character to be as acceptable to the public as those which are to be met with in periodical craft of larger burthen" (x). He admits that some annuals, especially the *Janus,* are "filled with literary pabulum of which it was composed, . . . for the most part, too solid for the digestions of the great mass of the readers to who[se] patronage such works are principally addressed" (x–xi). He contends that the essays in the *Janus* were more appropriate for the *Quarterly Review* than an annual.

DEMANDING ORIGINAL CONTRIBUTIONS

Editors of the annuals spent paragraphs in their prefaces answering the critics and defending the originality of the pieces published in their volumes. In response to such criticism and to add competing value to their own annuals as well as to distinguish the genre from other reading materials, editors established a common practice of claiming originality in the preface, such as the following claim from Reynolds: "[S]uch a list of authors has been obtained as perhaps never before graced the pages of any one volume of *original* contributions" (1829 *Keepsake,* iv).

In an effort to defend the *Forget Me Not* against criticism that the volumes were merely a miscellany or anthology, in the 1827 preface Shoberl derides the idea of republication and again reminds readers and critics of the importance of original materials:

> Flattering as were the opinions of critics in general on the last volume, still, owing to some unaccountable misconception, one or two writers belonging to the periodical press treated the Forget Me Not in their remarks as a mere selection from works previously before the public. In order to correct a notion equally false and derogatory, the Editor feels it incumbent on him to declare, in the most unqualified manner, that originality is an essential requisite in articles destined for the pages of this miscellany; and that, though in former years some translations were introduced, yet all the pieces in the present volume—so far from being borrowed from other publications, or selected from hoards of spurious or unauthenticated scraps—have been, with a few trifling exceptions (such as the short poems by the late Mrs. Piozzi and Mrs. Grant), written expressly for this work, and communicated by the authors themselves. (v)

Editor Thomas Pringle apologizes to his audience and warns them of previously printed materials in the 1833 *Friendship's Offering:* "In one slight point we have in the present volume not adhered strictly to our usual practice. We have admitted three little pieces that had previously been in print. These are, the pleasant prose article entitled 'Old Maids,' and two scraps of verse, 'The Tornado,' and a "Sonnet by Alfred Tennyson'" (vii). Pringle diminishes the act by referring to them as "little" and "scraps." He continues in the preface by citing the original publication site and rendering an mini-eulogy for the periodical's demise: "[A]ll originally inserted in the 'Englishman's Magazine' for August, 1831—a clever periodical, which amidst the 'chance and change' of the times and 'the trade,' was consigned, after the publication of a few numbers, to premature extinction" (vii)—almost as if he was unwilling to speak ill of the "dead."

Though this preface was published in the second generation of annuals (that is, after 1828), the habit of defending originality extended from the prior generation of annuals, an accusation that was not taken lightly by editors. In defending the inclusion and exclusion of pieces in the 1826 *Literary Souvenir,* editor Alaric Watts insists, "The literary contents of the following pages . . . have . . . been supplied, at my instigation, by a host of the most distinguished writers of the age" (vi). In the same preface, Watts assures his readers that "[t]he embellishments, too, have been executed . . . by the most eminent engravers, from *original* paintings and drawings by the first artists of the day" (vi).

Watts had a habit of answering criticism in his prefaces in a way that was defensive and incongruous with the polite literary goals of his annual. However, these declarations did not appear in the *Literary Souvenir*'s preface unprovoked. In reviewing the 1828 volume of the *Literary Souvenir,* for example, a critic scolds Watts and condemns the volume for Watts's "illiberal" prefatory remarks (regarding a competitor) and its unoriginal content:

> [W]hen the editor of a literary work complains of the vain-glorious puffs of his rivals in the same line, he ought to be pretty well assured before hand, that his own wares will bear, at least as severe a scrutiny as that, to which he wishes those of his opponents to be subjected. . . .
>
> It wo[u]ld be the mere empty sound of adulation, if we were to say, that Mr. Watts is at the present moment in any such condition. Had not the authenticity of the new Souvenir been unquestionable, we should have at once suspected that the title had been pirated, and that the book now before us was but an imitation and a very poor imitation, of the beautiful productions which, in preceding years, have attracted our attention, and have justified the applause we so willingly bestowed upon them. We should be equally happy to speak in terms of praise of each, succeeding work of the same nature; but this, of course, we can only do when it is equally deserving. (anonymous, *Monthly Review* [December 1827])[13]

Even though this review critiques a later volume of the *Literary Souvenir,* the originality issue included an accusation that had been leveled at editors since the initial production of annuals. In an earlier defense of originality in the 1826 preface, Watts answers just such a criticism (most likely from a review of the 1825 *Literary Souvenir* during the prior year):

> With regard to the literary portion of this volume, *I would wish it to be clearly understood that it is what it professes to be, original.* I am led to dwell upon this feature of my plan thus particularly, in consequence of having observed that more than one of the literary friends who have contributed anonymously to my pages, and of whose names I should have been extremely happy to have availed myself, had they permitted me so to do, have been publicly announced as the "contributors" to a work professing similar objects with the *Literary Souvenir,* not only against their consent, but without their having furnished a single line for its pages. As I perceive the names of other of my friends attached to productions, in the announcements of the work in question, which have already appeared repeatedly in print, it is not unfair to infer that they, too, have been pressed into the service of the parties in the same manner. Of course, a selection might, upon such a principle, include *all* the poets and novelists of the age, not excepting those recently deceased, for "dead men tell no tales." (x–xi; emphasis added)[14]

Watts did not accept unsolicited prose or poetry for his annual, expressing the intent that *The Literary Souvenir* would be a tightly controlled product of quality literature and artwork. He separated *The Literary Souvenir* from other reading materials and annuals by vociferously claiming originality in its contents and denouncing any disingenuous claims to authenticity. In the same volume in a postscript, Watts directly addresses accusations of republishing:

> Mr. Montgomery mentions in his Sheffield Iris, that the "Lines on leaving a scene in Bavaria," by Mr. Campbell in the L.S. for 1825, were originally published, about twenty years ago, in an obscure newspaper, long since defunct, entitled "The Alfred." Mr. M. considers the poem one of the most powerful compositions of its author.

> The little piece, from the same pen, inserted in the present volume, may, it is possible, have appeared under similar circumstances. I am not, however, aware that it has. The same remark will apply to the little epigram by Mr. Coleridge. Neither of these poems was furnished by their authors. The song ascribed to Sheridan was presented to me as original, by a distinguished living poet. (412)

However, this addendum undermines Watts's earlier defense against republishing literary material. Like Pringle, Watts uses language to diminish the affront: "obscure newspaper," "little piece," and "little epigram." In addition, he absolves the poets of responsibility and maintains his integrity, with concessions, by begrudgingly admitting the possibility of a republished poem. But Watts's acceptance of a secondhand poem from persons other than the authors smacks of the same surreptitious borrowing practice that Watts condemns in his preface. Interestingly, this postscript is almost completely buried at the end of the volume and is printed in the same fashion as an advertisement—something a reader might overlook.

Authors were not as ethical or as informed as Watts seems to have been. In a January 1827 *Monthly Review* article, the critic accuses editor and popular poet T. K. Hervey (who was also the editor of *Friendship's Offering*) of plagiarizing from the tale "Agatha," which immediately precedes his "Address to Floranthe" in the 1827 *Friendship's Offering:* "The lines . . . are evidently a plagiarism from the following sentence in the tale . . . which precedes this poem, and which Mr. Hervey must have had an opportunity, of course, of reading in the manuscript. . . . There are other plagiarisms in the poem, which it is not worth our while to specify as they must be obvious to every literary person" (anonymous, 89). This accusation, while serious, did not preclude the reviewer from recommending the volume to readers with a wish that more of Hervey's poetry would have appeared in the volume. This particular volume's contents are very plump and offer the consumer a larger selection of contents than most other annuals—which may have been the cause of duplicating lines in order to fill more pages.

The issue of originality, in the face of either republished or plagiarized material, is an ethical debate waged between editors and critics that did not hinder the retail sales of annuals. In fact, because of the lucrative remuneration afforded literati for their contributions to annuals, authors (including Wordsworth) sold their writing to literary annuals and magazines or were the victims of unauthorized publication. In the preface to the 1828 *Literary Souvenir,* Watts admonishes Coleridge for publishing his poem "Youth and Age" in both Watts's annual and William Pickering's *Bijou* (xvi). Watts may have been hasty in this judgment: Coleridge's dual publication may have been the result of an unauthorized submission. Wordsworth, in a letter to Alaric Watts regarding the 1832 *Literary Souvenir,* offers a poem for inclusion in the 1833 volume but warns, "[I]t has been sent to Sir Walter Scott and one or two of my other friends; so that you had best not print it till towards the latter sheets of your volume, lest it should steal by chance into publication, for which I have given no permissions. Should that happen I will send you some other piece" (Watts, *Alaric Watts,* 2:189–90). Other authors, like Felicia Hemans, reprinted their contributions to the annuals in their own volumes of poetry: "Evening Prayer at a Girls' School," for example, appeared not only in the 1826 *Forget Me Not* but also in two of Hemans' poetry volumes: *The League of the Alps Etc.* (1826) and *Forest Sanctuary Etc.* (1829) (Wolfson, *Felicia Hemans,* 437). By the late 1830s, the number of titles had grown so large that editors rarely defended the originality of contributors' writing. They simply acknowledged it in the preface or in a postscript, as done with the following: "It is proper to mention, that the beautiful address to Mrs. Siddons, by Joanna Baillie, is reprinted from a collection of Poems, edited by that lady" (*Literary Souvenir* 1830 [365]).

By 1830, editors of the annuals were very well aware that they could not control authors, nor could they request authors to abstain from earning money by multiply publishing their works. Watts found a middle ground by publishing a more visible postscript in his 1830 *Literary Souvenir* defending the intended originality of its contents: "In consequence of his having seen a song in the newspapers, from the pen of Mr. T.H. Bayly, entitled, 'The Last Man,' the Editor considers it due to the author of the sketch, entitled, 'The Last Man in Town,' in the present volume, to mention that it was in the types several months before the appearance of the Poem in question, and that it was written upwards of four years ago" (365). With this postscript, Watts not only defended his right to claim original work but also differentiated publishing and printing processes among literary annuals, periodicals, journals, and magazines. The literary annual was a work maneuvered through a year-long process of acquisition, editing, printing, and distribution, as opposed to the other formats, which had a very brief and quick acquisition, editing, and publishing process.

EXPORTING "BRITISHNESS" IN THAT FIRST GENERATION OF ANNUALS

Successful at "home," the literary annual became one of Britain's most flourishing printed exports, popular in the United States, France, Spain, Germany, and Italy (fig. 3.8). Two Spanish-language annuals, *Aguinaldo Puerto-Riqueño: Colleccion de producciones orijinales en prosa y verso* (published in Puerto Rico, 1843) and *Aguinaldo matanzero* (edited by Jose Victoriano Betancourt and published in 1847), emerged in the mid-nineteenth century. The Canadians also picked up on the popular format and published *The Christian Remembrancer for 1832, The Canadian Forget Me Not for 1837,* and *The Maple-Leaf, or Canadian Annual,* issued 1847–49 (R. Thompson, *American,* 166).

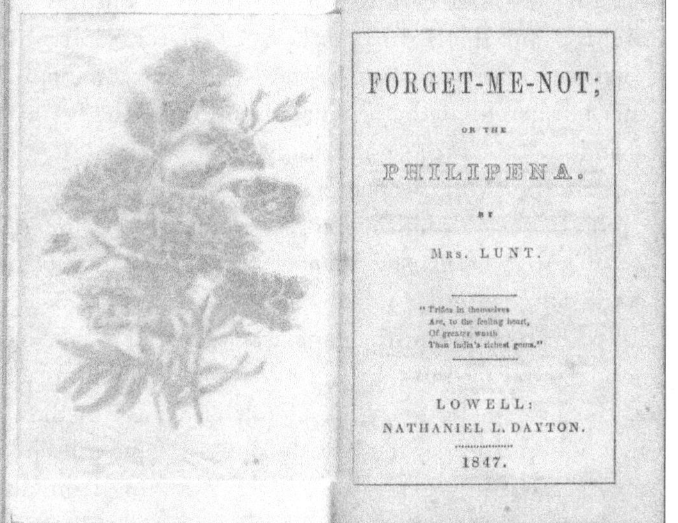
FORGET-ME-NOT;

OR THE

PHILIPENA.

BY

MRS. LUNT.

LOWELL:
NATHANIEL L. DAYTON.

1847.

Figure 3.8 American gift book, 1847 *Forget Me Not; or, The Philipena* (from the Katherine D. Harris Collection)

With the promise of a wider audience, Ackermann and other publishers ventured into partnership with American or European publishers before the French and American penchant for unauthorized reproduction of annuals became prominent. American publishers Carey, Lea and Carey partnered with Ackermann to produce a one-time American printing of the *Forget Me Not* for 1828. Though Carey, Lea and Carey were large distributors of literary annuals and in business with many London publishers, the company's name does not appear on any other *Forget Me Not* title page, which leads me to believe that either variant title pages were produced for the British and American audiences or the partnership was severed after the 1828volume. In addition, Carey, Lea and Carey maintained that business title for the period 1827–29 only, changing to Carey and Lea after Edward Carey's departure, according to Richard Gassan ("Carey"). Ackermann's ventures did not end with this publisher: Ackermann was renowned for his trade in Spanish annuals (including the translation of the *Forget Me Not* discussed in the previous chapter). Ackermann's publishing and printing success stemmed from more than the popular English and Spanish-translation of the *Forget Me Not*. His publishing house "dominated the export of British books in Spanish to the former colonies in the 1820s" (Vera, 3).

Thomas Hood's *Comic Annual* was well received in America in 1830 and sold between 1,000 and 1,500 copies, with a readership "of at least several times that number" because of the family audience (Clubbe, *Victorian,* 75) and the practice of sharing books. The British-published 1830 *Keepsake Français,* the first of this title and written entirely in French, used only one recognizable British author, Sir Walter Scott.[15] Alaric Watts claimed to start a French version of the *Literary Souvenir* replete with French culture but heralding the original intentions of the British literary annuals; he abandoned the project after only a few volumes (figs. 3.9 and 3.10).

The first American literary annual appeared in 1826 with the publication of several different titles, including the *Atlantic Souvenir* (the most popular), *Philadelphia Souvenir, Souvenir,* and *Wreath,* and remained viable commodities until 1902, when the last annual, *Book of Beauty,* was published.[16] In addition, the Americans created a hybrid nationalism in their annual industry. But they were not as self-conscious about their borrowing as the British. Editor S. G. Goodrich writes in the *Token*'s 1838 preface that in emulation of the British annuals, "[t]he present volume is therefore enlarged" (rising to quarto size, 5in. × 7 ¾in., from duodecimo or octavo) and states that "an attempt has been made to bring the graphic illustrations,

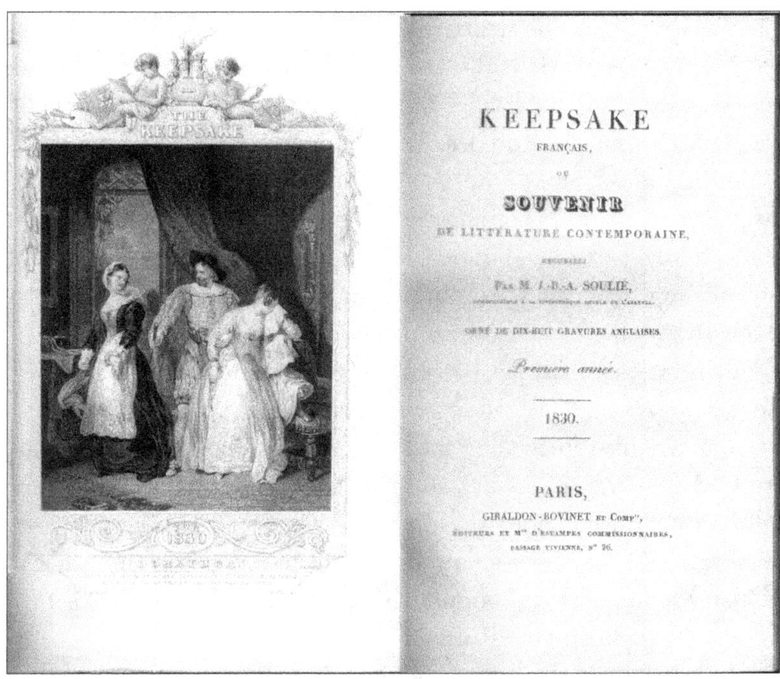

KEEPSAKE

FRANÇAIS,

OU

SOUVENIR

DE LITTÉRATURE CONTEMPORAINE,

PAR M. J.-B.-A. SOULIÉ,

ORNÉ DE DIX-HUIT GRAVURES ANGLAISES.

Première année.

1830.

PARIS,

GIRALDON-BOVINET ET COMP^ie,

ÉDITEURS ET M^ds D'ESTAMPES COMMISSIONNAIRES,

PASSAGE VIVIENNE, N° 26.

Figure 3.9 Frontispiece and title page, British-published 1830 *Keepsake Français* (from the Katherine D. Harris Collection)

TABLE DES MATIÈRES.

		Pages
La maison d'Aspen, tragédie	SIR WALTER SCOTT	1
Le regard	mad^e DESBORDES VALMORE	80
Épisode d'un voyage en Amérique	DE CHATEAUBRIAND	81
La mort d'un ange	JEAN-PAUL	89
L'ame du purgatoire, ballade	CASIMIR DELAVIGNE	95
Le soleil d'automne	JEAN POLONIUS	99
Les solitudes de l'Amérique	DE CHATEAUBRIAND	103
Le Brésil	DE L***	109
L'ange	CHABOT DE BOUIN	111
La source de l'Orbe	CHARLES DIDIER	113
Le château de Robert-le-Diable	CH. NODIER	115
Venise	JULES LEFÈVRE	122
Le pêcheur de l'Adriatique	ANTONIN DE SIGOYER	126
Le père Émilien, épisode d'un voyage	madame PERCY	129
Le dernier chant du poète	ANTONIN DE SIGOYER	143
Fragment	ALPH. DE LAMARTINE	145
Napoléon	AMABLE TASTU	146
Pensée	DE CHATEAUBRIAND	148
Adieux à Rome	BALLANCHE	149
La jeune hellénienne	ALFRED DE VIGNY	152
Le Dante	CHARLES NODIER	156
La sylphide	P. J. DE BÉRANGER	162
L'alouette	G. DE MANCY	165
Maxime et Zoé, ou le mauvais œil	M. MÉRIMÉE	166
L'athée	DE LA MENNAIS	170
Prière d'un damné	GASPARD DE PONS	173
Sonnet	SAINTE-BEUVE	174
Stances	ALPH. DE LAMARTINE	175
La princesse et les pèlerins	A. FONTANEY	177
L'abbé de La Mennais	VICTOR HUGO	178
Des femmes	madame HORTENSE ALLARD	180
Les fouilles de Rome	DE CHATEAUBRIAND	182
Turner	ERNEST FOUINET	184
Un Lac	*Ibid.*	185
Stances	ALPH. DE LAMARTINE	187
L'amour	BENJAMIN CONSTANT	193
Fragment	ALPH. DE LAMARTINE	195
*A Mademoiselle Marie N****	A. FONTANEY	196
Albaïzir, ou le serviteur fidèle	S.	199
Le passage du mont Saint-Bernard	CASIMIR DELAVIGNE	202
Misraël	ALEX. DUMAS	205
Vieille ballade	FRANCOIS Ier	209
Michel-Ange	DE STENDHAL	210
Le buisson	CH. NODIER	216
Médora	A. FONTANEY	218
Lettres de lord Byron	NOEL BYRON	222
Le cimetière de village	M. J.-B.-A. SOULIÉ	225
Le devin	ERNEST FOUINET	231
Le pêcheur de Sorrente	DELPHINE GAY	235
Fragment	BALLANCHE	238
Rêves d'un voyage	DE BÉRANGER	241
Le portrait	A. FONTANEY	243
Chœur de Moïse	DE CHATEAUBRIAND	246
Vers	A. DE LAMARTINE	250
La fiancée	ERNEST FOUINET	252
Monologue de Macbeth	ÉMILE DESCHAMPS	255
La jeune fille et le fossoyeur	madame M. WALDOR	257
La grande salle du château	ERNEST FOUINET	260
Superstitions de l'amour	A. DE LATOUCHE	264

TABLE DES GRAVURES.

Sujets.	Peintres.	Graveurs.	
Offrande du Keepsake	STOTHARD	S. MITAN.	
Portrait de lady Ellis.	LAWRENCE	C. HEATH.	
Frontispice	STEPHANOFF	ENGLEHEART.	
Georges d'Aspen et Isabelle	*Idem.*	MITCHELL	42
Isabelle et Gertrude	CHALON	F. BACON	57
Venise	S. PROUT	FREEBAIRN	122
La jeune Hellénienne	STEPHANOFF	GOODYEAR	152
La Sylphide	A. DEVERIA	C. ROLLS	162
La princesse et les pèlerins	WILKIE	C. HEATH	177
Eaux de Turner	TURNER	WALLIS	184
Idem.	*Idem*	*Idem.*	
Le fidèle serviteur	COOPER	GOODYEAR	199
François Ier	BONNINGTON	C. HEATH	209
Médora	CORBOULD	*Idem.*	218
Le devin	CHALON	MITCHELL	231
Le portrait	SMIRKE	PORTBURY	243
La fiancée	LESLIE	C. HEATH	252
La salle du château	*Idem*	MITCHELL	255

Figure 3.10 Table of contents from French annual, 1830 *Keepsake Français* (from the Katherine D. Harris Collection)

as nearly as may be, to the standard of the London annuals" (iii). The topics of the American engravings differed greatly from those of the British annuals: The American publishers included images not of pastoral life or proper ladies but scenes from the American landscape, including images of the Wild West and Native Americans. (These were the Americans' images of savagery and colonial conquest.) American publishers further complicated the annual's national boundaries by claiming British volumes as their own, canceling title pages and tipping in others that altered the year and the publisher—all without indicating that these were reissues.[17]

Studying the annuals has become more complicated recently because of the discovery that not all volumes offer their contents in the same order—poems are replaced or the meticulously ordered contents are reordered, causing variations in volumes of the same title.[18] These types of variations offer insight into the piracy that so often occurred when the printing plates of British annuals were sold to American publishers. This could also account for the popularity of certain poets, some of Britain's greatest exports during the Romantic era.[19]

Because Britain and America had no copyright agreement, many British authors did not receive income from the sale of their books in America. It was not until the 1842 Copyright Act, championed by Dickens, Wordsworth, and Thomas Hood, that British authors began to collect income from these sales.[20] Hood's influence on the act was through correspondence with Sir Thomas Noon Talfourd (a former member of the House of Commons and original proposer of the 1837 amendments to the law) and his letters to the *Atheneum,* titled "Copyright and Copywrong" and published in June 1842. The 1842 act provided copyright protection for forty-two years or the life of the author, a change from the twenty-eight years in the prior law (Clubbe, *Victorian,* 118), and was significantly authored by William Wordsworth himself—giving new meaning to the author as national treasure.[21]

The American literary annual phenomenon followed its own developmental path, differentiating itself from the British annual with content derived from local authors and political and cultural intonations of a post-revolutionary and pre–Civil War United States.[22] Many of their annuals became politically centered or more accessible to working-class citizens, as opposed to the decidedly middle-class nature of the British-published literary annuals. The business of annuals differed greatly, too, in the United States and eventually suffered from the rise of ladies' books and magazines.[23]

FOUR

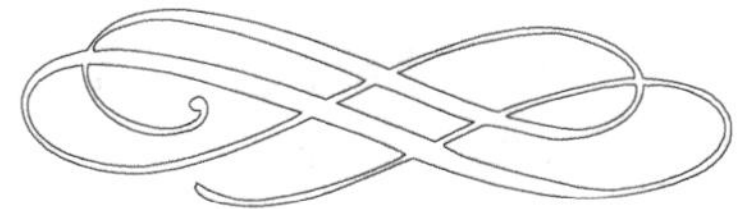

Second-Generation Annuals

A Ballroom Filled with Debutants and Comedians, The Keepsake *and* The Comic Annual

WITH THE DEVELOPMENT OF *THE LITERARY SOUVENIR* and other, less popular annuals, Ackermann's vision of function and utility disappeared and was replaced by the cult of beauty, an incredibly competitive market from 1828 through the 1840s. The author of the 1828 *Keepsake* preface acknowledges the competitive market for literary annuals but describes its entry as a "debutant" in a "family":[1]

> A Preface is often like a trump card, of which the most is made when the hand is weakest. Ours shall be brief, from the presumed strength, not weakness, of our hand; and because, *unlike* a trump card, a diffuse and cringing preface rarely gains a trick. It must not, however, be dispensed with: to commence our course by sailing against the stream would only be defective policy.
>
> We therefore introduce the Keepsake as a claimant for some portion of the protection freely awarded to other individuals of the family, of which our *debutant* is the youngest, and, we trust, not the least deserving member.
>
> It is unnecessary to dwell on the design and scope of the present work, the leading features of the class to which it belongs being

> too generally known to require even an allusion. Competition, the parent of excellence, has already given birth to a crowd of literary annuals, the number of which is still increasing. The deserved popularity of these volumes, united to a persuasion, that an addition to their number, on a similar but enlarged plan, would not be unacceptable to the public, suggested the idea of this new undertaking; the principal object of which will be, to render the union of literary merit with all the beauty of art as complete as possible. (v–vi)

The editor of this volume accepts that the number of annuals by 1828, fifteen in total, has proved the marketability of such a literary product and does not propose in his preface that he will strike upon something new. This literary annual will, instead, borrow from the tradition already established and improve upon it—the format has been borrowed and altered for the purpose of capitalizing on a trend. *The Keepsake*'s "newness" stemmed from its higher retail price: *The Keepsake* was the first annual to sell for a guinea,[2] as opposed to the twelve shillings for Watts's *Literary Souvenir.* The targeted consumers of the literary annual were middle-class families; the lower-middle-class families were excluded from the "cult of beauty" with the introduction of this guinea annual, which was later carried on by *Heath's Book of Beauty,* first published in 1833 and written/edited solely by Letitia Elizabeth Landon (L.E.L.). Landon being at the forefront of this "cult of beauty," it was only appropriate that she lead the annuals into a different generation, a second generation, which was preoccupied with beauty.

The Keepsake carried this cult of beauty to its height, offering an initial publication in 1828 in quarto and covered in red silk. With the 1828 *Keepsake,* annuals were introduced to the public in a larger, more luxurious 6 × 9 in. volume. However, the margins increased instead of the text, which gave readers the illusion of increased space and therefore more value (fig. 4.1). Frederic Reynolds recognizes his audience's yen for beautiful products and assures them in his 1829 *Keepsake* preface that "[t]he Engravings have been considerably augmented in size, and, it is presumed, in value; no exertion having been spared to render them superior even to those of last year. The type, too, has been altered, and the binding and gilding materially improved; in fact, as before stated, every effort has been made to render the Keepsake *perfect* in all its departments" (iv–v). The larger engravings allow readers to linger even longer over the various details.

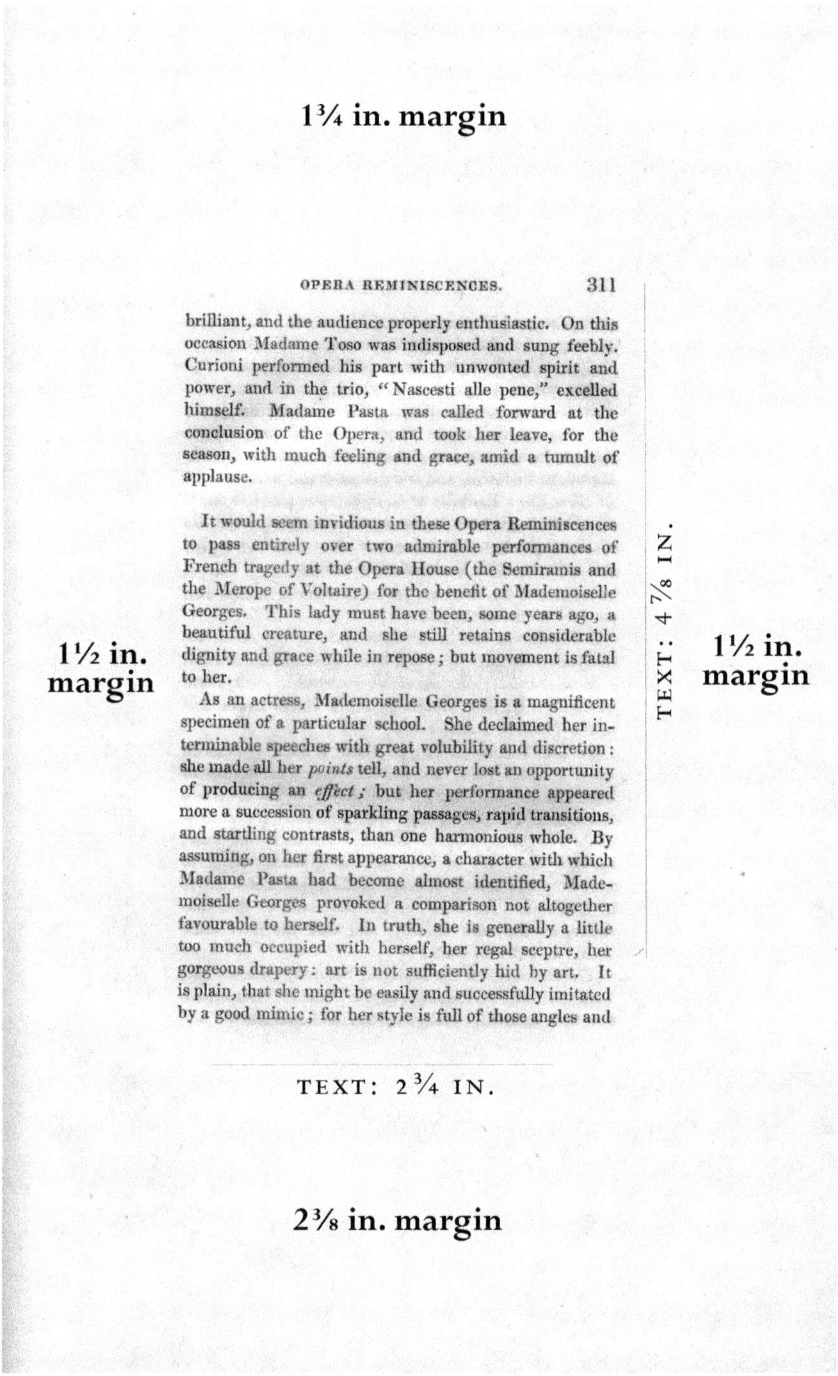

1¾ in. margin

OPERA REMINISCENCES. 311

brilliant, and the audience properly enthusiastic. On this occasion Madame Toso was indisposed and sung feebly. Curioni performed his part with unwonted spirit and power, and in the trio, "Nascesti alle pene," excelled himself. Madame Pasta was called forward at the conclusion of the Opera, and took her leave, for the season, with much feeling and grace, amid a tumult of applause.

It would seem invidious in these Opera Reminiscences to pass entirely over two admirable performances of French tragedy at the Opera House (the Semiramis and the Merope of Voltaire) for the benefit of Mademoiselle Georges. This lady must have been, some years ago, a beautiful creature, and she still retains considerable dignity and grace while in repose; but movement is fatal to her.

As an actress, Mademoiselle Georges is a magnificent specimen of a particular school. She declaimed her interminable speeches with great volubility and discretion: she made all her *points* tell, and never lost an opportunity of producing an *effect;* but her performance appeared more a succession of sparkling passages, rapid transitions, and startling contrasts, than one harmonious whole. By assuming, on her first appearance, a character with which Madame Pasta had become almost identified, Mademoiselle Georges provoked a comparison not altogether favourable to herself. In truth, she is generally a little too much occupied with herself, her regal sceptre, her gorgeous drapery: art is not sufficiently hid by art. It is plain, that she might be easily and successfully imitated by a good mimic; for her style is full of those angles and

1½ in. margin

TEXT: 4 ⅞ IN.

1½ in. margin

TEXT: 2 ¾ IN.

2⅜ in. margin

Figure 4.1 Ample margins on a page of text in a quarto volume, 1828 *Keepsake* (from the Katherine D. Harris Collection)

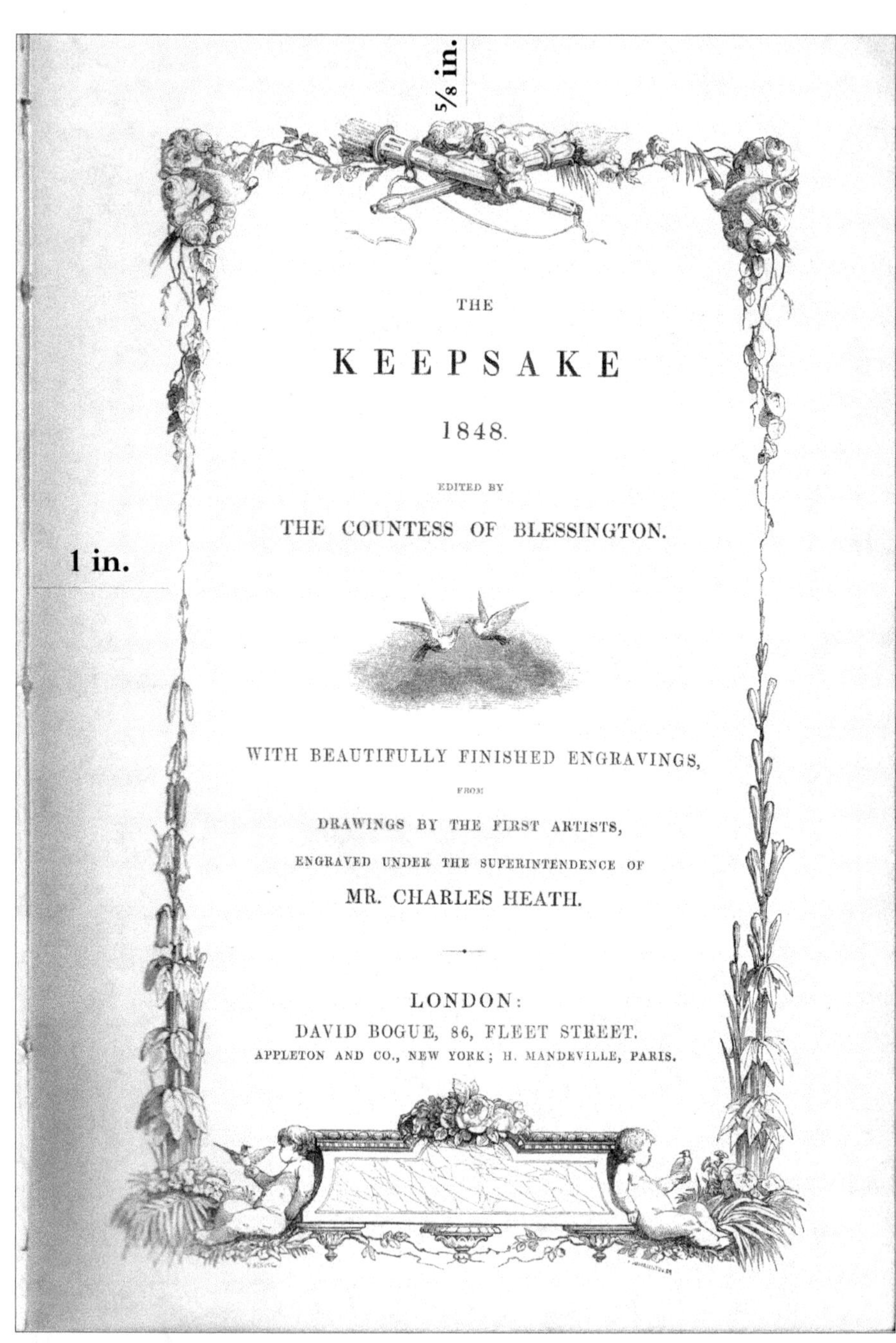

Figure 4.2 Ample margins on an engraving page in a quarto volume, 1848 *Keepsake* (from the Katherine D. Harris Collection)

Later volumes edited by the Countess of Blessington were produced with less margin and more textual coverage, which gave the volumes an air of more—more poetry, more prose, and larger engravings (fig. 4.2). In *The Keepsake,* consumers invested in a promise of more entertainment value due solely to the better use of space.

Leigh Hunt, writing for the 1828 *Keepsake,* assuages readers' and consumers' concerns by assuring them "not [to] be deterred by a size like that of the present one from taking it into fields and gardens; and in the house the size gives it an advantage over miniature publications, having more to show for itself, and to be adorned with; not to mention that we can make presents of it to our grandmothers, without insulting their venerable eyesight" (16). Even with Hunt's reassurances, the increased size was not conducive to portability, especially considering that the annual was a valuable

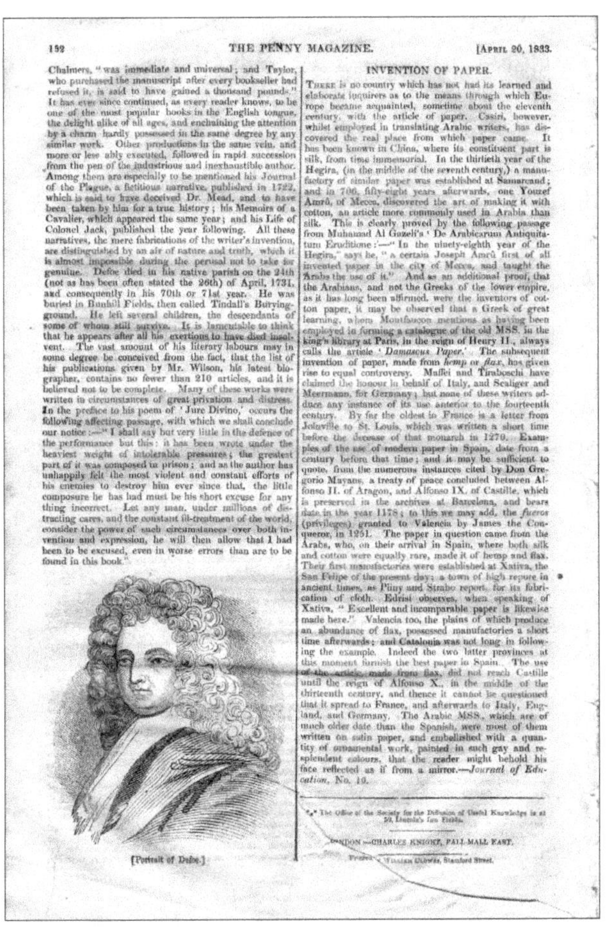

152 THE PENNY MAGAZINE. [April 20, 1833.

Chalmers, "was immediate and universal; and Taylor, who purchased the manuscript after every bookseller had refused it, is said to have gained a thousand pounds." It has ever since continued, as every reader knows, to be one of the most popular books in the English tongue, the delight alike of all ages, and enchaining the attention by a charm hardly possessed in the same degree by any similar work. Other productions in the same vein, and more or less ably executed, followed in rapid succession from the pen of the industrious and inexhaustible author. Among them are especially to be mentioned his Journal of the Plague, a fictitious narrative, published in 1722, which is said to have deceived Dr. Mead, and to have been taken by him for a true history; his Memoirs of a Cavalier, which appeared the same year; and his Life of Colonel Jack, published the year following. All these narratives, the mere fabrications of the writer's invention, are distinguished by an air of nature and truth, which it is almost impossible during the perusal not to take for genuine. Defoe died in his native parish on the 24th (not as has been often stated the 26th) of April, 1731, and consequently in his 70th or 71st year. He was buried in Bunhill Fields, then called Tindall's Burying-ground. He left several children, the descendants of some of whom still survive. It is lamentable to think that he appears after all his exertions to have died insolvent. The vast amount of his literary labours may in some degree be conceived from the fact, that the list of his publications given by Mr. Wilson, his latest biographer, contains no fewer than 210 articles, and it is believed not to be complete. Many of these works were written in circumstances of great privation and distress. In the preface to his poem of 'Jure Divino,' occurs the following affecting passage, with which we shall conclude our notice:—"I shall say but very little in the defence of the performance but this: it has been wrote under the heaviest weight of intolerable pressures; the greatest part of it was composed in prison; and as the author has unhappily felt the most violent and constant efforts of his enemies to destroy him ever since that, the little composure he has had must be his short excuse for any thing incorrect. Let any man, under millions of distracting cares, and the constant ill-treatment of the world, consider the power of such circumstances over both invention and expression, he will then allow that I had been to be excused, even in worse errors than are to be found in this book."

[Portrait of Defoe.]

INVENTION OF PAPER.

There is no country which has not had its learned and elaborate inquirers as to the means through which Europe became acquainted, sometime about the eleventh century, with the article of paper. Casiri, however, whilst employed in translating Arabic writers, has discovered the real place from which paper came. It has been known in China, where its constituent part is silk, from time immemorial. In the thirtieth year of the Hegira, (in the middle of the seventh century,) a manufactory of similar paper was established at Samarcand; and in 706, fifty-eight years afterwards, one Youzef Amrû, of Mecca, discovered the art of making it with cotton, an article more commonly used in Arabia than silk. This is clearly proved by the following passage from Muhammad Al Gazeli's 'De Arabicarum Antiquitatum Eruditione:'—"In the ninety-eighth year of the Hegira," says he, "a certain Joseph Amrû first of all invented paper in the city of Mecca, and taught the Arabs the use of it." And as an additional proof, that the Arabians, and not the Greeks of the lower empire, as it has long been affirmed, were the inventors of cotton paper, it may be observed that a Greek of great learning, whom Montfaucon mentions as having been employed in forming a catalogue of the old MSS. in the king's library at Paris, in the reign of Henry II., always calls the article '*Damascus Paper.*' The subsequent invention of paper, made from *hemp* or *flax*, has given rise to equal controversy. Maffei and Tiraboschi have claimed the honour in behalf of Italy, and Scaliger and Meermann, for Germany; but none of these writers adduce any instance of its use anterior to the fourteenth century. By far the oldest in France is a letter from Joinville to St. Louis, which was written a short time before the decease of that monarch in 1270. Examples of the use of modern paper in Spain, date from a century before that time; and it may be sufficient to quote, from the numerous instances cited by Don Gregorio Mayans, a treaty of peace concluded between Alfonso II. of Aragon, and Alfonso IX. of Castille, which is preserved in the archives at Barcelona, and bears date in the year 1178; to this we may add, the *fueros* (privileges) granted to Valencia by James the Conqueror, in 1251. The paper in question came from the Arabs, who, on their arrival in Spain, where both silk and cotton were equally rare, made it of hemp and flax. Their first manufactories were established at Xativa, the San Felipe of the present day; a town of high repute in ancient times, as Pliny and Strabo report, for its fabrication of cloth. Edrisi observes, when speaking of Xativa, "Excellent and incomparable paper is likewise made here." Valencia too, the plains of which produce an abundance of flax, possessed manufactories a short time afterwards; and Catalonia was not long in following the example. Indeed the two latter provinces at this moment furnish the best paper in Spain. The use of the article, made from flax, did not reach Castille until the reign of Alfonso X., in the middle of the thirteenth century, and thence it cannot be questioned that it spread to France, and afterwards to Italy, England, and Germany. The Arabic MSS., which are of much older date than the Spanish, were most of them written on satin paper, and embellished with a quantity of ornamental work, painted in such gay and resplendent colours, that the reader might behold his face reflected as if from a mirror.—*Journal of Education,* No. 16.

*** The Office of the Society for the Diffusion of Useful Knowledge is at 59, Lincoln's Inn Fields.

LONDON:—CHARLES KNIGHT, PALL-MALL EAST.

Printed by William Clowes, Stamford Street.

Figure 4.3 Less luxurious typeface and margins, 1833 *Penny Magazine* (from the Katherine D. Harris Collection)

object that conveyed delicacy and intimacy. Owners would have a difficult time carrying their precious object into the elements outside the drawing room. Nonetheless, Hunt assures owners, readers, and consumers of the annual's durability in pastoral settings, places that are not filled with urban trappings and are inviting to visit (but not to stay).[3]

The Keepsake's advantage in the annuals market was in being produced in only the quarto volume; the publishers did not have to market the volume in various sizes. In contrast to the cheaper reading materials, such as *The Penny Magazine,* which contained smudged type, truncated margins, closely printed double columns of text, and poor-quality engravings on thin, low-quality paper, the annuals were extravagant (fig. 4.3).

To increase sales, by 1830 publishers had separated the literary annual into subgenres, including the comic annual, religious annual, musical annual, landscape annual, and juvenile annual. Of notable popularity were the Christian annuals and gift books, especially those edited by Mrs. Sigourney, deemed "The Mrs. Hemans of America" by Bradford Allen Booth ("Taste," 300). In 1830 several musical annuals appeared, including *Apollo's Gift, or the Musical Souvenir, The Musical Bijou, Musical Forget Me Not, Musical Gem,* and *Musical Souvenir. The Musical Bijou,* published in 9 × 11.5 in. quarto form in blue paper boards (with at least three-inch margins for the poetry and prose pieces), appears to be the size of sheet music rather than the normal pocket-size of most annuals and includes twenty-seven poetry and prose pieces, five engravings, and seventeen pieces of sheet music (setting its poems to music) (figs. 4.4 and 4.5). This *Bijou* provides an evening's entertainment complete with literature to read, scenes to admire, songs to perform, music to play, and even verses to translate from French.

The annual acted as an educational experience, a place to inspire memories in its audience as opposed to simply chronicling memories for them. I. Pocock addressed the much-used sentiment of the genre in his poetic illustration of "The Parting,"[4] echoing Ackermann's original words:

> "Forget me not,—forget me not!"
> How often I have heard,
> The lads and lasses wanton wi'
> That sad and solemn word:—
> They picture too, the pretty flower,
> And posies make for rings;

Figure 4.4 "Poets Beware" sheet music, 1830 *Musical Bijou* (from the Katherine D. Harris Collection)

2

POETS BEWARE!

BY THOMAS HAYNES BAYLY.

Poets, beware! never compare
Woman with ought in earth or in air:
Earth may be bright, air may be light,
But brightness and lightness in woman unite.
Can you suppose eyes are like sloes,
Or that her blushes resemble the rose?
Where shall we seek for sloes that can speak,
Or roses that rival an eloquent cheek?

Surely you ne'er saw lilies so fair
As the forehead that peeps thro' the curls of her hair!
Surely her lips red rubies eclipse,
The coral she wears and the nectar she sips!
Birds, in the Spring, sweetly may sing,
But Woman sings better than birds on the wing:
Then, Poets, beware! never compare
Woman with ought on earth or in air.

Figure 4.5 "Poets Beware!" poem by T. H. Bayly, 1830 *Musical Bijou* (from the Katherine D. Harris Collection)

And rhyme it in their album books,
And twenty other things.

"Forget me not,—forget me not!"
I've often heard them say,
To those who thought they were beloved,
Yet loved as light as they.—
Ne'er thinking, silly heartless things,
Should only *one* be true,
How bitterly—how awfully!
Those words might make 'em rue.

(123)

These opening stanzas refer to the flower, albums, poetry in the annuals, and eventually the failure of romantic love—all subjects of many of the works in literary annuals. Though it is associated with the genre, the *Musical Bijou* is evidence of the genre's evolution and its move away from being pocket-sized gifts. Instead, this annual is obviously to be enjoyed by more than one person at a time. The gift continues to give as a musician plays the notes for others to witness the music, the engraving, and the poetry. This experiment in musical annuals proved to be short-lived: some disappeared altogether by 1833, and others were published sporadically through 1849.

The juvenile annuals made a spotty appearance on the market from 1828 to 1835 with Mrs. Watts's *New Year's Gift,* Mrs. S.C. Hall's *Juvenile Forget Me Not,* and Thomas Roscoe's *Juvenile Keepsake.* Apparently, the youth of England were in further need of instruction and moral guidance than what was offered in the typical literary annual. Alaric Watts's son and biographer notes that in constructing the *New Year's Gift,* Mrs. Watts believed that youths needed to "cultivate reason, . . . morality and Christian principles. . . . Religion, purely doctrinal, she left to other agencies" (1:312). However, imagination was suppressed in favor of reason: "She excluded, therefore, from the subjects of her little book all apocryphal personages, giants and fairies, in all of which children of that age were quite capable of believing to their prejudice, and not to their profit" (1:313).

In 1830, Thomas Hood published the first of the comedic annuals (with Charles Tilt of Fleet Street), *The Comic Annual; or The Anniversary of the Literary Fun.* Hood first produced the magazine *Whims and Oddities* in 1826 (published by Lupton Relfe, also the first publisher of *Friendship's Offering* through 1827), which established him as a "leading comic poet" (*Letters* [Morgan], 68; Clubbe, *Selected Poems,* 14). In answer to the public's request, Hood produced a second issue entitled *Whims and Oddities, Second Series* in 1827. The reference in the preface to the 1830 *Comic Annual* as a third series in *Whims and Oddities* called on an audience already familiar with Hood's reputation as a comic and allowed Hood to capitalize on his prior success—much the same as Ackermann with his *Forget Me Not* and *Repository of Arts.* It also highlights the association between Relfe and Hood: before Relfe published *Whims and Oddities,* he solicited Hood for contributions to *Friendship's Offering*—the relationship bears mentioning because it is an example of a small circle of writers and publishers in London during the 1820s and 1830s who traded favors. Hood had a relationship with the publisher Edward Moxon (*Letters* [Morgan], 74), the poet Letitia Landon, and the writer Charles Lamb long before he ventured into the literary annual business. And, much like all of his colleagues, he imposed on these relationships when compiling his annuals.

In his first volume, Hood strikes upon the ultimate parody of the annual and mimics the opening traditional proclamations resident in every annual's preface:

> [I]t is my humble hope and aim to contribute towards the laughter and lustiness of my fellow-creatures, by the production of The Comic Annual,—a work not equivocating between Mirth and Melancholy, but exclusively devoted to the Humorous—in plain French, not an "Ambigu," but an "Opera Comique." Christmas, indeed, seems a Tide more adapted for rowing in the Gig or the Jolly, than tugging in the Barge or the Galley, and accordingly I have built my craft. The kind friends who may patronise the present launch, are assured that it will be acknowledged by a renewed exertion, and that I seriously intend to come before them next year with "A braver Bark, and an increasing sail."
>
> The materials which were in preparation for a Third Series of "Whims and Oddities," have been thrown into the present volume—that work may, therefore, be still considered as going on, though its particular name is not exhibited—but it is a partner in

> the Comic Firm. Each future Series will in the same manner be associated with the whims and oddities of other authors;—and it will be my endeavour to feed every succeeding volume with the choicest morsels that can be procured. In short, the work will be pamper'd—like Captain Head. In the meantime, many little defects, incidental to a first attempt, will be observed and pointed out by the judicious critics;—to whom, consciously and respectfully, I bow, like Norval,—"with bended bow and quiver full of errors;" merely hoping, timidly, that as second thoughts are allowed to be best,—they will deal mildly with my first ones.
>
> In my illustrations, as usual, preferring Wood to Copper or Steel, I have taken to *Box* as the medium for making hits. For some of the Designs, I am indebted to private Friends, and in particular to one highly talented young Lady, who has liberally allowed me to draw upon her drawings, and with an unusual zeal for my woodcuts, has, I may say, devoted her head to the block. It is difficult to return thanks for such deeds, but I feel deeply indebted to the kindness by which her pencil was led.
>
> . . . The Literary Critics are requested to look upon the letter-press in the same spirit, and to remember, before killing "The Comic," that it is as the late Giraffe, "the only one of its kind in England." The work, indeed, at present, is like the celebrated Elephant that had no rival but himself. If, however, others of the kind should sprint up, all the Editor wishes for is an open field and fair play. (vi–x)

As noted before, the preface for each literary annual was a space for the editor to applaud the engravings and writings as the "best," defend against the annual's critics, and reassure readers of the next yearly installment. In this preface, Hood parodies the traditional preface, inserting silly wordplay ("pencil was led"), declarations of the originality of his humorous endeavor, and metaphors of ship building. In the typical explanation of the illustrations or engravings, Hood moves backward in technology and uses a simplified woodcut engraving (taken from a crude line drawing) for these volumes, which serves the sentiment of the volume. The engravings appear to be of no higher quality than a line drawing and misrepresent the artistry required to produce a woodcut engraving by reducing it to a parody of the materials (fig.

SINGLE BLESSEDNESS.

THE COMIC ANNUAL.

NUMBER ONE.

VERSIFIED FROM THE PROSE OF A YOUNG LADY.

IT'S very hard!—and so it is.
To live in such a row,—
And witness this, that every Miss
But me, has got a Beau.—
For Love goes calling up and down,
But here he seems to shun;
I'm sure he has been ask'd enough
To call at Number One!

B

Figure 4.6 "Single Blessedness" woodcut engraving and poem, 1830 *Comic Annual* (from the Katherine D. Harris Collection)

4.6). And the practice of borrowing or renting artwork from its owners to recast it as a steel or copper plate engraving is lampooned as a "Lady" subjects her drawings to be redrawn and overdrawn by Hood's own pencil.

Published in paper boards and a leather spine—deceptively similar to many other "family" members in the genre—this first *Comic Annual* contains eighty-two engravings, greatly outnumbering the thirty-eight pieces of prose and poetry. This unusual abundance of engravings is interspersed among the poem and prose pieces, most of which were written by Hood. Common practice in the early and contemporary annuals dictated that engravings be created first and passed on to authors for a verbal rendering—essentially extensions of the engravings (see chapter 5). Hood reversed this and used engravings to articulate a punch line and "head and tail pieces" to bookend a work.[5] The significance of this practice lies in the production cost of engravings; more engravings typically inflated the cost of a volume. But using original cuts by the engraver and woodcut engravings (as opposed to steel) not only reduced Hood's costs but also allowed for critique on the fetishizing of engravings in annuals.

"A True Story," included in this first *The Comic Annual,* concerns a Colonel Case and his servant Pompey, a "jaundiced black." Pompey learns that he and his master are packing for Ireland, a turbulent and violent land that Pompey has been reading about. Running to his master and begging him not to go, Pompey offers this explanation to the jaundiced Colonel Case: "'O Massa'—(so the explanation ran) / 'Massa be killed—'cause Massa *Orange Man,* / And Pompey killed—'cause Pompey not a *White Boy!*'" (48). The subjects of this satire include the British Empire, African servants and their "broken English," Irish-English relations, and current literature.

This last subject becomes apparent with the engraving concluding the poem, "She Walks in Beauty, Like the Night"—a parody of Lord Byron's famous poem (fig. 4.7). Byron, dead for six years already, was the focus of a severe amount of literary mania. Hood's parodic use of the line mocks Byron and his fans but really highlights England's mistreatment of African cultures. In the simple woodcut engraving, an African woman is drawn to literally represent darkness. Her dark skin is "like the night." She walks fanning herself with a banana leaf as the sun shines on her face. The shadow cast behind her indicates that she *is* the night, further separating this woman from Byron's lady who walks *in beauty.* For Byron, references to a woman, the night, and beauty are contained in a single complex line: "She walks in beauty, like the night" (line 1). The simile modifies "beauty," not the woman. The woman walks surrounded by beauty in the same way that darkness would envelop her if she were to walk through the night. In Hood's parody, Byron's line is represented as "She is like the night." Though a parody, the image exposes England's racism and the British colonies' abhorrent treatment of other cultures. The dark African with large lips and a beaming smile seems happy to represent night and all of its contingent tropes of darkness (such as savagery, evil, and deception). Vanessa Warne suggests that Hood specifically parodies "the female body as grotesque and align[s] femininity with deceptiveness" (10). While this image is not necessarily grotesque, it is an overexaggerated image of an African woman exposing herself willingly. She tilts her head almost coquettishly and carries a fan in mimicry of a lady's umbrella. She plays at being white or British (though still wearing bangled jewelry around her ankles, ears, and wrists)—a slur on the proper British lady who supposedly read this genre. Presented in 1830, this parody is an early rendering of the sexually transgressive "Hottentot" who would fascinate later Victorians.[6]

Hood mocks the genre from a position of knowledge, though: he was a contributor to many of the earlier annuals, including *Forget Me Not,*

48 A TRUE STORY.

Cried Case, with anger's tinge upon his yellow,—
Pompey, for answer, pointing in a mirror
The Colonel's saffron, and his own japan,—
"Well, what has that to do—quick—speak outright,
boy?"
"O Massa"—(so the explanation ran)
"Massa be killed—'cause Massa *Orange Man*,
And Pompey killed—'cause Pompey not a *White*
Boy!"

"SHE WALKS IN BEAUTY, LIKE THE NIGHT."

Figure 4.7 "She Walks in Beauty" tailpiece engraving (parody), 1830 *Comic Annual* (from the Katherine D. Harris Collection)

Friendship's Offering, and *The Literary Souvenir,* and was an editor of *The Gem* (1829–32). Hood's annual, with a second edition during its first year, continued through 1839 and was published each year (4 × 6.5 in.) with the same image on paper boards, lending a familiarity and consistency to that volume that was not always standard to other titles in the genre (fig. 4.8).[7] Hood's parody eventually became more political satire, as he points out in his 1837 preface, than parody of the literary annual. The advertisements for the 1837 volume published in British monthly, quarterly, and weekly magazines promised that the 1837 volume would contain "political pepper and spice" (Preface to *The Comic Annual*, 1837, v). However, because he was residing in Germany during the 1830s to escape his creditors, Hood informs his readers that *The Times* was delivered to him well beyond the time when social and political issues had been resolved. In an attempt to keep the *Comic Annual* contemporaneous with current issues, he excised a majority of the political satire that filled the volume—at least, he claims this in his preface. In actuality, Hood did not use the *Comic Annual* as a podium for political bullying; instead, he was more concerned with the working class and could be classified as merely socially aware rather than an advocate.[8] Despite this classification, by comparison to all other polite and heavily moderated annuals, the *Comic Annual* was as politically motivated as the American *Liberty Bell,* which championed the abolition of slavery.

Hood's irreverent and satirical entry into the literary annuals market encouraged other parodies of the genre, including imitators of his parody: in 1831, *The New Comic Annual,* a separate publication, made its debut and disappearance in the family, as did *The Comic Offering, or Ladies Melange of Literary Mirth,* which lasted through 1835, when *The Comic Almanac* appeared and was a fixture until 1853. The title page of *The New Comic Annual* attributes the writing to Sir John Falstaff, the infamous comic butt of Shakespeare's *The Merry Wives of Windsor.* In a nod to its original reference, the annual is specifically dedicated "to the Lovers of Gaiety and Glee, from the high-born Peer, to the low-born Peasant; and, especially to the '*better half*' of men—Their Merry Wives" (iii). Using puns to gain the easiest humor, the author irreverently parodies Hood's *Comic Annual* in both its appearance and its contents. The preface is peppered with verbal puns that characterize a begging dog, the figure/plate that opens the annual's preface (fig. 4.9):

Figure 4.8 Front board from Hood's 1833 *Comic Annual* (from the Katherine D. Harris Collection)

Your Humble Petitioner Sheweth,

That deeply impressed with that first law of nature, *"take care of No. 1,"* he prays, that this his first Annual, may be well seconded in *succeeding* Numbers. In so novel a position before the public, your petitioner feels that he assumes one which he cannot long uphold, unless by your encouragement upheld; neither, in thus raising himself in cur-ious mood to a New Title, wherein he stands alone, does he expect, however *upright* his appeal, to support that title long, unless by you supported in his waggish tale and doggrel verse.

Taking, therefore, the above stand, if not with cap in hand, his *mouth* bespeaks the world's charity and the critic's mercy.

Your Petitioner further sheweth, that full of faith in the one, and hope in the other, to his latest day, even on his *last* legs, shall his *great full tale* appear in graceful *lay* unfolded.

Your Petitioner humbly conceives, that he does not trust to a fragile reed, or rest upon a false staff, in thus ushering into the world his first Number by the merry title of—

FALSTAFF'S ANNUAL;

the joyous harbinger of "genial laughs," or glad contributor of social mirth; ripe for all seasons—the winter's hearth or summer's shade. But, should his bantling fade and fall with the autumnal leaf, still may future evergreens be his never-fading laurels; his broad merry face laughing sour crabs (who seek the fruit and look beyond the *bark*) into sweet *countenance*—of his Annual, as worthier of the Wreath of Comus than the Wrath of Critics.

If, however, your petitioner shall appear to have set out with a "frail bark," he must, nevertheless, trust to his present canvass, and hope for a future better sail! for, remember, my brother *cynics,* it is "ONLY ONCE A YEAR!" (v–viii)

The annual must have met with enmity or poor sales, because it never appeared again.

The standard entreaties that often punctuate an annual's preface here are reduced to a mongrel begging for scraps—much the same as the annuals' editors were reduced to doing to gain an audience in the 1831 saturated market. "Falstaff," in a long opening song entitled "Falstaff's Festival, or the Power of Mirth, An Ode in Honor of Comus," recounts the creation of *The New Comic Annual* in which Hood plays a prominent role. After

"*Le* PETIT CHIEN *du mendiant*." THE BEGGAR'S PETITION.

"You must endeavour to write in such a manner as to convert melancholy into mirth, increase good humour, entertain the ignorant, create the admiration of the learned, escape the contempt of gravity, and attract applause from persons of ingenuity and taste."

DON QUIXOTE.

YOUR HUMBLE PETITIONER

SHEWETH,

THAT deeply impressed with that first law of nature, "*take care of No. I*," he prays, that this his first Annual, may be well seconded in

Figure 4.9 "The Beggar's Petition" engraving, 1831 *[Falstaff's] New Comic Annual* (from the Katherine D. Harris Collection)

proving his comic worth and stating that "[s]ublime on nothing could he write" (2), Falstaff retired to St. Paul's Churchyard

> [a]nd there pour'd out his comic soul;
> Then from his waistcoat pocket took
> A full-length image of himself, the Falstaff of this Book.
> Hurst, Chance & Co. approve his lofty air;
> A Falstaff's Annual! they shout, is here;
> A Falstaff's Annual! again re-echoes there.
> Delighted quite,
> The merry Knight,
> In laughing mood
> Assumes the Hood,
> And laughs with all his might.
>
> (3)

Falstaff nods to Hood's introduction of the comic genre but declares that his annual can be sold alongside Hood's:

> Now here, at least, "too many Cooks
> Spoil *not* the broth;" no more than many books
> Pall the taste. How few soups savour,
> To palates fresh, of the same sort of flavour.
> . . . .
> Behold, behold, Sir Falstaff cries,
> Other Comics arise!
> For our brother last year,
> Hood, himself, did appear
> Siam's Elephant, *(tho' small his size,)*
> Without a rival one,
> "Clear stage and favour none."
> Like the Siam Youths, that by nature are twain,
> Let us one remain;
> United in our plan,
> Upon an "open field"
> Mutual "fair play" yield;
> *He* to the Tilt[9] of his fair enterprize,
> To our game *we,* of glorious Chance,[10]
> Our equal fame and fortune to advance.

> Two faces disdains the *Old Comic* to wear
> 'Neath one Hood—so the *New;* as in Knighthood, both are
> In one golden fight
> Of pun and fun; the Knight
> Seeks not from others their own *liveli*-hood to bar.
>
> (7–8)

Falstaff recounts an evening of frivolity in which he separates from his group and records his humorous musings in the middle of London's publishing district. The act of creating a new comic annual is compared to the original endeavor by Thomas Hood. However, these last few lines indicate (through puns, of course) that Hood and Falstaff are united not only under a unified comic knighthood but also under the same "hood," which refers to their battle against a common foe instead of each other. Though the rhetoric in Falstaff's preface is primarily directed to the public and critics, the puns in this ode are a request to Hood and a celebration of diversity within the comic subgenre—a request for cooperation in the name of "brotherhood" (an interesting reference to fraternity considering that the annual was definitely meant for the sisterhood of readers—see later discussions of femininity and the annuals).

In the 1831 *Comic Annual* preface, Hood answers these queries and makes a few suggestions regarding the sudden appearance of both the *Comic Offering* (edited by Louisa Sheridan) and this *New Comic Annual.* The preface bears quoting at length both for these answers and for the parody of himself and the genre that Hood commits.

> Now, I do not intend, like some votaries of freedom, to cast mud on the muddy, or dirt on the dirty,—but, while I am on the hustings, I will ask the Committee of that Uncandid Candidate, "The New Comic," whether it was quite honest to canvass against me under my own colours, and to pass off the enemy's poll-book as mine? The Code of Honour should be a kind of Coade's Cement between man and man,—but, to speak technically, some seem bound by it and some unbound. Mr. Hurst gave me his word, and shook hands thereon, that the delusive title should be altered;—and yet that bad title to a good name, "The New Comic," is still retained. Surely he feels both the brand and the blush in what Byron calls "that red right hand."

> Were there no other and fitter labels extant than such close parodies of mine? . . .
>
> The coupling, in advertisement, [of] "The New Comic" with a volume really mine, is a trick that smacks of the neighbourhood. There is as little difference as distance between the plying of 65, St. Paul's Churchyard, and the plying of the Fulhams and Brenfords close at hand.
>
> The Editor of the Edinburgh Literary Journal, was actually induced to swallow what Izaak Walton would call the *Cad*-bait,—and after a jolt in the "New" concern, was induced to criticise it as a ride in the old.
>
> Fain would I drop here the Steel Pen for a softer quill, to speak of an Editress who—distinguishing fair from unfair—has acted the perfect brunette towards me, and has brought a heavy charge against me "for work done." In the Announcement of "The Comic Offering"—a little book chiefly remarkable for a coat of damson cheese, seeming equally fit, like Sheridan's poor Peruvians, for "covering and devouring,"—it is insinuated that I am an author unfit for female perusal:—I, who have never that respect infringed which, with me, dwells "like fringe upon a petticoat." Miss Sheridan and modesty compel me to declare, that, many Ladies have deigned to request for their albums, some little proof of "the versatility" or prosatility of my pen:—yet what says the Announcement, or rather Denouncement: "But shall we permit a Clown or Pantaloon to enter the Drawing-room or Boudoir—no, *not even under a Hood!*"
>
> . . . I confess, besides, that on being so attacked by a perfect stranger, I did at first think it rather hard of her; but having now seen her book, I think it rather soft of her, and shall say no more. (v–ix)

Hood posits himself not as the protectorate of his readers, inevitably women, but as the entertainer and freely admits entering not only the publicly private drawing room but also the very private dressing room. Louisa Sheridan's objections are obviously that Hood's parodic annual is too coarse for a lady's viewing; she offers her annual as a remedy to include women in the jocularity. Hood's acerbic wit in this preface smacks of the immediate competition caused by his successful title—a competition that certainly mirrors the furor among "legitimate" titles as well.[11]

In 1832, the genre reached an apex in England, with sixty-three titles being offered. The landscape and geographical annuals, including *Heath's*

Picturesque Annual, Turner's Annual Tour, and *Geographical Annual,*[12] increased the British public's interest in landscape art and foreign vistas. *The Bengal Annual* and *The Oriental Annual,* both initially published in 1830, were produced and published in Calcutta, India, extending the boundaries of home to Britain's colonial empire. *The Young Gentleman's Annual* (1834) and *A Father's Present to His Son* (1831 and 1833) were published specifically to allow men to participate in the consumerism and gift exchange created by the annuals. Some annuals took the opportunity not just to instruct young women but also to expose the readers to long treatises on political issues. And although annuals were not originally intended as a political platform, many snuck through despite reviewers' protests: A religious annual, *The Amulet* (1826–36), often included articles on the abolition of slavery. Another annual, published in 1834, addressed this political issue in a commemorative volume: *Bow in the Cloud, or the Negro's Memorial: A Collection of Original Contributions in Prose and Verse, Illustrative of the Evils of Slavery and Commemorative of Its Abolition in the British Colonies*. By 1840, the number had fallen to thirty-five, and the number generally declined each year until 1857, when only three British titles were published. Before the annual's demise, the British publishers attempted gimmicks in publishing to produce almost unreadable annuals such as *Schloss's English Bijou Almanac,* which measured a half inch in height and came in a case with a small magnifying glass (figs. 4.10 and 4.11).

Figure 4.10 Title page, 1841 *Schloss's English Bijou Almanac* (from the Katherine D. Harris Collection; photo credit, Tom Davis)

Figure 4.11 Boards, 1841 *Schloss's English Bijou Almanac* (from the Katherine D. Harris Collection; photo credit, Tom Davis)

Ironically, as the British annuals lost their foothold in the consumer marketplace, the American titles began to thrive: In 1831, the Americans published only thirteen annuals. Not until 1842 did the American annuals equal the British in number. By 1846, fifty-six different annuals had been published in the United States, compared to the sixteen titles then being published in Britain. Of these sixteen, some early literary annuals continued successful production, including the *Forget Me Not, Fisher's Drawing Room Scrap Book,* and *The Keepsake* (Faxon, 129–40).

Whatever the evolution of literary annuals in the 1830s, Hood's humorous poke at a product of popular culture came because the literary annual genre was being harshly criticized by reviewers and literati throughout the English press. With this criticism and parody committed from within the "family" itself, the genre suffered such damaging criticism that its contents have been derided by many nineteenth- and twentieth-century critics and, consequently, ignored by literary critics and book historians alike until the late twentieth century.

Though the early twentieth century saw three volumes attempting to imitate the earlier annuals, these were but reminders of the popular phenomenon that had once struck England. William Jeremiah Burke, writing in 1935, describes the nineteenth-century annual as a fad and continues deriding them: "Today they amuse us, and if we stop to read them seriously as they were meant to be read, fatigue us, for they contain some of the worst poetry in the English language. They were calculated to pull the heart strings and bring tears to the eyes, to awaken noble sentiments and inspire kindly thoughts and deeds" (25).

Though trade criticism in the nineteenth century did not sustain the phenomenon—and mangled its validity in the twentieth century—its readers and consumers insisted on new publications each year and continuously fueled the production of these gems, amulets, and keepsakes. During the 1830s, the audience seems to have ignored the reviews, and readers were purchasing volumes in advance sales. Some of the more popular annuals evolved to accommodate the market and were rewarded with longevity and re-creation during the late nineteenth century in anthologies of the best works from literary annuals and new incarnations in the twentieth century in "new" keepsakes and forget me nots that borrowed the original format.

FIVE

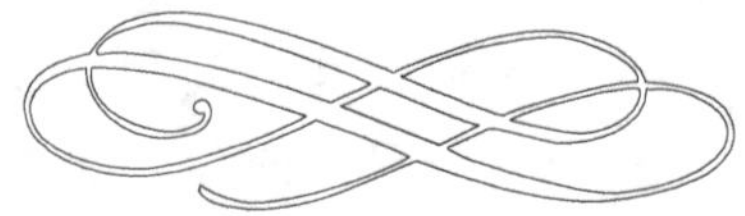

The Artistic Influence of the Annual's Engraving "Copyists"

ENGRAVINGS IN THE LITERARY ANNUALS WERE AN INTEGRAL element contributing to the initial success of the genre and are necessarily elemental in distinguishing a literary annual. Rudolph Ackermann's expertise in reproducing illustrations provided a foundation from which to create the first literary annual: the engravings would anchor the entire volume. In general, the annuals favored landscape paintings and portraits, exposing massive numbers of readers to artwork that they potentially would have never seen. The artwork was cut on a wood or metal plate, printed on the proof sheets, and passed on to an author to create a verbal illustration of the print.

Privileged over the writing and authorship, the engravings became the star not only of Ackermann's volumes but also, later, of their own subgenres. According to Luisa Calè, in 1788 Henry Fuseli began "to present the field of art as an encounter between painting and book" (5) to encourage a movement away from the twenty-year history of exhibiting portraits and landscape art exclusively at the Royal Academy. By combining art and literature in a single volume and doubling the impact with his Repository of Arts gallery shop, Ackermann exhibited the best efforts by British artists.

Ironically, the annuals resorted primarily to portraiture by the second generation, a step backwards from Ackermann's original impetus.

Publishers used a separate printer for the text and the engravings, usually sending the engravings to be printed on India paper for the final product.[1] The engravings were then glued to the verso of a page, with the following recto page remaining blank[2]—a time-consuming and laborious practice for printers and a costly necessity for publishers and editors.[3] This thinner paper provided a more porous medium and resulted in a crisper image—another element that added to the high quality expected of annuals.[4] This blank recto page also created a fetishized object surrounding the engraving. Because there was the luxury of blank space on its reverse side, the engravings could be removed without destroying the text; they became portable artwork that could be transported out of the original work and used for decoration.

When the genre began its quick ascent to popularity, the engravings originated from illustrations or paintings created by two entities. But only one was considered a true "artist," especially in the eyes of the Royal Academy: "To the Royal Academy, founded on hierarchical values which placed history painting at the summit, the engravers were only *copyists,* lacking originality and thus excluded from the highest honours. However, many engravers though conceding their work was not foremost in the orders of design, believed it was a distinct language of art with its own terms" (Celina Fox quoted in Ledbetter, "Copper," 28–29; emphasis added). In the annuals, membership in the Royal Academy is indicated by "R.A." following a name. This abbreviation never followed an engraver's name but quite often accompanied a painter/illustrator's name—a mark of the institutional validation of imagination.

According to Kathryn Ledbetter, engravers "made art possible for the masses, thereby causing an increased demand for art" ("Copper," 29). She cites an 1838 *Monthly Review* article that celebrates the engraver's artistry and applauds the annual's dissemination of art:

> As regards the important interests both of literature and the arts it must be allowed that the Annuals have had a manifest influence. . . . [N]ever before had such pictures as have filled the Annuals been published at so cheap a rate, although they cost the proprietors of them very large sums; never before had admiration been so awakened

> to pictorial embellishments; and never before were artists, proprietors, and purchasers so generally and multitudinously pleased; and thus all interests reciprocating and repaying one another produced, though it was at one time thought a mere transient fashion, a great and, we have no doubt, a permanently beneficial result in the history of true refinement. (quoted in Ledbetter, "Copper," 22–23)

Engravers, deemed "copyists," were accused of lacking originality and the ever-important concept of imagination that saturated the Romantic era. In reproducing these paintings, engravers attempt to either reproduce or re-present the "aura" of a particular work. Walter Benjamin defines "aura" as "the authenticity of a thing [that] is the essence of all that is transmissible from its beginning, ranging from its substantive duration to its testimony to the history which it has experienced"; aura is the "quality of its presence . . . in time and space, its unique existence at the place where it happens to be" (220, 221). In the annuals, then, what is authentic: the original painting or the engraving? If the Royal Academy is given a say in the answer to this question, then engravers are merely mechanically reproducing art in an apparatus that is inadequate. The engravers, however, produce a steel plate that will, in turn, mechanically reproduce the image for a mass audience. Benjamin declares that this mechanical reproduction is an attempt by the masses

> to bring things "closer" spatially and humanly, which is just as ardent as their bent toward overcoming the uniqueness of every reality by accepting its reproduction. Every day the urge grows stronger to get hold of an object at very close range by way of its likeness, its reproduction. . . . To pry an object from its shell, to destroy its aura, is the mark of a perception whose "sense of the universal equality of things" has increased to such a degree that it extracts it even from a unique object by means of reproduction. (223)

To Benjamin, the aura of artwork is not reproducible by mechanical means: "[T]he technique of reproduction detaches the reproduced object from the domain of tradition" (221). The piece of art that is created specifically for reproduction no longer holds authenticity, or aura. The piece of art then represents not ritual (or tradition, as he specifies) but politics. Melding Benjamin with textual theory, however, yields a new authenticity with each copy that is then re-presented multiple times and in multiple layers with each social interaction. The literary annuals, specifically, are living palimpsests, created through the production of artwork (painter, illustrator, engraver, printer) that is expressible in meaning as readers interact with the reproduction.

In rendering paintings into etched engravings, these craftsmen substituted brushstrokes, paint, and color with a tedious process involving reducing scale, scratching detail, and burning with nitric acid. Ian Bain notes that "the delicacy of the work and the necessary variation in acid biting could take a considerable amount of time: Charles Warren is known to have spent 'thirteen weeks of regular and incessant exertion' on a single small plate illustrating Scott's *The Lady of the Lake*" (22). The end result was an image that replaced depth with negative and positive line etchings and dramatic detail. According to Basil Hunnisett, "the engraver's goal was to translate artists' originals, frequently executed in colour, into black-and-white pictures, using all the nuances which could be achieved by fine lines exhibiting ranges of tone by thickness of ink printed on off-white semi-absorbent plate paper. The skill required to do this was based upon artistic abilities not very dissimilar to those which produced the originals; dissimilar only in that it did not require the qualities of originality and imagination which distinguish a Turner, Bartlett or Allom" (quoted in Ledbetter, "Copper," 28). Because Ackermann printed his annuals in-house, he would have employed several of these skilled craftsmen. The publishers understood that this labor was valuable and paid engravers what they were worth, according to Hunnisett.[5]

In a comparison of John Martin's *Seventh Plague of Egypt* and the engraving rendered by Henry Le Keux for the 1828 *Forget Me Not,* the perspective shifts only slightly, with the darkening sky pushed farther to the right side and minor elements altered to render the engraving more Egyptian than Roman (figs. 5.1 and 5.2). In Martin's oil painting, the central facet is a cross illuminated by the opening in the dark clouds.[6] In skewing the cloud's light and dark rotation, Le Keux refocuses the scene on Moses, who is stationed in the left foreground. Le Keux adds an Egyptian obelisk in place of a beveled building highlighted by the light sky closing in it. The building in the original clutters the scene, while Le Keux's rendering opens the space to symbolize the darkness descending on non-Christian relics. In addition, Le Keux excises an integral moment in the scene by removing the progressively smaller pyramids in the background. This directs attention toward the largest pyramid, which has a lightning bolt cracking

Figure 5.1 *Seventh Plague of Egypt,* oil painting by John Martin, 1823

Figure 5.2 "Seventh Plague of Egypt," engraving by Henry Le Keux, 1828 *Forget Me Not* (from the Katherine D. Harris Collection)

down from the swirling sky. The color and depth are rendered in exaggerated lines, and the suffering crowd of onlookers has been minimized, with only a few detailed expressions in the engraving. Otherwise, the engraving captures the terror and fury of the moment from Martin's oil painting.

Several engravers and illustrators regularly featured in literary annuals include Henry and John Le Keux, George and Henry Corbould, Edward Francis Burney, S. Prout (referenced above as lending his artwork), Richard and William Westall, and Charles Heath. Edward Burney, cousin to novelist Francis Burney, illustrated *Evelina*. Richard Westall, a painter and illustrator, often worked with his brother, William. The Corboulds worked together as artist and engraver to create original illustrations for the annuals—a family business inherited from their father (a landscape specialist) and continued to a son, Richard Henry Corbould, who illustrated for nineteenth-century novels. Similarly, the Le Keux brothers conducted family business as engravers:

> John Le Keux (1783–1846) and his younger brother Henry Le Keux (1787–1868) were apprenticed to the architectural engraver James Basire, and both produced a wide variety of architectural and views engravings for various publications, including works by Neale, Pugin, and J. M. W. Turner. Henry Le Keux abandoned engraving work for the crape manufacturing business in 1838, but John continued to execute commissions until shortly before his death in 1846. John's eldest son, John Henry Le Keux (1812–1896), also became an architectural engraver; his works include plates in Ruskin's *Stones of Venice* (1851) and *Modern Painters* (1888).[7]

Interestingly, artists, illustrators, and engravers did not gain as much press as did their engravings or the annuals' authors. In fact, engravings met with abbreviated criticism in reviews and were referred to only by title and artist's last name. Though most literary annuals published engraver and illustrator names in the table of engravings and alongside the engravings themselves, the literary contents gained most of the periodicals' negative and positive attention: "'The Bower Scene,' and 'The Coquette,' by C. Heath; 'The Brigand Chief and his Wife,' and 'The Contadina,' by W. Humphreys; and 'The View of the Castle of Monaco,' by E. Finden, are merely respectable as works of art. The real charms of the volume are to be found in its literature" (anonymous, review of 1827 *Friendship's Offering,* 87). Ironically, engravings were privileged in the production process of annuals and anchored the genre in its popularity. But the spectacle, and not the production, of engravings fascinated readers and consumers of annuals—a fascination that inevitably veils the engraving artists from the public.

Ackermann, and other publishers of literary annuals except Thomas Hood, used woodcut engravings until Charles Heath popularized, but did not invent,[8] the more efficient and detailed intaglio steel engraving in 1825.[9] Ackermann, ever diligent about producing high-quality artwork, switched to steel plate engravings, finding that "small prints with high quality detail could be produced on steel and in much greater quantities than by the traditional soft copper plates" (Ford, *Ackermann,* 65). Though a technical detail in the production of literary annuals, the move from woodcut to steel-plate engravings was significant in nineteenth-century book history and the production costs of literary annuals (fig. 5.3).

Philip Gaskell points out that the intaglio plates "were printed separately from the type, often on a different paper from the ordinary sheets, and show little or no impression on the verso . . . Intaglio plate marks were seldom allowed to show, but there is often a slight roughness to be felt on the surface of a picture printed from copper or steel" (272). The artistic skill required for steel-plate intaglio engravings paralleled that of the woodcut:

> Strictly speaking, a wood-*cut* is cut with a knife along the plank, while a wood-*engraving* is cut with a graver or burin on the cross-section, usually of a piece of box-wood. The latter makes for harder wood and therefore permits a much greater delicacy in the design. But the terms are used indiscriminately by most cataloguers (and many other people) for any illustrations printed from wood as distinct from metal. Both, indeed, are often used to describe illustrations which (as frequently since the 1860s) were printed from electrotype metal blocks taken from the original (but less durable) wood blocks; for it is often impossible to tell these from impressions of the original wood. (Carter, 221)

Intaglio differs from woodcuts and wood engravings by the negative and positive images created: "The engraving processes in which the image is incised into the plate, as opposed to those where the surface is cut away leaving the image in relief" (Carter, 127). During printing, "the lines of the design are filled with ink, the rest of the surface being wiped clean,

Figure 5.3 Comparison of "Sacontala" (steel-plate/intaglio engraving), 1825 *Forget Me Not*, drawn by H. Corbould and engraved by Geo. Corbould, and "A Spill Case" (woodcut engraving), 1830 *Comic Annual*, drawn by Thomas Hood (from the Katherine D. Harris Collection)

and damp paper is pressed hard on to the surface so that it lifts the ink out of the engraved lines. The technique of engraving the plate is similar to that of cutting a negative wood block, allowing the use of very fine lines and cross-hatched tones, but it gives a positive not a negative result" (Gaskell, 156). The steel plates did not disintegrate as quickly as the wood engravings, which allowed printers to render thousands of imprints before retiring a steel plate. Copper plates, the traditional method of printing engravings, could withstand only about one hundred impressions before the artwork was compromised by the plate printers' wiping of canvasses (and not the printing pressure). This new printing invention, in turn, decreased publishers' production costs (Bain, 19).

By distributing such massive numbers of prints, the annual engaged audiences "in popularising the public instruction in art" and reinforced the burgeoning movement to establish national art institutes. Anthony Dyson suggests that many factors "converged to contribute to the spread of a popular interest in art in Britain," including the literary annual and "the example of the upper classes; the proliferation of art institutes and exhibitions; the growth of the provincial cities and their competitive spirit; the campaigning of the artists themselves; the proselytising of enthusiastic newspaper editors and the enterprise of publishers of magazines and annuals: the rise of the art unions; important public projects such as the building of the new National Gallery and the Houses of Parliament; and Government sponsorship of public art education in response to commercial pressure from overseas" (quoted in Ledbetter, "Copper," 29). At the downturn of the annual's critical success, a reviewer in the November 1831 *The Monthly Review* suggests that though the annuals may not have contained the highest quality literature, the engravings at least introduced artistic standards: "They do, and have done, much for the diffusion of *sound principles of art,* by the exquisite engravings which they have been the means of presenting to the public, at a much more moderate rate than could have been possibly expected some twenty years ago" (371). In his autobiography, S. C. Hall, editor of *The Amulet,* points toward these engravings as vehicles to educate the nation's middle class and as a much more appealing sight than the ill-printed and colored prints that were sold for decoration: "They were displaced by engravings after the choicest works of our British painters, executed in such a manner as to educate the eye and give employment to the mind" (178).

To attract their readers, publishers paid exorbitant prices to "borrow" original paintings and have them rendered as engravings. A single portrait required anywhere between 20 and 200 guineas (that is, £21–210) for borrowing fees and up to 200 guineas for the engraver's fees (Hall, 177). The engravings in one volume of *The Amulet* (a religious annual edited by S. C. Hall, 1826–36) cost 1,200 guineas, or £1,260 (Hall, 178). In addition to the fees, editors demonstrated their gratitude by including an owner's name in the preface while all other contributors and artists were acknowledged in a general mention, such as "to George Morant, Esq. their particular thanks are due, for the loan of Prout's admirable picture of Vicenza, which has furnished the subject of one of the engravings" (Shoberl, Preface to 1829 *Forget Me Not,* v). Artists frequently loaned their own artwork and received not only public gratitude, but also free advertising for their work, which in turn increased the value of their paintings as well as their names. William Blake even contributed an engraving, "Hiding of Moses," to the *Remember Me! A New Year's Gift or Christmas Present for 1825* (fig. 5.4).

Figure 5.4 "Hiding of Moses," engraving by William Blake, from 1825 *Remember Me! A New Year's Gift or Christmas Present* (from the Katherine D. Harris Collection)

Often, painters did not share the Royal Academy's disdain for engravings or reviewers' disgust for the annual phenomenon. Painters frequently loaned their art to be "copied" for a larger audience. Lawrence, Wilkie, Stothard, Leslie, Turner, Collins, Uwin, Stanfirled, Danby, Stuart, Newton, and Roberts are but a few of the respected artists who lent their work to the popular form. These and other artists happily acknowledged their affiliation with the annuals and were grateful to be made "household words to thousands of persons who had never before heard of them" ("Annuals," 495). The anonymous author of the 1858 *Bookseller* essay "The Annuals of Former Days" provides evidence of the increase in the sale and collecting of art in relationship with the annuals:

> Previous to the appearance of the Annuals, there were few, if any, collectors of modern pictures in Manchester, Birmingham, Liverpool, or Leeds, and there is now scarcely a gentleman of wealth in any one of those cities who has not a gallery of modern works of art, many of them by the best masters; whilst the prices of our English painters have gone on increasing with the demand until they have reached, in many instances, six times the amount they used to ask for their works. In the sale of the effects of the late Mr. Rogers, a sketch by Leslie, for which the poet had given £40, produced £1,000; and another sketch, also by Leslie, purchased in 1824 for £10 was sold no great while ago, by Christie & Manson, for £350. (495)

Alaric Watts's son notes that the artworks published in the 1826 *Literary Souvenir* were indeed in demand:

> These works, then engraved for the first time, became so popular that larger engravings were subsequently made from them, as was the case with other subjects first introduced to the public in this work. As an illustration of the technical beauty of the engravings in this volume, I may mention that another subject by Stewart Newton, entitled "The Forsaken," engraved by Charles Heath, was so highly valued by *connoisseurs* for the engraver's work,—it possessed, I think, little other value,—that proofs of it, before letters, were purchased in this very year by Messrs. Colnaghi, the print-sellers, at a public sale, at an uniform price of 19s. each. (218)

This information comes directly from the footnote in the 1827 preface in which Alaric Watts professes that a single engraving "fetches a price considerably larger than that of the entire volume" (xii). Recognizing the boon to the art world, painters of great standing fostered exclusive relationships with annual editors; Charles Heath, the proprietor of several annuals, was regularly entrusted with producing volumes and actually committing to engraving many of J. M. W. Turner's works. Hunnisett notes that several apprentices were involved in creating an engraving:

> An alternative speciality was an artistic one, where engravers could contribute their best skills to part of a plate only. From trial proofs we know that four engravers worked upon a print issued in *The Keepsake* for 1830, page 322. This work, "The Prophet of St. Paul's" after A.E. Chalon, measured only 4 1/8 × 3 ¼ inches and depicted an old bearded palmist, seated at a table covered by an ornate cloth, examining a young lady's hand. She is attired in a light dress, and a negro servant stands beside her; close to the palmist is a globe. Notes indicate that "Part by J.H. Watt, Rhodes graved up white draper, D. Smith did remainder, and C. Heath flesh." (Hunnisett, 55)

Because of the long production process and the yearly publication schedule, owners and artists sometimes lent their paintings to more than one literary annual. Unfortunately, owners, concerned mainly about the fees, were not obliged to inform editors and publishers of their multiple indiscretions. In a review of the 1827 *Friendship's Offering* with Thomas K. Hervey as its editor, the critic notes that the painting *Alexander and Diogenes* was rendered as an engraving for both *Friendship's Offering* and Alaric Watts's *Literary Souvenir.* In addition, the same engraver, "E. Finden," rendered the painting for both literary annuals. Edward Finden, much like many other engravers, participated in a family industry including his brother William Finden, and they would have employed apprentices to create engravings (s.v. "Finden," LoveToKnow *1911 Encyclopedia*). Eventually, because of the high demand and increased production rate, the Findens would come to rely more on their assistants, all of which inevitably decreased the quality of their work. The same review notes that "the *name* of the same engraver Mr. E. Finden, is subscribed to both plates; but it is evident that one of them is the work of the master—the other of some of his pupils" (87).

Both Finden and Charles Heath employed a large number of the available engravers during the 1830s and 1840s. Both men created a factory-type creative process and divided the work on one engraving among several men. John Heath notes that an engraving of Mrs. Peel in the 1829 *Keepsake* bears Charles Heath's signature but was produced by a choir of assistants: "Lane reduced, Goodyear etchd [*sic*] figure, Webb etchd fur and feathers, J.H. Watt draper and hat, Rhodes worked up hat feathers, D. Smith background, and C. Heath flesh" (quoted in Ledbetter, "Copper," 26). Ledbetter notes that "Heath and Finden supported a burgeoning industry of skilled artists," which "helped to bring art and literature together for the masses" and enabled "the characteristic pictorial nature of Victorian culture" ("Copper," 26, 29).

Because of the use of engravings in literary annuals and the phenomenal reception and sales of literary annuals, Ian Bain notes that the popular engravers were accused of oversaturating the public with steel-plate engravings and overproducing the style to a point of "mechanical debasement" (25). Steel plates were used in printing illustrations until the 1860s, at which time publishers returned to woodcut engravings for their publications.

American publishers, unable to withstand the financial burden of commissioning new illustrations or paying substantial borrowing fees, "used only engravings which had appeared in British gift books," as is noted by Ralph Thompson in his study of the American literary annual vogue (42). The large literary annual publishing house of Carey and Hart sometimes bought the actual British plates or duplicates; at other times they bought the impressions at eight pounds per thousand impressions (Thompson, *American,* 42). Though the American literary annual tradition differed from the British phenomenon, the dilemma of financing and producing the engravings was equally burdensome on both sides of the Atlantic. Thompson notes that two plates in the British *Keepsake* for 1828 (founded by the engraver Charles Heath and the publisher William Ainsworth) were originally published in *Ten Epistles of Ovid,* translated by the Reverend William W. Fitzthomas (London: C. and R. Baldwin, 1807). This surreptitious borrowing is not surprising, considering that this inaugural volume of *The Keepsake* cost publishers over 11,000 guineas, or £11,550 (preface, 1829 *Keepsake*).

After the acquisition and engraving process, editors then committed to further reproduction of the original painting by requesting a poetic verbal rendering—a request that created competition among authors and forced and perhaps limited the creative process. Editor Frederic Shoberl had apparently solicited more than one poet to illustrate *Constancy,* a painting by P. Stephanoff. Both James Bird and Charles Swain submitted poems entitled "Constancy" to support the engraving (see appendix D for full text); because both poems were of fine quality, Shoberl included them in the 1829 *Forget Me Not* immediately following the engraving, explaining his decision in a footnote: "This and the following poem were written expressly to illustrate the engraving inscribed Constancy; and, the subject being so differently treated by the gifted authors, it has been deemed right to introduce the compositions of both" (161) (fig. 5.5). In this case, the authors competed against each other for space in a popular annual—a move that inevitably pitted their poetic abilities against each other.

Figure 5.5 "Constancy" engraving, 1829 *Forget Me Not,* painted by P. Stephanoff and engraved by F. J. Portbury (from the Katherine D. Harris Collection)

Behind the public scene, authors often approached artists to request permission to verbally illustrate a work—leaving the final approval with the artist. In a letter to William Bernard Cooke, an engraver of maritime views who did much work for Turner, Thomas Hood solicited Cooke for just such a "favor": "I cannot help regretting that your descriptive part of the work on Brighton is engaged—I am so fond of the coast, that any writing of that sort would be quite to my taste. I only mean by saying this—to place myself in your way in the event of any similar undertaking being proposed hereafter. If any verses should occur to me you shall have them" (*Letters* [Morgan], 95). Apparently, Cooke had approval rights of the verses that would accompany his illustration.

The annuals, though derided for their sentimental writing, served as a source of artistic community among the genre's consumers. The engravings became the focus for increasing the size of the books to accommodate a larger image; consumers constantly requested that the size be increased so they could see more details. In many cases, the engravings were excised from the book by owners and framed as a representation of the master artistry.

During the 1830s, consumers became increasingly fond of the engravings, to the point at which some annuals were filled with more engravings and less literature. In fact, the *Landscape Annual,* appearing in 1830, consisted of two volumes: one with the literature and the other with only the engravings. By 1830, because of the public clamor for more engravings and larger prints, the literary annual format began to change—again. In 1832, Letitia Elizabeth Landon and the publisher Fisher, Son, and Jackson created a faux scrapbook based on the annual format.[10] It consists of thirty-six engravings, named in a list of plates, and their accompanying "poetical illustrations," each only two pages long. However, *Fisher's Drawing Room Scrap Book* does not contain a table of contents—an element of the work that is essentially an advertisement for the contents in hand.[11]

The "scrap book" designation in the title creates a false sense of the personal, unlike the album, commonplace book, or scrapbook as they are defined in the previous chapter. This work is a preprinted, mass-produced work that focuses almost exclusively and quite self-consciously on the engravings. Each poem is specifically tailored to the engraving, as was normal practice in the annuals. And because the entire contents were under Landon's control, she added footnotes to each poem that explain the historical significance, "legend, and train of reflection" (Introduction,

1832 *Fisher's*, 3) of the engraving or poem. She offered more than the poetic beauty celebrated by other annuals; with her additional notes, Landon offers a well-rounded illustration of the engraving and did not leave the reader to guess at a particular word's meaning or the origin of the scene—contrary to the meaning behind the annual's title: *scrap book*.

By 1830, authors had begun to resent this practice of forced versifying. In *Fisher's Drawing Room Scrap Book* for 1832, Landon writes in the preface that "the ideas that seem at first so delightful are grown common, by passing through the familiarizing process of writing, printing, and correcting" (3). Even Landon in this same preface acknowledges that this type of commercialized poetics of "mere description is certainly not the most popular species of composition." Catherine Boyle and Zachary Leader, in *Romantic Period Writings,* suggest that this relationship between print and poetic product "hints at this 'familiarization' process by drawing attention to the poem as product, the result less of inspiration than of the contingencies of commerce and labor" (187). In *Fisher's Drawing Room Scrap Book* for 1833, an exasperated Landon throws up her hands in the first three lines of a poem accompanying the engraving "Macao, China":

Good Heaven! whatever shall I do?
I must write something for my readers:
What has become of my ideas?
    Of all the places in the world,
To fix upon a port in China;
Celestial empire, how I wish
I had been christened Celestina!
    The wish however's served for rhyme,
And here again, invention falters:
Had it but been a town in Greece;
I might have raved about its altars,
    And talked of liberty and mass,
Of tyrants and Romaic dances,
Of Athens with a German king,
And fifty thousand other chances:
    Or had it only been in Spain;
. . . .
    Or Italy, the land of song;

. . . .
Or France, which, like an invalid
. . . .
Or had it only been Madeira;
. . . .
I'm like a sailor sent to sea,
Sent with "no, nothing" for his sea-hoard;
What on earth can I find to say,
Of a pagoda or a tea-board?
No love, no murder, no description,
Their only "old association"
Is with the willow-pattern plates,
That on the dresser have their station.
I give it up in pure despair;
But well the muse may turn refractory,
When all her inspiration is—
A Chinese Town, and an English Factory.

([Leader], 208–9)

The poem does anything but illustrate the engraving. Landon's exasperation was most likely due to the fact that she provided the text for every *Fisher's Drawing Room Scrap-Book* until her death in 1839. However, this poem comes in 1833, only the second year of the annual's publication. Already, Landon was stretching for ideas in the forced-labor community of poet-for-hire, as was apparent when, in the poem following "Macao," Landon directs readers away from the engraving, "The Chinese Pagoda," and registers her regret in producing a poem with a forced subject.

Now, I who thought the first vexatious[12]
Despaired and knew not what to do,
Abused the stars, called fate ungracious—
Here is a second Chinese view!

I sent to Messrs. Fisher, saying
The simple fact—I could not write;
What was the use of my inveighing?–
Back came the fatal scroll that night.

"But, madam, such a fine engraving,
The country, too, so little known!"
One's publisher there is no braving—
The plate was work'd, "the dye was thrown."

. . . .

O Captain Elliot, what could make you
Forsake the Indian fanes of yore?
And what in mercy's name could take you
To this most stupid Chinese shore?

([Leader], 210–11)

Not only does she expose the labor of writing, but she also laments her distance, both emotionally and creatively, from the Chinese landscape. This poem resonates with the poet instead of the subject. In Landon's effort to fill space, she exposes herself to public view and voices discontent with and rebellion against the practice of privileging the engraving over authorial creativity. Though she submits to her publisher's wishes, in the end she subversively avoids their demand for a verbal illustration and rebels against the notion that poetry is decorative. Because her publishers allowed these poetic entries into the annual, they seem to have mounted the poems only as filler to each engraving's visual spectacle.

Other editors and many authors, including Thomas Hood, depended primarily on their income from literary annuals to survive. In 1835, Hood moved to Germany to escape creditors but continued to write most of the text for *The Comic Annual* as well as design the woodcut engravings. His was a forced labor dependent on popular success, as is pointed out by John Clubbe in his brief biography of Hood (*Selected,* 17, 19).

Later, Alaric Watts even converted his *Literary Souvenir* into a repository of artwork in 1835 with *The Literary Souvenir and Cabinet of Modern Art*. In the following year, "literary souvenir" lost dominance in the title and was usurped by the new primary function of *The Cabinet of Modern Art and Literary Souvenir*, an annual filled with engravings. The literary had finally lost to the visual in this groundbreaking annual title.

SIX

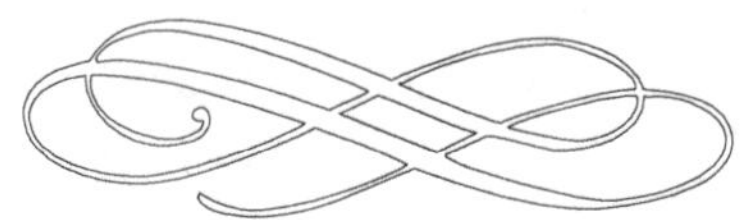

Accumulating Profits or Constructing Taste

Editorial Control of the Literary Annuals

BY 1830, THE TRADE IN ANNUALS HAD BECOME SO popular that various titles emerged with hopes and promises of continuing a yearly publication. But with titles like *Olive Branch* and *Zoological Keepsake* appearing and vanishing in a single year, more often than not that promise was broken. Many factors contributed to the success or demise of a particular title—external appearance, engraving quality, literary contents, popular authors, editorial arrangement, marketing, and reviews. Despite the overwhelming popularity of annuals, it is a common misconception that editors and publishers of annuals earned a large profit from their sales. They did, however, set standards for taste in the 1820s and 1830s by simultaneously garnering praise and causing apoplectic reactions by reviewers.

According to John Ford, Rudolph Ackermann printed 20,000 volumes of the *Forget Me Not* in some years and used a quarter of a million plates per edition (*Ackermann,* 64–65). *Friendship's Offering* provided publisher George Murray Smith with a substantial fortune: "The annual *Friendship's Offering* first published in [November] 1823—a type of literature upon which much ridicule has been expended—was a very successful enterprise on the part of the firm. It had a circulation of from eight to ten thousand copies, and was sold at the price of 12s" (*Recollections,* 9).[1] In the preface to the 1826 *Literary Souvenir,* editor Alaric Watts proudly declared the success of the initial publishing of his literary annual: "The sale of six thousand copies of the *Literary Souvenir* for 1825, under disadvantages of no ordinary nature, and the flattering testimony borne to its merits by nearly the whole of the periodical press, whilst they have afforded gratifying proofs of the correctness of my anticipations as to the probable success of such a publication, have also had the effect of stimulating my publishers and myself to produce, in the present volume, a work calculated to deserve, if not to secure, a still more extended degree of patronage" (v). In 1828, 12,000 copies of Charles Heath's *Keepsake* disappeared from booksellers' shelves in a few weeks. The following year, 20,000 copies of the 1829 volume sold in less than a month ("Annuals," 497–98).

The printed numbers and expected circulation of annuals seem to indicate that this genre was an incredibly lucrative venture for publishers and editors. In fact, Richard Altick, in studying the genre in relation to the Victorian period, found that "in one season, 1828, it was estimated that 100,000 copies were produced [of various literary annuals], at a retail value of over £70,000 [in the aggregate for the genre]" (362). While specific costs and circulation numbers were not recorded by a majority of the publishers, a few kept track of and published their costs (see table 6.1).

TABLE 6.1 PUBLISHERS' COSTS

Title & Year	*Cost*	*Circulation*	*Price*
Forget Me Not[a]	—	20,000	12*s*
Friendship's Offering (1824)	—	8,000–10,000	12*s*
Literary Souvenir[b] (1824–37)	£50,000	—	12*s*
1825	—	6,000	12*s*
1826	£2,000	—	12*s*
1827[c]	£2,620	10,700	12*s*
Keepsake (1828)	£10,550	12,000	£1.1*s*
Keepsake (1829)	£11,550	20,000	£1.1*s*
Literature only[d]	£2,000	—	£1.1*s*
Keepsake & Picturesque Annual (1832)[e]	£9,487	—	£1.1*s*

[a] Unspecified year; John Ford's history of Ackermann's publishing house (65).

[b] From A. Bose's 1953 article.

[c] From Watts' biography.

[d] From Ledbetter's article, "'White Vellum'."

[e] Ledbetter retrieved these figures from the Longman archives and notes them in her article "'White Vellum.'" Charles Heath is the proprietor of both of these annuals.

Between 1823 and 1835, literary annuals retailed between twelve shillings and three pounds. A. Bose speculates that if a twelve-shilling annual "sold less than 8,000 copies, the sale proceeds would barely equal the expenditure," and a guinea annual would have to "sell at least 12,000 copies" (51). In calculating payment to authors for the most lavish annual in 1829, Kathryn Ledbetter notes that Charles Heath and editor Frederic Mansel Reynolds "paid Scott £500 for each of his contributions, Southey 50 guineas, Wordsworth 100 guineas, and Coleridge £50, with 29 other contributors garnering fees unknown. . . . 'In total, the various financial inducements handed out in the course of this extraordinary promotion during 1828 amounted to some 1600 guineas [£1680]'" ("White," 39). Leonard Huxley, in a history of *Friendship's Offering*'s publisher, Smith Elder, notes that this annual was a "profitable venture" (12) but offers no figures to support the claim. Smith himself described the elation felt at the completion of the first printing in late 1823: "The actual publishing of "Friendship's Offering" was a notable event. For two or three days before the day of its appearance everybody remained, after the shop had closed. Tables were set out, and we sealed up each copy in a wrapper. When the work was all over we were regaled with wine and cake, and sang songs" (*Recollections,* 10).

Alaric Watts and Longman publishers are among the few to have kept records of retail sales. For *The Literary Souvenir,* retail booksellers subscribed or preordered the volumes, which were then presented in November (see appendix C). A senior partner at Longman recorded these subscription orders from various booksellers for the 1827 *Literary Souvenir* (see table 6.2; Watts, *Alaric Watts,* 1:248, 249).

The total number printed was 10,697 with the following actual sales: 10,169 small paper copies, 335 of which were presentation copies, 700 were sent for sale to America, and 7,712 were sold in England between November 1, 1826, and April 1827; 528 large paper copies were sold during the same time period, out of the 750 printed (Watts, *Alaric Watts,* 1:250). For the 1827 *Literary Souvenir,* costs increased only £620 from the previous year, but circulation numbers almost doubled from the initial 1825 volume.

Because of the annual's immediate success, editors improved on the product without altering the price. Watts reminded his readers in the 1826 preface to the *Literary Souvenir* that twelve shillings for this volume was relatively low considering the expense of obtaining works of such high quality:

> I need scarcely remind my readers that if, instead of such illustrations as these, from original paintings and drawings, most of which have

TABLE 6.2 LONGMAN SUBSCRIPTION ORDERS FOR THE 1827 *LITERARY SOUVENIR*

	Small	*Large*
Longman, Rees, and Co.	3,500	100
Baldwin, Cradock, and Joy	600	12
Simpkin and Marshall	200	6
George B. Whittaker	150	
Sherwood and Co.	150	4
James Duncan	50	
Rivingtons	25	
Smith, Elder, and Co.	50	
T. M. Richardson	80	
Lupton Relfe	75	
Harrison and Co.	25	
J. A. Hessey	25	3
Charles Tilt	25	2
R. Ackermann	50	2
Thomas Tegg	25	
Robert Jennings	25	4
F. G. Moon	25	6
Sampson Low	25	6
W. Pickering	6	
Hatchard and Son	25	
Total	6,433	201

> been procured with very great expense, I had chosen to introduce inferior plates, perhaps pleasing enough to persons possessing no great refinement of taste, taken from published prints, or obtained from cheap sources, more than double the number might have been given, at precisely the same cost. And when it is remembered that ten engravings, executed in the most finished style of the art, and upwards of four hundred pages of closely printed original Tales, Sketches, and Poems, by about forty of the most popular writers of the day, are supplied to the public at the cost of *twelve shillings,* I shall readily be believed when I affirm that many thousand copies must be sold before the proprietors can be even reimbursed for the expenses of such work. (viii–ix)

Watts almost shamed his readers into their luxury; he proclaimed that the annual was worth well beyond twelve shillings for the excellent literary and artistic contents provided within. If Watts comes across as a scolding patriarch, then Frederic Shoberl writes himself as a benevolent contributor for the common good. In the 1835 *Forget Me Not* preface, he wrote that "by using paper of larger size than heretofore, which admits of a proportionate increase in the dimensions of the plates, and by adopting a more substantial binding instead of the frailer materials hitherto employed, they have incurred an additional expense, for which, as the price of the work continues to be the same, they can look to nothing but the public patronage for remuneration" (4). In other words, Shoberl professed that the public's continued consumer sponsorship was all the thanks needed for creating a better package—a self-aggrandizing move that Shoberl hoped would endear his literary annual to the public. These declarations of bigger, better, and grander by many of the literary annuals' editors were an attempt to attract consumers in a market saturated with annuals. Watts made this move in 1826, Shoberl in 1835—a ten-year gap between improvements in format. Watts offered more when the annuals were coming to prominence; Shoberl offered more as the format altered once again to include more engravings and less literature, as was the public's desire.

Because the early circulation numbers supported the literary annual's future, an industry was born and encouraged with their production: "[The annuals] afforded employment in many ways to the industrious classes, at a period when it was perhaps of all others the most acceptable,—to those engaged in the manufacture of paper, to compositors, type-founders, pressmen, binders, to literary men, painters, engravers, booksellers, and others, these annuals have been a source of profitable occupation, during that very season of the year, which, heretofore, was the most apt to fall heavy upon those numerous and useful members of the community" (anonymous, *Monthly Review* [November 1831]: 371). A Cornhill retail bookseller reported selling "from a thousand to fifteen hundred of these attractive little volumes; netting . . . some four shillings (the twenty-fifth copy included) on every twelve-shilling and seven shillings on every guinea book" ("Annuals," 493). When volumes outlived their season, they ended up in a street bookstall being sold for sixpence as opposed to their twelve-shilling price. With this move, the annual became a literary product for a completely different class of reader. The bookstalls allowed people like George Eliot's Bob Jakin (*Mill on the Floss*) to purchase a *Keepsake* and several volumes of the *Portrait Gallery* without taxing his income. Though an annual's move into a bookstall was a sign of failure to many publishers and editors, the title would become reinvigorated through a new working-class audience, a new meaning being written onto the palimpsestic surface.

S. C. Hall, editor of the successful religious literary annual *The Amulet,* reported in the *Art Journal* that overall proceeds in 1829 topped £90,000 ("Annuals," 493). Twenty-five separate literary annual titles captured the public's eye and pocketbooks for 1829 (see table 6.3; see appendix A for titles in other years).

TABLE 6.3 LIST OF ANNUAL TITLES FOR 1829

Title	*Editor*	*Publisher*
Affection's Offering		
Amulet	S. C. Hall	
Anniversary	Allan Cunningham	
Bijou		William Pickering
Cabinet of Curiosities		
Casket		John Murray
Christian Forget Me Not		Thomas Holmes
Christmas Box	Crofton Croker	William Harrison Ainsworth
First Flowers		Poole
Forget Me Not	Frederic Shoberl	Rudolph Ackermann
Friendship's Offering	Thomas Pringle	Smith, Elder & Co.
Gem	Thomas Hood	William Marshall
Juvenile Forget Me Not	Anna Maria Hall	N. Hailes
Juvenile Keepsake	Thomas Roscoe	Hurst, Chance & Co.
Keepsake	Frederic Mansel Reynolds	Hurst, Chance & Co.
Literary Souvenir	Alaric Watts	Longman, Rees, Orme, Brown & Green
Musical Gem	Nicholas Mori and William Ball	
Nautilus		
New Year's Gift	Mrs. Alaric Watts	Longman, Rees, Orme, Brown & Green
Offering	Rev. Thomas Dale	
Poetical Album	Alaric Watts	Hurst
Souvenir Litteraire de France	Alaric Watts	Longman, Rees, Orme, Brown & Green
Times Telescope		Sherwood
Winter's Wreath		Geo. Smith and George B. Whittaker
Young Ladies Book	W. Harvey	

Alaric Watts and his wife, S. C. Hall and his wife, and the publishers Longman and Hurst Chance all appear more than once on this list and were the more prolific editors and publishers of the annuals during this year, which would indicate that they shared in a majority of the £90,000 earned for the 1829 season (see table 6.4). However, the industry of craftsmen divided the majority of the proceeds, leaving only £10,000 for publisher's profits and £30,000 for retail booksellers ("Annuals," 493).

The production costs, acquisition spending, and eventual glut of the literary annual market would cause the indebtedness and even bankruptcy of a few speculators. Despite these phenomenal numbers, producing a literary annual proved chaotic and difficult at best. However, even with the hindsight of failed productions, many authors reached for the opportunity to edit an annual, including John Gibson Lockhart (*Janus*),[2] Thomas Campbell, Thomas Hood (*The Gem, The Comic Annual*), Dr. Croly (*The Graces*), T. K. Hervey (*Friendship's Offering, Amaranth*), Thomas Dale (*Offering, Iris*), Thomas Pringle (*Friendship's Offering*), Allan Cunningham (*Anniversary*), Mary Russell Mitford (*Finden's Tableaux*), Caroline Norton (*The Keepsake, Fisher's Drawing Room Scrap-Book*), Letitia Elizabeth Landon (*Heath's Book of Beauty, Fisher's Drawing Room Scrap Book*), Crofton Croker (*Christmas Box*), Leitch Ritchie (*Friendship's Offering, Picturesque Annuals*), Alaric Watts (*The Literary Souvenir*), Agnes Strickland (*Juvenile Scrapbook*), Mary Howitt (*Fisher's Drawing Room Scrap-Book*), S. C. Hall (*Amulet*), Anna Maria Hall

TABLE 6.4 EARNINGS BASED ON £90,000 INCOME FOR THE TRADE IN ANNUALS FOR 1829

	Income (£)
Authors and editors	6,000
Painters for pictures or copyrights	3,000
Engravers	12,000
Copperplate printers	5,000
Letterpress printers	5,000
Paper manufacturers	6,000
Book binders	9,000
Silk manufacturers and leather sellers	500
Cost of advertisements paid by publishers	2,000
Incidental expenses paid by publishers	1,500
Total	50,000

(*Juvenile Forget Me Not, Finden's Tableaux, Fisher's Drawing Room Scrap-Book*), W. Harrison Ainsworth (*The Keepsake*) and Thomas Roscoe (*Juvenile Keepsake, Remembrance, The Landscape Annual*) ("Annuals," 494).

Though each editor followed a different plan, many were responsible for constructing the overall tone of the volume, including obtaining the artwork. Alaric Watts, editor of the *Literary Souvenir,* began work on the first volume in July 1824 and went to publication in November. By the time Hurst Robinson contacted him, they had already selected and contracted the artwork for the volume; that left only the written contents for Watts. Editing the volume took five months, which is an incredibly short amount of time to amass works from various authors—especially considering the geographical diversity of all authors and the rate of postal delivery (Watts, *Alaric Watts,* vol. 1, chap. 15). Frederic Shoberl, longtime editor of the *Forget Me Not,* abbreviated that time period with a request to T. J. Serle in a February 1835 letter:[3]

> My object, as you will perceive from his letter, is to obtain an article in illustration of a picture of his, which is engraving for the next volume of the Forget Me Not. The writer would be left at perfect liberty to use his own judgment in regard to the form of the article, & to make it a Dramatic Sketch, a Tale, or whatever he pleases. If a Tale, I think it would not much exceed twenty printed pages.
>
> Permit me to enquire if it would suit your convenience to undertake this illustration for which Messrs. Ackermann would, of course, make any reasonable remuneration. You would not be hurried in regard to time: for, if I could be furnished with the Article by the end of April, it would be quite early enough.

An early spring due date would allow Shoberl to prepare both the engraving and the accompanying prose for the November/December publication date of the 1836 *Forget Me Not.* Arguably, this attenuated rate of production for the author must have become de rigueur by 1835 or at the very least practiced by Shoberl, who had become an expert at producing the *Forget Me Not* on time for each year.

Because of the year-long labor "to get together one hundred contributions in prose and verse from popular authors" (Watts, *Alaric Watts,* 1:254), editors were able to shape the reputation and visibility of many literary figures, including Wordsworth, Tennyson, and Clare, often seducing them with ego rather than money, as in the following letter from Thomas Hood to James Hogg, dated April 22, 1828:

> It is my pleasant duty to address you on behalf of a New Annual [*The Gem*] which has been placed under my care—to obtain, if I may, your valuable name & assistance for its pages.—In the absence of all claim upon you for such a service, I can only make this request as for a personal favour & obligation which I shall be most happy in any way to acknowledge. It is my *earnest* wish to see you numbered with the Contributors who grace my list—already a goodly company—& the very respect & value I attach to their names make me the more desirous of your own in the association. (*Letters* [Morgan], 99)

In the same month, Hood also imposed on his friendship with John Clare for a piece of writing, hoping to "gather all those known to use of old in *the 'London'*—so pray let me have some of your best verses, *and I will take care that they shall be properly acknowledged*" (*Letters* [Morgan], 100; emphasis added). Felicia Hemans, a poet who had proved herself marketable in the literary annual genre, was the target of another of Hood's requests, in a letter dated June 21, 1828:

> I had the pleasure of addressing you some time since, but the letter, I fear, never reached its destination. The purport was to bespeak your valuable assistance, for a new Annual [*The Gem*] which has been placed under my Editorship:—for I am very anxious to place you amongst my poetical contributors. Sir Walter Scott[,] I am proud to say, heads the list,—& if you will so far oblige me, as I request, it will be a personal favour which I shall be most happy to acknowledge. (*Letters* [Morgan], 106)

Hood used literary names in his attempt to acquire further literary names for his first annual. Unfortunately, Hemans never contributed to *The Gem;* Hogg contributed only one poem, for the 1830 volume; and Clare contributed one poem for each of the 1829 and 1830 volumes. Much like Alaric Watts, Hood was well connected in London literary circles, because of his early employment as an apprentice engraver under Le Keux (a featured artist in *The Gem* and other annuals, as discussed in the chapter on engravings) and shortly thereafter with the *London Magazine* (Clubbe, *Selected,*

4–6);[4] with his editing and engraving experience, he was able to convince many well-known poets (including Tennyson) and artists (including Turner) to contribute to *The Gem*.

With this position, though, editors were taxed with the diplomatic refusal of at least five hundred contributions "that were offered and were not suitable" (Watts, *Alaric Watts,* 1:254). The effort required labor and expense on the part of the editor. With the annuals being so popular and having a reputation for publishing veritable neophytes, mailed entries were sent to editors begging for some entry into the latest volume. Eventually, because of the deluge of mail, editors publicly requested that no unsolicited poems, stories, and articles be sent to their attention:

> The very great increase of the correspondence of the "Literary Souvenir," and the expense and trouble to which the Editor [Alaric Watts] has been put, by the transmission to him of unsolicited communications for his Work, and subsequent and repeated applications respecting them, have rendered it necessary for him to announce, that no letters or parcels that do not appear to come from known correspondents, will be received, unless their carriage be paid; and that he cannot undertake to preserve and to return short pieces, whether or prose or verse, from anonymous or unsolicited contributors. (Watts, Postscript to 1830 *Literary Souvenir,* 364)

This request seems to indicate that editors were loathe to sift through the mounds of amateur writing that were continuously submitted; however, hopeful poets typically sent their entries through the postal system, with recipients (not senders) required to pay the postage.

An editor's position, seemingly rife with power, actually held little more than the empty promise of financial remuneration. Many editors received little or no compensation for their year-long efforts—or worse. During the initial popularity of annuals, in 1825–26, a financial panic struck that temporarily crippled major publishers, including William Pickering (publisher of the *Bijou* and *Carcanet*) and Hurst, Robinson and Co. (publisher of *The Graces* and *The Literary Souvenir*). In November 1825, Watts's biographer reports, "the number of bankruptcies in England had doubled those of the preceding January; and these were again to be doubled in the following month" (Watts, *Alaric Watts,* 1:219). In a two-month span (November–December 1825), seventy to eighty banks were included in the tally.

The book trade suffered business losses because of the use of bills of exchange. According to Bernard Warrington, "[B]efore the use of cheques became significant, this chaotic and unwieldy system of accepting, discounting and renewing bills has often been noted as a symptom of the failure of financial institutions to keep pace with business activity" (7). Apparently, Warrington notes, "members of the trade were constantly accepting and discounting each other's paper" (7). In January 1826, the Edinburgh publisher Constable and Co. folded, leaving its London agent, Hurst, Robinson and Co., vulnerable to bankruptcy. To save themselves, Hurst and Robinson ceased payment on all of their outstanding accounts and closed their doors (Watts, *Alaric Watts,* 1:222).

The collapse and dissolution of Hurst, Robinson and Co. caused a ripple effect in the industry: In 1826, it forced editor Alaric Watts to take his 1827 *Literary Souvenir* to Longman. Hurst revived himself in the book trade in various forms, though, including Hurst and Co. and Hurst, Chance and Co., the last of which was the publisher for Heath's *Keepsake* until it too was lost to Longman in 1831. Longman became the publisher for *Heath's Book of Beauty* (1833), *New Year's Gift* (1829), *Souvenir Litteraire de France* (1829), and *Young Gentleman's Library* (1829). Though Watts was able to secure a new publisher for his *Literary Souvenir,* his financial reputation was blackened with a debt to Hurst Robinson—a debt that he was never able to repay and that continued to accrue interest throughout his lifetime (Watts, *Alaric Watts,* 1:224). In addition, Watts experienced trouble with debt from his *Literary Souvenir* days (beginning in 1836) that was to plague him until 1850. The editor fronted much money and borrowed from his publishers at Longman, amassing more debt than he could recoup in profits from the annuals and the illustrated poetry books (Watts, *Alaric Watts,* 2:275). The preface to the 1827 *Literary Souvenir* spends eleven pages reassuring readers of the *Literary Souvenir*'s presence and continuation. Watts expressed concern in this preface that booksellers on the outermost borders of London would believe the rumors that Hurst had forbidden Watts from publishing under the *Literary Souvenir* title or that the annual would crumble along with the dissolution of the publishing firm. Watts iterated his dedication to the volume and promised (both readers and booksellers) that the contents and title were controlled not by a publisher but by him, the editor—a move that reveals his creative and editorial control of the annual, exposing the business of annuals to the public.

Heath contracted for the printing and distribution of *The Keepsake* with newly formed publisher Hurst, Chance and Co. instead of relying on them for foundational capital. For *The Keepsake,* Heath bore the expense of acquisition—a costly endeavor, considering that the first *Keepsake* cost £10,500 and the second £11,550. With the introduction of *The Keepsake,* the competition for "known" contributors became fierce. The £11,550 was dispensed primarily in payment to the authors (or their estates) who contributed to the 1829 volume, including William Wordsworth, Percy Bysshe Shelley (posthumously), Mary Shelley, Samuel Taylor Coleridge, Sir Walter Scott, and Robert Southey, some of whom contributed more than one piece (fig. 6.1). The bulk of those funds was used to acquire "original" poems and prose from authors like Scott, who was rumored to have been offered £800 to edit (and declined) and another £400–500 for his contributions to the 1829 *Keepsake.*[5] Reynolds began a new trend in acquisitions for literary annuals that held true through the 1860s with Thackeray's spending on *Cornhill Magazine* by Smith Elder, publisher of the successful literary annual *Friendship's Offering.*

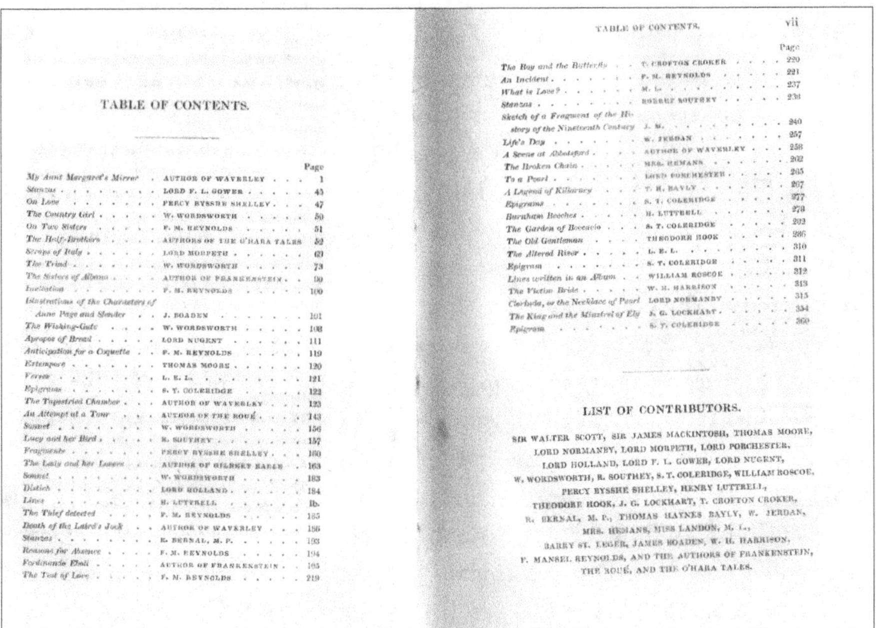

TABLE OF CONTENTS.

LIST OF CONTRIBUTORS.

SIR WALTER SCOTT, SIR JAMES MACKINTOSH, THOMAS MOORE, LORD NORMANBY, LORD MORPETH, LORD PORCHESTER, LORD HOLLAND, LORD F. L. GOWER, LORD NUGENT, W. WORDSWORTH, R. SOUTHEY, S. T. COLERIDGE, WILLIAM ROSCOE, PERCY BYSSHE SHELLEY, HENRY LUTTRELL, THEODORE HOOK, J. G. LOCKHART, T. CROFTON CROKER, R. BERNAL, M. P., THOMAS HAYNES BAYLY, W. JERDAN, MRS. HEMANS, MISS LANDON, M. L., BARRY ST. LEGER, JAMES BOADEN, W. H. HARRISON, F. MANSEL REYNOLDS, AND THE AUTHORS OF FRANKENSTEIN, THE ROUÉ, AND THE O'HARA TALES.

Figure 6.1 Notable literary names in table of contents of 1829 *Keepsake* (from the Katherine D. Harris Collection)

Unlike other editors, Charles Heath gambled his own money for *The Keepsake*'s success. And to corner the annual market with well-known names, Heath guaranteed their contributions by offering exorbitant fees; he could do this because he had assumed the responsibility for paying authors, illustrators, and engravers—a fiduciary duty commonly borne by the publisher.[6] These expenses, eventually curtailed by his new publisher, Longman, did not seem to faze Heath or curtail his industriousness, though. He continued to speculate in the field with several other literary annuals, gift books, and illustration books, including *The Belle of the Season, Flowers of Loveliness, Gems of Beauty, Book of Beauty, Turner's Annual, Pictorial Annual, Children of Nobility,* and *Turner's Rivers of France.* His financial disarray was never communicated to his editors and was consequently a surprise when his business declared bankruptcy. According to Jane Wilde, the Countess of Blessington—an editor of Heath's 1840s gift books and literary annuals—earned approximately £2,000 per year from the annuals (342) but was forced to sell her furniture and her magnificent mansion, Gore House, with Heath's failure. She died in 1848 following the strain.

Even after the 1825–26 Panic, editors became partners in literary annual ventures, waived a salary, and assumed partial financial responsibility in the hope that profits would pay them exceedingly well. But bankruptcy continued to plague their positions. S. C. Hall, editor of *The Amulet,* received no profit as editor of *The Amulet* (1826–37) for its ten-year run. The first two years, Baynes and Son published the annual; when Westley and Davis acquired the venture, Hall contracted to receive profits instead of a salary and was later saddled with burdensome debt when Westley and Davis collapsed in 1837, a responsibility that he was unaware of when he committed to the contract.

Another source that taxed the income of British editors and publishers was the American export or, more justly framed, the American pilfering of British annuals. Though British annuals achieved great success in America, British publishers, editors, and authors rarely received any income from those sales because there was no international copyright law in place until 1842 and no economical way to enforce any such laws (see chapter 3). Though Thomas Hood's *Comic Annual* sold well in America, he rarely controlled its reprinting (Hood, *Letters* [Marchand], 52). Some magazines, like *Knickerbocker's Magazine* in New York, would request the early proof sheets, from which they would reset the text and print excerpts. Reprinting the engravings was another dilemma altogether: generally engravings were woodcuts or steel plates and could not easily be reproduced by American artists from a proof sheet alone.

Frederick Faxon points out that the Americans, but apparently not the British, had a practice of removing the title page, then printing and tipping in a new title page with a different year so that the booksellers could sell the leftover stock from the previous year or take already published work and republish it (xiii). In addition, according to Faxon, many of the American volumes were published without a date (xvii). This absence of a demarcating year allowed publishers to produce a fluid stock that was not limited by a date and consequently could always be sold as contemporary, "new," or of the latest fashion—the very reason for buying a new volume each year. In the 1893 *Atlantic Monthly,* a contributor highlighted this yearly newness: "These books were not to be resold; a last year's Annual was not to be thought of as a present however attractive in itself. Its dates betrayed it. They were gifts, and often treasured up as the faded rose and the ivory Malbone miniature of her bridal days are treasured in the matron's cabinet, because they were haunted with the secret and subtle fragrance of bygone memories" (quoted in Faxon, xxvii).

Faxon cites the sloppy work of resellers for this discovery. Apparently, when the title was no longer offered, publishers would buy the stereotyped plates, reproduce the volume, and include a new title page or perhaps replace the engravings. However, the republished copies often had the former title in the preface or the original title page just after the new one. In changing the plates, a new list of engravings was not inserted. Faxon calls these "spurious" volumes and claims that Leavitt & Allen and Cornish, Lamport & Co. did most of this republishing (xviii). The *Amaranth* (1849), *Garland* (1850), *Keepsake of Friendship* (1851), *Magnolia* (1852), *Token of Friendship* (1853), *Casket* (1854), and *Memory's Gift* (1869) were all American literary annuals that contained the same contents but dissimilar editors: Emily Percival, G. S. Monroe, and Clara Arnold. Faxon assumes that these editors, all of whom were successful editors of previous volumes of these titles, were unaware that their names were being co-opted by the spurious volumes (xix).

Apparently, this practice was not confined to America and was prolific on the Continent. This meant that British publishers and editors did not receive remuneration for their expansion into the New World or the Continent and were left with counting income and readership only from Britain.

By 1830, the market had become saturated with the *Gems*, *Literary Souvenirs*, *Iris*es, and *Amulets* and reached a total of forty-three titles. In an 1828 essay that anticipated this glut, Leigh Hunt celebrated the competition, calling it a "contest of sunbeams which shall produce the finest gems; *whose* tree, or *whose* parterre, shall burst out into a flush of more splendid blossoms" (11).[7] This year also introduced the first parody from within the family (as discussed in chapter 4): Thomas Hood's *Comic Annual,* which was filled with gentle ribbing instead of the caustic criticism offered by review periodicals. Several flattering imitations appeared in the following year to capitalize on Hood's successful venture, including *The New Comic Annual* (1831), published by Hurst Chance with an unknown writer/editor; and *The Comic Offering* (1831–35), edited by Louisa Sheridan and published by Smith Elder, publisher of the popular annual *Friendship's Offering.* In 1834, Hood moved his *Comic Annual* to publishers A. H. Baily and Co. because of discrepancies and payment for sales in America. Hood's enmity toward Tilt turned into a lengthy lawsuit (which Hood conducted from his residence in Germany). Tilt issued the *Comic Almanac* (1835–53) in direct competition with Hood's *Comic Annual* and employed George Cruikshank as its illustrator, which most likely accounts for the imitator's long run. The business of literary annuals was such that publishers would not hesitate to "borrow" the format from former volumes, nor would they hesitate to produce separate titles to compete against one another in the literary annual market.

By issuing the volumes in various sizes or collecting only the engravings in a single volume, publishers, editors, and printers struck upon a product that could be manipulated, formatted, and resold as a more decadent product—regardless of the fact that they did not alter its contents. A volume of the engravings alone could be bought by consumers who enjoyed the artistic work over the literary. In an advertisement at the conclusion of the 1832 *Landscape Annual,* the publishers offered two Royal octavo volumes,[8] each bound in morocco (leather) at a price of a guinea (£1.1*s*)—one volume contained the writing and the other the engravings.[9] The India proofs could be had for £2.12*s.*6*d.*—only a slightly higher cost for the engravings alone than the two volumes of both text and engravings. However, a volume advertised as India proofs would have been considered higher-quality printing.

Even the simplistic woodcut engravings in Hood's *Comic Annual* were printed in large sheets and sold separately for sixpence per large sheet (Advert, 1835 *Comic Annual*). In the 1830 *Literary Souvenir,* the publisher,

Longman, advertised various forms of the volume as well as its contents: Large paper sets containing all contents of the 1825–29 volumes and decadent India Proofs of the plates sold for six pounds or each year separately for one pound, four shillings. Consumers were urged to complete their sets of the small paper volumes for twelve shillings each, with the exception of the 1825 volume at fifteen shillings, and readers were warned that "two volumes are already out of print, and are not likely ever to be re-printed." Individual proofs and sets of proofs in various formats, including Imperial Quarto, Octavo India, Imperial India Proofs, and Prints, cost between three shillings and seven pounds—a large selection that allowed consumers to mount their favorite artwork and further rendered the *Literary Souvenir* indispensable in the household.

Charles Heath, ever the entrepreneur, capitalized on the public's fascination with Scott's novels and the easily obtainable artwork popularized by the annuals. In an undated volume,[10] Heath commissioned a volume of excerpts of *The Waverley Album* combined with fifty-one line engravings by Heath himself, E. Finden, C. Rolls, and other prominent engravers. The volume, encased in embossed silk covers, sold for a guinea—a deliberate similarity to Heath's red-silked *Keepsake.* Even before the decadence of the annuals, Scott's novels sold for one pound, ten shillings and were incredibly popular. With this volume, Heath combined the popularity of form and content, excising the only element that would have marred the volume's longevity—a date. Without a year indicated on the title page, Scott's novels and Heath's engravings seem timeless, unlike the seasonal annuals that were considered expired by April of the following year.

Hood, likewise, capitalized on his successful humorous annual and reformatted the product to create a new object that lacked any altered content. Physically exhausted from producing all of the *Comic Annual*'s contents, engravings included, Hood ceased production in 1839 and republished particular pieces in *Hood's Magazine.* The magazine, while not claiming to be original, garnered Hood a livable income because of his recognizable name and the popularity of the *Comic Annual.* The genre, while still present in popular culture and thriving in America, was broken down and sold piecemeal, literally: the woodcuts from the *Comic Annual* designed by Hood were so popular that the publishers issued a separate volume.

In addition, publishers were reprinting selections from various annuals in a premature retrospective salute to the genre, beginning in 1834 with the American publication *The Beauties of the English Annuals for 1835,* published in New York by Wallis and Newel.[11] The publisher Moxon reissued *The Comic Annual* as *Hood's Own* in monthly shilling parts during the 1870s to resurrect the success of the original. A few monthly magazines misrepresented themselves as literary annuals but were in actuality a year's worth of numbers bound to mimic and capitalize on the literary annual style. They exposed themselves with an irregular pagination of two or more series of pages in a single bound volume, each series beginning with an Arabic numeral 1 instead of using small Roman numerals for prefatory material and continuing with Arabic numbering for the contents (Faxon, xv).

Kathryn Ledbetter and Patricia Pulham argue that annuals were eventually replaced by popular Victorian periodicals, including the *Academy, Westminster Gazette,* and *Macmillan's Magazine* (Pulham, 31), during the 1850s, when they were finally forced out of publication.[12] Ledbetter notes that "[p]eriodicals such as *Cornhill Magazine* and *New Monthly Magazine* offered original poetry and fiction at greatly reduced costs and the middle classes were seeking the three-decker novel at Mudie's [Library]" ("BeGemmed," 244), which opened in 1842 at a subscription rate of three guineas (that is, thirty-three shillings) per year.[13] Vanessa Warne proposes that "the rapid decline of the annuals . . . is linked to the changing cultural appetites and interests of the middle classes" (10), especially those related to the visual arts.

The legacy of the annuals continued, though, as seen in S. C. Hall's autobiography, in which he nostalgically applauded the literary annuals and their popular influence: in the late nineteenth century, when magazines, serialized fiction, and novels dominated the public's attention, he observed, "[N]o such engravings as [the annuals] contained are now produced; while the literary contents, principally tales and poems, are as pure gold compared with the tinsel of the modern magazine" (179).

CONSTRUCTIONS OF TASTE: CRITICS AND THEIR REVIEWS

At first, reviewers enjoyed the annuals, offering long excerpts and recommending particular annuals to their readers. Within five years, however, reviewers began to write with disgust about the genre—primarily with objections to the poetess aesthetic. Laura Mandell points out that "two myths pervade the study of this immensely important and influential body of writing. One is that canonical writers shunned this work, refusing to publish in well-paying annuals and choosing instead to create great, high art; the other is that poetess poetry is 'bad' writing" ("Uses of the Archive," *The Poetess Archive*). Both myths rely on the production of aesthetics, and the reviewers were the ones who first produced this demarcation about literary annuals.

In the 1811 *Reviewers Reviewed,* Josiah Condor declared that "the legitimate and original design of Criticism, was to illustrate the productions of genius, and by carefully collating them with the universal dictates of nature, to deduce from both a settled and defined code, to which all matters of taste might be referred" (3). Condor continued in his treatise by condemning most contemporary review periodicals for subverting taste, bypassing genius, and claiming prominence. For Condor, reviewers were gatekeepers, arbiters of good taste. In years following the publication of Condor's (and others') treatises on criticism, London experienced a profound explosion of print materials—all of which required reviews that would guide consumers in their selection of reading materials.

Review periodicals, abundant throughout the life of this popular phenomenon, include the *New Monthly Magazine, Blackwood's Magazine, Eclectic Review, Monthly Review, Literary Gazette, The Mirror, Gentleman's Magazine, British Critic,* and *Atheneum,* among others. Critics writing these review articles considered themselves, like editors of the annuals, protectors of public literary tastes. One reviewer described the duty of critic as knight-errant protecting the public against bad literature: "If the legitimate object of periodical criticism is to recommend to the public such works as deserve its patronage, and expose folly and false taste, we may, in the discharge of the first of these offices, be allowed to criticise the [1825] Literary Souvenir" (anonymous reviewer, *British Critic,* quoted in 1826 *Literary Souvenir*).[14] In their public duty, the critics initially applauded literary annuals, especially the *Forget Me Not* and *Literary Souvenir,* because they possessed "a tone of romance, which, set off as it has been by poetry of a very high order, can have no other possible tendency, than to purify the imagination and the heart" (anonymous reviewer, *Monthly Review* [November 1826]: 274).[15]

Poetry in literary annuals was intended to stimulate the reader's sentiments, educate their intellect, and validate their creativity. The prefaces proclaimed editorial intentions and marked the literature and the textual object alike as a delicate object of beauty. Alaric Watts contended that poetry in particular would cause this continued reengagement, even though poetry was considered to be more difficult than prose and not appropriate for this female audience. In the 1835 *Literary Souvenir* preface, Watts openly and decidedly privileged poetry over fiction, continuing the debates surrounding fiction's literary value: "[P]oetry, which without entering into minute detail, may illustrate, in a page, the true spirit of a picture; and . . . being a branch of the Fine Arts itself, is less out of place in such a work. A poem, moreover, if it be good for any thing, will bear reading a second time, which is more than can often be said of a prose tale" (vi–vii). Because the short story and the serialized novel had begun to co-opt much of the space in magazines and periodicals, Watts's defense not only protected annuals and encouraged readers to buy them for the economy of reading but also promoted the sale of any poetry volume.

This leisured audience had already been exposed to volumes of poetry: the standard for publishing poetry and accumulating an audience had been established by publishing single-author volumes of poetry on either the patronage or the subscription model. However, the genre peaked in 1820, according to Lee Erickson, when poetry titles began a slow decline (28; see table 6.5).

Because of these declining sales, publishers (including Smith Elder, John Taylor, Longman, and John Murray) refused to publish new poetry as well as second editions of major poets, including Percy Bysshe Shelley, John Keats, and George Gordon Lord Byron, regardless of their respective posthumous fame (Erickson, 33). In the few volumes that were published

TABLE 6.5 POETRY SALES IN THE EARLY NINETEENTH CENTURY

Year	*No. of titles*[a]	*No. of first editions*
1815–19	225 per year	155
1820	320	200
1821–24	205 per year	145
1825	205	110
1826	127	91
1832	110	77

Source: Erickson, *Economy of Literary Form.*

[a] Erickson refers to the various titles that were produced and not the numbers of volumes printed for each title.

during the late 1820s and early 1830s, publishers often asked a poet to underwrite her or his volume's publication to guarantee against unprofitable sales.[16] Erickson further argues that "despite lower printing costs, publishers found that most poetry appealed to an increasingly smaller portion of the reading public and so kept its price high," selling for approximately five shillings for over one hundred years (35). However, the single-author volume's demise does not account for the literary annual's success. Quite possibly, at a price of twelve shillings (and more), the annual's variety of authors, genres, and engravings appeased a broader audience than did a single-author volume of poetry.

Not every poet suffered lack of sales during the initial popularity of the annuals. In fact, Felicia Hemans gained a significant audience from her contributions to annuals and was able to command one thousand prints of her 1828 volume, *Records of Woman,* from her publisher, William Blackwood. Because of "the present state of sales for poetry," instead of advance payment as Hemans requested, Blackwood offered to "take on . . . the expenses of paper & printing" and arranged to share the profits with Hemans (Blackwood to Hemans, in *Felicia Hemans,* 497n2). The poet agreed to the plan, stating that "hope of profit" did not motivate this publication; instead, she had "expressed more of [her] own personal feelings than in any thing [she had] ever before written" (March 1828 letter to Blackwood, *Felicia Hemans,* 497). Blackwood's gamble on Hemans's poetry produced three hundred pounds in profits by late 1830 for *Records of Woman;* in addition, Hemans's volumes sold consistently with profits ranging between one hundred and three hundred pounds through 1835 for second and third editions (*Felicia Hemans,* 444).

According to the critic's edict, reviewers were required to protect the public from bad literary choices or corrupting printed materials—treating readers and consumers like children. Of course, this protectiveness occurs more prominently in the discussion surrounding female readers, such as the following: "We feel justified in pronouncing the [1828] Souvenir for the new year a failure, as compared with its predecessors" (anonymous reviewer, *Monthly Review* [December 1827]: 525). From the consumer's point of view, the review provided a shelter against poorly produced consumer products. After all, the cost of an annual starting at twelve shillings and going up to three pounds was a tremendous expense that required sound investment advice. Consumers and readers were anxious to know whether the current year's *Forget Me Not, Keepsake,* or *Literary Souvenir* merited its purchase price.

With the public's literary and economic welfare in mind, critics anonymously commented on the negative and positive aspects of each annual, offering both praise and condemnation in the same review.[17] Each annual was typically judged on several categories, including the artistic merit of the engravings, quality of the literature, and arrangement and flow of its contents. Because an annual consisted of thirty to fifty literary pieces on varying subjects and tones, the ordering of contents was especially important to propel the reader forward. One critic noted that the organization of the pieces in the 1826 *Friendship's Offering* read like a funereal procession instead of an uplifting and leisurely experience: "Altogether, we should judge of the poetry of this volume, that it is in too mournful a strain. The proportion of elegiac stanzas is very great: with reflections on death the volume opens, with these it teems in the middle, and with these it concludes. Was it as a *memento mori* to royalty, that the opening piece, entitled 'A Monarch's Death-Bed,' was made to follow immediately after the dedication to His Majesty? This is a curious piece of editorial bad taste in arrangement" (anonymous, *Monthly Review* [February 1826]: 169).

Reviewers were concerned that the prose, poetry, and engravings were not enough to fulfill an annual; instead, the volume was expected to contain ephemeral materials that tied the title to contemporary culture: "To that portion of the work which is in prose, we must object that it consists entirely of tales, and that of these the greater number are too slight, if not indeed too fantastic, in their texture. The uniformity of fictitious narrative might, perhaps, have been saved by the introduction of a few 'curiosities of literature,' indebted letters of distinguished men, an essay or two discussing some interesting question in literature or the arts, or speculating in a gay mood on the features of the past and the signs of the coming year" (anonymous, review of 1825 *Literary Souvenir, Monthly Review* [October 1825]: 280).

Continuously striving to offer the best product, Ackermann and Shoberl heeded these suggestions and incorporated curiosities of literature into the *Forget Me Not*. In the 1830 volume, Shoberl included an early poem by Byron (posthumously, of course) and twice accounted for its inclusion: once in the preface and once in a headnote to the poem. "It is the first attempt of the late Lord Byron's that is known to be extant; and we consider this piece as being the more curious, inasmuch as it displays no dawning of that genius which soon afterwards burst forth with such overpowering splendour. It was inspired by the tender passion, and appears in the shape of verses addressed to the object of his earliest, and perhaps his only real attachment, the 'Mary' whom he has celebrated in many of his poems" (iv–v). Shoberl judged the poem before the critics could, thereby circumventing the negative publicity that the poem might have caused. A full-page apologia immediately precedes the six-stanza poem itself, identifying the verses as a "literary curiosity" rather than as a specimen "of Byron's transcendent and original power":

> The following schoolboy rhymes are not inserted as an example for youthful imitation, but as a literary curiosity. Innumerable specimens of Byron's transcendent and original powers are already before the public; but the dawning impulses of superior minds have been rarely disclosed: consequently they possess a novel interest, as well as afford a clue to the dominant feelings which have ruled their destinies. To the philosophic eye, that deficiency of mere poetic interest, which might disgrace an inferior writer, invests the timid steps of the uncultivated muse with a peculiar charm, as it proves, in a striking degree, the ultimate triumph of perseverance and the omnipotent force of *genius.* To those who construe the fitful and wayward flights of an untamed imagination into a settled and desperate malignity of temper, it may be useful to submit a document which bears the genuine impress of generous feeling and simple piety. Minds of a more tender and enthusiastic temperament will learn to pardon the insensibility of Lord Byron's favourite "Mary," when they learn that every crevice of her youthful heart was preoccupied, and that her warmest affections centred upon the man of her choice. (38n)

This is one of those rare instances in which the editor spoke to the audience, as indicated by a smaller typeface, outside of the preface. Shoberl directed the reader to pardon the quality of the poem as well as Mary for not returning Byron's affection. With this literary curiosity, he fueled the already-extant Byron-mania centered on the man and his life as it relates to his work.

With this artistic selection, Shoberl also displayed his shrewd business sense by offering Byron and his writing as a variety piece—a move to assuage the critics. John Wilson was not one of those quieted critics, however. In his December 1829 review, published in *Blackwood's Edinburgh Magazine,* Wilson praised the 1830 *Forget Me Not*'s contents and soliloquized on the genre's salvation of readers who quested to find material between highbrow books and lowbrow periodicals. As he moved through the *Forget Me Not*'s contents, quoting and praising, he stopped abruptly to castigate Shoberl for including the aesthetically inferior Byron selection: "[W]hat an absurdity it is for a man of sense, taste, and judgment, like Mr. Shoberl, to suppose that any value can be given to his volume by [adding] such verses as the weakest, worst, and most worthless of 'Poems by a Minor' when we all know that, with one or two exceptions, Byron was ashamed of the very best of them; and that even the very best afforded no intimation of his future genius, which was the sudden growth of his inspired manhood." Here, Wilson complimented a deceased Byron while admonishing Shoberl's editorial selection.

Even with this castigation, Wilson seems to play protective uncle not only to the audience but also to the annual's authors—and the audience's protectors were many. Often, reviewers seemed to be speaking from a position of unanimity rather than an individual voice. In the November 1826 *Monthly Review,* an anonymous critic denounced the engravings in the 1827 *Forget Me Not* as "secondary productions" and declared that the editor and publisher had "disappointed our expectations" (284). Excerpts of the literature follow without much critique except the comment that "[t]he literary part of the volume is marked by a great variety of serious and pleasant matter, arranged evidently with a view to allure the reader from page to page, without surfeiting him with any particular subject. Yet, we do not think that there are many things in the whole collection which call for distinguished praise" (284). The reviewer speaks under the guise of "our," inferring a consensus of opinion—but among whom? This language not only represents but also seemingly includes public opinion, a tactic that strengthens the critical point of view and creates a conclusive atmosphere with the reader being protected. In this voice, the critic applauds arrangement but criticizes literary aesthetics. This consensus (language), disappointment, and lack of praise might be expected to have discouraged consumer patronage of the 1827 *Forget Me Not.* However, after excerpting portions of the better prose and poetry, the reviewer surprisingly recommended the work to his readers: "The specimens which we have given of the merits of the 'Forget-me-not,' in its verse and prose departments, have been selected from among the most favourable which we could find. We had intended to add [other pieces,] but we regret to find that our space is already filled up. We must refer the reader for it to the work itself, *assuring him, at the same time, that he will find abundant employment for a leisure evening, in a considerable mass of agreeable matter, which we have necessarily left wholly unnoticed*" (293; emphasis added). The review continues briefly with a list of appropriate poems and prose in the 1827 *Forget Me Not* to accompany a reader's various emotional states—a recommendation strengthened by the reader's inclusion in the consensus. The volume, after being appropriately criticized and excerpted, is deemed adequate for leisurely entertainment; considering that the original intent for literary annuals was polite literature, this volume has met its goal. The critic, aware of the limitations of the genre as well as its popularity, forewarned consumers of the entire volume's failure but pieced together a recommendation from its parts.

Aware that reviewers categorically reviewed new annual publications and recommended or denounced them on their qualities as a whole product or part of a product, in the first *Keepsake* (1828) editor Frederic Mansel Reynolds introduced his volume by preemptively guiding readers and critics to view the entire product instead of its separate pieces: "With regard to the literary department, we have only to state generally, that writers of the most approved talents have enlisted themselves in our cause, and have contributed the aid of some of their choicest lucubrations. Our desire has been, that its pervading characteristic should be an elegant lightness, appropriate to the nature and objects of the work. If this has been accomplished, without totally precluding subjects of deeper interest, which, like shadows on the surface of a sparkling lake, heighten the brilliancy of the gayer parts and the effect of the whole, we have nothing left to wish for" (vi–vii). Reynolds mapped out *The Keepsake*'s intent and implied that readers would be simultaneously dazzled by its beauty and blinded to its weaknesses. Because *The Keepsake* debuted five years after the first literary annual was published, Reynolds had enough time to observe the substantive format alterations to the genre and the failure of a half-dozen titles. Ackermann knew what would sell.

Realizing that annuals were a national phenomenon by 1826 (increasing in number by 200 percent from 1824), and an international sensation by

1828 (with a doubling of the number of 1826 titles), some reviewers began drawing national boundaries around the British annuals' production and accusing imitators of capitalizing on the public's ignorant frenzy to purchase, give, and own the beautiful objects. In a review of the 1828 *Bijou,* the anonymous critic used comparisons to false gems and decadent culture (not British) to denounce pretenders: "The volume strongly reminds us of that sort of Bijouterie so common in France, in which one or two genuine stones are inserted, for the purpose of passing off a great quantity of vile past and trumpery gold. To the unpractised eye, they all shine with equal lustre; but now and then a critic will step in, to detect the difference between them, and even to record it, for the purpose of keeping the rules of good taste free from the debasement of a false standard" (*Monthly Review* [December 1827]: 530).

The nationalism invoked by this review is ironic considering that a German publisher (Ackermann) borrowed from the French almanack and the German Taschenbüch to create the format of the first British-published annual. In another instance of unspoken nationalism, a reviewer tacitly elided the annual's German origins by condemning a few of the engravings and literary works in the 1828 *Literary Souvenir,* citing them as "scarcely fit to grace a German Almanack" (anonymous, *Monthly Review* [December 1827]: 520)—a reproach regarding the production quality of the annual. In another review, John Wilson completely disregarded the German tradition and claimed the invention of annuals as Britain's own: "What Donkey was the first to bray that the Annuals, the subject of this our Monologue, were introduced into this country from Germany? Gentle reader, did you ever see a German Annual, or Literary Almanack? . . . But you know better—you know that the Annuals are a native growth of the soil of England, springing up like white and red clover beneath lime (a curious fact) wherever the periodical ploughshare has drawn its furrows" (*Blackwood's* [December 1829]: 950). Not only invoking Britannia in his review, Wilson resorted to a pastoral, domestic metaphor to describe the invention of annuals, as if they could have been grown only in British soil. The comment invokes a sense of nationalism for the annual's form, advertising a distinctly British product to England's inhabitants.

In a review of the *Literary Souvenir* for 1825, an anonymous critic acknowledged the contribution of other nations yet reckoned that British ingenuity would improve the product beyond recognition and thereby create a new product instead of merely an improved one:

> It is not a little gratifying to us to observe the keen and enterprising spirit of emulation which actuates our countrymen, in carrying to the highest degree of improvement, any invention which they borrow from their neighbours. Three or four years ago we possessed no annual publication which, for beauty or ornament, or utility of design, could be compared with the embellished almanacks of Germany. We have now several pocket-volumes published yearly, the least elegant of which is greatly superior to any thing produced on the Continent, and the best of which preclude the possibility of rivalry any where out of England. When these undertakings were first commenced, they retained, for a season, the character of the almanack, adding to it a few pieces of poetry, a tale or two in prose, and two or three very indifferent engravings. Now, with the exception of a few minor productions, they exclude every feature which would seem to attach them to one year more than to another; poets and other writers of the highest classes of our literature contribute to their pages, and feel proud to avow contributions which the most precious resources of art are employed to illustrate. (*Monthly Review* [October 1825]: 279)

This patriotism echoes Ackermann's use of British national pride to market his lithographic books, advertised in the 1824 *Forget Me Not* (and discussed previously). This critic accepted the German, and hence Ackermann's, influence on the annuals but subsumed that identity into the rhetoric of British nationalism. The annual symbolizes "home," eliding its Continental influences. Another reviewer called annuals "very graceful links to the chain of sympathy and kindness that binds the different branches of families together . . . which exercises a most useful influence upon the taste, as well as upon the heart" (anonymous, *Monthly Review* [November 1831]: 371). In this metaphor, the annual comes to represent not only the woman and her drawing room but also the larger realm of "home." During the early nineteenth century, England began to expand its colonial holdings and actively establish its empire. The ultimately feminine figure of Britannia came to represent the country with the ascension of Queen Victoria in 1837. Using the annuals as a representative of British superiority engendered this larger national consciousness, defining a portable British product that testified to Britain's superiority. It naturally followed that these products would require their knight-errants to protect not just the literal family but also the metaphorical British homeland. The role of the critic expanded, again like the editor, to include gatekeeper: one who would safeguard the nation from illegitimate literary objects or pretenders.

By completely denying the annual's German and French origins, critics enfolded these cultures into British nationalism. This elision allowed critics to hold the *Forget Me Not* as a standard for comparison but still remain gatekeepers of the nation. The *Literary Souvenir,* introduced in 1825, earned high marks in comparison to the *Forget Me Not* and was "considered [to be] a dangerous rival to Ackermann's *Forget Me Not*" (anonymous review, *European Magazine,* quoted in 1826 *Literary Souvenir* advertisements). With competition among annuals' publishers for the limited number of consumers, the critic's inference that books were "dangerous" to each other imbues them with violence and characterizes their creators as if in constant struggle—an echo of the expansion of the British Empire. Where does that leave the consumers and readers, then? They were the fortunate recipients of the competition, gaining a wide selection of annuals from which to choose and being only cursorily aware of the battle, ensuring "so much excellence in their execution, that we know not which to prefer" (anonymous, *Monthly Review* [November 1825]: 448).

The reviewers lost complete control of the public by 1832 as the popularity of annuals skyrocketed despite critics' acrimonious efforts to stigmatize the genre as literarily inferior. A long list of complaints began to be compiled as early as late 1826, the most common including overindulgent language and unmemorable poetry, a sacrilege considering that the main purpose of the annuals was to create, encapsulate, or retain a memory. In November 1826, an anonymous reviewer criticized an article in the 1827 *Amulet* for being "written in a flowery and artificial style, which . . . soon cloys a taste accustomed only to wholesome and simple viands" (*Monthly Review,* 280).[18] Because the annuals were approaching the height of their popularity and consumer sponsorship, the critic effectually condemned the *Amulet* and its reading public. However, the review did not impede the *Amulet*'s sales, which supported a ten-year run that ended in 1836. The public seemed to enjoy the cloying taste of the annual!

Critics also accused annuals' editors of exchanging pages for favors—a practice thought to dilute contents and offer false fame:

> There are, indeed, very few of the compositions that can be set down as contemptible, although we are much disposed to place all those signed Montague Seymour (heaven knows who he is!) under that head. There are also three or four other writers, whose names appear in this volume, such as John Luscombe, Esq., David Lester Richardson, Esq., Alexander Balfour, Esq., and David Lyndsay, Esq. of whose existence we must confess we had no previous knowledge, and of whose talents we have formed, from their present labours (perhaps erroneously) no very flattering opinion. But their contributions are doubtless of a "friendly nature"—that is to say, they cost nothing; and they help, not only to fill up the volume, but to serve as so many foils to the better names upon which its literary popularity must depend. (anonymous, *Monthly Review* [November 1826]: 284–85)

This review of the 1827 *Forget Me Not* and many other similar reviews are evidence of the declining reputation of literary annuals in the press despite the genre's enormous popularity. These reviews supplied fodder for later scholars to dismiss the literary annuals and their noncanonical authors. Though these authors have not been institutionalized in anthologies, they were still incredibly popular among the early nineteenth-century reading public: David Lester Richardson became editor of the *Bengal Annual,* a literary annual produced and published in Calcutta, India—extending the reaches of the British Empire by reproducing an emblem of home; Alexander Balfour, who worked in Blackwood's publishing house, was a minor Scottish poet and a friend of Burns's; and David Lyndsay was a pseudonym that the cross-dressing poet Mary Diana Dods used for publishing in the annuals.[19] Other reviewers made note of the "crowd of Misses and Esquires, who . . . [gave] a world of trouble" to the annuals' editors, undoubtedly referring to the supposedly lesser-known poets and versifiers who "were never intended by nature for literary pursuits, and who dangle after them only for a drawing-room name" (anonymous, *Monthly Review* [December 1827]: 520; *Monthly Review* [December 1826]: 391). Though many annuals did become riddled with favor-poetry or name-seekers, many of the contributions are evidence of the shifting attitude in poetry: what was once privately produced by nonprofessional poets, most likely in an album, became publicly accessible and a marker of the genuinely urbane life of Britain's citizens.

In addition to condemning the contributors of annuals, critics also made a distinction between popular writing and "literature" by differentiating poetry from verse, the latter labeled such because it was judged as mediocre. A review of the 1827 *Poetical Souvenir* found that this pseudo-annual was not really an annual but a pretender designed and advertised as such to capitalize on the literary annual phenomenon. The critic distinguished between verse and poetry: "The volume is[,] as its title indicates, wholly composed of what the editors are pleased to call *poetry,* but which we must designate as verses, that are little better than the ballads suspended on the stalls. . . . The editors miscalculated in the first instance in imagining that a volume, consisting only of scraps of verse, was likely to meet the public taste; but still more disastrous was their mistake, when they supposed that such verses as they have produced, would be read by any body above the rank of a gypsy" (anonymous, *Monthly Review* [January 1827]: 112). Mediocre submissions penned by versifiers became a common complaint among reviewers and detractors of the literary annual. Many critics claimed that anyone could be published in the annual—a point that Alaric Watts vociferously denied—and, eventually, that the literati were prostituting their writing for profit. The annuals eventually became known as purveyors of society verse and no better than the daily gossip newspapers that published any social tidbit to sell papers.

Eventually, even well-known, established authors did not escape censure for their annual contributions. One critic addressed these authors specifically in a review of the 1828 *Bijou:* "The verses of Coleridge, C. Lamb, L.E.L., the Rev. J. Blanco, A. Cunningham, [and] Dr. Southey, do not exhibit a single line worth remembering. As to Barry Cornwall, his muse seems quite exhausted. She has arrived at the last stage of a decline, and we recommend him to have an inquest held upon her, as we suspect that she is really dead. . . . [¶] In conclusion, we should say of The Bijou, that although it contains a few real jewels, they are for the most part badly set" (anonymous, *Monthly Review* [December 1827]: 526, 530). In another review of the 1828 *Amulet,* the critic offered a generally positive review but pointed out that S. T. Coleridge's contribution, "Conversational Dialogues," was strangled by its own language: "[W]e would suggest to the distinguished author, the expediency of conveying his thoughts in a language that may be universally and easily understood. [¶] . . . [H]e must render them a little more accessible to people of common sense" (anonymous, *Monthly*

Review [November 1827]: 355–56). James Hogg, the "Ettrick Shepherd," also suffered a rebuke for the complexity of his poetic language in the 1828 *Forget Me Not:* "[I]t shews that our pastoral swain has already lost much of the characteristic simplicity of his reed" (anonymous, *Monthly Review* [November 1827]: 408).

Critics attributed the demise of poetic standards in the literary annuals to the habit of printing authors' names with their contributions, a practice that was foreign to the periodicals, journals, and magazines of the early nineteenth century. Before 1826, authors' names appearing on the content pages were masculine, only initials, or completely absent. With the introduction of the 1826 literary annuals, authors' names appeared more frequently beside their contributions—a practice that allowed consumers to purchase annuals based on a name.[20] Single-author volumes of poetry and various other publications made authors into national treasures and icons of public fame. Authors were becoming commodified names; Felicia Hemans, for example, benefited tremendously from her name and was able to sell works based on that alone. However, critics warned against relying on this commodification of names and the search for continued fame. A critic reviewing the 1827 *Literary Souvenir* chided Alaric Watts for allowing anonymity to disappear and literati to assume that fame was a constant:

> Indeed, the custom of affixing real signatures to writings intended for works of this description . . . has become a public nuisance. The weak ambition of having their names emblazoned in a handsome volume, which is likely to be seen and read by every young lady in the country, has not only reached the matured and acknowledged bards, but has moreover generated a dandy race of poetasters, who leave no means of solicitation untried, in order to get their gilt gingerbread sonnets placed side by side with those of Southey or Campbell. And the latter, as if to augment the evil, whenever they condescend to write for a compilation of this kind, appear really to exert all their industry in reducing their offerings to the lowest degree of insipidity. . . . Mr. Watts should issue his proclamation, stating that in future he would permit no signatures to the compositions of which his work may consist. . . . [Watts] will teach the magnates of Parnassus, that celebrity, in order to be preserved, must still be suitably courted. (anonymous, *Monthly Review* [December 1826]: 390–91)

Frederic Mansel Reynolds, editor of *The Keepsake,* proffered authorial anonymity as a game in his first volume:

> It cannot fail to be observed, as a feature peculiar to the Keepsake, that the articles are published anonymously. This course was adopted, partly from a regard to the wishes of individuals, which prevented the divulgence of names in some instances, and partly from an inclination to risk the several articles on their own merits, unaided by the previous reputation of the writers. Whether this deviation from custom will meet [with] approval remains to be known; though literary idlers will probably find amusement in tracing the hand of particular authors in their respective contributions. (1828 preface, vii)

One of four scenarios caused Reynolds to suppress the authors' names: authors did not want to rely on their previous reputations (good or bad); they were experimenting in a new form or style; they were new authors and thus did not have a reputation or a marketable name; or Reynolds wanted to associate a high literary quality with *The Keepsake* instead of popular authors' identities. Whichever the reasons, Reynolds returned the next year with a volume full of marketable literary names and a declaration that eleven thousand guineas had been spent on producing the volume, most of which had been paid to contributors. Authors' names were then listed in the table of contents, and again separately in a list of contributors,[21] some only thinly veiled, including the "Author of Frankenstein."

Editor Alaric Watts accounted for authors' anonymity in the preface to the 1827 *Literary Souvenir* as an attempt to protect them: "[S]everal contributors to the present volume would, but for my solicitation, have been induced to withhold from me the countenance of their names, in order to escape numerous applications of the same kind" (xiv). With this comment, Watts supposedly shielded his authors from annoying requests by other editors, and there were many. But, really, he was protecting his investment; authors would have readily sold their writing to other editors if asked. In addition, many writers of different genders and various levels of ability used publication in literary annuals as a way to validate their "talent." Proximity to well-known literary names also provided a sense of accomplishment.

Because reviews were initially important to the annual industry, they were not always left to objective critics. As much as many reviewers believed in their duty to judge for the benefit of the audience, the critical periodicals were not always a source of unbiased opinion. The reviewers' comments were sometimes based on friendships and literary alignments, as was typical of the time. In a February 1830 review of Letitia Landon's and Robert Montgomery's poetry volumes,[22] the *Monthly Review* critic exposed the manipulation of public response:

> Besides, such is the amazing activity of the press, and so numerous its demands for literary assistance, that there is scarcely any one who can write a book, who does not also contribute, in verse or prose, to the literary journals. It is the general interest of these *collaborateurs* to assist each other, and they do so to an extent, of which the uninitiated have no conception. . . . *They pass over, as an antiquated notion, the sacred regard which a true critic will always pay to the dignity and purity of his country's literature.* . . . Many of them are, in truth, the mere workmen of the booksellers, who write, as they are paid, by the volume; and who are ready either to get up a review, or a romance, at a moment's notice, and exactly in the tone which their employer prescribes. (anonymous, 160–61; emphasis added)

This critic lamented that reviewers were no longer the protectorates of the public against bad literature and shirked their duty to "expose folly and taste." Instead these new reviewers had become subjects of money, beholden to publishers and mesmerized by the commodification of the written word.

Prior to 1831, though, relationships among the literary workers were forced by the relatively small field in London during the early nineteenth century. For example, Thomas Hood, the popular comic author and editor of the literary annuals *The Gem* and *Comic Annual,* began his writing career as a subeditor for *London Magazine* during the early 1820s. During this time, he became close companions with authors, editors, and publishers, including Charles Lamb, Letitia Landon, John Hamilton Reynolds (who would become a longtime correspondent), Edward Moxon (publisher and editor), John Clare, James Hogg, Alaric Watts (editor of the popular *Literary Souvenir*), Robert Browning, Charles Dickens, and William Thackeray. Men were not the exclusive players; many women were part of the literary circles and were considered colleagues. In addition, these women did not write in a vacuum: Joanna Baillie, for example, admired Felicia Hemans's work, as did Maria Jane Jewsbury, William Wordsworth (whom Hemans visited at Dove Cottage), and Blackwood, the venerable publisher. Alaric Watts was a big fan of Jewsbury's work and sought her friendship. Letitia Landon was an early colleague of Thomas Hood's prior to the creation of the *Comic Annual* in 1830.

Most of these authors and other editors of literary annuals acted as editors of periodical magazines during their careers and were familiar with the publishers, styles, contributors, and industry of the review magazines: Frederic Shoberl, the *Forget Me Not* editor, edited the *New Monthly Magazine* in February 1814 (*Wellesley* 3:169); Alaric Watts also edited the *New Monthly Magazine* from January 1819 through May/June 1819 (*Wellesley* 3:169); Joseph Blanco White, a frequent Spanish contributor to the annuals, edited the *London Review* in 1829 (*Wellesley* 2:525); and Letitia Landon and Mary Russell Mitford both contributed many anonymous reviews to several periodicals. Thackeray, Dickens, and other Victorians were intimately familiar with these publications as well as the above-mentioned authors. In fact, Dickens and Thackeray honored Hood at the end of his life with an invitation to a literary men's dinner.

With the insularity of literary circles and journalistic work experience, it was inevitable that these writers would review each others' works and provide favorable comments—a practice made more sinister by publishers who "inspired" favorable reviews of their own books in their periodicals. "Puffery" or "trade criticism," as it was labeled, was also used to promote "authors and editors by inserting paid or 'stimulated' social gossip about them in the newspapers," as noted by Leslie Marchand in *The Letters of Thomas Hood* (83n5).[23] Both books and authors gained exposure through the press regardless of whether this exposure took the form of gossip, criticism, or benign excerpts. Often, publishers advertised their books in the *London Times* along with an excerpt from a favorable review, essentially an advertisement disguised as an article, and, as a *Monthly Review* critic pointed out in the February 1830 edition, "without adverting to the material fact that it was emphatically marked in that newspaper as the production of 'a correspondent,' a precaution which is generally used when the editor [of the newspaper] has a wish to oblige, but no desire to be held out to the world as responsible for the truth or justness of the article so inserted" (anonymous,

166). In all of these scenarios, the logic behind this publicity was to inspire curiosity about the author or his/her work and, hence, book sales.

The editors of the annuals were not beyond this practice. Thomas Hood, a critic of puffery, resigned his two-year post as editor of the *New Monthly Magazine* in 1843 (Wellesley 3:170) in protest of publisher Henry Colburn's blatant puffed gossip and literary reviews. Hood's public condemnation of the *New Monthly*'s publisher was a bold move, considering his desperate financial need and his own practice of puffery in the 1820s and 1830s. In an 1835 letter, Hood gratefully acknowledged the benefits of his friendship with C. W. Dilke, editor of the *Atheneum:* "I have said nothing yet of the Athm [*Atheneum*] or its notice [of the 1836 *Comic Annual* reviewed in the December 12 and December 19, 1835, issues]. The paper is a great treat to me. . . . Wright says the reviews of the Comic [Annual] are by [John Hamilton Reynolds]. I own I cannot detect his hand. . . . I could not have been better pleased had I *reviewed myself*" (*Letters* [Marchand], 56). This review revealed contents rather than critiquing them; the periodical followed a popular practice of providing "extract to opinion" (Clubbe, *Victorian,* 42) and thus uncovered or previewed the annual's contents for its readers. Alternatively, periodicals like the *Atheneum* (at a cost of two to four shillings, in comparison to the twelve-shilling annual) provided an economical view of the annuals for those who could not afford them (or were not given any), allowing these voyeurs to glimpse a lifestyle that afforded such disposable income and affectionate gifts.

Despite his later moral standards, Hood engaged in a mutual patronage to publicize and sell his books. He first appeared in the literary marketplace as a journalist and eventually published his Keatsian-style poetry to limited acclaim and even smaller positive critiques. In 1826, Hood successfully introduced himself to the reading public with *Whims and Oddities,* a collection of his magazine pieces.[24] Because sales of single-author volumes of poetry and prose were on the decline during the 1820s, Hood requested help from one of his literary friends—dancing around the practice of puffery. In an 1827 letter to Alaric Watts (editor of the popular annual *Literary Souvenir*), Hood wrote,

> I shall quote the Souvenir as you wish,—& moreover will write something (good I hope) certainly, for your next volume. . . .
>
> I have made an arrangement for the next Series of Whims & Oddities,—& Longmans are to bring out my Serious Poems. You

> shall have one of the first sets of sheets I can get. I expect it will be out in about a month—& any notice you can get for it will oblige me. Poetry I suspect is nowadays suspended animation & will require artificial inflation alias puffing. I do not mean this of your critiques. (*Letters* [Morgan], 80)

Hood carefully requested only a "notice" or a mention, without specifically soliciting a favorable review. Generally, a mention or an excerpted piece in any critical periodical served as publicity that could be used to entice consumers: "It has . . . furnished to Mrs. Hofland an opportunity of framing a light, interesting little tale; and as we owe that lady a mark of our attention, for the frequency with which she has administered to our instruction as well as our amusement, we shall extract the whole of this fragment" (anonymous, *Monthly Review* [November 1827]: 403). The author was rewarded with having her entire piece publicized for two shillings (the cost of the *Monthly Review*) as opposed to the twelve shillings for the entire *Forget Me Not.*

Like this one, many reviews excerpted materials from the annuals without rendering an opinion on the individual pieces (for example, *The Mirror of Literature, Amusement and Instruction* supplied extensive excerpts, including engravings, with very little else). Others reserved space for excerpts in return for professional favors. In a December 1826 review of the 1827 *Literary Souvenir,* the writer, nearing the end of the review, apologized to his audience: "Miss Benger's sketch of Elizabeth Woodville possesses a good deal of merit. . . . We should certainly have made room for some part of it, had we not been pledged by a prior engagement to 'The Grey Hair.' The stanzas are written by Mr. Watts" (395). In Hood's letter to Watts, the mutual patronage is explicit: to allow readers a preview of the *Literary Souvenir*'s contents in exchange for publicizing *Whims and Oddities.*[25] Hood and Watts had a genuine respect for each other's work. But driven by a need for income, authors and reviewers promised to influence the popularity and sales of the respective volumes through their journalistic connections—a sure sign of puffery or at least trade criticism.

Though the critical press began, in a sense, shaming the public for patronizing the genre, the annual's success continued unabated for much of the 1830s: "We have here a display of genuine taste,—an elegant compendium of our passing literary novelties, which no gentleman need be ashamed to place in the hands of a lady on a new year's day" (anonymous review, *New*

Monthly Magazine, quoted in 1826 *Literary Souvenir* advertisements). This review touches on the shame already encroaching on the literary annual phenomenon by 1825 but perpetuates the gift exchange inherent to the genre and the gendered relationship between benefactor and recipient, that is, a man offers elegance and propriety to a woman, who relies on his benevolence to instruct her. By 1832, consumers of annuals had choices, not simply in the look and tone of a volume but also in its designation within the genre (comedic, juvenile, religious). The genre's market and its original purpose had become diluted with all of these subgenres. In light of this competition, all editors constantly advertised, like Hood's begging mongrel, for their respective literary annual volumes. Surprisingly, one of the genre's early "fathers" became a source of this dilution, turning his protectorate role into a defense of himself and his editorial decisions.

Alaric Watts had initially envisioned his *Literary Souvenir* as an improvement on the genre's form and entered the relatively young market of annuals in November 1824 with only eight other titles competing for consumers in the 1825 season. Though Watts's alterations positively influenced the contents of literary annuals and the publication format, he was still bound by Ackermann's original intent: to please the intended recipient, women, with polite literature. Watts had been a vociferous proponent of his *Literary Souvenir* by professing its success in his prefaces. However, by the late 1820s, he had begun to use his prefaces and, later, his contributions to defend his publication as well as attack those who criticized or denigrated him or *The Literary Souvenir.* With debt constantly staining his name and the previous crisis with his publishing firm, Watts turned to the 1832 *Literary Souvenir* for an outlet against his supposed enemies. In "The Conversazione," a poem he composed for the 1832 *Literary Souvenir,* Watts ridicules and satirizes several literary figures. The 545-line poem covers thirty pages, an exceedingly long text for a literary annual, and contains twenty-eight footnotes. In general, these footnotes are not merely informational but publicize Watts's disputes with various people, his admiration for others, and his outright enmity for the practices of still others (mostly periodicals publishers and reviewers). While some of his venom is well aimed, the medium is perhaps inappropriate, according to one reviewer:

> As a poem it is a most miserable affair. As a satire it betrays more of bad temper and malignant feeling. . . . [W]e ask whether a work

> like the Literary Souvenir, intended for the drawing-room, very frequently within our own experience presented as a Christmas gift to youth of both sexes, and hitherto looked upon as a collection of amusing, light, and inoffensive articles, should be made the channel for such a scurrilous composition as this "Conversazione?" . . .
>
> *Poetry* like this is certainly not of the description, which we should wish to see in the hands of any young person, and we hope that the specimen, which we have given, will induce many persons to deliberate, whether they ought to admit the volume that contains it within their family circle. (anonymous, *Monthly Review* [December 1831]: 524, 525)

Watts's literary miscellany was originally intended to give readers a selection of polite material that delicately instructs. This critic reminded Watts of that standard and attempted to shield potential consumers from the *Literary Souvenir*'s straying poem. As was his practice by 1832, Watts responded to criticism of "The Conversazione" in his 1832 preface with only a vague reference to the satirical poem and its detractors. He emphasized that the literary annual was an appropriate venue in which to publish a "satirical squib," which was not intellectually or morally unsuitable for the general reader (viii). With this push outside the boundaries of polite literature, Watts asked his readers to grow with the *Literary Souvenir*'s evolution instead of resisting it despite the fact that the poem really is a diatribe in which he constantly quibbles over literary aesthetics. After all, *The Comic Annual,* a highly satirical and sometimes bawdy literary annual, was well into successful publication, along with several other satirical annual titles. Consumers did not seem to mind the public poetic quarrels—a quality that most likely improved sales.

The public was already inundated with newspapers that offered gossip and social misconduct as fodder for sales. In offering a rebuke to Watts, the reviewer warned him against becoming like the "Sunday papers of this metropolis," which were filled with "lies which they unblushingly invent and give to the world, concerning the proceedings and motives of public men. . . . [T]hey wantonly inflict upon sensitive minds, wounds of the most painful nature. They are no better than prostitutes, for they carry on an open trade in vice, the odious vice of scandal, for the base purposes of lucre. . . . [Watts] has shewn, in his 'Conversazione,' talents which would well fit him for that disgraceful employment" (anonymous, *Monthly Review* [December 1831]: 525–26). If Watts's poem pointed the literary annual toward an alteration in format that was immorally opportunistic, consumers would then become the knowing recipients of vice—and would most likely guzzle it gleefully, even those middle-class consumers to which the literary annual was inevitably aimed.

With this review, the critic was a herald to, rather than a protector of, the public's literary taste. Instead of speaking of the public as children in need of literary protection, this reviewer warned consumers that they were ultimately responsible for the types of publications offered because of their patronization: "Now then, we ask, can the patrons of such newspapers hold themselves free from responsibility, for the circulation of the vile falsehoods and infamous satires which those journals publish to the world from week to week? There is no sound moralist who will not agree with us in the opinion, that every person who buys one of these papers, or contributes in any way to support them by money or by approbation, participates in the guilt of the abandoned men who conduct them" (anonymous, *Monthly Review* [December 1831]: 526). Despite the reviewer's condemnations, consumers as described in this article are empowered with a responsibility to judge reading materials by a moral standard—a stance that most reviewers do not take. Perhaps this critic realized that the public did not need protection or that the reviews were not responsible for the consumer success and popularity of literary materials. Alternatively, this writer might have used his review as a soapbox for his views on the immorality of current publications—similar to many annual editors and their prefaces. The annuals did not become the sensationalized print that flooded the newsstands but had to be adapted in order to swim in the flood waters, hence the inclusion of poems that were not so neutral.

The shaming and abuse of literary annuals, evident in critical periodicals, was highlighted by those within the literary industry. Eventually, the unique commodification of gift exchange altered the annuals' format, sales, and reception. And inevitably, the unique set of readers, not the press, were the ones who influenced the long popularity of the genre.

SEVEN

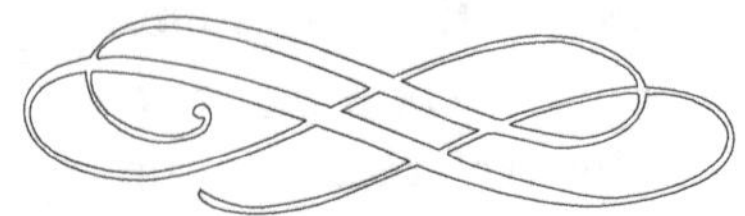

Feminizing the Textual Body

Women and Their Literary Annuals in Nineteenth-Century Britain

IN *WRITING WOMEN'S LITERARY HISTORY,* MARGARET EZELL challenges scholars to investigate and create a women's literary history beyond the eighteenth and nineteenth centuries. According to Ezell, most British literary history focuses on the long nineteenth century and its prolific pool of women authors. Women experienced the professional world of writing in all time periods, but not until the nineteenth century did they become part of the dominant pool of authors, editors, and publishers in the print world. Also during the nineteenth century, England saw a huge rise in the production of printed materials—a 400 percent increase from the eighteenth century—caused by various technological advances, including mechanized papermaking, typesetting with plate impressions, and, later, stereotyping. Though Ezell's call to action came ten years ago, we are still sorting through the nineteenth century's print media and discovering, or rediscovering, various categories of women's authorship, production, and reception.

Prior chapters deal with excavating the form from underneath piles of other media formats. Here, I show that readers and consumers of the annuals privileged its feminine aspects—not those promoted as such by patriarchal annual producers, but those aspects of these texts best suited to female writers and readers. The literary annual in its textual production is best seen as a female body, its male producers struggling to make it both proper and sexually alluring, its female authors and readers attempting to render it their own feminine ideal.

"FEMININE" TRADITIONS IN IDEOLOGY AND READING

Gauging reading practices has always been a difficult task, unless readers' notes or a reading journal are uncovered. However, with the annuals, the actual reader is even more difficult to assess because of the valuable nature of the annual—no markings would have been committed on the annual's pages except in the appropriately invited blank space, that is, an inscription page or early album pages. Yet so much was written during the time about women readers that we have a good sense of what editors felt they needed to do to market their wares. Kate Flint argues that the "woman" reader continued to be a problematic category even during the nineteenth century:

> From one point of view, reading was a form of consumption associated with the possession of leisure time, and thus contributed to the ideology, if not always the practices, which supported the ideal of the middle-class home. Yet it could also be regarded as dangerously useless, a thief of time which might be spent on housewifely duties. Although a means of extending one's knowledge and experience beyond the bounds of one's personal lot—hence, perhaps, becoming a fitter marital companion in the process—reading was often, none the less, unavoidably associated with woman's "inappropriate" educational ambition. (11)

To pose annuals as a cure rather than a disease, the initial editors and publishers of the annuals often competed to present the most beatific representation of family, woman, and the domestic in their annuals.

To escape censure for encouraging women to read, regardless of the status of the material, the editors had to provide guidelines for proper reading in their prefaces. They also dropped names, not only acknowledging the artists but also impressing upon the reader the importance of the volume's selections, especially considering that the competition for consumers was fierce within the first four years of the annual's appearance. In *Paratexts,* Gerard Genette points out that a preface, composed after the compilation of the entire work, is written to "ensure that the text is read properly" (197). The editorial preface emphasizes control of the reading experience by guiding the reader through the labor, importance, and purpose of that particular volume. In the first few sentences, editors generally expressed some sort of metaphor about the volume, whether a debutante (indicating a bourgeois class of leisure readers [as in Frederic Reynolds's preface to the 1828 *Keepsake*]), a card game (establishing jovial and somewhat illicit community [again, as in the 1828 *Keepsake* preface]), or a banquet (with images of consumption and overindulgence [as in Frederic Shoberl's preface to the 1830 *Forget Me Not*])—all "directing attention to the merits" (Shoberl, preface to 1828 *Forget Me Not*) of the works in each completed volume. The editors used these metaphors to "get the book read" and "to get the book read properly" (Genette, 197).

In addition, an editor guaranteed in his preface that his volume would provide not only unbiased direction for both reading and moral guidance but also a sustained presence in the reader's life. The presence was intellectual in the constantly recurring theme of moral guidance, and also physical: the book would sit conspicuously on personal library shelves or drawing room tables. In essence, the editor guaranteed that his volume would not prove ephemeral or transitory, like so many other fashionable pastimes. The preface assumed editorial control of reading practices at the same time that the volume established stability, a purpose partially borrowed from the conduct manuals.

Ackermann's *Forget Me Not* was originally intended as an example of propriety and beauty, clothed in the garb of a moral instructor. With this 1834 volume, Shoberl maintained that instruction in a format that resonated with the didactic form of an eighteenth-century conduct manual. For instance, one conduct manual from 1778 encouraged women "to conceal any blemishes and set off [their] beauties" using dress, dancing, music, and drawing (Gregory's *Father's Legacy to His Daughter*). However, the annuals lacked that self-conscious scolding inherent to the conduct manuals. By the 1820s, young women had already been exposed to Mary Wollstonecraft's cry for the education of women with the 1792 publication of *A Vindication of the Rights of Woman,* which blames the cult of female manners for oppressing women's intellectual capabilities. Wollstonecraft's early treatise was well-founded, as noted by Anne Renier: "[Because of the] rising standard of living, particularly among the middle classes prospering from the great industrial and commercial advances of these years, daughters were being given [an] education of sorts . . . to attract suitors. . . . The young lady was taught to play the piano or the harp, [but] her more serious studies went little further than a smattering of literature, a modicum of history and geography . . . and the rudiments of a foreign language" (16–17). Wollstonecraft indicted the cultural practice of young girls' partial education in *A Vindication of the Rights of Woman* at a time when women were publishing their words but not quite with the economic success of men. Wollstonecraft pointed out that men wrote the conduct books for women and girls and that male dictatorial authorship of female conduct created a totally unrealistic ideal of femininity: "One cause of this barren blooming I attribute to a false system of education, gathered from the books written on this subject by men who, considering females rather as women than human creatures, have been more anxious to make them alluring mistresses than affectionate wives and rational mothers" (112).

Conduct manuals, ranging as far back as the seventeenth century, focused on making "young women desirable to men of a good social position" and "represented a specific configuration of sexual features as those of the only appropriate woman for men at levels of society to want as a wife" (59), as Nancy Armstrong points out in *Desire and Domestic Fiction*. Their titles proselytized for this restraint, promising an education in "female" manners:

Lectures of Female Education and Manners (John Burton, 1793)
The Excellent Female (Amos Chase, 1791)
Letters on the Improvement of the Mind (Hester Chapone, 1802)
Letters on the Intellectual and Moral Character of Women (William Duff, 1807)
Self-Control (Mary Brunton, 1811)
A Father's Legacy to His Daughters (John Gregory, 1778)

Armstrong also suggests that conduct manuals, squarely opposed to the leisure of novel reading, focused on producing a woman who was educated only enough to perform her duties: "This writing assumed that an education ideally made a woman desire to be what a prosperous man desires, which is above all else a female. She therefore had to lack the competitive desires and worldly ambitions that consequently belonged—as if by some natural principle—to the male. For such a man, her desirability hinged upon an education in frugal domestic practices. She was supposed to complement his role as an earner and producer with hers as a wise spender and tasteful consumer" (59). Instead of coordinating servants, meals, and children, women of all ages would be encouraged to linger in bed or the dressing room to read a novel—or so that image was presented to the public by the conduct manuals.

Contrary to standard conduct manuals, in her introduction to the *Female Reader,* Wollstonecraft urged her woman reader to improve "of her mind and heart" as "the business of her whole life" and then presented a compilation of short stories (52). Wollstonecraft donned a masculine pseudonym, Mr. Creswick, for this publication, certain that advice from a woman author would not be considered authoritative for moral instruction of her own sex. Armstrong points out that conduct books were meant to reinforce "domestic ideology and [articulate] a specific understanding of the relationship between reading, sexuality, and social control" (quoted in Pearson, *Women's Reading,* 46). These manuals are teaching tools to enact an idealized femininity and do not offer a leisure-reading experience.

John Gregory's *Legacy* manual was written in the guise of a dying father who wants to bequeath the only thing that his daughters could inherit—advice on love, friendship, money, intellect, and fashion, among other things. Women were bound by coverture, laws that prohibited married women from owning property, voting, and earning money. A wife existed only as an extension of her husband. Marriage then became a game of flirtation and bargaining. Gregory's conduct manual was more lamentable because the girls would apparently be without their mother (because she was dead—a popular, if not disturbing, rhetorical device). He felt that his specter would live in his published words. According to Jacqueline Pearson, Gregory's manual finds that marriage is necessary to control femininity: "femininity is 'natural' and innate, yet a constant struggle is needed to maintain it" (*Women's Reading,* 47). Offering to haunt his daughters' lives ever after, Gregory's soon-to-be-deceased self gives some of the following advice:

Modesty:

> 1. One of the chief beauties in a female character is that modest reserve, that retiring delicacy, which avoids the public eye, and is disconcerted even at the gaze of admiration.—I do not wish you to be insensible to applause. If you

were, you must become, if not worse, at least less amiable women. But you may be dazzled by that admiration, which yet rejoices your hearts.

2. Converse with men even of the first rank with that dignified modesty, which may prevent the approach of the most distant familiarity, and consequently prevent them from feeling themselves your superiors. (24 & 25)

Beauty:

1. When a girl ceases to blush, she has lost the most powerful charm of beauty. That extreme sensibility which it indicates, may be a weakness and incumbrance in our sex, as I have too often felt; but in yours it is peculiarly engaging. Pedants, who think themselves philosophers, ask why a woman should blush when she is conscious of no crime. It is a sufficient answer, that Nature has made you to blush when you are guilty of no fault, and has forced us to love you because you do so.—Blushing is so far from being necessarily an attendant on guilt, that it is the usual companion of innocence. (26–27)

2. Dress is an important article in female life. The love of dress is natural to you, and therefore it is proper and reasonable. Good sense will regulate your expence in it, and good taste will direct you to dress in such a way as to conceal any blemishes, and set off your beauties, if you have any, to the greatest advantage. But much delicacy and judgment are required in the application of this rule. *A fine woman shews her charms to most advantage, when she seems most to conceal them. The finest bosom in nature is not so fine as what imagination forms.* The most perfect elegance of dress appears always the most easy, and the least studied. (55–56, emphasis added)

Propriety:

1. Wit is the most dangerous talent you can possess. It must be guarded with great discretion and good-nature, otherwise it will create you many enemies. Wit is perfectly consistent with softness and delicacy; yet they are seldom found

united. Wit is so flattering to vanity, that they who possess it become intoxicated, and lose all self-command. (29–30)

2. Humour is a different quality. It will make your company much solicited; but be cautious how you indulge it.—It is often a great enemy to delicacy, and a still greater one to dignity of character. It may sometimes gain you applause, but will never procure you respect. (31)

3. The intention of your being taught needle-work, knitting, and such like, is not on account of the intrinsic value of all you can do with your hands, which is trifling, but to enable you to judge more perfectly of that kind of work, and to direct the execution of it in others. *Another principal end is to enable you to fill up, in a tolerably agreeable way, some of the many solitary hours you must necessarily pass at home.*—It is a great article in the happiness of life, to have your pleasures as independent of others as possible. *By continually gadding abroad in search of amusement, you lose the respect of all your acquaintances, whom you oppress with those visits, which, by a more discreet management, might have been courted.* (51–52, emphasis added)

Virtue:

1. Virgin purity is of that delicate nature, that it cannot hear certain things without contamination. It is always in your power to avoid these. (35)

All of these "recommendations" cite public performance and caution the young women against exercising too much of any attribute. Each "legacy" instructs the daughters on propriety, appearances, and "getting a man." Previous conduct manuals by various authors were incredibly popular through 1820, at which point they were replaced by several other media forms focused on women's behavior. This tradition of training young women in conduct instead of educating them continued well into the nineteenth century.

With the conduct manual as one of its guiding principles, the literary annual presents itself a fragmented physical and mental conflation of both masculine and feminine qualities: the feminine, the annual's appropriate coverings or proper dressing of what is represented as a female friend; and the masculine social control via marketing strategies that locate its content within male-generated codes of propriety and morality. The book is represented as a feminine body regulated by masculine intellect. The way that the conduct manual's content, male-dictated forms of propriety and morality, appears in literary annuals is best understood through Althusser's notion of "interpellation."[1] The preface of the 1834 *Forget Me Not,* as one example, hails readers into a world regulated by propriety, moral education, and beauty. This relationship creates a community between work and reader. The reader constructs meaning through her own truth values, and with this a multiple presence is scripted onto the work itself, becoming part of the textual condition in which the only immutable law is the law of change (McGann, *Textual Condition,* 3, 4, 16). The already extant ideology incorporated into the annual combines with the reader's beliefs, creating an archive of intersecting ideology and intimate subjectivity in the annual itself.

In the preface for the 1831 *Friendship's Offering,* Thomas Pringle suggested the suitability of his literary annual by declaring that it would permanently reside in the "repositories of family literature" and "may be rendered fit to impress the mind, and to assist in forming the taste, exercising the judgment, and improving the heart" (vi). In this offering, Pringle enticed the reader with promises of education, information, entertainment, and literary and moral value—all contained within the prose, poetry, and engravings of that year's volume. In addition, editors encouraged their readers to preserve each year's volume—a reassurance that the material stability of the volume paralleled its literary stability. In recent literary criticism, scholars note that because the annual was meant as a gift, it represents only a fleeting or ephemeral moment. In his dissertation, Matthew Kutcher argues that "gift books" (erroneously identifying the literary annual, as discussed in chapter 2) are "completely invested in their contemporary moment and . . . were not intended to live long" (18). Because annuals were made of sturdier materials than magazines and other periodicals, their textuality actually signals their longevity. The annual could become a moral reference year after year and could physically survive because of its constructed physical superiority.

Flint has argued that male cultural critics' use of the figure of the woman reader "shows how notions about reading fed off attempts to define women's mental capacities and tendencies through their physical attributes, and, in turn, appeared to contribute to the validation of these very definitions" (11). A savvy entrepreneur, *The Literary Souvenir* editor Alaric Watts marketed his annual as "polite literature," despite his publisher's belief that poetry was "beyond many of the purchasers of this description of book" (Jack, 174). Members of this audience—women, girls, and children—were expected to be uneducated, or at least unsophisticated, consumers. However, a majority of women readers themselves requested, read, and submitted poetry. Because so much poetry existed within the volumes, critics accused annual editors of flooding the market with what this audience wanted: sentimental and supposedly unsophisticated poetry.

This poetry, presented as appropriate material for the annual's audience, represents an idealized femininity, which I call "patriarchal femininity," and is predicated on defining woman and feminine as passive, uneducated, domestic, impotent, or simple. Because the annuals were leisure materials, reading an annual supposedly did not require "severe application." Pearson states that "[g]enres which emphasised 'imagination' were gendered as feminine, those requiring 'severe application' as masculine. In effect this means gendering novels, romances, and some lyric poems as feminine, while men read 'better books,' epic, satire, classical literature, history and science" (19). The annuals were filled with original poetry instead of the more authoritative and authentic classic literature. The genre typically included Romantic-era contemporaries instead of the long-gone and proven literature of the great authors. The few deceased literati included in an annual were typically P. B. Shelley and Byron, not Shakespeare, Milton, or Pope. Even Byron was not often cited, because of copyright laws and exorbitant fees.[2] The poetry submitted and published in annuals was classified as simple, unsophisticated, sentimental, and emotionally hysterical at times—supposedly resembling its readers.[3] Editors, then, were the gatekeepers of this patriarchal femininity, morality, and literary aesthetic in the annuals.

Knowing his audience, editor Thomas Hood upheld this moral code when he dis-included Charles Lamb's poem "The Gypsy's Malison" at the last minute from the 1829 *Gem* because "it would shock all mothers" (Lamb, *Letters,* 5:158):

The Gypsy's Malison

Suck, baby, suck, mother's love grows by giving,
    Drain the sweet founts that only thrive by wasting;
Black manhood comes, when riotous guilty living
    Hands thee the cup that shall be death in tasting.
Kiss, baby, kiss, mother's lips shine by kisses,
    Choke the warm breath that else would fall in blessings;
Black manhood comes, when turbulent guilty blisses
    Tend thee the kiss that poisons 'mid caressings.
Hang, baby, hang, mother's love loves such forces,
    Choke the fond neck that bends still to thy clinging;
Black manhood comes, when violent lawless courses
    Leave thee a spectacle in rude air swinging.
So sang a wither'd sibyl energetical,
And bann'd the ungiving door with lips prophetical.

(Lamb, *Letters,* 158–60)

The gypsy curses the uncharitable household without specifying who exactly rejected her begging requests for some sort of sustenance. As the speaker, the old woman almost barks her condemnation with the striking consonants that begin lines 1, 5, and 9: *suck, kiss, hang.* The repetition of "black manhood comes" (lines 3, 7, and 11) condemns the child to a guilty adulthood, with his mother's life encouraging his eventual destruction. Considering that Hood compiled and organized *The Gem* to mimic the already successful *Forget Me Not, Friendship's Offering,* and *The Keepsake* as dedications to femininity, this particular poem does not suit its purpose. For one, the maternal image is blackened by a suffocating mother, and the second image of a woman is a transient, evil beggar. Neither celebrates femininity, domesticity, or maternity. Nor do the images provide moral instructions, except perhaps to avoid opening the door to the extremely marginalized "other," the poor, dark woman.

Hood replaced Lamb's sonnet with prose, obligingly attributing it to Lamb's authorship in *The Gem*'s table of contents. The replacement is a seemingly sympathetic dedication to widows and a call to eradicate the accompanying stigma:

> Hath always been a mark for mockery:—a standing butt for wit to level at. Jest after jest hath been huddled upon her close cap, and stuck, like burrs, upon her weeds. Her sables are a perpetual "Black Joke."

Satirists—prose and verse—have made merry with her bereavements. She is a stock character on the stage. Farce bottleth up her crocodile tears, or labelleth her empty lachrymatories. Comedy mocketh her precocious flirtations—Tragedy even girdeth at her frailty, and twitteth her with "the funeral baked meats coldly furnishing forth the marriage tables."

I confess, when I called the other day on my kinswoman G.—then in the second week of her widowhood—and saw her sitting, her young boy by her side, in her recent sables, I felt unable to reconcile her estate with any risible associations. The Lady with a skeleton moiety—in the old print, in Bowles's old shop window—seemed but a type of her condition. Her husband,—a while hemisphere in love's world,—was deficient. *One complete side—her left—was death-stricken. It was a matrimonial paralysis,* unprovocative of laughter. I could as soon have tittered at one of those melancholy objects that drag their poor dead-alive bodies about our streets.

It seems difficult to account for the popular prejudice against lone women. There is a majority, I trust, of such honest, decorous mourners as my kinswoman: yet are Widows, like the Hebrew, a proverb and a byeword amongst nations. From the first putting on of the sooty garments, they become a stock joke—chimney-sweep or blackamoor is not surer—by mere virtue of their nigritude.

Are the wanton amatory glances of a few pairs of graceless eyes, twinkling through their cunning waters, to reflect so evil a light on a whole community? Verily the sad benighted orbs of that noble relict—the Lady Rachel Russell—blinded through unserene drops for her dead Lord,—might atone for all such oglings!

Are the traditional freaks of a Dame of Ephesus, or a Wife of Bath, or a Queen of Denmark, to cast so broad a shadow over a whole sisterhood? There must be, methinks, some more general infirmity—common, probably, to all Eve-kind—to justify so sweeping a stigma.

Does the satiric spirit, perhaps, institute splenetic comparisons between the lofty poetical pretensions of posthumous tenderness and their fulfilment? The sentiments of Love, especially affect a high heroical pitch, of which the human performance can present, at best, but a burlesque parody. *A Widow, that hath lived only for her husband, should die with him. She is flesh of his flesh, and bone of his bone;* and

> it is not seemly for a mere rib to be his survivor. The prose of her practice accords not with the poetry of her professions. She hath done with the world,—and you meet her in Regent Street. Earth hath now nothing left for her—but she swears and administers. She cannot survive him—and invests in the Long Annuities.
>
> The romantic fancy resents, and the satiric spirit records, these discrepancies. By the conjugal theory itself there ought to be no Widows; and, accordingly, a class, that by our milder manners is merely ridiculed, on the ruder banks of the Ganges is literally roasted. (Hood, "The Widow," emphasis added)

Invoking the suttee, or sati, the practice of burning a Hindu wife alive with her husband's body, Hood suggests that wives lose or forfeit their identities when husbands die—or at least half of their physical selves. This limited view precludes a woman's individuality and life outside the home. The widow becomes vulnerable without her guiding masculine figure. Hood's commentary rests more upon the emotional state of widows than the social condition of a woman's role as a widow. However, his deliverance of "widow" from social mockery and dangerous amorous advances reflects a masculine attempt to rescue a fragile, vulnerable woman. He pleads to his audience for recognition. Though the piece seems geared toward altering the public's view of widowhood, in reality, it is addressed to the coterie of women readers and endeavors to provide an emotional solidarity and understanding of a woman's hardship. Hood's "The Widow" is definitely not a cry for autonomy on the widow's behalf.

Upon hearing of the rejection, Lamb wrote, "I am born out of time. I have no conjecture about what the present world calls delicacy. . . . I have lived to grow into an indecent character. When my sonnet was rejected, I exclaimed, 'Damn the age; I will write for antiquity!'" (*Letters,* 5:156). For Lamb, his poem represents a common motif of warning and charity. He plays upon the trope of the disenfranchised fortune-teller who is both helpful and dangerous in her freedom. Even more than the pastoral cottage dweller, the gypsy represents Nature because she must live directly from the land and others' contributions. Hood's replacement contribution is much more mild. Instead of questioning motherhood, the primary role for women within an idealized patriarchy, he offers a celebration of sorts of woman's martyrdom while keeping her within the confines of patriarchal definitions.

Editor Frederic Shoberl, however, welcomed Richard Polwhele's contribution "To a Young Lady Playing at Chess" for the 1834 *Forget Me Not.* Polwhele, a well-known poet by that time, offered a well-constructed, brief poem that hints at the author's 1798 diatribe, *The Unsex'd Females,* against Mary Wollstonecraft. Polwhele's *Forget Me Not* poem is obviously meant to equate the strategies of an intellectual game with the strategies of becoming the proper married woman. In the title, the young lady does not even engage in chess but plays "at" it, as if it were a child's game. The final stanza declares,

And now, in stale-mate or in scholars,
Whether you play for love or dollars,
    The game may terminate:
And, though your labour thus you lose,
You get your head from out the noose:
    But marriage is—*check-mate!*

(326)

This last stanza punctuates the game of marriage, which rescues the young lady.

In the poem, Polwhele's lady completes the game, with some ambiguous entity declaring checkmate, rescuing the woman from her current state as if she were a helpless victim: whether a victim of her own femininity or the game itself is unclear. However, the young lady is not clearly the winner here: the act of marriage terminates the young lady's intellectual pursuit. This femininity presented by Polwhele attempts to harness and finalize the social role of women. His female player only mimics being intellectual, never quite achieving it. In this scenario, Polwhele presents a fantasy of social control and mimics Lamb's critique of women's "unmasculine" intellect, or their complete lack thereof.

But not all critiques of femininity were as pejorative and protective: Felicia Hemans consistently contributed poetry to the annuals that challenged this patriarchal femininity. In the 1825 *Literary Souvenir,* Hemans delivers a poetic representation of a mother's dedication to her child in "The Mother and Child":

Where art thou, Boy?—Heaven, heaven! the babe is playing
    Even on the margin of the dizzy steep!
Haste—hush! a breath, my agony betraying,

And he is gone!—beneath him rolls the deep!
Could I but keep the bursting cry suppress'd,
And win him back in silence to my breast!

Thou 'rt safe!—Thou com'st, with smiles my fond arms meeting
Blest, fearless child!—I, *I* have tasted death!
Nearer! that I may *feel* thy warm heart beating!
And see thy bright hair floating in my breath!
Nearer! to still my bosom's yearning pain,—
I clasp thee now, mine own! Thou 'rt here again!

Figure 7.1 "Mother and Child" engraving, 1825 *Literary Souvenir*, painted by W. Brockedon and engraved by W. Humphrys (from the Katherine D. Harris Collection)

Inspired by an engraving, "The Mother and Child" (fig. 7.1) (as was the tradition with annuals), Hemans constructs a maternal ideal: The mother agonizes over her child's imminent death, but at the same time the language celebrates her maternal power, as is evidenced by the child's trust and innocence. In seeing her child playing near the cliff, the mother experiences death before the child can even sense any danger. Even when the child is safe back in her arms, the mother still feels a sense of loss, a "yearning pain" for the potential outcome. In the engraving, we see the mother's left breast exposed to the child, and also to readers as the voyeurs. The mother's face is partially hidden in the shadows of the darkened sky, drawing attention to her highlighted breast. The breast is not sexualized but is instead an enticement to the young, cherubic child. In fact, though the wind seems to propel all of the mother's clothing away from her body and toward safety, her left hand seems to be purposefully revealing her left breast instead of struggling to cover it against the wind's force. The mother understands that her breast holds more power than the outstretched arm. The boy's gaze and hand do not match the level of hers but are pointed toward her breast, his source of nurturing, comfort, and sustenance. The image invites the child, as well as the viewer, back into safety. The light falls onto the woman's chest and lurches through her arm to point the viewer to the light-encircled child. This use of light links the child and the breast in an unbroken moment of desire: desire for the breast by the child and desire to rescue by the mother.

With Hemans's poem, and more specifically in the accompanying engraving, the reader identifies with the child's persona because of the overwhelming projection of maternity, rescue, and safety. The waters below, always a baptismal trope, and the liminal space represented by the dangerous cliff are rejected as the mother entices child and reader into her arms and to her breast. In addition, the gaze of the reader is captured through the representative breast instead of being engaged through the mother's direct gaze.

The highlighted breast is merely a fragment of the female body. The reader, as voyeur, gazes on this fragmented female body that offers salvation. The scene asks the reader to identify not with this body but with the mother's frantic intellectual position, to join her in her attempt to control emotion and rational thought to resolve the dilemma. The reader experiences this intellectual problem with the mother, who must determine the best way to save the child instead of resorting to a typical hysteria.[4] Hemans's mother exhibits strength, reason, and duty in an alternative rendering of the feminine. The literary annual, too, entices the reader with representations of women's bodies despite not being sexualized and draws her (the reader) into its salvation. The question is, then, a salvation from what? Patriarchy, by providing an image of an autonomous woman? Femininity, by saving women from themselves?

The poetic moments by Polwhele and Hemans offer varying degrees of conduct to each annual's readers. While Polwhele's poem declares marriage triumphant and the woman defeated, Hemans's poem enacts an urgency in maternal instinct and autonomy. With her poem, the speaker, identified only as a mother, lacks the demarcating role of wife. No mention is made of husband, a physical home, or an ideological home. She is free from social constraints though burdened by her responsibility to her male child.[5] Polwhele's poem provides a marital social structure for the young lady who merely plays at these intellectual games. Hemans's poem exposes maternal drives without judging them.[6] In the case of Hemans's poem, the feminine is recuperated and empowered. The mother rescues her child from immediate threat and in doing so recognizes her responsibility for further "mothering," not just in physical safety but also intellectually—teaching the child to avoid harm on his own. This contradictory image of femininity offered by the annuals allowed women readers an opportunity to develop an alternative feminine ideal from within the patriarchal restrictions and thus for subverting patriarchal definitions of femininity.

The gaze in the "Mother and Child" engraving engages directly only the two characters within the scene. The reader is left as a voyeur to watch the captured moment. Even when gazing beyond the boundaries of an annual's scene, the usually female subject depicted in annual engravings often averts her gaze toward an invisible point beyond the scene. When the gaze of the subject is directed outside of the scene and specifically positioned so that the reader can lock eyes directly with the subject, the scene opens outside of the work and enfolds the reader into the moment, almost as if the reader and subject become intertwined in a doubled gaze that looks both inside and outside of the scene. The reader is incorporated into the scenic moment at the same time that the subject leaves the scenic page to engage the reader. Whichever the two-way path runs, the reader becomes an agent in the engraving's moment.

In *Romanticism and Gender,* Anne Mellor argues that the engravings in annuals (like Kutcher erroneously calling them "gift books") "promoted an image of the ideal woman as specular, as the object rather than the owner of the gaze" (111). However, Mellor does not address the engraving subjects who *do* engage a viewer's gaze—and there are more than a few. This engaged gaze appears only once in an annual engraving published prior to 1828:[7] "The Fortune Teller," in the 1825 *Friendship's Offering* (fig. 7.2). Essentially, the scene does not allow a reader to be a voyeur but incorporates her into the specular viewing. The viewer is invited into "The Fortune Teller" scene through the eyes of a smiling child who is getting her palm read by a standing woman, most likely a gypsy. The woman on whose lap the child sits holds the girl's hand out to the fortune-teller, but the child is not paying attention to the interaction. The fortune-teller directs her predictions and readings toward the sitting woman while the child seems at play with the viewer. Because of this directed gaze from the child, the viewer, too, is having her fortune told. The light and unbroken movement from the child's gaze through her arm and to the fortune-teller makes the viewer implicit in the scene.

The scene is one that marks each individual with a class standing: the child is well dressed and being handled with relative care; the sitting woman commands both the fortune-teller and the child by extending the child's right hand but without actually touching the fortune-teller; the teller stands with a supplicating bend to her shoulders in deference to the woman, not the child. The single right-handed finger that the teller holds up can either scold the child or offer advice. In all of this, the child is completely disengaged from the scene; smiling and playful, she is most fascinated with the reader. Her slack body belies her inviting, complicit gaze. The girl, whose body almost completely covers the sitting woman, overwhelms the scene. Her gaze and body are both a conduit incorporating the reader and a shield protecting the sitting woman from the fortune-teller. This child supplies a sense of community to the scene, drawing the reader into the captured moment with only a gaze.

Only a few engravings after 1828 directly engage the reader by offering a visual connection between reader and engraving scene. By 1830, however, women with this engaged gaze had begun appearing in many annuals' portraits. The period 1828–30 also signals a shift in the literary annual's purpose: annuals became books of beauty in which women's portraits

Figure 7.2 "The Fortune Teller" engraving, 1825 *Friendship's Offering*, painted by Sir Joshua Reynolds (from the Katherine D. Harris Collection)

dominated the annual's engravings and celebrated representations of femininity. This proliferation of portraiture and engaging scenes invited the readers/viewers into the fantasy world of the engraving, offering a path into and out of the idealized feminine scenes. One feature of this feminine alternative to patriarchal femininity is its openness to readers, in contrast to the annual's prescriptive content with its masculine bias.

PHYSICALLY CONSTRUCTING THE FEMININE

These feminine and masculine qualities, contradictory as they are, appeared not only in the ideology resident in the annuals but also in the annual's physical construction.

Ackermann's original *Forget Me Not* stood at only 3in. × 5in., the traditional duodecimo size. Though not uncommon at the time, this size provides portability and freedom from domestic space. Another genre, the novel, was also constructed in duodecimo or octavo, with its largest audience in mind: women readers. Richard Altick argues that these proportions were directly related to the size of ladies' skirt pockets to allow freedom and portability: "[O]ne of the reasons why the eighteenth-century novel was issued in handy 12mo [duodecimo] size was that it was read by so many women. When reading ceased to be confined to its traditional indoor locale and was practiced outdoors and in public vehicles, pocket- sized volumes became more and more necessary" (278). However, as a reviewer in the December 1827 *Mirror* noticed, the literary annual's initial size, rendering it perfectly portable, contradicted the feminine delicacy of the volume's paper and silk boards, which was "scarcely safe out of the drawing room or boudoir."

The December 1827 *Mirror* review also notes that the 1828 *Friendship's Offering* presented a unique alternative to all of the fragile coverings: a materially stable volume bound in sturdy embossed leather bindings. An annual could always be rebound in a personal selection, but the original binding was meant to be enjoyed indoors instead of strolling through the park—another unconscious attempt to mitigate a woman's freedom outside the home. Portability became a moot point when the size of annual volumes stretched to accommodate the public's demand for larger engravings, issued in larger octavo and the more luxurious quarto format.

In another move to present a consumable and controlled femininity, Frederick Mansel Reynolds and Charles Heath allegedly stumbled onto a warehouse of red watered silk, bought four thousand yards at three shillings a yard (Watts, *Alaric Watts,* 1:269–70), and covered the boards of the 1828 *Keepsake* with it—thereby producing a textual object constructed from material normally used for a woman's skirt.[8] By 1829, *The Gem, The Bijou,* and the *Literary Souvenir* all came to the debutante ball clothed in similar crimson silk. By 1832, Ackermann had changed his paper pasteboards to the crimson silk in solidarity with the other "ladies." Citing Cynthia Lawford's findings, Patricia Pulham notes that the rubber used "in the new backing techniques in which binders had invested 'was also being used in women's corsets to tighten the stays'" (14). The binding created the restrictions on both of these feminine bodies; however, the binding glue was not used until 1830, a significant amount of time after the annuals had become popular.

Similar to the clothing that garbed Shoberl's 1834 *Forget Me Not* (quoted earlier), these crimson-covered annuals marketed a private female body: a skirt not only creates a boundary between a woman's body and the public but also shields them from the improper touch of a profligate public. And a silk skirt indicates a certain amount of wealth and class standing. The long skirt, made of heavy silk and rustling about her legs, restricts her physically and reminds a woman of the moral boundaries of proper behavior, for lifting up her skirt is an act of not only defiance but also revelation to those around her. Access to a woman's skirt is similar to access to her dressing room, a view that Jonathan Swift inventories in filthy reality in "The Lady's Dressing Room," published in 1732. The space, both under her skirt and in her room, even in the early nineteenth century, is still confidential and private. The silk material used by Heath invokes that private space but titillates at the same time because a reader may open the skirted volume and venture inside.

According to the *Oxford English Dictionary,* in American slang *pocket-book*—a form on which the literary annual was modeled (as discussed in chapter 2)—also refers to "the female pudenda," a euphemism that, albeit anachronistically, sexualizes the literary annual's textual body. Admittedly, even a crimson-covered annual does not specifically suggest female genitalia, unless we infer that the color of the material refers to menstruation. However, fragmented forms of a woman's body and mind are incorporated into the ideology and physical aspects of literary annuals. In the following cases, an actual element from the female body is combined with memories and the textual object to create a rendering of passive femininity.

Both Leigh Hunt and John Wilson use a woman's hair to assuage the heartache associated with distance and yearning. Hunt, writing for the inaugural 1828 *Keepsake,* pragmatically suggests using hair as a bookmark: "After all, it is easy to combine with a literary keepsake the most precious of all the keepsakes—hair. A braid of it may be used instead of ribbon to mark the page, and attached to the book in the usual way of a register" (18). In place of a ribbon, the lock of hair suggests a connection both to the full body and to memories within the literary annual. Both are memorialized with the act of joining them together. The lock of hair becomes a fetishized piece of woman incorporated into the textual body itself and a fragmented representation of relationship. By mere fetishizing of the hair, Hunt creates a sexual ambiguity about the fragmented female body: the proximity of hair to a body that supposedly remains untouched represents touching what cannot normally and properly be handled—at least without a marriage proposal. By giving a lock of hair, the woman gives a piece of herself that is otherwise taboo and sequestered. She offers, essentially, a fantasy or phantasm of herself—a poignant offer when she cannot properly make a gift of any other part of her body, particularly in any sexualized way. The lock of hair metonymically represents but also constrains the feminine sexuality offered by the annual.

In John Wilson's 1829 "Monologue, or Soliloquy on the Annuals," the critic meditates on the current state and purpose of literary annuals, reserving high praise for Ackermann's *Forget Me Not*. Within the article, gender is demarcated with objects and acts of remembrance. The author writes of a scenario that differentiates a man's erotic fantasy from a woman's memories.

In the scenario, a woman's memory is stirred by images of a setting sun, but her fantasy is of "the friend of our youth . . . at our side, unchanged his voice and his smile; dearer to our eyes than ever, because of some slight, faint, and affecting change wrought on face and figure by climate and by years!" (951). Instead of a lover, the woman's vision indicates a relationship filled with tenderness, friendship, and innocence. The male figure is represented to her in writing: "Let it be but his name written with his own hand, on the title-page of a book; or a few syllables on the margin of a favourite passage which long ago we may have read together, 'when life itself was new,' and poetry overflowed the whole world!" Traditionally, individuals represented in writing are preserved in a historical moment; this particular moment inscribes the male figure with agency—his writing represents his intellectual and educated self. He has written himself into perpetual existence.

The female figure in Wilson's soliloquy, however, becomes the subject of desire and is represented through a lock of her hair:

> Or a lock of her hair in whose eyes we first knew the meaning of the word "depth" applied to the human soul, or the celestial sky! But oh! if death hath stretched out and out into the dim arms of eternity the distance—and removed away into that bourne from which no traveller returns the absence—of her on whose forehead once hung the relic we adore in our despair—what heart may abide the beauty of the ghost that, as at the touch of a talisman, doth sometimes at midnight appear before our sleepless bed, and with pale uplifted arms waft over us—so momentary is the vision—at once a blessing and a farewell! (951)

The fantasized female figure has absolutely no language, no written text from which to infer her meaning. She is a ghost figure that does not even have a corporeal existence. The hair becomes the singular representation of her self, and the male figure interpolates that self into a body that has no agency, constricted by its ephemeral and incorporeal state. The male figure in the woman's memory at least has a face and eyes, but the female here has only a forehead and a relic of her own sexuality in that lock of hair. Unsupervised and mute, she appears to him in the most sexualized place, his bedroom. His vision, a fantasy really, passes over him in an orgastic moment.

As discussed in chapter 2, when the annuals first appeared on the market, publishers and editors borrowed particular elements from other successful genres, including the album and the almanac. Much like an album, the 1824 *Friendship's Offering* includes blank diary pages that invite the reader or consumer to mark and incorporate herself into the textuality of the annual. Through writing, this person becomes an agent in the physical production of the work—very similar to that agency offered by an album's blank pages. During 1824, Alaric Watts produced his 1825 *Literary Souvenir,* purposefully excluding blank pages and information. Interestingly, the *Forget Me Not* never included blank diary pages for its consumer. Ackermann always excluded the reader from the physical production of his annual; however, the *Forget Me Not* evolved to allow the reader to assert her own ideology, especially with the inclusion of poems by Landon or Hemans.

After Watts's changes, the only remaining blankness appeared on the inscription page: an area embellished and partially controlled by someone other than the final recipient. Unlike the dedication page, which is preproduced and printed simultaneously on all copies, the inscription page gestures to a unique relationship between presenter and recipient (fig. 7.3). The dedication page, though, signals a larger, more public homage to one particular individual—almost as if the printed dedication page provides an example for an inscriber's inscription.[9] The 1825 *Friendship's Offering* and 1826 *Literary Souvenir* were the first to offer dedications to various entities, usually inscribed to the current monarch or some patron. Interestingly, the *Forget Me Not* never contained dedication pages, whereas a dedication page was included with every volume of both *Friendship's Offering* and *The Literary Souvenir* except their first (1824 and 1825, respectively).[10] Commanding attention on a full page immediately following the verso of the title page, the dedication in the 1826 *Literary Souvenir* reads as follows:

to
her grace the
Duchess of Bedford
this volume
is most respectfully inscribed
by her grace's
obliged and very obedient servant
the editor

When present, the dedication page replicates supplications reminiscent of the patronage system. The page itself was protected from possible excision during the rebinding process because of its protected positioning behind the title page. However, because the inscription page precedes both the title page and the frontispiece, it could fall victim to a binder's cut during rebinding. In addition, the inscription page is not authorized or codified by being included in the table of contents. This makes the inscription page dispensable regardless of its ability to engender a unique textuality for each volume.

Gerard Genette categorizes both of these types of pages as paratexts: "devices and conventions" that mediate "between book, author, publisher and reader" (i). According to Genette, an inscription "enhances the work's material value by making this book different" (142). With a signature and/or a date inscribed on the opening pages of an annual, the inscriber authorizes him/herself into the life of the work as well as the life of the recipient. A relationship is actuated, and the inscriber grants himself/herself agency through the authority of a handwritten annotation. The inscriber writes the relationship into existence on this page.

Alternatively, the inscribee is, according to Genette, "always a potential reader at the same time that he is a real person, and one of the presuppositions of the inscription is that the author expects, in exchange for the gratification, a reading" (141). Though marked upon the page and thereby becoming part of the archive that is a literary annual, the inscription necessitates another agent, the recipient (the inscribee). The inscribee will then become the possessive and meaningful reader who will interact with the work in all of its bibliographic, linguistic, and paratextual modes (fig. 7.3).

In this scenario between inscriber and inscribee, gender inherently dominates the exchange. Regardless of the actual biological sex of the two, the recipient accepts the inscription without alteration ideally—a

Figure 7.3 Embossed inscription plate, 1826 *Forget Me Not* (from the Katherine D. Harris Collection)

relationship that mirrors the masculine and feminine roles inscribed into the literary annual itself. However, even these gendered actions are interrupted by an editor's instructions. In the 1829 *Anniversary,* editor Allan Cunningham includes instructions for constructing the best inscription, complete with a sample of script:

> The Vignette on the opposite page is intended to suit the PRESENTATION of the Volume with the recurrence of ANY PARTICULAR DAY in the Year. It will be observed that the ancient "ANNIVERSARIE" has been taken to adapt it to the purpose. . . .
>
> It will be better to use the pencil, rather than the pen, for the purpose of inserting the names of the parties required.
>
> As the first inspection of a design, of the conundrum class, sometimes occasions a momentary misconception or perplexity, it may be as well to remark that the wording, *when found out and filled up,* will resolve itself into something similar to the following:
>
> TO LADY TEAZLE, *on the* ANNIVERSARIE *of* HER WEDDING *day, from* SIR PETER.

Sir Peter Teazle is a cuckold in Richard Sheridan's 1777 farce, *A School for Scandal.* Married to a country squire's young daughter, Teazle becomes the victim of deceit, affairs, and gossip among the city's fashionable crowd. This inscription, though genuine in its instruction, invokes Sheridan's facetious and revolving relationships.

By using a pencil, the inscriber does not commit to a permanent mark, in reference to the numerous trysts portrayed in Sheridan's play—even if using the apparatus to avoid mistakes. Pencil markings will temporarily identify the writer but are in danger of fading or being replaced. Using pencil also creates a volume that is eternally transferable through a chain of recipients and presenters. And on this page, a physical palimpsest of erased names records the provenance of the volume. By encouraging readers to write inscriptions in pencil, Cunningham encourages the infidelity of the female recipient, who will pass it on to others rather than keeping it forever. However, the erasability of the inscription sets up the durability of the volume as it is passed from hand to hand. Despite being represented in the pejorative, then, this feminine object has longevity and historical presence, attributes rarely afforded to "feminine" forms.

THAT SUBVERSIVE FEMININE VOICE

Around 1830, the annuals became so popular that not even the press's vitriolic diatribes could dissuade consumers and readers from participating in the craze. The frenzy occurred at the same instant that women began to take control of the annual's contents as both editors and contributors.[11] In discussing the *Lady's Magazine,* Pearson asserts "that women 'liked to read what women had written'" because the readers contributed all of the magazine's contents until 1820 (*Women's Reading in Britain*, 97). Regarding Victorian publications more generally, Margaret Beetham argues that periodicals offer readers a mirror for their own identity, a theory that allows elasticity in a reader's identity: "Maintaining a regular readership means offering readers a recognizable position in successive numbers, that is[,] creating a consistent 'reader' within the text. The reader is addressed as an individual but is positioned as a member of certain overlapping sets of social groups, class, gender, region, age, political persuasion or religious denomination" (121). Both Beetham and Pearson point to the reader as a consumer and patron of particular forms of media. With the annuals, women were certainly its consumers and audience. In their "imagined community"[12] of readers, the women saw images of themselves.

Felicia Hemans's poem "A Brigand Leader and His Wife" and its accompanying engraving, both published in the 1827 *Friendship's Offering,* offer a portrait of a seemingly poetically constructed conservative woman. This poem exemplifies the tension between the constructed social or public role of women and domesticity's suffocating role in a heroic world of male chivalry:

> There's one, that pale beside thee stands,
> More true than all thy mountain bands!
> She will not shrink in doubt and dread,
> When the balls whistle round thy head;
> Nor leave thee, though thy closing eye,
> No longer may to her's reply.
>
> . . . .
>
> And, oh! not wholly lost the heart,
> Where that undying love hath part;
> Not worthless all, though far and long

From home estranged, and guided wrong:
Yet, may its depths by Heaven be stirr'd,
Its prayer for thee, be pour'd and heard!

(stanzas 3 and 6)

A woman follows her husband to the far reaches of war only to be left alone upon his death. The speaker describes a "home estranged" and a woman "guided wrong," a woman who attempted to maintain domesticity by following the ultimate figure in her life, her husband. The home a woman so carefully cares for is "an ideal that is yearned for," as Angela Leighton argues in the introduction to *Victorian Women Poets* (xxxvi). In a foreign land, Leighton continues, where "home is unhomely, the woman's place [has] shut her out" (xxxvi). The poem's little "flower" stands alone, "A friendless thing, whose lot is cast, / Of lovely ones to be the last" (stanza 5). Yet she still maintains her place as dutiful wife, even in the absence of her husband's ruling authority: "Sad, but unchanged through good and ill, / Thine is her lone devotion still" (stanza 5). Hemans describes this woman in all of her domestic piety, inherently naive and constructively limited. The wife is "pale" and fragile like a "flower," though stalwart in her devotion as she "stands" beside her husband while "balls whistle round" her head. Hemans duplicitously combines national pride in the British fighting force with absurd heroics on the wife's part. The wife endangers her own life, literally standing behind her husband as he fights for his life and fails. The violent danger whizzing by her should signal the wife to fight for her own life, but there is no indication that she can or will. She simply passively stands beside his cold body, remaining pious.

In *Romanticism and Gender,* Anne Mellor points out that "the thematic content of Hemans's poetry pits a masculine public code of heroic chivalry against a feminine private code of domesticity, only to reveal the inadequacy of each" (10). The accompanying engraving, "The Brigand," shows the wife peeking over her gun-bearing husband with one hand draped on his shoulder and the other covering her breast in a pose that suggests her feminine inability to protect herself (fig. 7.4). The complication is that this woman stands only partially concealed by her husband in the middle of a battlefield. She has removed herself from the enclosed safety of home and exposed herself to the open field of violence. The partial enclosure cannot protect her or her husband from the flying bullets that threaten

Figure 7.4 "The Brigand" engraving, 1827 *Friendship's Offering*, painted by Charles L. Eastlake and engraved by William Humphrys (from the Katherine D. Harris Collection)

their existence. The makeshift "home," easily ruptured by these penetrating bullets, will soon fall apart when the brigand leader receives a fatal wound. The wife stares in disbelief at her husband's lifeless body. The "home" does not protect him, because it is a false structure. The woman, who represents the "home," cannot provide structural safety for her husband; she cannot protect him from death. Instead, she witnesses his death in frozen despair.

This witnessing is the important moment in the poem, however. The brigand leader's wife is the source of history inside the patriarchal system. She, not her husband, is left standing. She does not fade away, as Hood suggests in his 1829 "The Widow" piece (discussed earlier). In this patriarchal world, if men are the source of history, then who authorizes this account? The most obvious answer is the narrative source—the wife. The brigand leader is objectified by the historical account. In contrast, the wife witnesses, remembers, and recounts the narrative of the history and becomes, more importantly, the reproductive agent, history's subject. However, the wife reproduces epistemologically instead of biologically. She will now live forever both within the poem and outside of it. Her life continues after the poem ends, because the reader never receives any information about her other than her survival. In contrast, the brigand leader's life ends with the poem's conclusion. Felicia Hemans uses war, a masculine poetic trope, to free a woman from the bondage of marriage and leaves her to survive and transmit her stories of a feminized war experience. In essence, the public history becomes her private, domestic experience, that is, her experience is conflated with the external "masculine" society but feminized and internalized by her participation. History is borne by the "mother," this feminine figure, and is re-created despite her "other" present in the poem. The brigand leader's wife is disempowered in the sense of warfare, but she gains power by transmitting a historical narrative. "The Brigand Leader" provides an example of woman's subversion of the patriarchal system through the trope of English warfare. The engraving is titled only "The Brigand"; Hemans is the one who identified and defined the role of the woman in the image.[13]

In the same volume but fifty pages later, James Bird mused about the same engraving but valorized the soldier's death in "The Dying Brigand." Both poets contemplated the role of women, but Hemans criticized the masculine tropes of warfare (and also received the place of prominence within the volume). A study of both these poems and the entire volume suggests that Romantic traditions, both masculine and feminine, competed for a reader's attention.

The brigand leader's wife witnesses and historicizes as an omniscient speaker, but in Maria Jane Jewsbury's lamentations in "A Tale of a Mother's Grave," published in the 1831 *Friendship's Offering,* an androgynous voyeur witnesses a son's grief for his stalwart mother and the mother's blind devotion to his masculinity. The speaker witnesses the carriage approaching a graveyard and remarks that a sexton exited, along with a middle-aged man who was "like a child / That fears to walk alone" (stanza 6). The sexton blesses the grave, unaware of the son's relationship:

> "God rest thy soul, poor Ellen!"
> And with a faltering hand
> The old man plucked a weed that grew
> From out the osier-band;
> And he who in the chariot came
> Fell on his knees and did the same.
>
> "Poor Ellen!" said the sexton,
> "The parish laid her here,

We little thought that one like you
Would give her grave a tear,
It may be that some time or other
She was your servant?"—"No—my mother!"

"Would thou wert back, my Mother!
For I never knew thy worth,
Till I had wandered far and long
Upon this weary earth—
Till I had lived full half my span,
And grown a melancholy man!"

This son has wandered with no central location to call home. But he forsook his earlier home by not cherishing its presence:

"I thought thee harsh and wayward,
Too often when a boy;
Alas, I never knew how small
Thy share of earthly joy!
The pangs and fears that wrung thy breast,
When I was safely laid to rest.

"Our fare was hard and scanty,
And I with murmurs ate,
Whilst thou, though born to riches vast,
In hunger silent sate;—
It was thy hand that earned our crust,
And now—that blessed hand is dust!

"I am grown rich, my Mother,
I have done deeds of fame,
And thought to make thee now forget
My boyhood's blight and shame:
I come—and spoils of land and sea
Can only deck a GRAVE for thee!"

Jewsbury highlights this absence of the home while emphasizing the decentering of the self, effected because of the absent mother. Even while covertly questioning the institutions of home and maternity, Jewsbury incorporates a narrative that again treats the absent woman as object. She is the unsung hero and the future recipient of his spoils. But he did not appreciate her presence and cannot now reward her, because she is absent. In place of her presence, the son wants to erect a tomb elegant enough to represent his mother's silence:

> "Yes—I will build with marble,
> And gild with gold thy tomb;
> But wert thou in that lowly cot
> Amongst the wall-flowers' bloom,—
> The very cot I once disdained—
> How much of heaven on earth were gained!"

Apparent are feminine tropes of flowers, silence, death, and responsibility for grief, this falling on the only masculine representation. In the relationship between woman poet and woman reader, the reader can derive from this poem a sense of disruption in angelic domesticity. The son left because of dissatisfaction with his mother's abilities and stern qualities, thereby questioning her authority and asserting his own masculine will. In the end, he worships her but only because she is physically absent. This poem boldly pays homage to a mother's role and her authority in relation to masculine ideology. But it also enacts the existing figure of woman as muse. The mother inspires her child with her death, not her life.

The witness to the son's anguish sneaks off after viewing the outpouring of grief, resentment, and retribution. The son's dialogue is cast in quotation marks to give a sense of reporting instead of poetic interpretation. The reader's source leaves the scene, almost as if the scene is never resolved. In fact, Jewsbury concludes the poem with a stanza admonishing readers to appreciate their mothers—a somewhat didactic turn to the poem. Regardless, without the benefit of an "I," the female reader has no sense of changing ideologies of femininity. In contrast, in Letitia Landon's "Song," the author displays a sophisticated understanding of the feminine realm while discreetly subverting its codes in much the same way that Hemans quietly proclaims in "The Brigand Leader and His Wife." Published under the initials "L.E.L.," the poem captures a transcendent poetic experience:

I *wrote* my name upon the sand;
    I thought I *wrote* it on thine heart.
I had no touch of fear, that *words,*
    Such *words,* so graven, could depart.
The sands, thy heart, alike have lost
    The name I trusted to their care;
And passing waves, and worldly thoughts,
    Effaced what once was *written* there.
Woe, for the false sands! and worse woe,
    That thou art falsest of the twain!
I, yet, may *write* upon the sands,
    But never on thine heart, again.

(1827 *Friendship's Offering,* 180; emphasis added)

Love is the most apparent subject matter. However, the speaker presents love not only from herself as subject but also as the recipient of the grief. She is both subject and object of the poem, dominated with "I" and personal pain. Kathleen Hickock argues that, typically, poetry of the nineteenth century was about love "connect[ed] with some kind of sorrow" (20). However, the result of this love gives agency to the woman, and demonstrates that "[w]omen were frequently reminded that the burden of sacrifice and self-effacement in love was theirs" (Hickock, 20–21). L.E.L.'s effacement in the name of love is reminiscent of Hemans's (later) devotional love at the personal expense of the brigand leader's wife. Landon's poem also reminds readers of the classic Romantic hero, interpreting everything through the poetic "I."[14]

The woman in the poem surpasses mere chagrin at being the jilted lover; she grants herself existence outside of the lover's embrace by promises of the future and loving again: "I, yet, may write upon the sands, / But never on thine heart, again." Her sense of self is not constituted merely by love, but love is not the only transitional element: "home" or a sense of the domestic seems inconsistent and transitory in alignment with the sand, which is constantly being wiped clean.

Like Hemans, "Rosa," a partially anonymous author, contributed a poem to the 1827 *Friendship's Offering.* Rosa's "Hope and Memory" uses the popular trope of war. But the woman does not participate in war; instead, the sounds of an approaching war rupture her blissful peace as she sleeps in a pastoral setting. Noticeably missing from this scene are the boundaries of the enclosing domesticity of Hemans's "The Brigand Leader and His Wife."

> "Oh! Why?" I exclaim'd, "do these sounds intrude,
> My blissful visions breaking?
> For, never, in this sweet solitude
> Should thoughts of war be waking."
> . . . .
> But, it pass'd;—and, again, the soften'd tones
> From the distance came so sweetly,
> That I griev'd, when I heard the latest ones,
> To think, they had gone so fleetly.
>
> (stanzas 6 and 8)

The woman revels in her "sweet solitude" in "a lonely, but lovely spot" where she "stray'd" (stanza 1). She escapes a "home" to wander unfettered—"[t]he world, and its cares, forgetting" (stanza 1)—voluntarily, unlike Hemans's wife of the brigand officer, who is "[f]rom home estranged." This woman roams freely, liberated by her own truth; Hemans's wife silently proclaims, "Thine is her lone devotion still." Through Hemans's narrative, the wife does not speak, though the poem comes from her point of view. In Rosa's narrative, the wandering girl briefly has a voice, expressing her dissatisfaction with being disturbed and the violent promise of impending war. Infused between these seemingly benign descriptions of the "sounds" of war is a poetics of resistance to violence. Instead of being captivated with the possession and interpretation of the events, the women in these two poems try to situate themselves among the violence or to ignore it wholly, as in the case of "Hope." In "Women Reading, Reading Women," Jacqueline Pearson suggests that women assume both subject and object position in writing this poetry: "Yet reading might equally allow the woman access to a dangerously public domain of discourse. As the 'meeting place of discourses of subjectivity and socialization,' the issue of reading disturbed commentators who found threatening both women's command of their subjectivity and their access to extra-domestic world" (80). L.E.L. exemplifies Pearson's epistemological theories of shifting readership in "Song" by representing "I" as both lover and loved, as well as griever and recipient of grief while the lover wanders away: "The sands, thy heart, alike have lost

/ The name I trusted to their care" (lines 5–6). Woman achieves agency through her relationship with the poet instead of assuming objectivity: "If women were not encouraged to be active readers or writers, they were urged instead to be muses and inspire male poets, or were defined as passive texts to be read" (Pearson, "Women Reading," 84). In a direct reaction to the insurgence of published poetry by women, Frederic Rowton compiled *The Female Poets of Great Britain,* published in 1848. However, in the preface, Rowton unapologetically reviewed some of the feminine poetry compiled from the literary annuals and proclaimed that women's poetry merely reinforces a gendered hierarchy where masculinity dominates: "They will show, if I mistake not, that while Man's intellect is meant to make the world stronger and wiser, Woman's is intended to make it purer and better. . . . It is for man to ameliorate our condition; it is for woman to amend our character. . . . They aim, not at separating the two half minds of the world, but at making them act in concert and unison" (xxxix). L.E.L.'s "Song" undercuts Rowton's ideology in the first line by granting agency to a feminized speaker. This woman writes, and thereby claims, her own name: "I wrote my name upon the sand; / I thought I wrote it on thine heart." She inscribes and memorializes her name upon the emotional seat of a body. She privileges her own name over that of a man's because she does not write the man's name over her own heart. By inscribing her name on his body, she declares ownership of him. She realizes the misplaced inscription too late to retract it, discovering that she has inscribed herself onto a transmutable surface. The sand washes away her pen; but she reinforces the inscription by writing and narrating the act.

Despite the mistake, the narrative "I" willfully chooses the surface and acknowledges that she will reinscribe her name, but on another surface: "I, yet, may write upon the sands, / But never on thine heart, again." The misdirected pen will not wither and die as a result of this washing of the ink; the pen will move again and make a mistake again. But it will not ever stop its writing: the pen empowers the subject of the poem. By allowing the "I" to wander and rule her own feelings, L.E.L. disavows the "muse" cycle, which entraps women in a passive position.

With Ackermann's original intentions, Alaric Watts's politicization, and the variations on the literary annual as a genre that was exported throughout the world, the readers became incredibly important to the success and failure of these volumes. Male editors, reviewers, and publishers attempted to control—with the exception of Ackermann, who was more interested in advancing technologies of print and literary and artistic consumerism. Almost inadvertently, women readers were empowered with the literary annual space, a space where women authors and poets soon gained enough standing to control the editorial choices. It is odd, then, that the second generation of annuals became much more feminized than Ackermann's original subversion of British constructions of femininity. But Ackermann's insights and business savvy are what led him to feature popular literature and art rather than further articulating the historical, traditional, or classic views. The *Forget Me Not* opened the genre to subtly deny this stilted version of femininity.

CONCLUSION

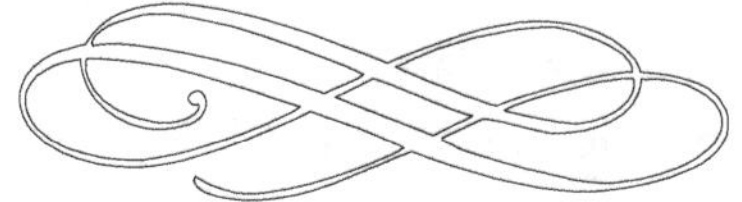

The Literary Annual's Evolution from Nineteenth-Century Gothic to Twentieth-Century Homage

I BEGAN THIS PUBLISHING, TEXTUAL, AND BIBLIOGRAPHICAL history of the early literary annuals to highlight their influence and that of their creator, Rudolph Ackermann. After years of research, I finally concluded that a definitive and conclusive history of the annuals was impossible. The genre subsumed literary forms and created others. As an example, what follows is a brief analysis of Gothic short stories in the annuals, an editorial and literary move that bolstered the annual's popularity among Gothic novel readers and authors. This popularity was recognized, finally, in the early twentieth century when during the Modernist literary era publishers and editors decided to pay homage not just to the literary annual but specifically to Rudolph Ackermann's contributions to the creation of the annual.[1]

The literary annuals gave rise to various genres and forms of literature during the early nineteenth century. In some genres, the editors and publishers merely pilfered from earlier publications and popular genres. Others were buoyed by the success of the annuals. Regardless of the popular opinion and the imagined community appropriated by the literary annual publishers, these seemingly inconsequential publications indelibly marked the publishing world. Ackermann's entire business plan relied on a faith in popular culture—a faith that resulted in revising this idea of taste. He published the materials that readers liked to share and made them into spectators and then purveyors of popular culture. With this, we cannot ignore some of the more disdained literary genres, especially the Gothic novel and the short story. Ackermann and Shoberl became adept at inserting these qualities into the *Forget Me Not,* more so than any other literary annual.

Gothic short stories in British literary annuals published between 1823 and 1831 take us further than scholars studying the eighteenth and nineteenth centuries may be comfortable with—to extend our discussions about the Gothic in such a way that the tradition does not die at 1820, as Robert Mayo argued in "The Gothic Short Story." We move past the deaths of Shelley, Keats, and Byron—the spokespersons for the second wave of traditional Romanticism. Queen Victoria would not ascend to the throne for another six years, and Tennyson had not yet become poet laureate of England. Scholars have touted 1820–30 as a "dead zone"—without any literary guiding light. However, many studies have shown that the magazines were filled with literary fodder, more specifically, the Gothic short story.

I chose to limit my study of literary annuals to these nine years because in 1831 not only did Mary Shelley publish the second edition of her popular novel, *Frankenstein,* with its famous introduction, but also the literary annual craze had reached its peak, with titles such as *The Keepsake, The Literary Souvenir, Friendship's Offering,* and, finally, *Forget Me Not.* Because parody is usually the marker of solidifying (and then moving beyond) a literary tradition, 1830 marks the year that the literary annual genre was solidified with Thomas Hood's parody, *The Comic Annual.*

Jane Austen's parody, *Northanger Abbey,* published in 1818 but written two decades earlier in reaction to the overblown sentiments of Mrs. Radcliffe's and Matthew Lewis's novels, solidified the High Gothicism of the 1790s. Mary Shelley's *Frankenstein* (1818), John Polidori's *The Vampyre* (1819), and Charles Robert Maturin's *Melmouth, the Wanderer* (1820) followed closely on the heels of Austen's satirical fun, along with several successful melodramas on the London stage. By 1818, though, the Gothic tradition had already transformed itself because of Sir Walter Scott's reworking of Gothicism in his historical romances, including *Waverley*

(1814). Even William Wordsworth participated in this evolution with his poem "The Ruined Cottage" (published in 1814 in *The Excursion*). Marilyn Gaull states that by 1820 Austen's satire had lost its popular appeal but not without solidifying the Gothic tradition's basic premise—to horrify and terrify its innocent readers (xi).

Critiqued as leading to false notions of reality, the Gothic novel was thought to overexcite young women and mislead them to think that life was as romantic and suspenseful as any Gothic novel. Samuel Taylor Coleridge reviewed Lewis's *The Monk* without enthusiasm:

> The horrible and the preternatural have usually seized on the popular taste, at the rise and decline of literature. Most powerful stimulants, they can never be required except by the torpor of an unawakened, or the languor of an exhausted, appetite. The same phaenomenon, therefore, which we hail as a favourable omen in the belles lettres of Germany, impresses a degree of gloom in the compositions of our countrymen. We trust, however, that satiety will banish what good sense should have prevented; and that, wearied with fiends, incomprehensible characters, with shrieks, murders, and subterraneous dungeons, the public will learn, by the multitude of the manufacturers, with how little expense of thought or imagination this species of composition is manufactured.

With this rebuke against sensational texts, reviewers attempted to save an entire generation of young women. Obviously, the critical disdain and the warnings did not work. In 1831, Mary Shelley revised her successful novel about the re-creation of life—downplaying the slightly incestuous relationship between Victor and Elizabeth—and added an introduction that accounts for creative imagination in much the same way that Victor Frankenstein justifies his scientific creations. With these publications beginning in 1818, the "New Gothic" tradition was cemented as the latest type of Gothicism (as Robert B. Heilman has suggested): "novels that turned from old forms of external terror to 'an intensification of feeling'" (C. Alexander, 409).

According to Robert Mayo, by 1810, the Gothic short story was well established as fiction ("Short," 448) and came in the form of Gothic romance, historical romance, sensational fiction, and sentimental horror.

These stories were published in *Blackwood's* and *London Magazine,* as well as the *Lady's Magazine* and *Lady's Monthly Museum,* even prior to 1800. As Mayo describes it, between 1790 and 1820, the Gothic short story usually consisted of a maximum of 2,500 words to fit magazine page limitations, differing in its "machinery of terror" ("Short," 454), and fragmentary at best. However, the Gothic short story was well adapted to the magazine format because these stories' "moral tone accorded well with the didactic claims of the miscellanies . . . and no matter how desperate the pressure of events, found room for a moral" (Mayo, "Romance," 765). Mayo claims that the Gothic short story then fell out of favor by the 1820s. But Christine Alexander and Franz Potter question this assertion and ask that another literary form be considered the new venue for Gothic short stories. That form is the literary annual, which became "infected" with Gothicism from its very inception.

Alexander notices the appearance of this new type of Gothicism in the Brontës' novels and attributes it to their juvenile explorations of Scott's novels, *The Lady's Magazine,* and a popular but much maligned literary genre, the literary annuals, specifically, *Friendship's Offering* for 1829, *The Literary Souvenir* for 1830, and the *Forget Me Not* for 1831.[2]

By 1820, Sir Walter Scott's historical realism had been reappropriated in a manner that resurrected the Old or High Gothic tradition, according to Potter (95)—a move that Alexander has renamed the New Gothic. Alexander finds that this New Gothic tradition governs many of the short stories published in the annuals and links the specific plots of several of these stories to much of Charlotte Brontë's juvenilia as well as *Jane Eyre:* "The Gothic frees her to achieve two apparently contradictory ends: on the one hand to imitate the Annuals and indulge in her love of the exotic, the licentious, and the mysterious, and increasingly to indulge in her fascination with the darker recesses of the mind and its relationship to natural phenomena; and on the other hand to assume the anti-Gothic stance that Heilman noted was so characteristic in the novels" (427). Though Alexander finds much of the Brontës' New Gothic influence in the annuals, what she does not discuss is the parallel disdain that both the early Gothic novel and the annuals suffered at the hands of reviewers.

Because the annuals contained short stories that were particularly Gothic, the genre was doubly damned. However, reviewers more often focused on the poetry rather than critiquing the short stories for their

Gothicism. This occurred because the Gothicism inherent to these prose pieces was not Matthew Lewis's sensationalism or even Mary Shelley's pseudo-science. Instead, the pieces contained the supernatural excitement of early Gothic novels. However, the conclusions to these short stories were often more appropriate for the literary annual and the young minds of the readers—they were disappointingly didactic or explained away through circumstance, which makes them more Mrs. Radcliffe than Monk Lewis—in exhibiting a penchant for "natural terror" rather than the supernatural.

These stories signal this shift in the Gothic tradition, from an old to a new intensity of feeling that was localized in a familiar setting, much the same as later novels such as *Dracula, The Woman in White,* and *Wuthering Heights.* With this, the literary annuals acted as catalysts, along with many other periodicals for this evolution in literary tradition—even despite the disdain from critics and literati.

The quality of writing in these short stories varies; however, Mary Shelley, William Harrison Ainsworth, and William Howitt exerted the most control over their prose and avoided some of the tropes of Gothic short fiction, such as compacted beginnings, liberal typographical interventions, underdeveloped characters and action, abrupt conclusions, and didactic overtones. Sir Walter Scott's "My Aunt Margaret's Mirror" in *The Keepsake* for 1829 is the longest story, at forty-four pages. Mary Shelley's "False Rhyme" in *The Keepsake* for 1830 is the shortest, at only three pages. The stories in *The Literary Souvenir* are significantly shorter than those in the *Forget Me Not*. Often, *The Literary Souvenir*'s stories are didactic in nature. Gothic short stories did not appear with any frequency in *Friendship's Offering,* an annual that seems to have focused more on poetry than any other literary form; in fact, Gothic short stories were completely absent from the 1824 and 1828 volumes of *Friendship's Offering.*

"The Ghost Laid," by William Harrison Ainsworth in *The Keepsake* for 1828, concludes abruptly but is decidedly ironic about the short story form and forced labor of writing to an engraving. The narrator mentions the image in a moment that breaks free from the narrative. The story concludes abruptly by admonishing the reader for wanting more details about the afterlife of the characters—whether they lived happily and contentedly or were subjected to further horrors. In a parody of the short story format and Gothic fiction, Ainsworth, as was typical of his writing, lends levity to both the annual and his tale.

Another example, "The Elves of Caergwyn," is a brief twelve-page story among the three hundred pages of poetry and prose in the 1831 *Forget Me Not*. It is not a fragment as with many other Gothic tales, but it does adhere to some of the conceits generally employed by authors of Gothic romance. Mayo defines this genre for us: "*[R]omance* was the hallmark for barbarous superstition, unreason, moral depravity, and bad taste. And Gothic romance, above all, outrageously violated the canons of 'truth to real life,' and offended a morality in which the appeal to reason, common sense, and decorum was a conspicuous feature. The pious pretenses of the literature of terror—the unwavering chastity of the heroines, the inflexible devotion of the heroes, the strict avoidance of the real supernatural, and the wholesale operation of poetic justice in the final chapters" ("Romance," 787). Mayo describes the particularities of the Gothic short story as lacking "plot framework . . . [with] little or no exposition, no resolution of events, and no accounting, usually, for the mysteries and horrors which have been devised" ("Short," 451).

"The Elves of Caergwyn" is not filled with overt examples of the supernatural, nor does it violate those "true to real life" requirements of novels. Instead, this piece resorts to a traditional Gothic framework of an undefined castle in an isolated land. The hero, Launcelot—reminiscent of medieval romance—validates the Gothic elements by arriving on a "very stormy evening in the autumn of 17–" (75). He returns to the land of his father, who ran off after he was jilted by a neighboring lady. No one knows him—at least until he presents letters of introduction to the now-old husband of the lady. One would expect that a battle or a revenge would ensue, but that is not so. Instead, Launcelot falls in love with the daughter, Anne, and privately sues for her hand in marriage. The twist is that a much-disliked and old landowner, Sir Purvill, is the intended betrothed by way of a long-standing family agreement. Launcelot, instead of battling for Anne's attention and favor, takes longing glances as Purvill disreputably manhandles Anne in front of her parents. But a deal is a deal. Our hero wanders off to a glen to sing his desires away and is interrupted by giggling. He follows the sounds and happens upon a cave where he spies tiny men and is then shot at by an unknown figure.

The rest of the story wraps up the opening scenes, in which Launcelot has stumbled into a witch's house for shelter from a storm. He overhears the witch taking money from a local peasant who has requested that a curse be placed on Purvill. The denouement comes in the form of discovering that Purvill is the one who shot at Launcelot, but not in the spirit of jealousy. Instead, the witch's curse plagues Purvill with voices and causes all of the house guests to restlessly lie awake every night. Purvill, suffering from dementia, flees the haunted, isolated land and thereby forfeits his right to marry Anne. Launcelot wins the girl!

The supernatural element of the elves is never explained away but is accepted by Launcelot. When he overhears the witch's curse, he thinks nothing more of it. Our narrator does not even connect those elements by the story's conclusion. Instead, Launcelot and Anne produce a prodigious line of great people—as our narrator brings us back to the idea that this story is a legend. Neither Launcelot nor Anne is a strongly motivated character. Instead, they seem to conform to the niceties of social interaction, declaring love only through their eyes.

This story is far from the incest, rape, and demons of Lewis's *The Monk*. However, its setting smacks of Radcliffe's isolation and continues with a pastoral setting that is also part of the natural terror that Radcliffe presents. By 1831, the audience would have been acutely aware of the revolution in poetics, namely, Wordsworth and Coleridge's *Lyrical Ballads* as well as the movement toward social responsibility by Shelley and Byron. Fancy and imagination had received a significantly different definition from Edmund Burke and Anna Letitia Barbauld predicated on the sublime. In this 1831 story, fancy has been imprisoned. The narrator proposes that a private viewing of this legend will free the reader's fancy: "Many are the stories extant among the aged peasants of their tricksy gambols; and those who love a tale of their days and deeds for some stormy winter evening, when the fancy is set free, and there are none stern or unimaginative enough to chide or check her flights, may perhaps read, with some interest, my legend of the Elves of Caer-gwyn." The implication is that there are still restrictions on a young woman's freedom of imagination. But the remaining stories in this volume contradict that notion. The literary annuals were intended to replace the conduct manuals and supplement the ladies magazines. The annual was also intended as a permanent keepsake, marking friendship and love as well as material wealth.

Richard Polwhele continuously published poems that defined women as players in the game of marriage, but only until they were married. After marriage, they were no longer participants—much the same way that Anne is portrayed in our story here. Conversely, women poets, specifically Felicia

Hemans, presented empowered and intellectual female characters who displayed this "intensity of feeling" rather than suffering through supernatural terrors. The entire movement of the literary annuals was to highlight intensity of feeling—we get this from Launcelot throughout the short story in the 1831 *Forget Me Not* not only in the cave scene where he encounters both the elves and his rival but also through the narrator's omniscient access to Launcelot's woeful plight. Everyone lives happily ever after in a socially defined relationship at the conclusion of the tale, but the narrator, inserting himself as an "I" at the conclusion of the tale, really conveys the intensity of a place or a space that is often the subject of that High Gothicism.

Here we have a melding of that old and new Gothicism that Alexander and Potter point toward. The proximity to the often schizophrenic goals of the literary annuals causes just such a mixture. By 1831, the goal of the literary annual was not so much to educate or to model propriety. Instead, it was the middle class's beautifully packaged version of entertainment that did not shield readers from the impropriety of the Gothic tradition but invited readers to secretly enjoy it. They could hide behind the beauty of the literary annual form and point to its ornamented hard covers—indeed, fancy and imagination were freed.

In total, between 1823 and 1831, ninety-six Gothic short stories were published in twenty-eight volumes, totaling approximately 1,554 pages (fig. 8.1). In some years, a literary annual might dedicate 30 percent of its three hundred pages to Gothic short stories, while in other years there were only 5 percent.

Both *Friendship's Offering* and the *Forget Me Not* were originally published with paper boards and were perhaps perceived as more ephemeral than *The Keepsake,* published with silk-covered boards, or *The Literary Souvenir,* published in leather or cloth boards. Maintaining a resonance of eighteenth-century literary forms, the *Forget Me Not* and *Friendship's Offering* were published in duodecimo and octavo through 1831 and did not indulge in larger paper until later years, if at all. *The Literary Souvenir* offered octavo and quarto versions, and *The Keepsake* was published only in quarto. Though the paper size evolved through the life of most literary annuals, the printed space (the printing plate) remained octavo, and the page began to incorporate large margins around the text blocks in 1825 with *The Literary Souvenir.* This was done to facilitate printing and, for some, printing on India paper and tipping-in engravings that were larger than the text blocks, all of which signals the eventual shift away from the annual's literary contents and toward its visual contents.

	A	B	C	D	E	F	G	H	I
1	Annual	Year	No. of Gothic Stories	Gothic Stories No. of Pages Total	Volume Pages Overall	% Pgs dedicated to Gothic Short Stories	No. of Gothic Engravings	No. of Engravings Overall	No. of re-print pgs (w/engravings as individual pg
2	FMN	1823	1	21	392	5.4%	0	12	9
3	FMN	1824	3	36	366	9.8%	0	13	16
4	FMN	1825	2	36	393	9.2%	0	12	15
5	FMN	1826	8	135	386	35%	3	13	63
6	FMN	1827	6	116	395	29.4%	0	13	57
7	FMN	1828	4	50	417	12%	0	13	24
8	FMN	1829	8	114	418	27.3%	2	14	56
9	FMN	1830	10	125	418	30%	1	14	62
10	FMN	1831	8	135	371	36.3%	1	14	65
11	**FMN Totals**	**9 vols.**	**50**	**768**	**3556**	**21%**	**7**		
12	FO	1824	0	0	222	0%	0	6	0
13	FO	1825	1	14	305	4.6%	0	26	6
14	FO	1826	2	34	397	8.6%	1	13	17
15	FO	1827	1	26	354	7.3%	0	11	13
16	FO	1828	0	0	384	0%	0	13	0
17	FO	1829	1	13	418	3.1%	1	13	8
18	FO	1830	1	12	384	3.1%	0	13	6
19	FO	1831	2	31	408	7.6%	1	13	18
20	**FO Totals**	**8 vols.**	**8**	**130**	**2872**	**4.5%**	**3**		
21	LS	1825	5	66	394	16.8%	1	13	39
22	LS	1826	4	73	410	17.8%	0	12	36
23	LS	1827	5	67	402	16.7%	1	12	32
24	LS	1828	3	39	406	9.6%	0	14	19
25	LS	1829	5	115	362	31.8%	2	12	55
26	LS	1830	4	50	364	13.7%	0	12	24
27	LS	1831	2	31	346	9%	1	12	15
28	**LS Totals**	**7 vols.**	**28**	**441**	**2684**	**16.4%**	**5**		
29	KS	1828	2	31	312	9.6%	2	19	22
30	KS	1829	4	109	360	30.3%	4	19	67
31	KS	1830	3	54	352	15.3%	4	18	37
32	KS	1831	1	21	322	6.5%	1	18	11
33	**KS Totals**	**4 vols.**	**10**	**215**	**1346**	**15.9%**	**11**		
34									
35	**TOTALS**	**28 vols**	**96**	**1554**			**26**		
36									40

Figure 8.1 Gothic short story spreadsheet

Charles Heath, founder of the most popular and successful literary annual, *The Keepsake,* selected the accomplished Gothic novel writer William Harrison Ainsworth as his first editor, preceding Frederic Mansel Reynolds in that role. Ainsworth was the only one of the many editors of annuals to contribute Gothic short stories to the annuals represented in this collection; he contributed to all but the *Forget Me Not.*

Though the *Forget Me Not* was not the most popular literary annual by 1831, it published by far the most Gothic short stories of the four literary annuals discussed here. Beginning with a single 21-page Gothic short story in the 1823 volume, the *Forget Me Not* incorporated eight stories, totaling 135 pages and representing 35 percent of the 1826 content. In 1830, the *Forget Me Not* again approached 30 percent of the annuals' content dedicated to Gothic short stories, totaling ten in number and 125 pages. The *Forget Me Not* published more than 400 pages of content each year from 1828 through 1830, equaled only by the *Literary Souvenir*'s overall pages for 1826–28. The more popular *Keepsake* maintained less than 300 pages of content between 1828 and 1831 but included four Gothic short stories (totaling about 109 pages) in 1829, which is 30 percent of the content. *Friendship's Offering*'s contents ranged anywhere from 222 to 418 pages but consistently contained the lowest number of Gothic short stories. Alaric

Watts's *Literary Souvenir* was the *Forget Me Not*'s greatest competitor for both the number of Gothic short stories and the number of pages dedicated to these stories. By 1829, the popularity of the Gothic short story had become apparent: *The Keepsake, Forget Me Not,* and *The Literary Souvenir* each dedicated 30 percent of their content to Gothic short stories.

In total, the *Forget Me Not* included fifty Gothic short stories and 768 pages over nine years; *The Literary Souvenir* included twenty-eight Gothic short stories and 441 pages over seven years; and *The Keepsake* included ten Gothic short stories and 215 pages over four years. In comparison to the total number of pages produced overall by each literary annual title, the *Forget Me Not* reserved 21 percent of its pages for Gothic short stories, as compared to the *Literary Souvenir*'s 16.4 percent and *The Keepsake*'s 15.9 percent. In total, the collection of transcriptions contains ninety-six stories and twenty-five engravings from twenty-eight volumes of literary annuals.

From twelve to nineteen engravings were included in each of these literary annuals. Charles Heath, a well-known engraver, was adamant that *The Keepsake* would offer a higher number of engravings than any other annual. In the inclusion of engravings, *The Keepsake* leads, with a total of eight engravings accompanying its Gothic short stories between 1828 and 1831. In fact, *The Keepsake* for 1830 included two engravings with Mary Shelley's story "The Mourner." The *Forget Me Not,* over a period of nine years, included only seven engravings to accompany its stories. Many of the engravings accompanying these Gothic short stories maintain a tone or topic according to the literary annual title: the *Forget Me Not* focused on bucolic scenes, while *The Keepsake* employed the horror-stricken scene or that sublime awe-fulness so redolent of Gothicism.[3]

The Gothic short story in the annuals has yet to be mined for scholarly inquiry, most likely because of the access issues already discussed. But Ackermann understood the public's demand for these types of reading materials, and he did not hesitate to supply that demand despite the critical views of the Gothic genre and the insistence on a proper female education.

MODERNIST HOMAGE TO ACKERMANN'S LITERARY ANNUAL

With these Gothic short stories squarely entrenching literary annuals in popular culture, much of the second half of their popularity and fervor centered on visual representations of beauty, eventually revising the entire genre toward the Victorian era.

In previous chapters, I address the bibliographic and literary history of an entire genre. However, I only briefly mention instances of individual volumes' unique bibliographical codes, such as variant rebindings, and discuss the potential for each volume to become its own archive, resident within the genre's overarching archive of mass-produced femininity but also unique for its marks, whether consisting of the aging process, inscriptions, or annotations. The bibliographic code, as George Bornstein points out, "corresponds to the aura and, like it, points to the work's 'presence in time and space'" (31). The aura authenticates the object's fragmented moments of production, creation, and dissemination in a historical continuum. In this (or any) archive, though, what moment is being preserved? The moment of writing or printing, the author's essence/presence, the reader's consumption, a commodified exchange after the passage of time, a moment of commodified touch, or a moment of possession? Which layer should be privileged, archived, or preserved?

Emily Dickinson's poetic collages pose such a dilemma. According to Jeanne Holland in "Scraps, Stamps and Cutouts," Dickinson's poetry is really a sign of a domestic "found" technology. Her publishing apparatuses consisted of various papers and scraps lying about her house. She used these materials with increasing regularity as her reclusiveness increased. She began to mix the scraps together to create a manuscript of found texts and original poetry (such as a stamp and words cut out from a George Sand review and pasted onto paper, with her poem written around the textual intrusion).

In examining Dickinson's textual practices, Holland finds that these are the poet's attempts to transcend a physical body—both Dickinson's physical body and the body of a material text. Holland focuses on the fixity (or not) of the printed word and the movability of its meaning according to a manuscript. Holland privileges the handwritten form and suggests that Dickinson's manuscripts are "artifacts"—material objects that mark a cultural moment in history.

These nonbook objects often contain vital insight into an author's or artist's work and are referred to as "ephemera," which literally means anything having a very short life. In archival science, the term *ephemera* refers to any printed, written, or existing object that supplies an essence of the author's work. The object may be of a transitory nature, but it is regarded as an essential element to reconstructing the life and work of a person. The fleeting moment of creation is acquired, organized, processed, and catalogued as that frozen temporal moment. At this brief juncture, and in a very small notation, even the most insignificant property becomes a repository for some sort of knowledge, which librarians, archivists, and collectors then explode as a gateway into the other works of the author. Archives are so filled with papers, objects, different editions of books, copies, and misprints because they each tell another fragmented moment in the unique life of a cultural object. This containment of total knowledge creates a certain comfort and hope to humankind in Borgesian terms:

> In the vast Library there are no two identical books. From these two incontrovertible premises he deduced that the Library is total and that its shelves register all the possible combinations of the twenty-odd orthographical symbols (a number which, though extremely vast, is not infinite): Everything: the minutely detailed history of the future, the archangels' autobiographies, the faithful catalogues of the Library, thousands and thousands of false catalogues, the demonstration of the fallacy of those catalogues, the demonstration of the fallacy of the true catalogue, the Gnostic gospel of Basilides, the commentary on that gospel, the commentary on the commentary on that gospel, *the true story of your death,* the translation of every book in all languages, the interpolations of every book in all books. (Borges, "Library of Babel")

The objects and handwritten notations by an author or the notorious reader represent the many levels of historical accumulation, which can then be archived. This is merely a fraction of what the archivist attempts to preserve. The ephemera is the smallest site of writing and language, yet it encases a vast amount of intrinsic value and knowledge and represents an attempt to reconstruct the artist in fragmentary pieces of reality. The specific marker, that which was intended to be fleeting or ephemeral, becomes a stepping-stone to unlock the secrets of the future, the present, and the historic.

In Dickinson's work, Holland points to the conflation of materials, text, and production of the eventual work that must be visually re-presented to readers so that they can fully understand that the "work" evolved from a poem into an artistic insertion of representations of history and culture at a given moment. Ideology seeps into the production of the text from the author herself, as opposed to being inserted by an outside source, such as the editor. In this sense, the work becomes the Foucauldian model of "author-function" defined in "What Is an Author?":

> Referring only to itself, but without being restricted to the confines of its interiority, writing is identified with its own unfolded exteriority. This means that it is an interplay of signs arranged less according to its signified content than according to the very nature of the signifier. Writing unfolds like a game that invariably goes beyond its own rules and transgresses its limits. In writing, the point is not to manifest or exalt the act of writing, nor is it to pin a subject within language; it is, rather, a question of *creating a space into which the writing subject constantly disappears.* (102; emphasis added)

Foucault's model of discursivity fuels much of Jerome McGann's sociological evaluation of a work. Foucault believes that the author becomes faceless (not nameless) as she writes and is preceded by the discourse that influenced her. The author, for Foucault, is not the primary source. The sociology of the text (the primary theoretical apparatus employed for my dissertation) welcomes the author back into the study, but it does not privilege that author. Instead, the reader, various institutions, and the book object itself are invited into the study of the work. Though a differentiation between text and work seems circular in logic, the distinction is created to avoid privileging the author or the actual literary text over any other entity within the sociology of the text.

Dickinson's artifact/object/work combines her writing, reference to another writer, the production of an icon within, and the use of "domestic" tools to create an image surrounded by language. All of these things produce a work that is layered with meaning and, in essence, is an "archive" of Dickinson's moment of creation and that immediate cultural moment. Readers do not have access to that cultural moment unless they review the manuscript complete with manufactured text. I use Dickinson's manuscript as an example of the knowledge that language cannot represent in the reproduction of these works. The original is always the closest representation of the moment (not necessarily the author).[4]

More concretely, because memories and moments are ephemeral and subjective, each person who engages with a book alters its meaning, even if only minutely. Derrida suggests that these moments of archivization are infinite throughout the life of the artifact: "The archivization produces as much as it records the event" (17). Archiving occurs at the moment that the previous representation is layered with new "saved" knowledge. Traces of the old document exist, but cannot be differentiated from the new—a living palimpsest.

When this is kept in mind, the textual object and its bibliographic codes are constantly open for reinterpretation. For these reasons, I contend that the textual object, the physical book, is also an archive of creation, memories, and moments—especially the literary annual, which was intended to represent memories—and is constantly being reevaluated and re-presented with each individual use as well as institutional preservation. Not only does the reader add meaning to an individual literary annual volume, but also the re-presentation of the genre continually layers meaning onto the history (and future) of literary annuals. I found this type of re-presentation in early twentieth-century volumes that mimicked the literary annual.

The legacy of the literary annual continued in the twentieth century, but not only through literary criticism; it also reappeared in its material form. Hoping to capitalize on the successful formula, publishers in the twentieth century resurrected the literary annual genre (in form and content) with both nostalgic anthologies of selections from the annuals and imitations with completely original content. In 1930, editor Dorothy Wellesley introduced a seven shilling, sixpence imitation, with visual reminiscences of the *Forget Me Not*. This volume, *The Annual, Being a Selection from the* Forget-Me-Not*s,* Keepsake*s and Other Annuals of the Nineteenth Century,* with an introduction by Vita Sackville-West, was published in London by Cobden-Sanderson and in a form only slightly larger than the first annuals.

The volume is wrapped in green paper boards and laid out like the originals—including inscription and list of embellishments pages. The volume includes selections primarily from *Forget Me Not* and *The Keepsake* but also includes those from the popular *Friendship's Offering, Talisman, Amulet,* and *Bijou*. The volume contains ten engravings, including an inscription page, a frontispiece engraving, and a vignette title page, as well as seventy-five contributions by various authors, including Mary Shelley, Wordsworth, Hogg, Southey, Hood, Landon, Blessington, Coleridge, Tennyson, and Scott. The "new" volume pays homage to the *Forget Me Not* by using the 1830 volume's cover image on its back board (fig. 8.2).

Figure 8.2 Similar designs on front and back boards, 1930 *Annual* (*bottom*) and 1830 *Forget Me Not* (*top*) (from the Katherine D. Harris Collection)

In the introduction, Sackville-West reminded readers of Ackermann's introduction of and influence over the annual's creation and congratulated him (belatedly, of course) for his ingenuity: "The form was compact, the binding dainty. . . . [Ackermann] had hit the public taste exactly" (iv). Using Ackermann's flower metaphor, Sackville-West offered a bouquet to her readers at the same time that she compelled them to remember its history:

> A perusal of the present representative selection, this nosegay picked from the flowerbeds of many publishers over a period of many years, will surely convince the reader that the enterprise was marked out for a roaring trade. We may read, today, indeed, in a spirit tinged by an amusement and a curiosity lacking in our grandparents; our absorption may, today, have become tainted with something of an antiquarian interest. We smile, where our grandparents saw no reason for a smile. We gain as much as we lose. Still, be it for one reason or another, we continue to find these contributions irresistible. (iv–v)

In essence, Sackville-West obeyed the original request to "forget me not" by re-creating the production and reception history of not only the contents but also the physical literary annual form. Though the volume imitates instead of mimicking Ackermann's *Forget Me Not* and others, its form is less opulent: the paper is of a lesser quality; the printing is murky and faded; and the engravings are printed directly to the page instead of being printed on India paper and tipped in, as well as being smaller in size. In addition, this volume technically qualifies as an anthology and not an annual.

The New Forget-Me-Not: A Calendar (1930), advertised on the back flyleaf of *The Annual,* was a borrowing of the early annual form, with "useful information" and polite literature included in the volume: "Modelled upon its illustrious Victorian predecessor, the *New Forget-Me-Not* pays a tribute to the swarm of nineteenth-century Annuals which so prettily pleased our ancestors, and *tells for our benefit the polite history of our times.* Forty eminent persons have each contributed an original chapter on the leading events, social, sporting and artistic, which fill the English year. The practical side of the calendar is not neglected, and space is provided for a record of the engagements and incidents of each day" (emphasis added). This volume was touted as containing original pieces (as opposed to Wellesley's anthology), as being illustrated by the well-known Rex Whistler, and as being published by the same publisher, Cobden-Sanderson. However, this ad layered contemporary history over Ackermann's creation and claimed the invention for the twentieth century. In the introduction to the *New Forget-Me-Not,* the new annual is juxtaposed with its original: "Thinking of these tinted niceties . . . we have been at some pains to produce for our times this *New Forget-Me-Not*. The times are more hurried, sentiment is less freely confessed—we grant such variations. Our almanack is intended to answer modern feelings, and—here we have varied the *Forget-Me-Not* constitution—by providing a daily register, we have accepted the new pace of our old friend the Year" (vii–viii). With its weekly calendar pages and ample writing space on each page, this six-shilling annual begged for completion by its owners, much like the first few *Friendship's Offering* volumes (1824 and 1825) (fig. 8.3). The hurried lifestyle and lack of sentiment indicative of the early twentieth century are the only differences between the volumes and the periods cited by the editor. Indeed, the contents are structured in four areas: winter, spring, summer, and autumn—replicating the original 1823 *Forget Me Not* format (which Ackermann dropped immediately in the 1824 volume). Sackville-West's version is filled with contemporary topics: cinema, war, and Madame Tussaud's. Max Beerbohm contributed a piece titled "Punting" that ends in murder in a decidedly Modernist fashion.

In the following year, *The New Keepsake* was published, buoyed by the success of the two previous ventures: "Encouraged by the reception of 'The New Forget-Me-Not' and 'The Annual,' works in which the view was expressed that the world is not in too great a hurry to enjoy a yearly feast of elegance and feeling, literary and artistic—that, indeed, like those other hastening mortals the Early Victorians, we all stand in need of the ingenious refreshments of the parterre and the sundial—encouraged, we say, by the welcome given to the two books named, we bring out our 'New Keepsake'" (iv–v). But the calendar was excised from this annual, with the rationale that it "introduced a menace of duty and punctuality not harmonious with an intention of pleasant escape" (v). Apparently, twentieth-century consumers and readers did not relish the new pace mirrored in *The New Forget-Me-Not*.

Interestingly, the alteration of content followed the evolution of the original annuals. The external format, however, did not parallel the unusual materials used to bind the annuals. The editor of *The New Keepsake* acknowledged that this volume could never equal the original *Keepsake* in its

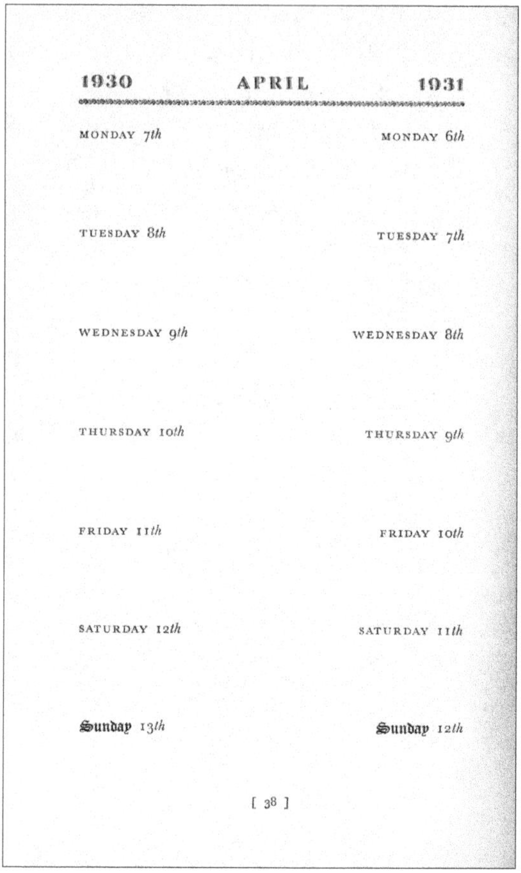

1930	APRIL	1931
MONDAY *7th*		MONDAY *6th*
TUESDAY *8th*		TUESDAY *7th*
WEDNESDAY *9th*		WEDNESDAY *8th*
THURSDAY *10th*		THURSDAY *9th*
FRIDAY *11th*		FRIDAY *10th*
SATURDAY *12th*		SATURDAY *11th*
Sunday *13th*		Sunday *12th*
	[38]	

Figure 8.3 Weekly calendar page, 1930 *New Forget-Me-Not* (from the Katherine D. Harris Collection)

red watered-silk binding and its pages full of poetry, prose, travel scenes, and beautiful images from England's most prized authors and artisans.

All of these new annuals resurrected the physical format and capitalized on a successful genre from a prior century. The first volume imitated the nineteenth-century annuals in physical form with content from the originals; the second volume published contemporary authors with a strict theme of the seasons; and the third volume eschewed restrictions on content and published the best writings of contemporary authors—a progression in these three volumes much the same as occurred in the original annuals. These volumes invoked a historical memory of the annuals themselves. Though reception of these "new" annuals is not clear, Sackville-West reminded readers of the eventual disdain suffered by the original annuals in an attempt to shame readers into disavowing those sentiments in the new and modern twentieth century:

> But we may be permitted to wonder whether some severer spirits expressed, within the privacy of their homes, that disapproval of which Leigh Hunt gives us but an inkling [in his article 'Pocket-books and Keepsakes' in the 1828 *Keepsake*]? Were there some who deplored the lucky-dip character of the Annual, and resented the inclusion of their literary mentors among a lot of parcels smothered in bran? Did some fastidious scholar sniff audibly while his lady fluttered the pages and sighed with delight as she discovered some unknown gem by Lord Tennyson, suitably illustrated by a dry-print engraving?[5] History is silent. And possibly, our shot at a venture is a shot without a mark. It was, after all, a day when the lady ruled in the boudoir—if in the boudoir only—and Mr. Ackermann foresaw that the path of literature might remuneratively be made easy. (ix–x)

In this note to readers, Sackville-West acknowledged the marketing and commodification of a literary form as well as both the popular and literary reception of annuals. By recording the reception of the genre, she may have hoped to avoid the same disdain from the educated reader—a marketing ploy used during the rise of the annual in the nineteenth century. While Sackville-West, Wellesley, Whistler, and Cobden-Sanderson used the business plan forwarded by Ackermann, right down to acknowledging their predecessors and the prior year's success, they inadvertently added to the palimpsest, already begun by Ackermann, in their use of a literary format. The twentieth-century producers of the "new" annuals re-created, wrote over, and simultaneously erased a genre to rebuild it with bibliographic and linguistic traces of the original. The commodity resurfaced and was remade, allowing exposure of the genre and its new contents.

The longevity of the original annuals was not repeated with these reinstituted volumes, however. The targeted audience for these volumes went beyond the ladies who ruled drawing rooms, especially considering the progress of the women's movement by 1929. Cobden-Sanderson produced only the three volumes before abandoning the experiment. Indeed, these publications could have been instigated by the sporadic scholarship in the nineteenth-century annual being published during the first thirty-five years of the twentieth century. Alternatively, the authors included in two of the "new" annuals, members of the Bloomsbury Group, could have insisted on the new product. Those questions have yet to be answered, along with many others about the publishing history of the literary annuals.

Appendix A

Chronological Index of British and American Literary Annual Titles

The *Forget Me Not* was published from 1823 to 1847 (with a final singular issue produced for 1856). By 1847, British literary annuals had lost much of their popular appeal; however, the American production of literary annuals doubled the number of British publications during the period 1846–57. By 1857, the literary annual genre had begun to lose public interest on both continents.

To illustrate the early and rapid rise in popularity of the annual, the title of each annual is listed under the year published. Beyond 1835, only the number of annuals published in 1846 and 1857 is listed (instead of the titles).

1823

English. (1) *Forget Me Not.*

1824

English. (3) *Forget Me Not; Friendship's Offering; The Graces.*

1825

English. (9) *Blossoms at Christmas; First Flowers; Forget Me Not; Friendship's Offering; Hommage aux Dames; Literary Coronal; The Literary Souvenir; Poetical Album;*[1] *Remember Me.*

1826

American. (4) *Atlantic Souvenir; Philadelphia Souvenir; Souvenir; Wreath, a Collection of Poems.*

English. (9) *Amulet; Blossoms at Christmas; First Flowers; Forget Me Not; Friendship's Offering; Janus; Literary Souvenir; Pledge of Friendship; Poetical Album.*

1827

American. (2) *Atlantic Souvenir; Memorial.*

English. (9) *Amulet; First Flowers; Forget Me Not; Friendship's Offering; Literary Souvenir; Pledge of Friendship; Poetical Album; Poole's Royal Sovereign; Royal Sovereign.*

1828

American. (10) *Amaranth* (Boston); *Atlantic Souvenir; Juvenile Sketchbook; Juvenile Souvenir; Legendary; Memorial; Moral and Religious Souvenir; Oasis; Talisman; Token.*

English. (15) *Amulet; Bijou; Carcanet; Christmas Box; First Flowers; Forget Me Not; Friendship's Offering; Juvenile Forget Me Not; Keepsake; Literary Souvenir; Pledge of Friendship; Poetical Album; Times Telescope; Troubadour; Winter's Wreath.*

1829

American. (15) *Atlantic Souvenir; Cabinet; Casket* (Boston); *Gift* (Boston); *Holiday Tales; Jackson Wreath; Offering; Pearl; Remember Me, a Religious and Literary Miscellany; Tales and Poetry from the English Souvenirs; Talisman; Token; Unique; Visitor; Western Souvenir.*

English. (25) *Affections Offering; Amulet; Anniversary; Bijou; Cabinet of Curiosities; Casket; Christian Forget Me Not; Christmas Box; First Flowers; Forget Me Not; Friendship's Offering; Gem; Juvenile Forget Me Not; Juvenile Keepsake; Keepsake; Literary Souvenir; Musical Gem; Nautilus; New Year's Gift; Offering; Poetical Album; Souvenir Litteraire de France; Times Telescope;*[2] *Winter's Wreath; Young Ladies Book.*

1830

American. (9) *Atlantic Souvenir; Casket, or Youth's Pocket Library; Garland* (New York); *Lily; Offering of Sympathy; Pearl; Talisman; Token; Youth's Keepsake.*

English. (43) *Ackermann's Juvenile Forget Me Not; Affections Gift; Affections Offering; Amulet; Anniversary; Apollo's Gift; Bengal Annual; Bijou; Cabinet Album; Carcanet; Christian Souvenir; Comic Annual; Emanuel; Excitement; Fisher's National Portrait Gallery; Forget Me*

Not; Friendship's Offering; Gem; Gem of Art; Iris; Johnson's Shooter's Annual; Juvenile Forget Me Not; Juvenile Keepsake; Juvenile Landscape Annual; Keepsake; Keepsake Français; Landscape Annual; Laurel; Literary Bluebook; Literary Gem; Literary Souvenir; Looking Glass; Lyre; Musical Bijou; Musical Forget Me Not; Musical Gem; Musical Souvenir; New Year's Gift; Olive Branch; Remember Me; Times Telescope; Winter's Wreath; Zoological Keepsake.

1831

American. (14) *Amaranth* (Newburyport); *American Comic Annual; Amethyst* (Baltimore); *Atlantic Souvenir; Child's Annual* (Philadelphia); *Hyacinth* (New York); *Keepsake Americaine; Lily; Pearl; Scrap Table; Spirit of the Annuals; Tablet; Token; Youth's Keepsake.*

English. (62) *Ackermann's Juvenile Forget Me Not; Affection's Gift; Affection's Offering; Amulet; Apollo's Gift; Bengal Annual; Cabinet Album; Cadeau; Cameo; Chameleon; Comic Annual; Comic Offering; Dramatic Annual; English Keepsake; Excitement; Father's Present to His Son; Fisher's National Portrait Gallery; Forget Me Not; Friendship's Offering; Gem; Humorist; Infant's Annual; Iris; Juvenile Forget Me Not; Keepsake; Keepsake Français; Ladies' and Gentlemen's Polite Assistant and Useful Remembrancer; Ladies' Poetical Album; Landscape Annual; Literary Souvenir; Looking Glass; Love's Offering; Lyre; Marshall's Christmas Box; Mirror of the Graces; Mother's Present to Her Daughter; Mr. Matthews' Comic Annual; Musical Bijou; Musical Forget Me Not; Musical Gem; New Comic Annual; New Musical Annual; New Year's Gift; Olive Branch; Phrenological Bijou; Pledge of Friendship; Poetical Offering; Regent; Remember Me; Remembrance; Royal Repository and Picturesque Diary; Sacred Harp; Sacred Offering; Scrap Table; Simpson's Gentleman's Almanack; Le Souvenir; Talisman; Times Telescope; Tit-Bits; Vocal Annual; Winter's Wreath; Youth's Keepsake.*

1832

American. (12) *Affection's Gift* (New York); *Annual; Atlantic Souvenir; Christian Offering; Compliment for the Season; Keepsake Americaine; Lady's Cabinet Album; Lily; Odd Volume; Pearl; Token; Young Lady's Own Book.*

English. (63) *Ackermann's Juvenile Forget Me Not; Affection's Gift; Affection's Offering; Amaranth; Amethyst; Amulet; Bengal Annual; Botanical Annual; Bouquet; Cabinet Album; Cabinet for Youth; Cabinet of Literary Gems; Cadeau; Chameleon; Comic Annual; Comic Offering; Continental Annual; Diadem; Easter Gift; Easter Offering; Evergreen; Excitement; Fisher's Drawing Room Scrap Book; Fisher's National Portrait Gallery; Forget Me Not; Friendship's Offering; Gem; Geographical Annual; Heath's Picturesque Annual; Hibernian Keepsake; Hive; Humorist; Infant's Annual; Juvenile Album; Juvenile Forget Me Not; Keepsake; Landscape Album; Landscape Annual; Literary Souvenir; Looking Glass; Love's Offering; Marshall's Christmas Box; Musical Bijou; Musical Gem; New Year's Gift; Nosegay; Poetical Offering; Portfolio; Recordanza; Regent; Remember Me; Rose of Four Seasons; Sacred Harp; Sacred Lyre; Sacred Offering; Shipp's Military Bijou; Sister's Gift; Spiritual Gleaner; Vocal Annual; Waverley Album; Winter's Wreath; Yorkshire Literary Annual; Youth's Cornucopia.*

1833

American. (10) *Annual; Child's Gem; Miscellanies; Odd Volume; Pearl; Premium; Religious Souvenir; Token; Young Lady's Sunday Book; Young Man's Guide.*

English. (39) *Affection's Gift; Amethyst; Amulet; Aurora Borealis; Bengal Annual; Biblical Annual; Bouquet; Cadeau; Chameleon; Christmas Tales; Comic Annual; Comic Offering; Dramatic Souvenir; Elgin Annual; Ellis's Missionary Annual; Excitement; Father's Present to His Son; Fisher's Drawing Room Scrap Book; Fisher's National Portrait Gallery; Forget Me Not; Friendship's Offering; Geographical Annual; Heath's Book of Beauty; Heath's Picturesque Annual; Infant's Annual; Juvenile Forget Me Not; Keepsake; Landscape Annual; Literary Souvenir; Looking Glass; Missionary Annual; Musical Gem; New Year's Gift; Offering; Regent; Sacred Musical Offering; Sacred Offering; Turner's Annual Tour; Wreath of Friendship.*

1834

American. (17) *American Juvenile Keepsake; Annual; Casket, or Youth's Pocket Library; Child's Annual* (Boston); *Daughter's Own Book; Ladies and Gentlemen's Pocket Annual; Lady's Cabinet Album;*

Lily; Oasis; Offering; Pearl; Religious Souvenir; Rosary; Token; Unique; Youth's Keep-Sake; Youth's Sketch Book.

English. (40) *Album Wreath; Amethyst; Amulet; Annual Souvenir; Bengal Annual; Biblical Annual; Bouquet; Bow in the Cloud; Comic Annual; Comic Offering; Coronal; English Annual; Excitement; Fisher's Drawing Room Scrap Book; Forget Me Not; Friend's Annual; Friendship's Offering; Gage d'Amitié; Gem of Art; Geographical Annual; Heath's Book of Beauty; Heath's Picturesque Annual; Juvenile Forget Me Not; Keepsake; Landscape Album; Landscape Annual; Literary Gift Book; Literary Souvenir; Looking Glass; Midsummer Keepsake; New Year's Gift; Offering; Oriental Annual; Regent; Sacred Annual; Sacred Offering; Souvenir; Turner's Annual Tour; Wreath of Friendship; Young Gentleman's Annual.*

1835

American. (14) *American Juvenile Keepsake; Annual; Beauties of the English Annuals; Bouquet* (Philadelphia); *Gift* (Concord); *Lady's Cabinet Album; Lily; Odd Volume; Parent's Present; Portfolio for Youth; Premium; Religious Souvenir; Token; Youth's Keep-Sake.*

English. (43) *Amulet; Angler's Souvenir; Annual Token; Biblical Keepsake; Christian Keepsake; Comic Almanac; Comic Annual; Comic Offering; Continental Landscape Annual of European Scenery; Continental Tourist; English Annual; Excitement; Finden's Tableaux; Fisher's Drawing Room Scrap Book; Forget Me Not; Friendship's Offering; Gage d'Amitié; Geographical Annual; Heath's Book of Beauty; Heath's Picturesque Annual; Juvenile Amulet; Juvenile Forget Me Not; Juvenile Keepsake; Keepsake; Lady's Keepsake and Maternal Monitor; Landscape Annual; Landscape Souvenir; Literary Souvenir; Looking Glass; Marshall's Christmas Box; Musical Gem; New Year's Gift; New Year's Token; Nursery Offering; Oriental Annual; Orient Pearl; Pledge of Affection; Present; Regent; Sacred Offering; Souvenir; Turner's Annual Tour; Youth's Cabinet.*

* * *

1846

American. (56)
English. (16)

* * *

1857

American. (15)
English. (3)

Source: K. Harris, "Chronological Index of British Literary Annual Titles," in *Forget Me Not* hypertextual archive with the primary source from Faxon, *Literary Annuals and Gift Books*, 129-40.

Appendix B

Prominent Contributors to British Literary Annuals

The following is a survey of Romantic and Victorian authors who regularly published in the literary annuals. I acknowledge the problematic use of descriptions such as "canonical," "primary," "popular," "prominent," and so forth in restricting this list. However, for lack of a better word, "canonical" refers to authors regularly studied in Introduction to Romanticism courses. This listing was compiled from Andrew Boyle's *An Index to the Annuals (1820–1850)* and Frederick Faxon's *Literary Annuals and Gift Books: A Bibliography, 1823–1903*. My corrections and additions to the above sources are in brackets.

BAILLIE, JOANNA (1762–1851)

Literary Souvenir [1825–35]

To Mrs. Siddons, 1830, 361 (reprint)
(Boyle, 15)

BARBAULD, MRS., *née* Aiken (1743–1825)

Amulet [1826–36]

Words: An Enigma, 1828, 90
Lines to Mr. W. . . , 1828, 321
Bouts Rimés in Praise of Old Maids, 1828, 357

Juvenile Forget Me Not [1828–32]

The Misses (addressed to a careless girl), 1830, 1
(Boyle, 17)

BROWNING, ELIZABETH BARRETT (1806–1861)

Keepsake [1828–61]

My Kate, 1855, 16
Amy's Cruelty, 1857, 75

Finden's Tableaux [1837–44]

India: A Romance of the Ganges, 1838, 29
The Romaunt of the Page, 1839, 1
The Dream, 1840, 1
Legend of the Brown Rosarie, 1840, 15
(Boyle, 42)

BROWNING, ROBERT (1812–1889)

Keepsake [1828–61]

Ben Karshook's Wisdom, 1856, 16
May and Death, 1857, 164
(Boyle, 42)

BULWER, EDWARD GEORGE BULWER-LYTTON (afterwards Baron Lytton) (1803–1873)

Friendship's Offering [1824–44]

The Poet's Dream, 1832, 73

Literary Souvenir [1825–35]

Too Handsome for Anything, 1829, 45
A Manuscript Found in a Madhouse, 1829, 56

Amulet [1826–36]

Arasmanes; or, The Seeker, 1834, 11

Keepsake [1828–61]

Ode, The Last Separation, 1841, 58
Jealousy, 1842, 221

The Lawyer Who Cost His Client Nothing, 1848, 1
The First Violets, 1849, 17
The Confirmed Valetudinarian, 1851, 153
The Modern Wooer, 1855, 116

[Heath's] Book of Beauty [1833–47; continued as *Book of Beauty*, 1848]

The Choice of Phylias, 1834, 1
Chairolas, 1836, 3
Juliet's Tomb in Verona, 1837, 32
The Three Sisters, trans. from the Phoenician, 1838, 4
Ode to a Leafless Tree in June, 1839, 14
The Wife to the Wooer, 1840, 11
First and Last: An Ode, 1841, 235
An Episode in Life, 1843, 3
Content and Desire, 1844, 146
Youth's Dirge, 1845, 249

Drawing-Room Scrapbook [a.k.a. *Fisher's Drawing Room Scrap Book,* 1832–54]

The Hon. Mrs. Norton, 1847, 83
(Boyle, 43)

BYRON, LORD (1788–1824) [all printed/published posthumously]

Forget Me Not [1823–47, 1856]

To My Dear Mary Anne, 1830, 38

Friendship's Offering [1824–44]

Stanzas to her who best can understand them, 1826, 102
To Lady Caroline Lamb, 1826, 230

Literary Souvenir [1825–35]

Lines written in the Livre des Etrangers of the Union Hotel at Chamouni, 1827, 231
To Ianthe (Dedication of "Childe Harold's Pilgrimage"), 1830, 96

Pledge of Friendship [1826–28]

Solitude, 1827, 127
Sun of the Sleepless, 1827, 275

Keepsake [1828–61]

Letters from Byron to several friends, 1830, 216

Anniversary [1829–30]

Letter on economy, 1829, 254

Gem [1829–32]

Conrad and Gulnare, 1832, 204

[Heath's] Book of Beauty [1833–47; continued as *Book of Beauty,* 1848]

Thou art not false, but thou art fickle, 1847, 1
(Boyle, 45)

CLARE, JOHN (1793–1864)

Forget Me Not [1823–47, 1856]

Song, 1829, 68
On a Child Killed by Lightning, 1829, 272
The Deity, 1832, 298
Pleasures of Life, 1844, 275

Friendship's Offering [1824–44]

The Maid of the Hall, 1827, 339
To a Friend, E.L.E., 1828, 170
Evening Pastime, 1829, 60
Nature, 1829, 60
The Wren, 1829, 151
A Spring Morning, 1829, 416
To the Redbreast, 1830, 211
The Thrush's Nest, 1831, 127
Sonnet, 1833, 113
The Nightingale's Nest, 1833, 358
Our Own Fireside, 1835, 176

Literary Souvenir [1825–35]

First Love's Recollections, 1826, 203
Song, 1826, 410
Ballad, 1827, 379

Crowland Abbey, 1828, 196
Sonnet, 1828, 364

Amulet [1826–36]

Sonnet, 1826, 24
Sonnet, 1826, 255
Sonnet to a Young Lady, 1827, 261
Spring, 1828, 279
The Quiet Mind, 1828, 301
Autumn, 1828, 396
Mortality, 1829, 145
Fame, 1829, 266
Death of Beauty, 1829, 293
To the Memory of Bloomfield, 1829, 318
May Morning, 1834, 298

Pledge of Friendship [1826–28]

Life, Hope, and Death, 1827, 104
The Summer Morning, 1827, 198
To Harry Stoe Van Dyk, 1828, 385

Juvenile Forget Me Not [1828–32]

The Grasshopper, 1829, 118

Anniversary [1829–30]

Ode to Autumn, 1829, 75

Gem [1829–32]

To the Memory of ****, 1829, 322
Boston Church, 1830, 123

Ackermann's Juvenile Forget Me Not [1830–32]

The Birds and St. Valentine, 1830, 57
(Boyle, 58–59)

COLERIDGE, SAMUEL TAYLOR (1772–1834)

Friendship's Offering [1824–44]

My Baptismal Birthday, 1834, 163

Fragments from the Wreck of Memory:
1. Hymn to the Earth, 1834, 165
2. English Hexameters Written in 1799, 1834, 167
3. The Homeric Hexameter, 1834, 168
4. The Ovidian Elegiac, 1834, 168
5. A Versified Reflection, 1834, 168
Love's Apparition and Evanishment, 1834, 355
Lightheartedness in Rhyme, 1834, 356

Literary Souvenir [1825–35]

The Exchange, 1826, 408
Lines Suggested by the Last Words of Berengarius, Ob anno Dom, 1088, 1827, 17
Youth and Age, 1828, 1
What Is Life? 1829, 346

Amulet [1826–36]

New Thoughts on Old Subjects, 1828, 37
Fragments of a Journey over the Brocken, 1829, 130
Three Scraps:
1. Love's Burial-Place, 1833, 31
2. The Butterfly, 1833, 32
3. A Thought Suggested, 1833, 32

Bijou [1828–30]

The Wanderings of Cain: A Fragment, 1828, 17; *Cameo,* 150
Work without Hope, 1828, 28; *Cameo,* 6
Youth and Age, verse, 1828, 144
A Day Dream, 1828, 146; *Cameo,* 9
The Two Founts, 1828, 202
Christabel, 1829, 285

Keepsake [1828–61]

Epigrams, 1829, 122
To a Critic, 1829, 261
Epigrams, 1829, 277
The Garden of Boccaccio, 1829, 282
Epigram, 1829, 311

Epigram, 1829, 360
Song, 1830, 264
The Poet's Answer, 1830, 279
(Boyle, 63–64)

DICKENS, CHARLES (1812–1870)

Keepsake [1828–61]

A Word in Season, 1844, 73
To Be Read at Dusk, 1852, 117
(Boyle, 81)

DISRAELI, BENJAMIN, First Earl of Beaconsfield (1804–1881)

Amulet [1826–36]

A Pilgrimage to the Holy Sepulchre, 1833, 61

Keepsake [1828–61]

Fantasia, 1845, 163
Shoubra, 1846, 30

[Heath's] Book of Beauty [1833–47; continued as *Book of Beauty,* 1848]

The Carrier Pigeon, 1835, 128
The Consul's Daughter, 1836, 74
To a Maiden Sleeping after Her First Ball, 1837, 186
Calantha, 1837, 252
A Syrian Sketch, 1838, 249
Portrait of Lady Mahon, 1839, 16
Portrait of Viscountess Powerscourt, 1839, 93
The Valley of Thebes, 1840, 3
Munich, 1841, 13
Eden and Lebanon, 1842, 220
The Midland Ocean, 1843, 89
(Boyle, 81–82)

EDGEWORTH, MARIA (1767–1849)

Friendship's Offering [1824–44]

The Mental Thermometer, 1825, 185

Amulet [1826–36]

On French Oaths, 1827, 297

Janus [1826]

Thoughts on Bores, 1825, 58 (contributed anonymously)

Christmas Box [1828–29]

Garry Owen; or, The Snow Woman, 1829, 33
(Boyle, 86)

HAZLITT, WILLIAM (1778–1830)

Amulet [1826–36]

The Spirit of Philosophy, 1836, 234
(Boyle, 119)

HEMANS, FELICIA (1793–1835)

[94 entries; some works published in more than one literary annual]

Forget Me Not [1823–47, 1856]

Evening Prayer at a Girl's School, 1826, 156
The Cliffs of Dover, 1827, 69
Night-Blowing Flowers, 1827, 237
The Sister's Dream, 1828, 1
Evening Song of the Tyrolese Peasants, 1828, 137
The Ivy of Kenilworth, 1828, 223
The Sculptured Children, 1829, 11

Friendship's Offering [1824–44]

The Brigand Leader and His Wife, 1827, 36
Last Rites, 1827, 105
Fading Flowers, 1827, 145
The Tomb of Madame Langhans, 1827, 246
Lines upon the Tomb of Madame Langhans, 1827, 249
Music of Yesterday, 1829, 6

Literary Souvenir [1825–35]

The Mother and Child, 1825, 64
The Grave of Korner, 1825, 118
Aymer's Tomb, 1826, 81
The Child and the Dove, 1826, 245
The Troubadour and Richard C'ur de Lion, 1826, 357
The Breeze from Shore, 1827, 10
The Better Land, 1827, 65
Ivan the Czar, 1827, 164
Corinna at the Capitol, 1827, 189
The Distant Ship, 1827, 289
Madeline, 1828, 22
The Wings of a Dove, 1828, 62
The Voice of Home, 1828, 99
Ancient Song of Victory, 1828, 145
The Memory of the Dead, 1828, 251
Italian Girl's Hymn to the Virgin, 1829, 40
Second Sight, 1829, 123
To a Departed Spirit, 1829, 190
The Magic Glass, 1830, 39
The Sisters of Scio, 1830, 181
The Mirror in the Deserted Hall, 1830, 356
On a Picture, 1833, 36
(Boyle, 120–23)

HOGG, JAMES, "The Ettrick Shepherd" (1770–1835)

Forget Me Not [1823–47, 1856]

The Skylark, 1828, 27
The Descent of Love, 1828, 217

St. Mary of the Lows, 1829, 25
Eastern Apologues, 1829, 309
A Sea Story, 1831, 19
Maggy o'Buccleugh, 1832, 182
The Battle of the Boyne, 1832, 299
Seeking the Houdy, 1833, 399
Scottish Haymakers, 1834, 327
The Lord of Ballach, 1836, 352

Friendship's Offering [1824–44]

The Minstrel Boy, 1829, 209
Auld Joe Nicholson's Bonny Nannie, 1829, 263
Ballad, 1829, 415
Verses to a Beloved Young Friend, 1829, 417
A Scots Luve Sang, 1830, 185
The Fords of Callum, 1830, 187
A Bard's Address to his Youngest Daughter, 1830, 312

Literary Souvenir [1825–35]

Invocation to the Queen of the Fairies, 1825, 122
Love's Jubilee, 1826, 121
The Border Chronicler, Charlie Dinmont, 1826, 257
Stanzas for Music, 1827, 247

Pledge of Friendship [1826–28]

A Night Piece (written in 1811), 1827, 231

Amulet [1826–36]

A Lay of the Martyrs, 1830, 145
A Tale of Pentland, 1830, 219
A Cameronian Ballad, 1831, 173
A Hymn to the Redeemer, 1835, 118
Morning Hymn, 1836, 42
The Judgment of Idumea, 1836, 79

Bijou [1828–30]

An Aged Widow's Own Words, 1828, 26
Ane Waefu' Scots Pastoral, 1828, 108

Woman, 1829, 92; *Cameo,* 146
Superstition and Grace, 1829, 129

Anniversary [1829–30]

The Carle of Invertime, 1829, 100
The Cameronian Preacher's Tale, 1829, 170

Gem [1829–32]

A Highland Eclogue, 1830, 194

Juvenile Forget Me Not [1828–32]

A Child's Prayer, 1830, 114
A Child's Hymn for the Close of the Week, 1831, 78

Ackermann's Juvenile Forget Me Not [1830–32]

A Child's Prayer, 1830, 176
What Is Sin? 1830, 223
The Poachers, 1831, 99
Hymn for Sabbath Morning, 1831, 172
The Shepherd Boy's Song, 1832, 157

Remembrance [1831, 1838, 1843]

A Boy's Song, 1831, 74
The Two Valleys, 1831, 121
The Covenanter's Scaffold Song, 1831, 256
(Boyle, 130–31)

HUNT, LEIGH (1784–1859)

Amulet [1826–36]

Abon Ben Adhem and the Angel, 1834, 176

Keepsake [1828–61]

Dreams on the Borderland of Poetry, 1828, 234 [contributed anonymously]

Finden's Tableaux [1837–44]

Albania, the Love-Letter, 1837, 7
(Boyle, 147)

JEWSBURY, MARIA JANE ["M.J.J."] (1800–1833)

Forget Me Not [1823–47, 1856]

Youth, 1825, 233
Winter Welcomed, 1828, 112
Two Scenes in the Life of a Favourite, 1828, 139
On Receiving a Bunch of Flowers from the Author of the "Excursion," 1830, 46
The Paysanne in the City, 1830, 182
The Boor of the Brocken, 1830, 185
A Lover's Ballad, 1846, 48
The Sleeping Slave, 1846, 190

Friendship's Offering [1824–44]

Trysting Times, 1830, 311
A Tale of a Mother's Grave, 1831, 126
A Birthday Ballad, 1831, 283

Literary Souvenir [1825–35]

The Young Author, 1825, 85
Song of the Hindoo Women, 1825, 205
The Military Spectacle, 1825, 243
Arria, 1825, 330
To a Poet's Infant Child, 1826, 78
The Rivals, 1826, 99
A Farewell to the Muse, 1826, 379
The First Wanderer, 1827, 112
Marie Antoinette and Mirabeau, 1828, 142
The Death of Saint Louis, 1828, 385
The Singing Bird at Sea, 1830, 247
Love Breezes, 1831, 253
The Dreamer, 1831, 319
The Stars, 1837, 214

Amulet [1826–36]

The Hero of the Coliseum, 1828, 17
The Return of the Vaudois, 1828, 69

The Errors of the True Christian, 1828, 200
The Sisters of Bethany, 1830, 155
The Lost Life, 1830, 187
The Florentine, 1831, 111
The History of a Trifler, 1831, 149
The Stricken King, 1831, 228
Song, 1831, 280
Sophie, 1832, 175
The Dying Girl to Her Mother, 1832, 190
A Lament and a Reply, 1834, 250

Pledge of Friendship [1826–28]

Egypt's Last Plague, 1828, 194
The Palace of the Two Kingdoms, 1828, 335

Christmas Box [1828–29]

Address to a Plum Pudding, 1829, 12

Winter's Wreath [1828–32]

The Hunters of the Tyrol, 1830, 73
The Bergsman and His Guest, 1830, 128
The Revenu, 1831, 116
The Orphan, 1831, 267

Juvenile Forget Me Not [1828–32]

The Youthful King, 1829, 17
Recreation and Dissipation, 1829, 37
Epitaph on a Dog, 1829, 64
Aunt Kate and the Review, 1830, 86
The Lapland Boy, 1830, 144
The Little English Boy, 1830, 146
A Godmamma's Epistle, 1831, 28
The Nut-Cracker, 1831, 81
A Little Boy's Letter from London, 1831, 133
Stanzas, 1831, 166
The Young Gleaner and His Counsin [*sic*], 1832, 157
To a Young Brother, 1833, 192
Temper in Trifles, 1834, 124
The Bride, 1837, 60

Gem [1829–32]

Sir Willoughby the Brave, 1830, 264

New Year's Gift [1829–36]

The Little Boy's Address to His Rocking-Horse, 1829, 30
The Lapdog and His Doctor, 1829, 188
The Birds and the Beggar of Bagdat, 1830, 101
The Passage of an Indian Army, 1831, 111
A Godmamma's Letter to a Little Boy, 1831, 142
I Am Far from Home, 1831, 145

Iris [1830–31]

The Funeral among the Mountains, 1830, 4
The Wizard, 1831, 27

Ackermann's Juvenile Forget Me Not [1830–32]

The Story of Pigeons, 1830, 183
The Two Soliloquies, 1830, 235
The Little Masquers, 1831, 19
Memoirs of a Butterfly, 1831, 54
The Defence of Saragoza, 1832, 151
The Sleeping Forest Child, 1832, 171

Drawing-Room Scrapbook [a.k.a. *Fisher's Drawing Room Scrap Book,* 1832–54]

To L.E.L. after Meeting Her for the First Time, 1839, 24
(Boyle, 152–54)

LAMB, CHARLES (1775–1834)

Christmas Box [1828–29]

Verses written in the first leaf of Lucy Barton's Album, 1828, 15 [contributed anonymously]

Bijou [1828–30]

Verses for an Album, 1828, 24; *Cameo,* 137

Gem [1829–32]

On an Infant Dying as Soon as Born, 1829, 17

A Widow, 1829, 25[1]
(Boyle, 161)

LANDON, LETITIA ELIZABETH ("L.E.L.") (1802–1838)

Editor of *Fisher's Drawing Room Scrap Book* and *Heath's Book of Beauty* [163 entries; some works published in more than one literary annual]

Forget Me Not [1823–47, 1856]

Ellen, 1824, 11
Lines on the Mausoleum of the Princess Charlotte at Claremont, 1824, 36
Second Sight: A Dramatic Scene, 1825, 22
The Parting Charge, 1825, 55
The Lute, 1825, 72
The Ruined Cottage, 1825, 120
The Indian Orphan: A Tale, 1825, 176
The Choice, 1826, 18
Prince Ahmed and the Fairy: A Sketch from the "Arabian Nights," 1826, 347
"Appealing by the magic" [title pages, 1827, 1828, 1829, 1830]
Love's Motto, 1827, 1
The Stag, 1827, 127
The Sword, 1828, 29
The Bridal Morning, 1828, 103
Song, 1828, 216
The Rose and the Laurel Leaf, 1830, 380
The Disconsolate, 1831, 215
The Thunder-Storm, 1832, 151
Giulietta: A Tale of the Fourteenth Century, 1833, 299
Madeira, 1835, 65
The Confession, 1836, 195
The Sleeping Beauty, 1837, 263
Alice Lee, 1839, 231
Love's Signal Flower, 1844, 9

Friendship's Offering [1824–44]

The Suicide's Grave, 1825, 197
Home, 1825, 200

Ballad, 1825, 237
The Sailor, 1825, 238
Hindoo Girl by an Urn, 1826, 25
Raphael's Death-Bed, 1826, 73
The Emigrants, 1826, 185
The Spirit and the Angel of Death, 1827, 1
Song, 1827, 180
The Banner of Five Byzants, 1828, 13
The Lyrist, 1828, 181
Venus Taking a Bow from a Sleeping Cupid, 1828, 188
The First Ball, 1828, 188
The Boon, 1836, 37
The Festival, 1836, 73
The Black Seal, 1836, 361
Parting Words, 1837, 71
The Bridal Day, 1837, 181
The Secret Discovered, 1837, 320
The Soldier's Bride, 1844, 140

Literary Souvenir [1825–35]

The Decision of the Flower, 1825, 1
Christine, 1825, 65
The Criminal, 1825, 375
The Tomb of Romeo and Juliet, 1826, 50
The Forsaken, 1826, 159
L'Amore Dominatore, 1826, 247
Retirement, 1826, 385
Lines Written Beneath a Portrait of Lord Byron, Painted by Mr. West, 1827, 33
The Minstrel's Monitor, 1827, 103
The Inconstant, 1827, 248
Cupid and Pysche [*sic*], 1827, 337
The Lost Star, 1828, 20
Juliet after the Masquerade, 1828, 57
Ballad, 1828, 136
The Declaration, 1828, 217 (may possibly be by W. Leeds)
The Adieu, 1828, 346
Love Tormenting the Soul, 1828, 402

May Morning, 1836, 84
The Mother's Warning, 1836, 166
The Evening Star, 1836, 199
Le Chapeau Noir, 1836, 226

Pledge of Friendship [1826–28]

Love's Happiness (from "The Improvisatrice"), 1827, 25
The Soldier's Funeral, 1827, 160
Rosalie (from "The Improvisatrice"), 1827, 205
Separation, 1828, 111
Othman, 1828, 289
Song, 1828, 378

Bijou; Cameo [1828–30]

The City of the Dead, 1828, 13; *Cameo,* 74
Sans Souci, 1828, 81; *Cameo,* 244
Tivoli, 1829, 7
Lines, the Feast of Life, 1829, 118; *Cameo,* 33
Mont Blanc, 1829, 225

Juvenile Forget Me Not [1828–32]

The Miniature, 1831, 37
The Dead Robin, 1832, 21
The Evening Prayer, 1832, 65
Mable Dacre's First Lesson, 1832, 79
The Shamrock, 1833, 25
The Grandmother, 1833, 65
The Indian Island, 1833, 67
The Rose of Eden Dale and Her Hothouse Flowers, 1833, 223
The Little Mountaineer, 1836, 31
The Lesson, 1836, 150
The Watchful Friend, 1837, 186
Dry Feet, 1837, 219

Keepsake [1828–61]

'Lady, thy face is very beautiful,' 1829, 121
The Altered River, 1829, 310
The Death Song, 1831, 143

Legendary Fragments, 1831, 172
The Forgotten One, 1831, 205
The Return, 1831, 273
Edith, 1832, 94
Good Angels, 1832, 129
An Early Passage in Sir John Perrot's Life, 1832, 179
Do You Remember It? 1832, 239
Marius at the Ruins of Carthage, 1833, 65
The Adieu, 1833, 103
One Peep Was Enough, 1833, 301
The Head, 1834, 93
Fenella's Escape, 1836, 215
Remembrance, 1837, 28

Juvenile Keepsake [1829–30, 1835]

The Mariner's Child to His Mother, 1830, 101

Ackermann's Juvenile Forget Me Not [1830–32]

To Amelia Read on Her Thirteenth Birthday, 1830, 177

Drawing-Room Scrapbook [a.k.a. *Fisher's Drawing Room Scrap Book,* 1832–54]

From 1832 until her death in 1839, L.E.L. contributed all the verse not otherwise ascribed to *Fisher's Drawing Room Scrap Book,* as well as the following poems inserted by later editors.

Interior of a Moorish Palace, 1840, 9
Kate Is Craz'd, 1840, 10
The Portrait of Lord Byron, 1840, 11
The Shrine and Grotto of Santa Rosalia, 1840, 15
The Mosque at Cordova, 1840, 17
Thomas Clarkson, Esq., 1840, 20
Scene in Lebanon, 1840, 23
Baptismal Font, Cathedral at Palermo, 1841, 6
Neftah in the Jereed, 1841, 13
Temple and Fountain at Zagwhan, 1841, 43
The Missionary's Wife, 1841, 54
Homes of Splendour, 1849, 59

[Heath's] Book of Beauty [1833–47; continued as *Book of Beauty,* 1848]

L.E.L. contributed all the articles and verse in the first volume (1833) of *Heath's Book of Beauty* and the following in subsequent volumes.

Lady Caroline Maxse, 1836, 62
The Lady Egerton, 1836, 191
Amina, 1836, 258
A Scene in the Life of Nourmahal, 1837, 232
Mrs. Wombwell, 1838, 33
Mrs. Maberly, 1839, 179
Miss Cockayne, 1839, 275

Finden's Tableaux [1837–44]

Arabia, the Arab Maid, 1837, 23
(Boyle, 162–66)

LANDOR, WALTER SAVAGE (1775–1864)

Keepsake [1828–61]

Lines on Torquay, 1841, 128
A Stiolion, 1842, 216
A Story of Santander, 1843, 154
Lines, 1844, 185
Sent with Flowers, 1845, 15
Lines, 1846, 29
Dream of Youth and Beauty, 1847, 247
Risposta al "Mi Vien da ridere di Gabuzzi," 1847, 269
On Leaving My Villa, 1848, 259
Beatrice Cenci and Pope Clement VIII, 1852, 2
To Mdlle. Luigina de Sodre, 1853, 124

[Heath's] Book of Beauty [1833–47; continued as *Book of Beauty,* 1848]

Imaginary Conversation, Rhadamistus and Zenobia, 1834, 129
Philip II and Dona Juana Coelho, 1834, 196
Steele and Addison, 1835, 150
Parable of Asabel, 1836, 261
Imaginary Conversation, 1837, 95

Farewell to Italy, 1837, 259
The Dream of Petrarca, 1838, 254
Two Dramatic Scenes, "Anne Boleyn," 1839, 182
Galileo, Milton and a Dominican, 1840, 45
To Miss Rose Paynter on Seeing Her Sit for a Portrait, 1840, 229
Lines, 1841, 102
To Zoe, 1842, 279
Vittoria Colonna and Michel Angiolo Buonarotti, 1843, 177
Aesop and Rhodope, 1844, 154
To Lady Charles Beauclerk on Her Marriage, 1844, 233
A Vision, 1844, 239
Second Conversation, 1845, 2
Veglia di Partenza, 1847, 250

(Boyle, 166–67)

MITFORD, MARY RUSSELL (1787–1855)

Editor of *Finden's Tableaux* [102 entries; some works published in more than one literary annual]

Forget Me Not [1823–47, 1856]

Alice: A Dramatic Scene, 1826, 5
A Village Sketch, 1826, 304
Grace Neville, 1827, 57
Sonnet, 1827, 174
Sonnet, 1827, 267
The Bridal Eve, 1827, 363
The Wedding Ring, 1828, 79
The Country Apothecary, 1828, 113
Lost and Won, 1829, 217
The Country Kitchen, 1829, 329
The Trial of Charles the First: An Historical Scene, 1830, 73
The Death of Charles the First: An Historical Scene (Drama), 1831, 248
Old Master Green: A Village Sketch, 1832, 73
Old Mathew, the Matseller, 1833, 343
The Will, 1834, 177
Vintage Song, from Otto of Wittelsbach, 1844, 47
Woman's Destination, 1845, 47

Friendship's Offering [1824–44]

The Lady of Beechgrove, 1826, 91
Hay-Carrying: A Village Story, 1827, 160
The Siege: A Dramatic Scene, 1827, 290
The Rustic Wreath, 1828, 50
The Election, 1829, 8
Patty's New Hat, 1829, 256
The Cobbler over the Way, 1830, 99
To Mr. Lucas, 1830, 338
The Cousins: A Country Tale, 1831, 1
The Incendiary: A Country Tale, 1832, 1
Match-Making, 1833, 1
The Carpenter's Daughter: A Country Tale, 1834, 80
The Beauty of the Village, 1835, 160

Literary Souvenir [1825–35]

My Godfather, 1826, 393
An Acted Charade, 1827, 120
The Queen of the Meadow, 1827, 177
Sonnet, On Leaving a Favourite Picture, 1827, 223
Sonnet, The Fishing Seat—White Knights, 1827, 287
The Last of the Barbers, 1828, 148
Mademoiselle, Thérèse, 1828, 207
The Stolen Kiss: A Dramatic Scene, 1828, 317
The General and His Lady: A Sketch, 1829, 204
The Young Novice, 1829, 289
A Village Romance, 1830, 105
The Runaway, 1832, 312

Amulet [1826–36]

The Vicar's Maid: A Village Story, 1826, 130
Sonnet, 1826, 329
The Chalk Pit, 1827, 145
Sonnet, 1827, 236
The Morning Walk, 1828, 15
The Village Schoolmistress, 1828, 53
Fanny's Fairings, 1828, 246
Little Moses, 1829, 380

A Castle in the Air, 1830, 347
The Residuary Legatee, 1831, 230
A Day of Distress, 1832, 163
The Absent Member, 1835, 97
Hunting Scene, from Inez de Castro, 1836, 156

Pledge of Friendship [1826–28]

Sweet Is the Balmy Evening Hour, 1827, 35
The Two Kinsmen: A Dramatic Scene, 1828, 81
Olive Hathaway: A Village Sketch, 1828, 95
Sonnet, Written after Reading Dr. Currie's "Life of Burns," 1828, 160
Sonnet, 1828, 234
To a Friend with a Tuft of Heart's-Ease, 1828, 359

Bijou; Cameo [1828–30]

Jessy of Kibe's Farm, 1828, 65; *Cameo,* 120
The Lover's Invocation, imitated from an unpublished French poem, 1828, 191; *Cameo,* 7

Winter's Wreath [1828–32]

On the Death of a Friend, 1829, 20
The Two Sisters, 1829, 46

Anniversary [1829–30]

Going to the Races, 1829, 46

Gem [1829–32]

Tom Hopkins, 1829, 99
Harry Lewington and His Dog, 1829, 193
Little Miss Wren: A Sketch, 1830, 125
The Rat-Catcher: A Sketch, 1831, 201

Remembrance [1831, 1838, 1843]

The Haymakers, 1831, 36

Comic Offering [1831–35]

Young Master Ben, 1832, 55
Spinning-Wheel Song, 1833, 43

Finden's Tableaux [1837–44]

England, the King's Ward, 1838, 4
Florence, the Wager, 1838, 13
Ceylon, the Lost Pearl, 1838, 32
Scotland, Sir Allan and His Dog, 1838, 44
Carlisle, the Signal, 1838, 52
The Buccaneer, 1839, 6
The Baron's Daughter, 1839, 33
The Cartel, 1839, 39
A Story of the Woods, 1839, 46
The King's Page, 1840, 9
The Proud Ladye, 1840, 22
The Roundhead's Daughter, 1840, 32
The Beacon, 1840, 46
The Bride, 1840, 53
The Woodcutter, 1840, 53
The Return from the Fair, 1841, 14
The Rustic Toilet, 1841, 25
The Gleaner, 1841, 44
The Village Amanuensis, 1841, 55
The Stolen Letter, 1841, 61
Hop-Gathering, 1841, 63
(Boyle, 193–95)

POLWHELE, REV. RICHARD (1760–1838)

Forget Me Not [1823–47, 1856]

The Syrian Princess: A Fragment of an Unpublished Tragedy, 1826, 161
Impromptu, 1827, 94
Lines, 1827, [229]
The Enthusiast on the Waters, 1829, 89
Concha Veneris, 1829, 230
The Cave of Lemorna: A Legendary Tale (written fifty years before and found among his mss.), 1831, 51
Forest Scenery, 1833, 149
A Scene in Cornwall, 1833, 220
To the Evening or Tree Primrose, 1833, 211

To a Young Lady Playing Chess, 1834, 325
The Parents to Their Children, 1835, 229
The Departed Friend, 1836, 116
The Last Evening Primrose, 1836, 194
The Rose of Sharon, 1837, 90
Love and Mercy, 1837, 265
A Good Conscience, 1838, 258
A Fragment, 1841, 120

Friendship's Offering [1824–44]

Epigram from Claudian, 1827, 214
The Sympathising Zephyr, 1827, 214

Literary Souvenir [1825–35]

The Rill Lost in a Thicket, 1826, 162
The Old Oak, 1826, 206

Pledge of Friendship [1826–28]

Indifference, 1827, 81
Lines Written in Illness, 1828, 162
Sonnet, Written in 1800, 1828, 295

Amulet [1826–36]

An Impromptu, 1829, 73
Rhapsody from Zechariah, 1829, 189
(Boyle, 225–26)

REYNOLDS, FREDERIC MANSEL (d. 1850)

Editor of the *Keepsake*

Keepsake [1828–61]

To ——, 1829, 49
On Two Sisters, 1829, 51
To ——, 1829, 79
Invitation, to a Beautiful but Very Small Young Lady, 1829, 100
An Anticipation for a Certain Coquette, 1829, 119

To a Spinster, 1829, 142
The Thief Detected, 1829, 185
Reasons for Absence, 1829, 194
Test of Love, 1829, 219
An Incident, 1829, 221
Impromptu, 1829, 239
To ———, 1829, 264
Moral Song, 1831, 213
The Bourbons 1830, 1835, 276
The Well of Beauty, 1835, 291
A Mother's Love, 1837, 250
Stanzas, 1842, 278
The Divorce, 1843, 236
The Impatient Man and His Deaf Family, 1846, 103

[Heath's] Book of Beauty [1833–47; continued as *Book of Beauty,* 1848]

Stanzas, 1834, 202
Inscription in an Annual, 1837, 260
A Character, 1838, 278
The Convict, 1839, 92
Love's Waywardness, 1841, 237
Berengaria, Consort of Richard I, 1848, 89
Philippa of Hainault, 1848, 205
Catharine, Consort of Henry V, 1849, 62
Elizabeth, 1849, 254
(Boyle, 239)

RUSKIN, JOHN, R., J. R., J. ρ*;* κ.Φ*; Μ*ονοτοϖος (1819–1900)

Friendship's Offering [1824–44]

Salzburg, 1835, 37
Fragments, 1835, 317
The Months, 1836, 290
The Last Smile, 1837, 102
Leoni: A Legend of Italy, 1837, 217
The Scythian Grave, 1838, 116
Remembrance, 1838, 119

Christ Church, Oxford, 1838, 287
A Scythian Banquet Song, 1839, 25
Aristodemus at Platea, 1839, 140
The Scythian Guest, 1840, 52
The Broken Chain, 1840, 137
To ***, 1840, 244
The Tears of Psammenitus, 1841, 37
The Two Paths, 1841, 73
The Old Water-Wheel, 1841, 107
Farewell, 1841, 168
The Departed Light, 1841, 217
Agonia, 1841, 288
The Broken Chain, 1841, 311
The Last Song of Arion, 1842, 48
The Hills of Carrara, 1842, 178
The Broken Chain, 1842, 359
The Broken Chain, 1843, 61
The Battle of Montenotte, 1844, 59
A Walk in Chamouni, 1844, 141

Keepsake [1828–61]

The Old Seaman, 1845, 63
The Alps Seen from Marengo, 1845, 270
Mont Blanc, 1846, 35
The Arve at Cluse, 1846, 234

[Heath's] Book of Beauty [1833–47; continued as *Book of Beauty,* 1848]

La Madonna dell' Acqua, 1845, 18
Written among the Basse Alps, 1846, 109
The Glacier, 1846, 110
(Boyle, 248–49)

SCOTT, SIR WALTER (1771–1832)

Forget Me Not [1823–47, 1856]

Description of the Ua More, 1826, 256
Written for Miss Smith, 1834, 197

Friendship's Offering [1824–44]

Song of the Chieftain's Daughter (from *Waverley*), 1834, 16

Literary Souvenir [1825–35]

Epilogue, 1825, 373

Christmas Box [1828–29]

The Bonnets of Bonnie Dundee, 1828, 27 (contributed anonymously)

Bijou [1828–30]

Letter from Sir Walter Scott to Sir Adam Ferguson, Descriptive of a Picture Painted at Abbotsford by David Wilkie, Esq., 1828, 33; *Cameo,* 180

Keepsake [1828–61]

My Aunt Margaret's Mirror, 1829, 1
The Tapestried Chamber; or, The Lady in the Sacque, 1829, 123
Death of the Laird's Jock, 1829, 186
Description of the Engraving Entitled "A Scene at Abbotsford," 1829, 258
The House of Aspen: A Tragedy, 1830, 1
A Highland Anecdote, 1832, 283
Lines to a Lady Cochrane, 1853, 96

Gem [1829–32]

The Death of Keeldar, 1829, 13

Diadem [1832, 1839]

The Foreign-Bred Chief (as Narrated to a Party at Abbotsford), 1838, 41 *(Boyle, 258)*

SHELLEY, MARY WOLLSTONECRAFT (1797–1851)

Forget Me Not [1823–47, 1856]

Lacy de Vere, 1827, 275 [previously unattributed[2]]

Winter's Wreath [1828–32]

Proserpine: A Mythological Drama, 1832, 1

Keepsake [1828–61]

The Sisters of Albano, 1829, 80

Ferdinando Eboli, 1829, 195
The Mourner, 1830, 71
The Evil Eye, 1830, 150
The False Rhyme, 1830, 265
Transformation, 1831, 18
Absence, "Ah! he is gone and I alone," 1831, 39
A Dirge, "This morn thy gallant bark, love," 1831, 85
The Swiss Peasant, 1831, 121
The Dream, 1832, 22
The Brother and Sister: An Italian Story, 1833, 105
The Invisible Girl, 1833, 210
The Mortal Immortal, 1834, 71
The Trial of Love, 1835, 70
The Parvenue, 1837, 209
Euphrasia: A Tale of Greece, 1839, 135
Stanzas, "How like a star you rose upon my life," 1839, 179
Stanzas, "O, come to me in dreams, my love!" 1839, 201

[Heath's] Book of Beauty [1833–47; continued as *Book of Beauty,* 1848]

The Elder Son, 1835, 83
(Boyle, 260-61)

SHELLEY, PERCY BYSSHE (1792–1822)

Pledge of Friendship [1826–28]

Death and Sleep, 1827, 282

Keepsake [1828–61]

On Love, 1829, 47
Fragments:
1. Summer and Winter, 1829, 160
2. The Tower of Famine, 1829, 161
3. The Aziola, 1829, 162
(Boyle, 261)

SOUTHEY, ROBERT (1774–1843)

Friendship's Offering [1824–44]

From the Italian, 1826, 144

Inscription for a Tablet on the Caledonia Canel, 1826, 167
Inscription for a Monument at Arroyo, in Molina, 1827, 147
Funeral Song, for the Princess Charlotte of Wales, 1828, 1
Ode on the Death of Queen Charlotte, 1829, 106

Literary Souvenir [1825–35]

Fidelity, 1825, 81
Mary Queen of Scots and Chatelar, 1825, 102
Ibid., 1826, 116
To ——, 1825, 372
Lines to the Memory of a Young Officer, 1826, 341
A Soldier's Epitaph, 1827, 89
Epitaph, 1828, 77

Amulet [1826–36]

Lines Written upon the Death of the Princess Charlotte, 1829, 91

Bijou [1828–30]

Scotland: An Ode, 1828, 81

Keepsake [1828–61]

Lucy and Her Bird, 1829, 157
Stanzas, 1829, 238

Anniversary [1829–30]

Epistle to Allan Cunningham, 1829, 9
Inscriptions for the Caledonian Canal, 1829, 194
At Fort Augustus, 1829, 195
At Banavie, 1829, 197
(Boyle, 270)

STRICKLAND, SUSANNAH [Mrs. Moodie in Boyle] (1803–1885)

[Strickland was an influential and prolific Canadian writer during the nineteenth century; her papers are housed in the National Library of Canada, and her writing has been the subject of much scholarly work.]

Forget Me Not [1823–47, 1856]

The Rover's Farewell to His Mistress, 1829, 369

Love and Ambition, 1831, 144
Winter Calling Up His Legions, 1831, 321

Friendship's Offering [1824–44]

There's Joy When the Rosy Morning, 1829, 148
The Captive, 1831, 184
A Canadian Song, 1834, 96

Pledge of Friendship [1826–28]

Stanzas on War, 1828, 357

Juvenile Forget Me Not [1828–32]

The Rose That Was Discontented with Her Guardian Thorns, 1829, 228
Awake, 1831, 104
The Woodlane, 1831, 145

Gem [1829–32]

The Disappointed Politician, 1832, 34

Juvenile Keepsake [1829–30, 1835]

The Young Tyrolese, 1829, 146
The Mock Coral Necklace; or, the Young Spanish Emigrants, 1830, 157

New Year's Gift [1829–36]

Hints to Juvenile Gardeners, 1829, 167
Lady Lucy's Petition, 1830, 114

Iris [1830–31]

The Heir of Jeroboam, 1830, 95
Nathan and David, 1831, 89
The Deluge, 1831, 170

Ackermann's Juvenile Forget Me Not [1830–32]

The Son of Arminius: A Tale of Ancient Rome, 1830, 241
The Captive Squirrel's Petition, 1831, 59
Visit of the Sea Fish to the River Fishes, 1831, 210
The Boudoir, 1832, 31
The Vanquished Lion, 1832, 97

Marshall's Christmas Box [1831–32]

Black Jennie: A Tale founded on Facts, 1832, 3
The Messenian Maiden's Dream, 1832, 45
The Release of the Caged Lark, 1832, 91
The Picture Lost at Sea, 1832, 152

Comic Offering [1831–35]

My Aunt Dorothy's Legacy, 1832, 118
(Boyle, 203–4)

TENNYSON, LORD ALFRED, First Baron (1809–1892)

Friendship's Offering [1824–44]

Sonnet, 1832, 367
Sonnet, 1833, 29 [This sonnet first appeared in *Englishman's Magazine,* August 1831.]

Keepsake [1828–61]

St. Agnes, 1837, 247
Stanzas, 1851, 22
Stanzas, 1851, 122

Gem [1829–32]

No More, 1831, 87
Anacreontics, 1831, 131
A Fragment, 1831, 242
(Boyle, 287)

WATTS, ALARIC ALEXANDER ("A.A.W.") (1797–1864)

Editor of *Literary Souvenir* [and *Poetical Album*]

Literary Souvenir [1825–35]

The Death of the First-Born, 1825, 74
Kirkstall Abbey Revisited, 1825, 155
A Woman's Farewell, 1825, 204

The Sleeping Cupid, 1825, 392
Richmond Hill, 1826, 39
Love's Wealth, 1826, 48
My Own Fireside, 1826, 75
The Bachelor's Dilemma, 1826, 88
The Poet's Den, 1826, 153
The May Flowers of Life, 1826, 201
The Return, 1826, 241
The First Kiss, 1826, 280
The Death of Pompey the Great, 1826, 314
A Remonstrance, 1826, 382
The Grey Hair, 1827, 62
A Girl in a Florentine Costume, 1827, 109
To My Child Sleeping, 1827, 257
For Ever Thine, 1828, 85
Stanzas, On Seeing Flags, 1828, 110
On Burning a Packet of Letters, 1829, 37
Invocation to the Echo of a Sea-Shell, 1829, 120
King Pedro's Revenge, 1829, 159
Ditto, 1829, 166
The Youngling of the Flock, 1829, 199
Meet Me at Sunset, 1829, 313
The Anniversary, 1830, 60
To Caroline Bowles, 1830, 120
A Remonstrance, 1830, 199
We Met When Life and Hope Were New, 1830, 265
A Sketch from Real Life, 1830, 307
To a Child Blowing Bubbles, 1831, 31
The Martyrs of Royallieu, 1831, 249
The Review of the Victims, 1832, 37
The Conversazione, 1832, 222
Sketches of Modern Poets:
1. Wordsworth, 1832, 289
2. Campbell, 1832, 291
3. Coleridge, 1832, 293
4. Charles Lamb, 1832, 294
A Lyric of the Heart, 1833, 21
The Sister of Charity, 1834, 63
The Painter's Dream, 1835, 1

The Nine Sisters, 1835, 48
The Sisters, 1835, 97
Gertrude, 1835, 119
The Exile's Return, 1835, 154
The Lament of Boabdil el Chico, 1836, 37
Love and Spring, 1836, 123
*Notices on the Works of: (all pub. anonymously)
Henry Howard, R.A., 1835, 20
Thomas Stothard, R.A., 1835, 26
Richard Westall, R.A., 1835 61
George Barret, 1835, 113
E.V. Rippingille, 1835, 171
G. P. Lewis, 1835, 220
Thomas Uwins, A.R.A., 1836, 23
Williams Collins, R.A. 1836, 43
Sir William Beechy, R.A. 1836, 97
On the Picture of Lady Pamela Fitzgerald, 1836, 155
Penry Williams, 1836, 208
Robert Edmonstone, 1836, 193
Leopold Robert, 1837, 147

Pledge of Friendship [1826–28]

The First-Born, 1827, 238

Keepsake [1828–61]

The Silent Toast, 1846, 42
I Love Thee! 1853, 87

New Year's Gift [1829–36]

To a Dear Little Boy after an Interval of Absence, 1829, 120

Iris [1830–31]

Sonnet, Written in the Burial-Group of Bolton Abbey, 1830, 221
On the Death of a Young Lady, 1830, 326

[Heath's] Book of Beauty [1833–47; continued as *Book of Beauty,* 1848]

The Anniversary, 1846, 101
(Boyle, 301–2)

WORDSWORTH, WILLIAM (1770–1850)

Literary Souvenir [1825–35]

Sonnet on Sir Walter Scott's Quitting Abbotsford for Naples, 1833, 1

Pledge of Friendship [1826–28]

Thoughts, 1827, 96

Winter's Wreath [1828–32]

To the Skylark, 1828, 27
Memory, 1828, 206

Keepsake [1828–61]

The Country Girl, 1829, 50
The Triad, 1829, 72
The Wishing Gate, 1829, 108
Sonnet, 1829, 156
Sonnet, 1829, 183
(Boyle, 312–13)

Appendix C

Editors and Publishers of British Literary Annuals, 1823–31

This table has been compiled from my inspection of annuals, Faxon's *Literary Annuals and Gift Books: A Bibliography, 1823–1903* (with my corrections and emendations) and Boyle's *An Index to the Annuals (1820–1850).* Faxon provided a bibliographic description, publisher, editor, and years. However, many of the volumes were described based on second- and even third-hand knowledge, which has created many errors in the index.[1]

Luckily, many of these titles can be found throughout the United States in university and other research collections, including the New York Public Library's general research collection and The Pforzheimer Collection of Shelley and His Circle, Yale University, the University of South Carolina, the American Antiquarian Society (predominantly American titles), Brown University, the Library of Congress, Fales Library (New York University), and the Katherine D. Harris Collection (my private collection). I have reviewed several of the more popular titles in the collections of the New York Public Library (and from my personal collection). Some of the annuals have been rebound in library bindings. However, the NYPL Rare Book and Pforzheimer Collections house volumes in their original paper boards and/or in the fashion of nineteenth-century contemporary bindings.

I have included some of the more popular titles just barely beyond the 1830 boundary to emphasize the evolution of the genre. For example, *Heath's Book of Beauty* was a late entry into the annual publishing field; however, this annual was borne of the demand for beauty in the annuals and was the progenitor of subsequent imitators.

For a complete review of the numerous titles published through 1835, see appendix A. For a full list of titles through 1902, see Faxon's chronological index (129–40).

Annual title	Year	Size (inches)	Publisher	Editor
Ackermann's Juvenile Forget Me Not (1830–37)	1830		R. Ackermann	Frederic Shoberl
Affection's Gift (1830–33, 1844)	1830			
Affection's Offering (1830–33, 1844)	1830			
Amaranth (c. 1832)	1832	5 × 2	Renshaw & Co.	
Amulet (1826–36)	1826	5 × 3 & large paper	W. Baynes & Sons	S. C. Hall
	1827	5 × 3	W. Baynes & Son and Wightman & Cramp	S. C. Hall
	1828	5 × 3	W. Baynes & Son and Wightman & Cramp	S. C. Hall
	1829	5 × 3	Frederick Westley & A. H. Davis and Wightman & Co.	S. C. Hall
	1830	5 × 3	Frederick Westley & A. H. Davis	S. C. Hall
	1831	5 × 3	Frederick Westley & A. H. Davis	S. C. Hall
	1832	5 × 3	Frederick Westley & A. H. Davis	S. C. Hall
	1833	5 × 3	Frederick Westley & A. H. Davis; William Jackson (New York)	S. C. Hall
Anniversary (1829–30)	1829	7 × 5 & large paper: 9 × 5	John Sharpe	Allan Cunningham
	1830[2]			
Apollo's Gift, or the Musical Souvenir (1830–31)	1830	Quarto	Willis & Co.	Ed. Clementi & M. and J. B. Cramer
Bijou (1828–30)	1828	6 × 4	Wm. Pickering	William Fraser
	1829	6 × 4	Wm. Pickering	William Fraser
	1830	6 × 4	Wm. Pickering	William Fraser
Blossoms at Christmas (1825–26)	1825	5 × 3	J. Poole	
	1826			
Cabinet Album (1830–32)	1830		Hurst & Co.	
Cabinet of Curiosities (1829)	1829			
Carcanet (1828, 1830)[3]	1828		Wm. Pickering	Sir Harris Nicolas
	1830		Wm. Pickering	Sir Harris Nicolas

Casket (1829)	1829	8 × 5	John Murray	
Christian Forget Me Not (1829 or 1830)	1829			Thomas Holmes
Christian Souvenir (1830, 1842)	1830	8 × 5		
Christmas Box (1828–29, 1832)	1828	6 × 4	Wm. Harrison Ainsworth	T. Crofton Croker
	1829	6 × 3	John Ebers & Co.	T. Crofton Croker
Comic Annual (1830–39, 1842)	1830	6 × 4	Charles Tilt	Thomas Hood
	1831	6 × 4	Charles Tilt	Thomas Hood
	1832	6 × 4	Charles Tilt	Thomas Hood
	1833	6 × 4	Charles Tilt	Thomas Hood
Continental Annual (1832)	1832	7 × 4 & large paper, proof before letters	Smith Elder & Co.	William Kennedy
Emanuel (1830)	1830		Maunder	Rev. Wm. Shepherd
Excitement (1830–45)	1830			
First Flowers (1825–29)	1825		Poole	
	1826		Poole	
	1827		Poole	
	1828		Poole	
	1829		Poole	
Fisher's Drawing Room Scrap-Book (1832–54)	1832	11 × 8	Fisher, Son and Jackson	Letitia Elizabeth Landon[4]
Fisher's National Portrait Gallery (1830–33)	1830			Wm. Jerden
Forget Me Not (1823–47)	1823	5 × 3	R. Ackermann	Frederic Shoberl
	1824	5 × 3	R. Ackermann	Frederic Shoberl
	1825	5 × 3	R. Ackermann	Frederic Shoberl
	1826	5 × 3	R. Ackermann	Frederic Shoberl
	1827	5 × 3	R. Ackermann	Frederic Shoberl
	1828	5 × 3	R. Ackermann	Frederic Shoberl
	1829	5 × 3	R. Ackermann	Frederic Shoberl
	1830	5 × 3	R. Ackermann & Co.	Frederic Shoberl
	1831	5 × 3	R. Ackermann	Frederic Shoberl
	1832	6 × 3	R. Ackermann and Carey & Lea, Philadelphia	Frederic Shoberl
Friendship's Offering (1824–44)	1824	5 × 3	Lupton Relfe	Thomas K. Hervey
	1825	5 × 3	Lupton Relfe	Thomas K. Hervey

Annual title	Year	Size (inches)	Publisher	Editor
Friendship's Offering (1824–44) (*cont.*)	1826	5 × 3	Lupton Relfe	Thomas K. Hervey
	1827	5 × 3	Lupton Relfe	Thomas K. Hervey and B. E. Pote
	1828	5 × 3	Smith, Elder & Co.	Charles Knight
	1829	5 × 3	Smith, Elder & Co.	Thomas Pringle
	1830	6 × 3	Smith, Elder & Co.	Thomas Pringle
	1831	6 × 3	Smith, Elder & Co.	Thomas Pringle
	1832	6 × 3	Smith, Elder & Co.	Thomas Pringle
	1833[5]	6 × 3	Smith, Elder & Co.	Thomas Pringle
Gem (1829–32)	1829	6 × 3 & large paper: 7 × 4	Wm. Marshall	Thomas Hood
	1830	6 × 4	Wm. Marshall	Thomas Hood
Gem of Art[6] (1830, 1834)	1830	Folio		
The Graces or Literary Souvenir[7] (1824)	1824		Hurst, Robinson & Co.	Rev. George Croly
Heath's Book of Beauty (1833–47)[8]	1833	7 × 4	Longman, Rees, Orme, Brown and Green & Longman	Letitia Elizabeth Landon[9]
Hommage aux Dames (1825)[10]	1825		John Setts, Jr.	
Iris (1830–31)	1830	6 × 4	Sampson Low & Hurst Chance	Rev. Thomas Dale
Johnson's Shooter's Annual (1830)	1830		Johnson	
Juvenile Forget Me Not (1828–32)[11]	1828			
	1829	6 × 4	N. Hailes	Mrs. S. C. Hall
	1830	6 × 4	N. Hailes	Mrs. S. C. Hall
	1831	6 × 4	Frederick Westley & A. H. Davis	Mrs. S. C. Hall
	1832	6 × 4	Westley & Davis	Mrs. S. C. Hall
	1833	6 × 4	R. Ackermann	Mrs. S. C. Hall
Juvenile Keepsake (1829–30, 1835)	1829	6 × 4	Hurst, Chance & Co.	Thomas Roscoe
	1830			
Juvenile Landscape Annual (1830)	1830			
Keepsake (1828–61)	1828	7 × 4	Hurst, Chance & Co.	Founded by engraver Charles Heath and publisher William Ainsworth (*Christmas Box*)

	1829	7 × 4	Hurst, Chance & Co.	Frederic Mansel Reynolds
	1830	7 × 4	Hurst, Chance & Co.	Frederic Mansel Reynolds
	1831	7 × 4	Hurst, Chance & Co.	Frederic Mansel Reynolds
Keepsake Français (1830–31)	1830		Whittaker	Mrs. A. A. Watts
Landscape Annual (1830–39)[12]	1830	7 × 5 & large paper; proof impressions on India paper	Robert Jennings & William Chaplin	Thomas Roscoe
Laurel (1830)	1830		Sharpe	
Literary Bluebook (1830)	1830		Marsh	
Literary Gem (1830)	1830	7 × 4		
Literary Souvenir (1825–35)[13]	1825	5 × 3 & large paper: 7 × 4	Hurst, Robinson & Co.	Alaric Watts
	1826	5 × 3 & large paper: 7 × 4	Hurst, Robinson & Co.	Alaric Watts
	1827	5 × 3 & large paper: 7 × 4	Longman, Rees, Orme, Brown & Green	Alaric Watts
	1828	5 × 3 & large paper: 7 × 4	Longman, Rees, Orme, Brown & Green	Alaric Watts
	1829	5 × 3 & large paper: 7 × 4	Longman, Rees, Orme, Brown & Green	Alaric Watts
	1830	5 × 4 & large paper: 7 × 4	Longman, Rees, Orme, Brown & Green	Alaric Watts
	1831	5 × 3 & large paper: 7 × 4		Alaric Watts
Looking Glass: A Caricature Annual (1830–36)	1830	Folio	McLean	
Lyre (1830–31)	1830			
Musical Bijou (1830–32, 1836, 1837, 1849–52)	1830	9 × 11	Goulding and D'Almaine	F. H. Burney
Musical Forget Me Not (1830–31)	1830	Quarto		
Musical Gem (1829–33, 1835, 1845)	1829	Quarto		Nicolas Mori and William Ball

Annual title	Year	Size (inches)	Publisher	Editor
Musical Gem (1829–33, 1835, 1845) (*cont.*)	1830	Quarto		Nicolas Mori and William Ball
Musical Souvenir (1830)	1830			
Nautilus (1829)	1829			
New Year's Gift (1829–36)	1829	5 × 3	Longman, Rees, Orme, Brown & Green	Mrs. A. A. Watts
	1830	5 × 3	Longman, Rees, Orme, Brown & Green	Mrs. A. A. Watts
Offering (1829, 1833, 1834)[14]	1829			Rev. Thomas Dale
Pledge of Friendship (1826–28, 1831)	1826		Marshall	
	1827		Marshall	
	1828		Marshall	
Poole's Royal Sovereign (1827)	1827	4 × 3	J. Poole	
Remember Me[15] (1825–26, 1830–32)	1825	5 × 3	I. Poole	
	1826	5 × 3	I. Poole	
	1830		Darton & Clark	
Remembrance, The (1831, 1838, 1843)	1831		Jennings & Chaplin	Thomas Roscoe
Royal Sovereign (1827)	1827		Toole	Toole
Souvenir Litteraire de France (1829)	1829		Longman & Co.	Alaric Watts
Times Telescope (1828–31)	1828		Sherwood	
	1829		Sherwood	
	1830		Sherwood	
Troubadour: A Vocal Souvenir (1828)	1828			
Winter's Wreath (Liverpool) (1828–32)[16]	1828			
	1829	6 × 3	Geo. Smith & George B. Whittaker	
	1830	6 × 3	Whittaker, Treacher & Co.; Wardle in Philadelphia	
	1831	6 × 3	Whittaker, Treacher & Co.; Wardle in Philadelphia	
Young Gentleman's Library (1829)	1829	5 × 3	Longman, Rees, Orme, Brown & Green	M. B. Pinnock
Young Ladies Book (1829)	1829			W. Harvey
Zoological Keepsake (1830)	1830	Duodecimo		Marsh

Appendix D

Full Text of Nineteenth-Century Writings from Chapters 3 and 4

FROM CHAPTER 3

The Graces

Simplici myrto nihil allabores Sedulus curæ. *Hor.*
I lay upon a bank with harebells strown;
For now the ruddy Sun was growing pale,
And here and there a star was glittering lone,
And odour-breathing from the blossomed vale
Came slowly as a sigh the evening gale.
Then all was hush'd,—but where with folded wing
Above me cooed the turtle-dove her tale,
And, thro' the grass, a little bubbling spring
Wooed gentle Summer-sleep with its low murmuring.

But whether that sweet spot was haunted ground,
Or that the world-sick fancy loves to stray
Thro' regions on our weary Earth unfound;
No sooner sleep upon my eyelids lay,
Than seemed to light the East a lovelier day;
And, lo! upon the dappled clouds afar
Came winged and rosewreathed forms, that with fond play
Danced round and round a slow descending car,

And from it stooped upon the flowery bank
Three shapes of beauty; yet they wore no plume.

In reverent worship at their feet I sank:
"We come," said they, and Echo said "We come,"
In sounds that o'er me hovered like perfume.
"We come, The Graces three! to teach the spell,
That makes sweet woman lovelier than her bloom."
Then rose a heavenly chant of voice and shell:
"LET WIT! AND WISDOM! WITH HER SOVEREIGN BEAUTY DWELL!"

(*The Graces,* 1824, v–vi)

FROM CHAPTER 4

Constancy

By James Bird

She dwelt in her dear native vale, where the light
Of her loveliness shone like the planet of night,
That makes all clad in beauty more beautiful still,
Adds new charms to the valley, new grace to the hill!

O'er that spot nature's bounty profusely had thrown,
From her garner of treasures, rare gems of her own!
And its beautiful glades were as happy as fair,
For the pride of the valley, young Ada, was there!

Oh! the charm of her smile was so sunny and bright;
Her form, like seraph's, all graceful and light,
And her eloquent eye softly told that its ray
From the sun of her soul had just darted away!

Yes! she breathed the fair sylph of that sweet shaded spot,
Bloom'd the chaste, lovely flower of her vine-cover'd cot,
Where the beauty of nature enchantingly smiled—
Where the mother was blest in the love of her child.

And of Ada's fond heart, there was *one,* who possess'd
All its hope—the devotion, the truth of her breast,
And whose love was to her as the flower to the bee,
Or the leaf that ne'er fades on the evergreen tree!

But the pride of her soul, the brave Seymour, was far
From the bowers of her home, 'mid the tumult of war;
With the fervour of youth, o'er the wide-rolling wave,
He had rush'd to the fight, with the noble and brave.

He departed!—The ocean divided them now,
And the care for his absence was mark'd on her brow,
Where anxiety's fear, the soft shading of sorrow,
Veil'd the bliss of to-day 'neath the hope of to-morrow!

Time fled—and he came not—and, and again,
Had the summer sun smiled o'er the deep, heaving main;—
Oh! How drear was the night, and how cheerless the day,
While he dwelt from her own lovely valley away!

Now the sweet blooming spring brought delight to the earth,
And the bud and the floweret rejoiced in their birth;
And though bright glow'd the scene which around her was spread,
Yet the spell of her heart, its enchantment, had fled!

He sent not—return'd not—she heard of his fame,
And her heart burn'd with joy at the tidings which came;
For the star of her being was cloudless or dim,
As Fate dealt her storm or her sunshine to him!

How slow wane the hours when the form we most prize
Far away!—far away!—is estranged from our eyes!
And the moments to Ada thus painfully wrought
The sad dread of suspense, the dejection of thought.

"He is gone!—and for ever!—if living, no more
Dwells his thought on the scenes he so valued before.

Seymour shares not the laurels he wins for his brown
With the heart that hath loved, and that worships him now!

"Yes! They tell me, my dear humble home from his thought
Is all vanish'd away like a dream that is nought.
No!—No!—he may fall in the morning of youth,
But his heart is the temple of virtue and truth!"

Thus she pensively mourn'd—and, though many a swain
Had bow'd down at the shrine of her beauty in vain;
Where her worshippers knelt, and exultingly told
Of their spacious domains and their treasures of gold,

Yet she heeded them not!—As the flower that will turn
To the light of its life, wheresoe'er it may burn;
So to Seymour her heart turn'd its hope, though the ray
That could cherish that hope from her sight was away.

The sun was slow wending to seek for his rest,
In the sapphirine bower of his realm in the west,
While his beams softly play'd on the light waving trees
That now whisper'd their joy at the kiss of the breeze!

In that hour lovely Ada dejectedly sate
By the door of her cottage, she mused on her fate;
And though sweetly her bird trill'd his song to her ear,
Its soft music had lost the rich notes that could cheer.

And the book she most loved, which had often re-press'd
The dominion of sorrow that vanquish'd her breast;
Its page, once so prized, fail'd to comfort her now,
Or to chase the despair that o'ershadow'd her brow!

Hope died in her soul:—hark! a footstep is nigh,
And a shadow has caught the bright glance of her eye—
She turns—her breath quickens—before her he stands,
Her own Seymour!—the book from her tremulous hands

Now fell, as she sprang, like an arrow that flies,
Or a dove that darts swift to her mate in the skies,
While her heart all its truth, all its ardour confess'd,
As her fast changing cheek softly sank on his breast.

At that moment, the rose, which she wore in her bosom,
Fell down at her feet with its redolent blossom;
As though *now* all its charms had no fragrance nor worth,
Since that bosom possess'd all its treasure in earth!

Oh, Ada! dear Ada! the noon of thy youth
Shall be bless'd for thy constancy, virtue, and truth.
And, Seymour! brave Seymour! thy honour shall be
Thy sure passport to joy—beauty's garland to thee!

Oh, woman! what bliss, what enchantment, we owe,
To the spell of thy heart, to thy solace below,
To thy truth so enduring—thy kindness and care
In the morning of joy, in the night of despair!

To thy soul's chosen Love thou unchanged wilt remain,
In health and in sickness, in pleasure and vain;
And, when closed are his eyes in Death's mortal eclipse,
Even then, still is his the last kiss of thy lips!

And over his grave thou wilt mournfully keep
Thy lone vigil of sorrow, to pray and to weep:
Yes! to pray—that his errors of heart be forgiven,
And that *thou* may'st yet meet him unsullied in heaven!

(1829 *Forget Me Not,* 157–61)

Constancy

By Charles Swain

"It is—it is the trumpet's note!—
Bright Hope once more is mine!

I see the glorious banners float,
The martial weapons shine!
I hear, like an approaching storm,
The warriors' heavy tread:
Albert! I seek in vain thy form:
O God!—canst thou be dead?

"One—but one little moment more,
My heart forget to ache;
That time hath blessed joys in store—
Or griefs—to bid thee break!
Long years, since our farewell, have past
In misery and in gloom;
And, oh! if it should prove our last,
Welcome my shroud and tomb!

"Alas! How could I live—yet know
That thou, my love, wert slain;
That, gash'd and cold, thy noble brow
Lay on the battle-plain:
That the fond voice, 't was bliss to hear,
In death had pass'd away:—
O, Albert, haste—or doubt and fear
Thy Genevieve will slay!

"Who calls?—the wind my ear deceives—
Again—'tis from the grove—
And, hark!—a step among the leaves—
'Tis he!—my life—my love!
O, welcome—welcome—to this breast,
Thou prized of all the most!—
This kiss—these tears—will speak the rest—
Alas! I thought thee lost!"

"My own fond girl—my graceful flower—
My beautiful—my pride—
How have I long'd for this blest hour,

When on the ocean wide!
And is, indeed, thy youthful heart
Still constant as my own?—
Then we have met, no more to part;
To live for love alone!

"O, I have many a tale to tell
Of woes and perils o'er;
Of fair and gallant youths that fell
Upon the Turkish shore!—
Of dreadful battles on the land,
And tempests on the sea;—
Still saved, by Heaven's protecting hand,
My Genevieve—for thee!"

"Yet thou look'st pale—thine arm is bound—
And faded is thine eye;
Ah me! I fear, from sight and sound,
Thou com'st but home—to die!—
But, no!—I will not speak of this,
Nor keep one thought of pain;
This hour is one of soul-felt bliss,
And many may remain!"

(1829 *Forget Me Not,* 162–64)

Notes

INTRODUCTION

1. Also quoted in Erickson, *Economy of Literary Form,* 30.

2. For further discussion about the Poetess Tradition, see Laura Mandell's introduction to the Poetess Archive Database (http://idhmc.tamu.edu/poetess/about/index.html#term).

3. For an example of Wordsworth's contribution to *The Keepsake* and the financial remuneration received for essentially allowing Charles Heath to use his name, see Douglas, "Wordsworth as Businessman."

4. Scott very famously declined a substantial amount of money to edit *The Keepsake,* a fact that has been mined by literary scholars as evidence of Scott's (and others') disdain for being associated with literary annuals. See Hill, "Scott, Hogg," esp. 19.

5. Here, I am purposefully reductive in my discussion of textual theory. My work relies on various schools of thought: bibliography, textual materialism, social textual criticism, and *l'histoire du livre,* a French tradition of book history. For a complete discussion of these various schools of thought, see "Society and Culture in the Text" in Greetham's *Theories of the Text,* esp. 367. In this introduction, I use *text* to refer to the characters on a printed page; *work* refers to the sociological product, as McGann defines it in *A Critique of Modern Textual Criticism.*

6. For an analysis of McGann's social text, see Mack and Rome, "Marxism, Romanticism and Postmodernism."

7. Papyrus, made from plants, is the precursor to paper. Its function was limited, however: only one side could be used for writing, which wasted materials and space. Papyrus was effective as a roll, but as a brittle substance, it was difficult to bend and sew into bindings. Parchment, made from animal skin, was more expensive but more efficient for writing and as binding material. In addition, parchment was recyclable: "Parchment had the added advantage of being capable of re-use, with a rescraping of the surface to produce a palimpsest. The text on papyrus could be rewritten while the ink was still wet, when a rag could remove any errors, but as the ink dried, it became more difficult to alter the text. And papyrus could certainly not take the harsh scraping that was necessary to produce a genuine palimpsest" (Greetham, *Textual Scholarship,* 60, 61).

8. For this project, *literary* refers specifically to poetry, prose, fiction, and nonfiction writing that employs the use of imagination and creative ability for composition.

9. Discussions of various forms of paratexts surface in several of the following chapters.

10. For an example of scholarship on literature as an archive, see Pasco, "Literature as Historical Archive."

11. For further reading on an annual focusing on slavery issues, see R. Thompson, "Liberty Bell."

12. The book as a body is an idea that has long been advanced by early modern scholars. The page itself was initially prepared from animal skin, a representation of the body. See Gellrich, *Idea of the Book.*

13. Faxon's bibliographical index (*Literary Annuals and Gift Books: A Bibliography, 1823–1903*) includes only physical descriptions of every American and British annual that Faxon and his team could visually inspect—in all, approximately two thousand British annuals.

14. Ledbetter and Hoagwood, "Introduction to *The Keepsake*."

15. The 1829 volume of the *Keepsake,* the subject of many scholarly articles and a dissertation by Kathryn Ledbetter, contained a large number of literati, including Percy Bysshe Shelley (posthumously), Mary Shelley, William Wordsworth, Samuel Taylor Coleridge, and Sir Walter Scott. Letitia Elizabeth Landon was also a major contributor to the 1829 *Keepsake.* For contributions by Landon and by Wordsworth, see Ledbetter and Hoagwood, "Introduction to *The Keepsake,*" in *L.E.L.'s Verses and "The Keepsake" for 1829: A Hypertext Edition.*

16. Whereas Clare published at least thirty-nine poems in some of the most successful British annuals from 1826 to 1844 (most prolifically between 1826 and 1830), Tennyson contributed only eight poems from 1831 to 1851, including "St. Agnes" in the 1837 *Keepsake.*

17. See Victorian Women Writers Project, http://webapp1.dlib.indiana.edu/vwwp/welcome.do; Internet Archive, www.archive.org/; the Poetess Archive, http://idhmc.tamu.edu/poetess/index.html; and the NINES federated projects, www.nines.org/about/scholarship/scholarly-projects/.

18. Wolfson, *Felicia Hemans.*

19. Each literary annual editor painstakingly selected the order of writings and engravings to produce a flow or movement to the volume—something that is lost in the anthologizing of the poetry.

20. Other avenues of inquiry include looking at the annual's impact on publication forms in the nineteenth century, e.g., Charles Dickens's *Christmas Book,* which began publication in 1843 and could have capitalized on the seasonal success begun by the annuals.

CHAPTER 1

1. Samuels suggests that this savvy, German-born entrepreneur can only be known by the business records that he left behind. Without a centralized archive of his letters, we can only surmise the accuracy of the *Notes and Queries* article's (1869) description. Very few accounts exist of Ackermann's workplace, with the exception of a single 1798 mention by colorist John Sell Cotman, and another provided by his son, Miles Edmund. John Ford, Ackermann's only biographer, paints a picture of a well-liked humanitarian in *Ackermann 1783–1983.*

2. According to Colin Franklin, Ackermann was a friend of Alois Senefelder's, a German who invented lithography in 1798 and then published (in English by Ackermann in 1819) *A Complete Course of Lithography.* Lithography allows the artist to draw directly onto stone without the intervention of a line engraver. Around 1819, Ackermann employed William Combe to write an argument against a proposed tax on the type of stone used for lithography, the best of which came from Germany (Franklin, "Prison Manuscripts," 57–58). Combe's treatise employed Ackermann's favorite technique, encouraging leadership in a quickly evolving world economy: "Lithography, though well known, as it is most extensively to the very great Advantage of the places where it has been more particularly cultivated and encouraged—It is however but new in this country, though if cultivated and

encouraged promises uncommon improvement in a branch of the fine Arts, which have taken such deep root in the British soil, and form such beneficial article in the trade of it" (Franklin, "Prison Manuscripts," 58).

3. Because of his relationship with Ackermann, Papworth contributed five prose descriptions of architecture, the type of descriptions that moved Ackermann to elevate architecture to artistic rendering in the *Forget Me Not:* "Regent Street" (1824), "Porch of the Chartres Cathedral" (1836), "The Doge's Palace, Venice" (1837), "Monuments of the Scaligers" (1846), and "Ratisbon Cathedral" (1847). Each essay is accompanied by an engraving of the same title.

4. Allen Samuels proposes that Ackermann's relationship with Rowlandson extended the influence of the Picturesque movement in London during the early nineteenth century because Ackermann "promoted art as illustration" ("Publishing the Picturesque," 242).

5. A publisher's list of Ackermann's offerings in the *Edinburgh Review* 41 of June 1827 lists *Flowers,* a folio study in thirty floral specimens with lithographic illustrations. Because Linnaean botany dominated the naturalist's landscape and women were being encouraged to engage in this type of science, this folio edition is further evidence of Ackermann's business acumen and knowledge of his clientele. Also listed, and now perhaps more famous, is Robert Blair's *The Grave: A Poem, Illustrated by Twelve Etchings Executed by Louis Schiavonetti from the Original Inventions of William Blake.*

6. Ackermann collaborated with celebrated artist Auguste Charles Pugin to great success on this project; see Hill, "A. C. Pugin."

7. For an in-depth view of Ackermann's business, see Ford, "Ackermann Imprints and Publications." For a discussion that locates Ackermann in larger nineteenth-century history, see chapter 1 ("Rudolf Ackermann and the Politics of a British Culture Industry") in Kutcher, "Flowers of Friendship." For an overview of the history of lithography in the early nineteenth century and Ackermann's contributions, see Beall, "Interdependence."

8. By selling subscriptions, essentially a preorder of a magazine or book made by individuals as opposed to booksellers, publishers could ideally determine budgets and profits before committing an issue to print.

9. Pugin allowed three paintings to be rendered into engravings for the *Forget Me Not* in addition to his other work with Ackermann: "The Pavilion, Brighton, West Front" (1826); "The Pavilion, Banqueting Room" (1826); and the "Presentation" (1834). The Pavilion artworks are accompanied by an anonymously authored prose description, "The Pavilion, His Majesty's Palace, at Brighton," and a third engraving not drawn by Pugin. For the influence of Pugin's son on the Gothic Revival in architecture (carrying on his father's legacy) during the first half of the nineteenth century, see Hill, "Reformation to Millennium."

10. Literary annuals were at first produced for a subscriber but were quite rapidly converted to consumer publications that were preordered by various booksellers, depending on the authors, editors, and publishers involved in a title. Orders also increased if the annual had a reputation for selling well during the previous year. Of course, reviews and circulation numbers were important in these decisions. Though many scholars have been able to track circulation numbers as offered by the original publishing houses or revealed in an editor's preface, assessing actual ownership, gift giving, or readership of literary annuals has been virtually impossible. Inscriptions give us some idea about a particular volume's

provenance and ownership, but the literary annuals are not held in a cohesive enough collection to permit an assessment of these issues.

11. French and German scholars have evaluated and indexed the impact of the almanac and pocket-book on literary annuals published in various countries. The French studies include John Grand-Carteret's *Les almanachs français* (1896), B. H. Gausseron's *Les Keepsakes et les annuaires illustrés de l'époque romantique* (1896), and Frédéric Lachèvre's *Bibliographie sommaire des Keepsakes et autres recueils collectifs de la période romantique, 1823–1848* (1929) and *Bibliographie sommaire de l'Almanach des Muses (1765–1833)* (1928). The German studies include Paul Merker's *Reallexikon der deutschen Literaturgeschichte* (1926–28), Hans Köhring's *Bibliographie der Almanache, Kalender und Taschenbücher für die Zeit von ca 1750–1860* (1929), R. Pissin's *Almanache der Romantik* (1910), Hans Grantzow's *Geschichte des Göttinger und des Vossischen Musenalmanachs* (1909), and Wolfgang Seyffert's *Schiller's Musenalmanache* (1913). V. A. Heck has created a list of European annuals in *Almanache, Kalender, Taschenbücher, Anthologien* (R. Thompson, *American Literary Annuals,* 165–66).

12. For a discussion of the Christmas trade and commodification of books, see Nissenbaum, *Battle for Christmas;* Piper, *Dreaming in Books,* chap. 4; and Kooistra, *Poetry, Pictures and Popular Publishing,* chap. 4.

13. In *The Evolution of the Book,* Frederick Kilgour describes stereotyping as "[a] process for producing a metal printing plate by infusing a plaster mold of typeset text with lead-rich type metal to produce an exact reproduction of the original type[, which] is useful for printing newspapers, as well as books for which reprinting is anticipated" (106).

14. Though the steam press became standard operating machinery in the production of newspapers and was a catalyst for dailies' and weeklies' lower retail prices, it did not replace the more expensive hand labor in book printing until the 1830s; see Altick, *English Common Reader,* 277. See also Eisenstein, *Divine Art, Infernal Machine.*

15. Altick describes the "working class" as lower-middle and lower classes who were "ranks of unskilled labor," as opposed to the "old-established middle class (merchants and bankers, large employers of labor, superior members of professions" (*English Common Reader,* 82). With the movement from cottage industries to mechanized labor, more people were moving to urban areas during the late eighteenth and early nineteenth century. The working class, as the largest-growing consumer class during that time, was a heterogeneous mixture of reading publics as well as economic levels—with their income, some in this class could be grouped with the lower middle class, a working class of literate and skilled laborers. The reading materials in demand depended heavily on the income of these skilled laborers: "[P]eople who benefitted from the spread of elementary education and whose occupations required not only that they be literate but that they keep their reading faculty in repair. And because these people shared more in the century's prosperity than did the unskilled laborers, they were in a somewhat better position to buy cheap books and periodicals as these became available" (Altick, *English Common Reader,* 83). "Cheap books and periodicals" were less costly to produce and more effective in rapid production.

16. This long-lasting genre focused particularly on the eccentricities of upper-class lifestyle. In "The Silver Fork Novel," Tamara S. Wagner labels the genre both escapist and censorious of the "frivolities and often supercilious emphasis on the aesthetic rather than the moral that characterised aristocratic high society" (para. 1). According to Wagner, the genre

lasted throughout the nineteenth century but was popular during the late 1820s and 1830s because of publisher Henry Colburn's advertising and recruiting skills. William Hazlitt (who coined the term), William Makepeace Thackeray, and Thomas Carlyle criticized the silver fork society and the itinerant novels in various works, including *Vanity Fair* and *Sartor Resartus* (Wagner, "Silver Fork Novel," para. 1–2). For further reading on silver fork society and literature, see Adburgham, *Silver Fork Society.*

17. For a discussion of the twopenny newspaper's cultural capital, see Maidment, "'Penny' Wise, 'Penny' Foolish?"

18. These authors, titles, and dates were amassed from primary research of newspapers, periodicals, and printed materials published between 1789 and 1860. Some references were taken from J. R. de J. Jackson's enumerative bibliography, *Romantic Poetry by Women;* appendixes in Altick, *English Common Reader* (381–96); and "On Cheap Periodical Literature" in *The Gentleman's Magazine* (June 1825): 483–86.

19. In 1814, Ackermann again engaged in relief support, this time on behalf of orphans and widows affected by the Battle of Leipzig. The king of Saxony recognized his work and awarded him the Order of Civil Merit. Printed posthumously, *A Short Account of Successful Exertions in Behalf of the Fatherless and Widows after the War in 1814* (written by Frederic Shoberl) provides correspondence and accounts of Ackermann's efforts. This pamphlet was apparently published to "increase the Subscriptions for the Fatherless and Widows of 1870 and 1871" by relaying the generosity of Ackermann in supporting victims after an assault on Leipzig in the *Narrative of the Most Remarkable Events Which Occurred in and near Leipzig . . . 1813* (again written by Shoberl). Sir Walter Scott wrote to Ackermann commending him on his endeavors and speaking of his own actions. He called Ackermann's *Narrative* "the most striking picture I ever read of the realities of war" (14, from March 26, 1813, letter in *Narrative of the Most Remarkable Events*). Ackermann also took in French and Spanish immigrants to work in his printing house, but this is a well-documented fact—and some suggest that it was perhaps not so benevolent.

20. Ackermann and subsequent literary historians capitalize and italicize the word *Taschenbuch* when writing about its influence on the *Forget Me Not.* In English, this grammatical structure implies that the word is a title. In German, though, all nouns are capitalized.

21. For further information on Taylor and his Anglo-Germanic influence in England, see Herzfeld, "William Taylor of Norwich."

22. For a discussion of *Mimili* as it relates to German nationalism, authorial control, and German parodies, see Kontje, "Male Fantasies, Female Readers."

23. "Biedermeier," 88.

24. The original engravings accompanying Clauren's text are available at Internet Archive, http://archive.org/details/mimilieineerzhooheunuoft.

25. Shoberl's translations include *A History of the Female Sex* (1808) and Kotzebue's play *The Patriot Father* (1830) from German and *Travels to Jerusalum and the Holy Land through Egypt by the Viscount Chateaubriand* (1833) and *The Hunchback of Notre-Dame* (1833) from French.

26. Translated by Professor Scott Westrem, CUNY Graduate Center.

27. Ackermann lost control of the volumes in 1831 when he turned over the business to his sons. Though his sons were educated in a London-based German-speaking school, they did not harbor the same loyalty to the homeland as their father did.

28. Hootman's database, *Index of British Literary Annuals* (www.britannuals.com/), "consists of artist and author indexes of 4,700 illustration items and 13,200 literary items from 283 British literary annuals" dating from 1823 to 1850, including the comic annuals. This is the only digital resource available to data mine the voluminous amounts of material published in the British literary annuals. Subtitles are inconsistently included in Hootman's database, which makes it difficult to assess the real effect of translations in the annuals. This is an area where further work is necessary after an appropriately encoded digital database has been established.

29. For a discussion of Joseph Blanco White's work, see Almeida, "Blanco White." John Ford proposes in *Ackermann 1783–1983* that José Joaquîn de Mora wrote and translated materials for *No Me Olvides* between 1824 and 1826—probably based on a review (*Foreign Review* 1 [1828]: 323–24).

30. For this Spanish translation of the successful *Forget Me Not,* Ackermann reused the plates and their accompanying prose or poetry in *No Me Olvides.* In both 1828 volumes, the table of contents for *No Me Olvides* does not include authors' names. In this annual, Ackermann published a translated volume and consented to erasing the original authors' names—a continuation of the debate surrounding anonymous contributions that plagued the first few years of British literary annual production.

31. For further discussion of Ackermann's Spanish publications, see Ford, "Ackermann"; Vera, *British Book Trade;* and Peers, "Literary Activities."

CHAPTER 2

1. Editors' introduction to *Alciato's* Book of Emblems: *The Memorial Web Edition.*

2. Alexander Pope condemns Quarles's emblems in *The First Epistle of the Second Book of Horace* (line 387), a heated accusation about the emblems' propensity toward allegory. Rodney Stenning Edgecombe claims that emblems fell outside the eighteenth-century Augustan logic and were shunned by the Romantics because of their desire for "open-ended kinds of moralizing" ("Emblems and Ecphrases," 105).

3. For a discussion of the relationship between ekphrasis and literary annuals, see Warne, "'Purport and Design.'"

4. See comparison of picturas in these emblem volumes at Emblem Project Utrecht, http://emblems.let.uu.nl/c161805.html#pi.

5. The subscription page notes that Ackermann took six copies himself, presumably for sale in his Repository of Arts shop. Included in the subscribers are several London-based publishers, booksellers, authors, artists, and literary annual contributors, including Captain Baillie, William Blake, Richard Cosway, Captain D'Arcy, Henry Fuseli, Charles Heath, John Neale, Messrs. Robinson and Co., Messrs. White and Co., and Messrs. Vernor, Hood and Sharpe.

6. Bernard Barton and B. W. Procter (writing under the pseudonym Barry Cornwall) were prolific contributors to the annuals.

7. In another letter to B. W. Procter (dated 1829 but sent after the letter with the album request/instructions), Lamb revealed his suspicion about Emma Isola's lineage: "What I told you, dear Procter, about my young friend was nothing but the exact truth. But I sunk the circumstance that her mother was a negro, or half-caste. . . . Mary corrects me, and

will have it that the lady's mother was a Hindostanee half-caste, and no negress, but was I to send you wool-gathering over the vast plains watered by the Ganges, or the more bewildering wilds of Timbuctoo, to search for images?" (*Letter,* 5:157–58).

8. The literary annual volumes that I have inspected lack any marginalia—not even an errant pencil mark. Cindy Dickinson notes that the Free Library of Philadelphia has in its collection an 1854 American gift book, *The Floral Forget Me Not,* which contains extensive marginalia made by Lizzie S. Turner over the course of nine years (Dickinson, "Creating a World," 53, 61). Typically, antiquarian collectors (both private and institutional) trade on the condition of a book; any text with marginalia (unless proved important) would decrease the book's value. Because of this industry standard, literary annuals sold through antiquarian dealers most likely do not contain marginalia—a situation that creates difficulty in studying the reception of annuals by the general reading public. While not a literary annual, *The Floral Forget Me Not* gift book is rare evidence of the interactive relationship between reader and textual object.

9. *The Mirror of Literature* 16, no. 474 supp. (January 1831) is dedicated to excerpts from Thomas Moore's 823-page tome on Lord Byron, *Letters and Journals of Lord Byron with Notices of His Life.*

10. See Charles Knight's description in the *Cyclopaedia of London* of Almanac Day (November 22), when all the porters came out of the Stationers Hall to deliver almanacs (588). For a description of the Stationers' Company, see page 587 of the *Cyclopaedia of London* and the engraving "Almanac Day at Stationers' Hall" on page 715 of the 1869 *Book of Days.* See also Bernard Capp's study of the British Library's collection of Potter almanacs in volume 4 of *Electronic British Library Journal* (2004).

11. In "Almanacs," published in the *New Quarterly Magazine* in 1876, Mortimer Collins offers a review of thirty morocco-bound almanacs owned by a single "bibliomaniac" and collected from 1796 to 1826. His review includes commentary on the owner's limited annotations and the reception of each different type of almanac (*Ladies' Diary, Gentleman's Diary, Vox Stellarum, Mertinus Liberatus, Old Poor Robin,* and others). See also Brian Maidment's assertions in "Re-arranging the Year" that almanacs represented a radical predictiveness in 1830s and 1840s England.

12. See also Eric Robinson's work ("John Clare and Weather Lore") on literary references to *Old Moore's Almanac.*

13. See Malcomson, *Popular Recreations.*

14. For a look at almanac publication from 1830 through the Victorian era, see Anderson, "Almanacs."

15. Knight edited the 1828 *Friendship's Offering* knowing full well that the annual's audience was predominantly middle-class women.

16. For a history of mathematics as it developed in *The Ladies' Diary,* see Albree and Brown, "Valuable Monument." See also Costa, "*Ladies' Diary.*"

17. In the 1816 volume that I reviewed, these two pages are the only two marked in the text, and they contain brief notes and the dates of a priest's ordaining.

18. *Old Poor Robin* (1770–1828), another Stationers' Company almanac, is decidedly parodic and is the precursor to the *Comic Almanack* for 1835 and 1843, illustrated by George Cruikshank. Both of these are precursors and contemporaries to Thomas Hood's successful *Comic Annual,* discussed in a later chapter.

19. See William Taylor's notes on the evolution and popularity of the *Almanach des Muses* in *Historic Survey of German Poetry,* 2:17–18, 59, 79.

20. In the reproduction of the 1830 *Forget Me Not* and the two *Hommage aux dames* volumes here, because of fading, the colors of each volume look dissimilar. However, physical inspection of the 1819, 1823, and 1828 volumes bears witness to the color similarities between the *Forget Me Not* and the *Hommage*'s paper boards. Interestingly, the first American literary annual, *The Atlantic Souvenir* (published in 1826), also used green glazed paper boards and a slipcase with the same image. Publishers Carey and Lea sold this annual to another publisher in 1832, who, in turn, merged the title with *The Token* for the 1833 volume. The Thomas Cooper Library at the University of South Carolina holds the 1827 and 1829 volumes of *The Atlantic Souvenir,* each with green glazed paper boards. The American Antiquarian Society holds the 1826–28 volumes with the same glazed boards. These volumes, in their original bindings, are difficult to find. Apparently, the urge to rebind volumes was as rampant in America as it was in England.

21. Surviving from 1822 through 1849, the *Mirror of Literature, Amusement and Instruction* receives ample attention from Jonathan Topham in "John Limbard."

22. See Internet Archive for a copy of the 1803 volume and others: www.archive.org/stream/poeticalregiste18unkngoog.

23. See May 12, 1799, letter to Thomas Southey in *Selections from the Letters of Robert Southey,* 1:71. For a copy of Cats's emblems, see Emblem Project Utrecht: http://emblems.let.uu.nl/c1627front000.html.

24. See January 4, 1799, letter to Robert Southey in Robberds, *Memoir of . . . William Taylor,* 1:240–45:

> Do you include any class of poetry, the comic as well as the serious, the ænigma as well as the ode? It would be well to do so, and to forbid nothing but excessive length. You must advertise for contributions in the Monthly Magazine at least, and evolve your plan in a short dissertation. The first German *Musenalmanach* was published in 1770, under the protection of Burger, assisted by Gotter and Kastner. This form of work is copied from a Parisian one, both in name and plan; but by whom it was set on foot in France, I do not know. I suspect it to have grown out of the "Ladies' Memorandum-books," which commonly contain an anthology of songs and riddles, and which would easily mould into a regular receptacle for those poemets, those insect ditties, those dragon-flies (perish the name! they are a beautiful animal), those libellas of Helicon, which aspire only to a summer's existence, to sport a double pair of wings, to orb their rings of love, and die in a bathing-place. (1:244)

25. See Haller, *Early Life of Robert Southey,* 225.

26. In *Coleridge, Schiller, and Aesthetic Education,* Michael John Kooy describes Schiller's 1796–1800 Musenalmanachs as vehicles for his moral philosophy (18–23):

> The goal Schiller began to formulate with Goethe in the 1790s was nothing less than the establishment of a new German literature of a European standard and quality, based on indigenous but not parochial traditions. This new work

> would be as important to the feelings and aspirations of the populace as Greek and Latin literature had been to those of the ancients. Weimar classicism as it took shape in the late 1790s, through the efforts of Goethe, Schiller and Herder, was thus classical not in the sense of reproducing the styles and forms characteristic of the Greek stage (though of course both Schiller and Goethe had their neoclassical moments), but rather in the sense of recreating in modern Germany the civic spirit that had routinely accompanied the production and performance of classical literature and drama. That meant above all the creation of a new canon. (21)

27. Taylor earned a much-lauded reputation as a Germanist because of his literary translations; see Chandler, "William Taylor's Pluralist Project."

28. For example, Watts wrote in the preface to the 1828 *Literary Souvenir,* "I have just learned (too late, however, to notice the circumstance in the entire impression of this volume), that 'Youth and Age,' by Mr. Coleridge, is about to be published in another annual work. I can only say, that I received it from the author, as a contribution to the Literary Souvenir" (xvi). The *Bijou* also published Coleridge's poem in its 1828 volume; and the *Cameo,* a reprint of the materials in the *Bijou,* then ran the poem in its 1828 volume. This issue of originality and editorial control is discussed in depth in a later chapter.

CHAPTER 3

1. Often unjustly described as a hack in contemporary literary scholarship, Combe is one of those lost authors caught between the Age of Enlightenment and the Romantic period. His work on *The Tours of Dr. Syntax* is unparalleled as satiric verse during this period. See Franklin, "Prison Manuscripts."

2. Only in the 1823 volume is the title labeled an advertisement rather than a preface. Whether Combe, Shoberl, or Ackermann wrote the preface is unclear: conflicting reports mention either Combe or Shoberl as the editor. For the sake of clarity, I have elected to assume that Shoberl and Ackermann collaborated on the preface.

3. Circulating libraries were a haven for single women during the late eighteenth and early nineteenth century; however, these libraries did not carry literary annuals. They were for subscriptions to mostly novel reading.

4. The Three Graces has a long history stemming from Platonic iconography and shifting through the Renaissance to three women depicted in the nude holding hands in an unbroken circle. For a brief history of the Three Graces, see Brandt, "Teaching Spenser." See images of Canova's sculpture at the Victoria and Albert Museum online (www.vam.ac.uk/images/image/12649-popup.html) and the Hermitage Museum online (www.hermitagemuseum.org/html_En/08/hm88_0_1_38_1.html). For earlier depictions of the Three Graces, see the Museum of Antiquities collection *The Three Graces,* c. 323–146 BC (www.usask.ca/antiquities/Collection/Three_Graces.html), Raffaello Sanzio's 1504 oil painting *The Three Graces* (www.wga.hu/frames-e.html?/html/r/raphael/2firenze/1/21graces.html), and Peter Paul Rubens's seventeenth-century painting held in the Museo del Prado (www.museodelprado.es/coleccion/galeria-on-line/obra/las-tres-gracias/).

5. Included in this set of information are "Transfer Days at the Bank," charades instructions, "Hackney Coach Fares," "Rates of Watermen," and holidays.

6. The 1825 *Forget Me Not* is the only anomaly that I have witnessed: both images pasted to the slipcase differ from those offered on the paper boards. Typically, the *Forget Me Not* boards herald the lion and unicorn, a royal seal. This remains one of those mysteries about the *Forget Me Not* that can be solved only by investigating Ackermann's and Shoberl's correspondence and missing business records.

7. The cost of covering books in cloth became more expensive in the mid-nineteenth century during the American Civil War, when Britain experienced a "cloth famine." Publishers returned once again to paper boards (Gaskell, *New Introduction to Bibliography,* 248).

8. For a case study of a West End bookbinder working in early nineteenth-century London, see Boisset-Astier, "French Bookbinder in London."

9. In England it was unusual for any binding to have a horizontal label on the back until about 1660. Retailers' bindings were hardly ever lettered until boards and printed labels came in late in the eighteenth century. The expense of binding Bibles did not hold true after 1800, when Bible work had become a cut-price business.

10. See Tanselle, "Book-Jackets, Blurbs, and Bibliographers"; see also McMullen, "Precursors of the Dustwrapper."

11. Until recently, Mark Godburn maintained a blog archive (http://earlydustjackets.blogspot.com/) about his discoveries in various archives. Currently, his blog dates back to 2010, which means that this particular discovery from October 4, 2010 ("A Short History of Sealed Wrappings") is no longer available online, but I have a pdf copy of the blog post in my possession. In it, Godburn supposes that the dust jacket, or wrapping, represents a gift already wrapped for the consumer and thus entices the owner to unwrap it. I have to disagree with this supposition; but this is another mystery to solve about the annuals that will be based on the findings from publishers' business records and correspondence. The post also includes a description of the wrapping and its provenance through auctions. The quoted information comes from a mention in the online magazine *Fine Books and Collections* (www.finebooksmagazine.com/fine_books_blog/2009/04/earliest-known-dust-jacket-found-at-oxford.phtml). Godburn reports that much of his findings and blog posts will be published in his forthcoming book, *Nineteenth Century Dust Jackets,* by the Private Libraries Association, due out in late 2014 or early 2015. Godburn discusses the literary annuals and dust jackets in chapters 1 and 2 (according to an August 18, 2014, e-mail from Godburn to me).

12. Scholars of literary annuals have typically begun their work here with *The Keepsake* for 1828 as the arrival of literary annuals.

13. "Puffs" are pieces published in periodicals, magazines, and journals that produce false interest in an author or publication. Publishers often planted social gossip or favorable reviews in magazines about their own publications or authors to create public interest and sales. This practice is discussed in chapter 5.

14. Scholars have made much of the anonymity inherent to the early literary annuals. Whether the lack of authors' names in the tables of contents was due to the editor's choice or the authors' shame is unclear. For more on anonymity and authorship in the early nineteenth century, see Dawes, "Anonymity."

15. Victor Hugo contributed a piece to this volume as well.

16. For a lengthy discussion of literary annuals, erroneously called gift books, see McGill, introduction to *American Literature.*

17. In comparison to that of the British annuals, the printing quality of the American volumes seems to have degenerated. For instance, in the 1838 *Token,* the engravings were printed directly onto the page instead of being printed on India paper and glued onto the page. In addition, the images were not printed using intaglio methods (apparent because the ink sits on the paper and feels raised when touched). Because of these elements, *The Token* seems to have moved away from Ackermann's prescribed elements of a literary annual, a move that is indicative of the American annuals across the board.

18. *The Literary Souvenir* has one such example with a Philadelphia publisher appended to the title page of one volume and a switched poem that differs from the British version of the same volume.

19. Of course, transatlantic relationships among American and British authors were not always contentious. Lydia Huntley Sigourney, editor of the *Religious Souvenir* and frequent contributor to the American annuals, maintained correspondence with William Wordsworth after an initial request to contribute to her American annuals. See Green, "William Wordsworth."

20. In the same year, Mudie's Circulating Library was founded, allowing for widespread commercialization of a novelist's name as well as popularizing the extended three-volume novel.

21. See Rhodes, "Copyright"; Bossche, "Value of Literature"; and Rose, *Authors and Owners.*

22. See Levy, "Lydia Maria Child."

23. For a description of the American literary annual phenomenon, see Thompson, *American Literary Annuals and Gift Books, 1825–1865.* Dickinson's "Creating a World of Books, Friends and Flowers" explores the relationship between gift giving and inscription in American gift books. See also E. Bruce Kirkham's index of contributors, authors, printers, and publishers in Kirkham et al.'s *Indices to American Literary Annuals and Gift Books, 1825–1865.* In a brief 1942 article, "Taste in the Annuals," Bradford Allen Booth laments that he will never finish his index of contributors to American annuals and offers his research to anyone who will take on the project; to attract scholars, Booth produces a list of major contributors in the article and categorizes the popularity of authors based on their contributions. Earl Hutchison's article on the American literary debt to gift books (more appropriately categorized as literary annuals) claims that "journalism histories ignore[d] the gift book phenomenon" (470) until his 1967 article, "Giftbooks and Literary Annuals: Mass Communications Ornaments." See also Richard Gassan's online project detailing the life of the American publisher Carey and Lea: "Carey and Lea: Printer and Publisher." Thompson's, Hutchison's, and Gassan's studies detail the financial impact of the American literary annual genre. See also Isabelle Lehuu's *Carnival on the Page,* which suggests that the during the American pre–Civil War decades, all new reading materials (including annuals) "shared a festive and somewhat transgressive quality" (3) For studies about specific American literary annuals, see, for example, R. Thompson, "Emerson and *The Offering* for 1829." For a more recent study, see Gassan, "First American Tourist Guidebooks."

CHAPTER 4

1. There has been much speculation about the identity of the editor (whether Charles Heath, the proprietor, or Frederic Mansel Reynolds, the 1829 editor), and consequently the author of the Preface, of the first *Keepsake,* but there is no decided conclusion—hence my ambiguous reference to the "author of the Preface" within the text.

2. A guinea equals twenty-one shillings or one pound, one shilling.

3. For more regarding polite culture and urban settings, see Kutcher, "Flowers of Friendship."

4. The table of contents indicates a "J. Pocock"; however, the printed name accompanying the poem text is "I. Pocock."

5. Head and tail pieces are engravings that signal the start and conclusion of a piece of writing. Usually, they were positioned on the same page as the last in the writing. They were not full-page images.

6. For a concise and authoritative discussion of the Hottentot figure in nineteenth-century England, see McClintock, *Imperial Leather.*

7. All volumes were issued with the same image on the front board; however, the image on the back board differed with every year.

8. See the introduction to *Selected Poems of Thomas Hood,* in which editor John Clubbe offers evidence of Hood's "neutrality in politics" (22).

9. Using a play on words here, the author refers to Charles Tilt, the publisher of *Comic Annual.*

10. Again using his favorite device, the author refers to Hurst, Chance & Co., publisher of *The New Comic Annual.*

11. Sheridan's *Comic Offering* was published by Smith Elder—publisher of the successful and popular *Friendship's Offering.*

12. The *Geographical Annual* actually contained no literary material, only maps. The intention was to republish an updated collection of these maps yearly as new discoveries were made. One reviewer classified this annual as "a perennial rather than an annual" and removed the *Geographical Annual* from any membership in the lurid class of literary annuals that were epidemic on bookstore shelves (anonymous, *Monthly Review* [December 1831]: 549). By 1831, the annuals were becoming more and more despised in trade criticism.

CHAPTER 5

1. India paper can be distinguished from other papers by running a finger around the edge and picking up the corner of a very thin sheet affixed to the page. Most engravings that I have run across in my research have been printed on India paper: "A confusing abbreviation for *India Proof Paper,* which is identical with China paper used for proofs of engravings; hence, India paper proofs or India proofs" (Carter, *ABC for Book Collectors,* 125).

2. The verso is the left-hand page of an open book. The recto is the right side.

3. In *Steel-Engraved Book Illustration in England,* Basil Hunnisett notes that arranging, organizing, and embedding the printed engravings required great amounts of labor, which was not necessarily conducive to quick reproduction:

> The first prints taken from a plate are always valued for their fresh and clear appearance, having a higher price put upon them in consequence. The use of steel plates reduced this value, since many more prints could be produced before the plate showed signs of wear; it was claimed that thousands of prints could be printed with little observable difference between the first and last. This gradually affected printing-house staffing, since the early proofs were always taken by specially skilled workmen, known as provers, working slowly and carefully to produce the finest specimens. Between two and six provers were employed, according to the size of the shop. . . . With steel plates, a prover's attention was not so necessary for the plain proofs; their principal function was then the production of India proofs. Thin India paper, fine, opaque and of good quality was used to take the actual ink, showing off the impression to the best possible advantage. But, because of its thinness, it needed to be backed by thicker plate paper. The India paper, cut to almost the same size as the original plate, was given a coating of fine paste, laid on the inked plate first and the thicker paper placed on top of that. Both passed through the press together, and the India paper adhered firmly to the damp backing sheet. . . . Because of the time taken to paste and print these proofs, output was restricted to about thirty or forty in one day. (186–87)

4. The exception is *The Comic Annual,* an annual that parodied the genre with both its literature and its woodcut engravings (which could be included with text during the printing process). See chapter 4 on engravers and engraving in the literary annuals.

5. Hunnisett writes that "it was not uncommon for an engraver to receive 150 guineas for a single plate, probably due to the short time allowed for completion. A volume of *The Amulet* cost nearly 1200 guineas for twelve plates, one of which, 'The Crucifixion' after Martin and engraved by Le Keux, brought the engraver 210 guineas. Of this sum, 180 guineas [were] for engraving and thirty guineas for making the reduction. Two other engravings cost 260 guineas, leaving about 700 guineas for the remaining nine plates. . . . Line engraving, as the highest form of the art, would expect to attract more, if only for the labour involved" (*Steel-Engraved Book Illustration,* 68).

6. John Martin (1789–1854) was known as a panoramic artist and was one of the most popular painters of the day. He often exhibited his work but seldom walked among the community of artists. Lacking membership in the Royal Academy, he was "never fully recognized by his peers" and was criticized by the likes of Thomas Lawrence, Sir David Wilkie, and John Ruskin, who deemed Martin's work "mere vulgar sensationalism" (Lambourne, *Victorian Painting,* 159). While his popularity waned further into the nineteenth and early twentieth centuries, his paintings now are valued in the thousands.

7. This family description originates from the Le Keux Correspondence collection at Beinecke Library, Yale University, which also contains valuable correspondence between the Le Keuxs, publisher Rudolph Ackermann, and editor Alaric Watts.

8. Steel-plate engravings were patented in 1819 by the American Jacob Perkins (Bain, "Gift Book," 19).

9. Instead of lending his artistic abilities to every literary annual, Heath aligned himself with only a few, including *The Amulet, The Literary Souvenir, The Landscape Annual,* and *Forget Me Not.* After 1828, he engraved very little, focusing instead on promoting his own productions, including *The Keepsake, Heath's Picturesque Annual,* and *Heath's Book of Beauty.* His sons, Frederick and Alfred, executed the majority of requests for engravings during that time.

10. Landon continued writing and editing this annual until her death in 1839. Afterwards, various women (including Caroline Norton) wrote and edited *Fisher's Drawing Room Scrap Book* through 1854.

11. Genette does not consider the table of contents to be paratextual, and it is not included in *Paratexts.*

12. Here, Landon refers to the previous poem and engraving, "Macao."

CHAPTER 6

1. Actual circulation numbers and expenses are difficult to locate. Publishers' records have been lost, destroyed, or compiled erroneously over the years. At the University of Edinburgh's Centre for the History of the Book, Director Bill Bell has reviewed the unpublished manuscript of the younger George Smith's memoirs, *Recollections of a Long and Busy Life.* In "The Secret History of Smith and Elder," Bell points out that Smith's version of the publishing house's history is myopic at best in an attempt to construct a public face for the firm (167). According to Bell, Leonard Huxley's *The House of Smith Elder* (1923) is the most authoritative and "thorough account of the firm's history to date" (168). Bell claims that even the more recent history by Jennifer Glynn, *Prince of Publishers* (1986), fails to note the skewed history presented in Smith's *Recollections* (Bell, 178n3).

2. Lockhart is also credited with having assigned John Keats to the Cockney poetasters in an August 1818 vituperous article published in *Blackwood's Edinburgh Magazine.* In the article, Lockhart comments that "Mr. Keats is still a smaller poet, and he is only a boy of pretty abilities, which he has done every thing in his power to spoil" (160).

3. Shoberl included with the letter an etching of "Cromwell & His Daughter" in the form of a proof engraving (letter to T. J. Serle, f. 158), which was printed in the 1836 *Forget Me Not* and accompanied by a nine-page prose work of the same title.

4. Among the *London Magazine* contributors with whom Hood became friendly are John Clare, "Barry Cornwall" (a.k.a. Bryan Waller Procter), Thomas DeQuincey, Charles Lamb, William Hazlitt, Frederic Mansel Reynolds (editor of *The Keepsake*), and Allan Cunningham (Clubbe, *Selected Poems,* 6).

5. Judith Pascoe and Andrew Boyle offer varying sums in their accounts of Scott's offer: either £400 or £500 for his involvement with *The Keepsake* (Pascoe, "Poetry as Souvenir," 173; Boyle, preface to *Index to the Annuals,* 1:iv).

6. Several authors, including Tennyson and Clare, detailed their problems with obtaining payment from the publishers. See Stephen Colclough's discussion of an unpublished Clare letter that addresses this topic, in "Clare and the Annuals."

7. The market reached its apex in 1832 with sixty-three titles vying for seasonal attention.

8. The designation "royal" indicates the paper size used for printing, in this case, a midsize sheet, 25 × 20 in. (Gaskell, *New Introduction to Bibliography,* 224).

9. I have not had the opportunity to inspect the engraving volume of a *Landscape Annual,* but the engravings presumably went through the same printing process as other annuals: printed intaglio with steel plates onto India paper and then glued onto the page.

10. Though undated, the volume's publisher, format, and binding indicate that it was published after 1831, ca. 1838. Heath's primary publisher after 1831 was Longman, the publisher of that volume.

11. Publishers were most likely capitalizing on the popularity of the literary annual's contributors. After the annuals phenomenon swept through most drawing rooms, authors of all abilities became well-known and a commodity in any publishing house.

12. For a discussion of Victorian women's magazines, see Beetham, *Magazine of Her Own;* and Beetham and Boardman, *Victorian Women's Magazines*; see also Phegley, *Educating;* and Adburgham, *Women in Print.*

13. See Griest, *Mudie's Circulating Library.*

14. This review was appended to the 1826 *Literary Souvenir* as a testimonial to the annual's superiority in a growing field of titles (only one in 1823, nine by 1825). After attesting to the periodical's legitimacy, the review continues in glowing praise of the annual: "The leading character of the articles is superior, the design is excellent, and, if rightly prosecuted, the *Literary Souvenir* may take the highest rank among periodical publications. The most eminent literary characters of the day are among its contributors. With such writers, and published annually, the work has every chance of attaining to steady excellence and enduring reputation. The limitations of our work will not allow us to quote a sixth part of what we could, otherwise, dwell on with great pleasure: there is much that is beautiful in the longer tales. The engravings which accompany the *Literary Souvenir* are extremely beautiful."

15. The *Monthly Review,* a London monthly magazine published from 1826 to 1845, was publicized as a gentler review periodical compared with the *Edinburgh Review* and *Quarterly Review.* Published by Charles Knight during 1826, the periodical was more dedicated to summary and quotation (*Waterloo Directory* online). However, this gentler nature does not seem the case with many of the reviews cited herein.

16. For an account of the business negotiations for publishing a poetry volume with Longman in the period 1825–27, see Douglas, "Wordsworth as Businessman."

17. Contributors to the *Monthly Review* are not identified (or the periodical even indexed) in *The Wellesley Index* or the *Curran Index* (an online update to *Wellesley*). As a consequence, the inevitable relationship between reviewers and editors, publishers, and authors cannot be fully disclosed here.

18. This review is a testament to the confusing recommendations offered by the review press; this critic, though harsh in the review, began the article with exaltations of the literary annual genre.

19. All of these authors except David Lyndsay are indexed in Boyle, *Index to the Annuals.* The information about Dods/Lyndsay was contributed to my hypertextual archive through the Victoria Listserv. See Bennett, *Mary Diana Dods.*

20. See Hootman, "British Literary Annuals," which indexes contributors and titles in British literary annuals. Hootman's study includes a statistical analysis of the contributions by gendered author's name. However, his work is limited in scope, as he admits in his introduction:

his work is not a survey of every British literary annual but is instead limited to the economically successful annuals, e.g., *The Keepsake, Friendship's Offering,* and *Forget Me Not.*

21. Authors contributing to this volume include Sir Walter Scott, Thomas Moore, William Wordsworth, Robert Southey, Samuel Taylor Coleridge, Percy Bysshe Shelley, Felicia Hemans, and Letitia Elizabeth Landon.

22. Landon and Montgomery were two very prolific contributors to the literary annuals in addition to their work for periodicals and their own volumes of poetry.

23. The novel *The Dante Club,* by Matthew Pearl (2004), supplies an example of how trade criticism entered the everyday lives of publishers and authors: this work of historical fiction includes brief scenes of an early nineteenth-century American publisher discussing the submission of trade criticism and puffery to buoy his authors' latest works or even just their ideas of a potential book. The tradition disturbs these authors in their search for either valid criticism or public signs of affection.

24. *Whims and Oddities* continued to be published through 1829 but underwent a restructuring with the 1830 volume; its contents were bound, illustrated, and expanded as *The Comic Annual* to conform to the massively popular literary annual phenomenon.

25. This letter also serves as witness to the fact that the decline in poetry volumes was caused by the rise in popularity of annuals—a genre that attracted those with a modest expendable income who could spend it on only one luxury.

CHAPTER 7

1. For a complete definition of "interpellation," see Althusser, "Ideology," 1–60.

2. Most annuals included "found" letters or early juvenilia by Byron instead of his more popular works. The owners of these "found" items could grant copyrights more easily than a publisher would—for Byron, believing in the poet-statesman, gave publishers the copyrights to his works as they were produced.

3. Even the contributions of William Wordsworth, Samuel Coleridge, Percy Bysshe Shelley, and Lord Byron were heavily criticized.

4. During the nineteenth century, hysteria was thought typically to be caused by "reproductive disorders, menstrual irregularities and suppressed sexual desire" (Freedman, "Two Case Studies," 110–11). However, two French case studies by Jean-Baptiste Louyer-Villermay note that the women suffered hysteria not from being coddled or from some sexual desire but from lack of sustenance and their "impressionable type of personality" (Freedman, "Two Case Studies," 110–13). See Elaine Showalter's discussion of British culture and female hysteria in *The Female Malady.* See also extended discussions about the relationship between literature and madness in Felman, *Writing and Madness* and in Gilbert and Gubar, *Madwoman in the Attic.*

5. The child's pubis is directed toward the viewer but is not specific in its genitalia; Hemans supplied the child's biological gender.

6. After all, how did the child get that close to the edge in the first place? Is it a symptom of neglect?

7. This survey of engravings in annuals is limited to annuals that were successful and lived in long runs that could be collected (e.g., *The Literary Souvenir, Forget Me Not, Friendship's Offering,* and *The Keepsake*). Other annuals, including the *Juvenile Forget Me Not* and *Amulet,*

are not included, because they represent different topics with variant audiences, e.g., children and religion. Hood's short-lived *The Gem* is included because Hood edited all four volumes (1829–32), which lends a consistency to the work; in addition, he continued his work as the sole author and engraver of the *Comic Annual.*

8. Silk is vastly different from the stiff cloth coverings typically used at this time. For a discussion of cloth coverings, see Gaskell, "Book Production: The Machine-Press Period, 1800–1950," in *New Introduction to Bibliography,* 189–310.

9. According to her review of over three hundred literary annual inscriptions ("Women, Literary Annuals"), Paula Feldman discovered that a majority of an (admittedly small) sampling of literary annuals were given as gifts between family members and awards for school performance instead of between lovers.

10. The 1825 *Friendship's Offering* was the only annual to include a color-illuminated title page.

11. Men (or at least male names) dominated as contributors and editors until 1830, when, according to Harry Hootman's index of popular annual titles, the female names listed in the tables of contents came to outnumber male names. I specifically refer to *male names* and *female names* because women authors sometimes shielded themselves behind masculine pseudonyms or simple initials. For more on anonymity and authorship, see Griffin, *Faces of Anonymity.* Despite this differential, women authors consistently appeared in the annuals, beginning with the 1824 *Friendship's Offering,* in which Mrs. Opie was one of the few authors identified by name. In the 1824 *Forget Me Not* and 1825 *Friendship's Offering,* Letitia Landon is the only identifiable and recognizable female author, but in retrospect only: her identity was temporarily shielded by her initials, "L.E.L.," an anonymity that would soon be pierced by her vast popularity among annuals' readers.

12. In *Imagined Communities,* Benedict Anderson argues that very large communities are formed simply by the act of reading similar materials: "[The community] is imagined because the members of even the smallest nation will never know most of their fellow-members, meet them, or even hear of them, yet in the minds of each lives the image of their communion. . . . [I]t is imagined as a community, because, regardless of the actual inequality and exploitation that may prevail in each, the nation is always conceived as a deep, horizontal comradeship. Ultimately it is this fraternity that makes it possible, over the past two centuries, for so many millions of people, not so much to kill, as willingly to die for such limited imaginings" (6–7). Though Anderson is discussing the nation-state and national consciousness, the communion perceived among a particular group establishes a camaraderie.

13. Toward the end of her life (d. 1835), Hemans began to critique an idealized feminine ideology that could no longer sustain the "cult of domesticity" or the Romantic ideal of beauty. The disintegration of this domestic ideal is apparent in her poem "Casabianca," published in 1826. She moved to female heroines with *Records of Woman,* which resituates history through the perspective of female heroes, including "The Indian Woman's Death Song" and "Madeline: A Domestic Tale." In these poems, Hemans reverses gender roles, and as a result, she found a very receptive audience for both her annual contributions and her volumes of poetry—perhaps in spite of the British nineteenth century's construction of gender.

14. For further discussions of Landon's Romantic identity, see Riess, "Laetitia Landon"; Blain, "Letitia Elizabeth Landon"; Furr, "Sentimental Confrontations"; Linkin, "Romantic Aesthetics"; Linley, "Sappho's Conversations"; and Lootens, "Receiving the

Legend." Also see Anne Mellor's, Susan Wolfson's, and Jerome McGann's works on the female poet—especially McGann's *Poetics of Sensibility* and *Romantic Ideology* and Mellor's *Romanticism and Gender.*

CONCLUSION

1. This material is adapted from the introduction to Harris, *The Forgotten Gothic: Short Stories from British Literary Annuals, 1823–1831,* published by Zittaw Press in 2012. The publisher graciously provided permission to reprint the introductory materials in this study.

2. *The Forgotten Gothic* collection builds on Franz Potter's initial assessment of sixty Gothic short stories in the annuals in *The History of Gothic Publishing*, uses a clear definition of "Gothic" for selecting Gothic stories, and focuses on the most popular British literary annuals: *Forget Me Not* (1823–47), *Friendship's Offering* (1824–44), *The Keepsake* (1828–57), and *The Literary Souvenir* (1825–35).

3. All of these engravings are included in Harris, *Forgotten Gothic.*

4. By this, I am not psychologizing the moment to implicate Thomas Tanselle's version of "authorial intention." Instead, I contend that the "moment" can never be restructured through artificial means in an archive.

5. In all likelihood, the engraving was produced and passed on to authors—even Tennyson—for a verbal illustration. Here, Sackville-West privileged the author instead of the engraving, a reversal of the original practices, which was perhaps done to tease readers with well-known literary names.

APPENDIX A

1. Faxon includes the *Poetical Album* in his bibliography of literary annuals; however, it does not fit the criteria (as previously discussed); I include the volume here with this note about the error.

2. The *Times Telescope* is an almanac, not a literary annual, but has been included in Faxon's bibliography; I include the volume here with this note about the error.

APPENDIX B

1. Note in Boyle, *Index to the Annuals:* "This, although signed with Lamb's name, was written by Hood [editor of *The Gem*], who had omitted Lamb's contribution 'The Gipsy's Malison,' 'as it would shock all mothers.'" Lamb was perplexed by Hood's decision and wrote to B. W. Procter (a frequent correspondent and friend) asking him to review the poem. (See letter dated January 29, 1829, the text of "The Gypsy's Malison," and Hood's replacement prose piece, "A Widow," discussed in chapter 7). See also the anonymous review in *The Athenaeum* of Walter Jerrold's biography, *Thomas Hood: His Life and Times,* in which the literary swap is discussed at length.

2. Boyle does not attribute the "Lacy de Vere" short story to Mary Shelley. However, recent scholarship has accepted that Mary Shelley wrote it. See Crook, *Mary Shelley's Literary Lives,* vol. 4.

APPENDIX C

1. Some of these errors are replicated in Harry Hootman's database of literary annuals. It is best to inspect each volume personally or visit digital archives of these materials.

2. This volume was partially prepared but never published.

3. The second edition was published in 1830.

4. Letitia Elizabeth Landon edited/contributed to only this first volume.

5. *Friendship's Offering* absorbed *Winter's Wreath* with this issue.

6. *Gem of Art* used 100 steel plates selected from *The Keepsake,* Heath's annuals, etc.

7. In 1825, this title was continued as the *Literary Souvenir* by Alaric Watts.

8. This title was continued as the *Book of Beauty* in 1848.

9. The Countess of Blessington took over editing this title after Landon's death in 1838.

10. A French almanac of the same name was printed for several years (1813–?).

11. This is not Ackermann's *Juvenile Forget Me Not* but is often confused with his title.

12. This title was issued in two volumes: the literature and engraving volumes were separate.

13. This title was replaced by *Cabinet of Modern Art* in 1836–37 and in 1842.

14. The 1829 volume was followed by the *Iris;* the 1833 and 1834 volumes were new editions titled *Juvenile Keepsake.*

15. This title is not listed in Faxon, *Literary Annuals*.

16. This title merged with *Friendship's Offering* for 1833.

Bibliography

SUBSTANTIAL LIBRARY COLLECTIONS OF BRITISH LITERARY ANNUALS

English Gift Books and Literary Annuals, 1823–1857. Chadwyck-Healey Microfiche Collection, Library of Congress, Washington, DC.

Fisher, Thomas, Rare Book Library. The McLean Collection in the Robertson Davies Library, Massey College, Toronto, ON.

The Pforzheimer Collection of Shelley and His Circle. Stephen A. Schwarzman Building, New York Public Library, New York.

Rare Books and General Collection, British Library, London.

Rare Books and Special Collections, University of South Carolina, Columbia.

Special Collections, Miami University of Ohio, Oxford, Ohio.

Special Collections, E. J. Pratt Library, Victoria University, Toronto, ON.

ONLINE RESOURCES FOR BRITISH LITERARY ANNUALS

Eckert, Lindsey. *Nineteenth Century British Literary Annuals: An Online Exhibition of Materials from the University of Toronto*. bookhistory.fis.utoronto.ca/annuals.

Harris, Katherine D. *Forget Me Not: A Hypertextual Archive of Ackermann's 19th-Century Literary Annual; An Edition from The Poetess Archive*. www.orgs.miamioh.edu/anthologies/FMN.

Hoagwood, Terence, Kathryn Ledbetter, and Martin M. Jacobsen. *LEL's "Verses" and* The Keepsake *for 1829*. www.rc.umd.edu/editions/lel/.

Hootman, Harry. *Index of British Literary Annuals*. www.britannuals.com.

The Poetess Archive Database. Gen. ed., Laura Mandell. http://idhmc.tamu.edu/poetess/.

PRIMARY MATERIALS

Ackermann, Rudolph. Letter to John Clare, March 13, 1829. British Library, Eg. 2248 ff. 128.

Advert. In *The Comic Annual*, edited by Thomas Hood, at back of volume. London: A. H. Baily and Co., 1835.

Advert. In *Forget Me Not: A Christmas and New Year's Present for 1823*, edited by Rudolph Ackermann and Frederic Shoberl, at back of volume. London: R. Ackermann, 1823.

Advert. In *Forget Me Not: A Christmas and New Year's Present for 1824*, edited by Frederic Shoberl, at back of volume. London: R. Ackermann, 1824.

Alciato, Andrea. *Book of Emblems.* 1531. In *Alciato's* Book of Emblems: *The Memorial Web Edition in Latin and English,* edited by William Barker, Mark Feltham, and Jean Guthrie. Memorial University of Newfoundland. December 2002. www.mun.ca/alciato/index.html.

"Almanac Day at Stationers' Hall" [engraving]. In *Book of Days, a Miscellany of Popular Antiquities,* edited by Robert Chambers, 715. London: W. R. Chambers, 1869.

Almanac de Gotha. Gotha: C. G. Ettinger, 1812.

Almanach des Muses. Paris: Vallat la Chapelle, 1767.

Almanach des Muses. Paris: Delalaine, 1781.

Angelica's Ladies Library, or Parents and Guardians Present. London: J. Hamilton, 1794. Facsimile, www.archive.org/stream/angelicasladiesoounkngoog.

"The Annuals of Former Days." *Bookseller* 1 (November 29, 1858): 493–99.

Anonymous. "The Annuals for 1832." *Monthly Review* (November 1831): 370–89.

———. "The Annuals for 1832." *Monthly Review* (December 1831): 523–49.

———. "Miscellaneous Intelligence." Review of 1832 *Continental Annual* and *Literary Souvenir. Monthly Review* (November 1831): 463–64.

———. Review of 1823 *The Graces, or Literary Souvenir*. *Blackwood's Edinburgh Magazine.* (December 1823): 669–72

———. Review of 1825 *Literary Souvenir. Blackwood's Magazine.* (Quoted in 1826 *Literary Souvenir* adverts.)

———. Review of 1825 *Literary Souvenir. British Critic.* (Quoted in 1826 *Literary Souvenir* advertisements.)

———. Review of 1825 *Literary Souvenir. Buckingham's Oriental Herald.* (Quoted in 1826 *Literary Souvenir* advertisements.)

———. Review of 1825 *Literary Souvenir. European Magazine.* (Quoted in 1826 *Literary Souvenir* advertisements.)

———. Review of 1825 *Literary Souvenir. Monthly Review* (October 1825): 279–97.

———. Review of 1825 *Literary Souvenir. New Monthly Magazine.* (Quoted in 1826 *Literary Souvenir* advertisements.)

———. Review of 1826 *Friendship's Offering. Monthly Review* (November 1825): 448.

———. Review of 1826 *Friendship's Offering* and 1826 *Janus. Monthly Review* (February 1826): 161–74.

———. Review of 1827 *Amulet* and 1827 *Forget Me Not. Monthly Review* (November 1826): 274–93.

———. Review of 1827 *Literary Souvenir. Monthly Review* (December 1826): 387–403.

———. Review of *No Me Olvides. London Literary Gazette* 570 (December 22, 1827): 824.

———. Review of *No Me Olvides. The Foreign Review and Continental Miscellany* 3 (1829): 262.

———. Review of 1827 *Friendship's Offering. Monthly Review* (January 1827): 86–94.

———. Review of 1827 *Poetical Souvenir. Monthly Review* (January 1827): 112.

———. Review of 1828 *Amulet. Monthly Review* (November 1827): 347–60.

———. Review of 1828 *Bijou. Monthly Review* (December 1827): 526–30.

———. Review of 1828 *Forget Me Not. Monthly Review* (November 1827): 400–411.

———. Review of 1828 *Literary Souvenir. Monthly Review* (December 1827): 519–20.

———. Review of L.E.L.'s *Venetian Bracelet* and Robert Montgomery's *Satan: A Poem. Monthly Review* (February 1830): 159–72.

———. Review of 1832 *The Amulet, Friendship's Offering, The Winter's Wreath,* and *The Juvenile Forget-Me-Not. Monthly Review* (November 1831): 370–89.

———. Review of 1832 *Literary Souvenir, Keepsake, Heath's Picturesque Annual, Continental Annual, New Year's Gift,* and *Geographical Annual. Monthly Review* (December 1831): 523–49.

———. Review of 1909 *Thomas Hood: His Life and Times.*

"Article 15." *Foreign Quarterly Review* (1828): 642–45.

Barbauld, Anna Letitia. "On a Lady's Writing." In *The Longman Anthology of British Literature,* vol. 2A, edited by Susan Wolfson and Peter Manning, 33. New York: Longman, 2003.

Barton, Bernard. "The Heart's Motto." In *Forget Me Not: A Christmas and New Year's Present for 1824,* edited by Frederic Shoberl, 1–3. London: R. Ackermann, 1824.

———. "To the Flower Forget Me Not." In *Forget Me Not: A Christmas and New Year's Present for 1825,* edited by Frederic Shoberl, 1–3. London: R. Ackermann, 1825.

Bayly, Thomas Haynes. "Poets Beware!" In *The Musical Bijou: An Album of Music, Poetry, and Prose, for MDCCCXXX,* edited by F. H. Burney, 2. London: Goulding and D'Almaine, 1830.

Beauties of the English Annuals for 1835. New York: Wallis and Newel, 1834.

B.E.P. Preface to *Friendship's Offering: A Literary Album,* edited by B.E.P., iii–vii. London: Lupton Relfe, 1827.

Bird, James. "Constancy." In *Forget Me Not: A Christmas and New Year's Present for MDCCCXXIX,* edited by Frederic Shoberl, 157. London: R. Ackermann, 1829.

———. "The Dying Brigand." In *Friendship's Offering: A Literary Album,* edited by B.E.P., 70–71. London: Lupton Relfe, 1827.

Bird, John. "A Faithful Guardian." In *Forget Me Not: A Christmas and New Year's Present for MDCCCXXIX,* edited by Frederic Shoberl, 65–67. London: R. Ackermann, 1829.

Blake, Williams. "Hiding of Moses" [engraving]. In *Remember Me! A New Year's Gift or Christmas Present for 1825.* I. Poole, 1824.

"The Brigand" [engraving]. In *Friendship's Offering: A Literary Album,* edited by B.E.P., 36. London: Lupton Relfe, 1827.

Byron, Lord George Gordon. "Original Letter of Lord Byron's to the Ettrick Shepherd." 1816. In *Forget Me Not: A Christmas and New Year's Present for MDCCCXLIV,* edited by Frederic Shoberl, 353–54. London: R. Ackermann, 1844.

———. "To My Dear Mary Anne." In *Forget Me Not: A Christmas and New Year's Present for MDCCCXXX,* edited by Frederic Shoberl, 38–40. London: R. Ackermann, 1830.

Cats, Jacob. *Moral Emblems with Aphorisms, Adages, and Proverbs, of all Ages and Nations, from Jacob Cats and Robert Farlie.* London: Longman, Green, Longman and Roberts, 1860. Facsimile, www.archive.org/stream/moralemblemswithoocats.

———. *Proteus: Sinné-en Minne-Beelden. Emblemata, Amores Moresque, spectantia. Emblemes Touchants les Amours et les Moeurs Meliora, latent. Tundatur, olebit.* Middelburg, 1618. http://emblems.let.uu.nl/c1618_introduction.html

Chorley, H. F. "The Elves of Caergwyn." In *Forget Me Not; A Christmas, New Year's, and Birthday Present for MDCCCXXXI,* 73–95. London: R. Ackermann, 1831. In *The Athenaeum,* no. 4198 (April 11, 1908): 441–42.

Clare, John. "Song." In *Forget Me Not: A Christmas and New Year's Present for MDCCCXXIX,* edited by Frederic Shoberl, 68. London: R. Ackermann, 1829.

Clauren, H. [Karl Heun]. *Mimili.* In *Vergissmeinnicht ein Taschenbüch.* Leipzig, 1818.

———. *Mimili.* In *Der Freimüthige.* Dresden: 1815–19.

———. "Mimili." In *The Flowers of Literature Consisting of Selections from History, Biography, Poetry, and Romance*, vol. 3. London: Thomas Tegg, 1824.

———. "The Soldier's Reward: A Tale of the Mountains." In *The Portfolio for 1824,* vol. 3, no. 74, 217–19, and no. 75, 232–33. London: William Charlton Wright, 1824.

[Coleridge, Samuel Taylor.] *Critical Review,* 2nd ser., vol. 19 (February 1797): 194–200. Reprinted in *The Monk: A Romance,* by Matthew Lewis, edited by David MacDonald and Kathleen Scherf, 398–402. Orchard Park, NY: Broadview, 2004.

Collins, Mortimer. "Almanacs." *New Quarterly Magazine* 5 (October–January 1876): 413–30.

Condor, Josiah. *Reviewers Reviewed.* Oxford, UK: Bartlett, 1811.

"The Contemplation" [engraving]. In *Forget Me Not: A Christmas and New Year's Present for 1826,* edited by Frederic Shoberl. London: R. Ackermann, 1826.

"La Contemplation" [engraving]. In *Hommage aux Dames,* edited by Charles Malo. Paris: Chez Janet, 1828.

The Country and Town Ladies' Memorandum Book, or Polite Pocket Museum. London: Otridge and Rackham, 1822.

Cunningham, Allan, ed. Inscription instructions in *The Anniversary or Poetry and Prose for MDCCCXXIX* [on inscription page]. London: John Sharpe, 1829.

Dickens, Charles. *The Pickwick Papers.* 1837. Edited by James Kinsley. New York: Oxford University Press, 1988.

Dyce, Alexander. *Specimens of British Poetesses.* London: T. Rodd, 1825.

Edinburgh Review. Publisher's insert. Vol. 41 (June 1827): n.p.

Eliot, George. *Middlemarch.* New York: New American Library, 1981.

Ellis, Sarah Stickney. *The Women of England: Their Social Duties and Domestic Habits.* 1839. In *Victorian Prose: An Anthology,* edited by Rosemary J. Mundhenk and LuAnn McCracken Fletcher, 53–57. New York: Columbia University Press, 1999.

Emmerson, Eliza. Letter to John Clare, February 26, 1829. British Library, Eg. 2248 ff. 121.

"The Enchantress" [engraving]. In *Heath's Book of Beauty.* London: Longman, 1833.

"Evening Dress." In *The Repository of Arts, Literature, Commerce, Manufactures, Fashions, and Politics* 5 (January 1811): 49. London: R. Ackermann, 1811.

"Falstaff's Festival, or the Power of Mirth: An Ode in Honor of Comus." In *New Comic Annual for 1831,* 1–10. London: Hurst, Chance, 1831.

"Fashion Prints and Evening Dresses." *Candice's Collections.* www.candicehern.com/collections/01/prints-dresses.htm.

The Female Spectator. Introduction. In *The Longman Anthology of British Literature,* vol. 1C, edited by David Damrosch and Stuart Sherman, 2402. 2nd ed. New York: Longman, 2003.

Finden, E. "Love's Motto" [engraving]. In *Forget Me Not: A Christmas and New Year's Present for 1827,* edited by Frederic Shoberl. London: R. Ackermann, 1827.

"The Fortune Teller" [engraving]. In *Friendship's Offering; or, The Annual Remembrancer: Christmas Present, or New Year's Gift for 1825,* edited by Thomas K. Hervey. London: Lupton Relfe, 1825.

Friendship's Offering; or, The Annual Remembrancer: Christmas Present, or New Year's Gift for 1824, edited by Thomas K. Hervey. London: Lupton Relfe, 1824.

Friendship's Offering; or, The Annual Remembrancer: Christmas Present, or New Year's Gift for 1825, edited by Thomas K. Hervey. London: Lupton Relfe, 1825.

Gaskell, Elizabeth. *North and South.* 1854. Project Gutenberg E-Text, July 2003. http://manybooks.net/pages/gaskelleetext03ecgns10/130.html.

The Gentleman's Magazine. "On Cheap Periodical Literature." June 1825: 483–86.

Goodrich, S. G. Preface to *The Token and Atlantic Souvenir: A Christmas and New Year's Present,* edited by S. G. Goodrich, iii–iv. Boston: American Stationers' Company, 1838.

"The Graces." In *The Graces or Literary Souvenir,* edited by Rev. George Croly, vii–x. London: Hurst Robinson, 1824.

The Graces or Literary Souvenir. Edited by Rev. George Croly. London: Hurst Robinson, 1824.

Gregory, John. *A Father's Legacy to His Daughter.* 1778. In Boston: James B. Dow, 1834.

Hall, S. C. *Retrospect of a Long Life from 1815 to 1883.* New York: Appleton, 1883.

Haywood, Eliza. "The Author's Intent." *The Female Spectator* 1, no. 1 (April 1744). Reprinted in *The Longman Anthology of British Literature,* vol. 1C, edited by David Damrosch and Stuart Sherman, 2402–4. 2nd ed. New York: Longman, 2003.

Hemans, Felicia. "The Brigand Leader and His Wife." In *Friendship's Offering: A Literary Album,* edited by B.E.P., 36. London: Lupton Relfe, 1827.

———. *Felicia Hemans: Selected Poems, Letters, Reception Materials.* Edited by Susan J. Wolfson. Princeton, NJ: Princeton University Press, 2000.

———. "The Mother and Child." In *Literary Souvenir; or, Cabinet of Poetry and Romance,* edited by Alaric A. Watts, 64. London: Hurst Robinson, 1825.

Hervey, Thomas K. Preface to *Friendship's Offering; or, The Annual Remembrancer: Christmas Present, or New Year's Gift for 1824,* edited by Thomas K. Hervey, iii–v. London: Lupton Relfe, 1824.

———. Preface to *Friendship's Offering; or, The Annual Remembrancer: Christmas Present, or New Year's Gift for 1825,* edited by Thomas K. Hervey, viii–v. London: Lupton Relfe, 1825.

Hommage aux Dames. London: John Setts Jr., 1825.

Hommage aux Dames. Edited by Charles Malo. Paris: Chez Janet, 1813–30.

Hone, William. *The Year Book of Daily Information and Recreation.* London: Thomas Tegg, 1841.

Hood, Thomas, ed. *The Comic Annual; The Anniversary of the Literary Fun.* London: A. H. Baily, 1835.

———. "Copyright and Copywrong." *Atheneum* (April 13, 1837): 263–65.

———. *The Letters of Thomas Hood.* Edited by Peter F. Morgan. Toronto: University of Toronto Press, 1973.

———. *Letters of Thomas Hood from the Dilke Papers in the British Museum.* Edited by Leslie A. Marchand. New York: Octagon, 1972.

———. Preface to *The Comic Annual; The Anniversary of the Literary Fun,* v–x. 2nd ed. London: Charles Tilt, 1830.

———. Preface to *The Comic Annual; The Anniversary of the Literary Fun,* v–x. London: Charles Tilt, 1831.

———. Preface to *The Comic Annual; The Anniversary of the Literary Fun,* v–xiv. London: A. H. Baily, 1837.

———. "A True Story." In *The Comic Annual; The Anniversary of the Literary Fun,* 44–48. 2nd ed. London: Charles Tilt, 1830.

———. *Whims and Oddities.* London: Lupton Relfe, 1826.

———. "The Widow." In *The Gem,* edited by Thomas Hood, 24–27. London: W. Marshall, 1829.

Hunt, Leigh. "Pocket-Books and Keepsakes." In *The Keepsake for 1828,* edited by Frederic Mansel Reynolds, 1–18. London: Hurst, Chance, 1828.

Jewsbury, Maria Jane. "A Tale of a Mother's Grave." In *Friendship's Offering: A Literary Album and Christmas and New Year's Present for 1831,* edited by Thomas Pringle, 126. London: Smith Elder, 1831.

Johnson, Samuel. ["On Fiction"]. *The Rambler,* no. 4, 1750. In *The Longman Anthology of British Literature,* vol. 1C, edited by David Damrosch, 2732–35. 2nd ed. New York: Longman, 2003.

"June" [engraving]. Drawn by Burney and engraved by J. S. Agar. In *Forget Me Not: A Christmas and New Year's Present for 1823,* edited by Rudolph Ackermann and Frederic Shoberl. London: R. Ackermann, 1823.

The Keepsake. Edited by the Countess of Blessington. London: D. Bogue; New York: Appleton; Paris: Mandeville, 1848.

Knight, Charles. *Cyclopaedia of London.* London: Charles Knight, 1851.

———. "Reading the News." In *Friendship's Offering: A Literary Album, and Christmas and New Year's Present, for MDCCCXXX,* edited by Thomas Pringle, 75–79. London: Smith Elder, 1830.

The Ladies' Diary; or, Complete Almanack for 1768. London: Company of Stationers, 1768.

The Ladies' Diary; or, Complete Almanack for 1821. London: Company of Stationers, 1821.

The Ladies' Diary; or, Complete Almanack for 1822. London: Company of Stationers, 1822.

The Lady's Magazine. London, 1770–1837.

Lamb, Charles. "The Gypsy's Malison." In *The Letters of Charles Lamb,* 5:158. Boston: Bibliophile Society, 1906.

———. *The Letters of Charles Lamb,* vol. 5 (1825–34). Introduction by Henry H. Harper. Boston: Bibliophile Society, 1906.

Landon, Letitia Elizabeth. "Appealing, by the magic of its name." Title page of *Forget Me Not,* edited by Frederic Shoberl. London: R. Ackermann, 1827–47.

———. "Chinese Pagoda." *Fisher's Drawing Room Scrap-Book; with Poetical Illustrations by L.E.L.* London: Fisher, Son and Jackson, 1832. In *Romantic Period Writings, 1798–1832: An Anthology,* edited by Zachary Leader and Ian Haywood, 210–11. London: Routledge, 1998.

———. Introduction. *Fisher's Drawing Room Scrap-Book; with Poetical Illustrations by L.E.L.* London: Fisher, Son and Jackson, 1832.

———. *Heath's Book of Beauty.* London: Longman, Rees, Orme, Brown, 1833.

———. "Lismore Castle." In *Fisher's Drawing Room Scrap-Book,* edited by Letitia Elizabeth Landon. London: Fisher, Son and Jackson, 1832.

———. "Macao." *Fisher's Drawing Room Scrap-Book; with Poetical Illustrations by L.E.L.* London: Fisher, Son and Jackson, 1832. In *Romantic Period Writings, 1798–1832: An Anthology,* edited by Zachary Leader and Ian Haywood, 208–9. London: Routledge, 1998.

———. "Song." In *Friendship's Offering: A Literary Album,* edited by B.E.P., 180. London: Lupton Relfe, 1827.

Le Keux, Henry. "Seventh Plague of Egypt" [engraving]. In *Forget Me Not for 1828,* edited by Frederic Shoberl. London: R. Ackermann, 1828.

Le Keux Correspondence. James Marshall and Marie-Louise Osborn Collection, Beinecke Rare Book and Manuscript Library, Yale University. http://webtext.library.yale.edu/xml2html/beinecke.lekeux.con.html#a2

The Literary Souvenir, or Cabinet of Poetry and Romance. Edited by Alaric A. Watts. Dedication page. London: Hurst Robinson, 1826.

Lockhart, John Gibson. "Cockney School of Poetry." *Blackwood's Edinburgh Magazine* (August 1818). Reprinted in *British Literature, 1780–1830,* edited by Anne K. Mellor and Richard E. Matlack, 159–61. New York: Harcourt Brace, 1996.

Martin, John. "Seventh Plague of Egypt." Collections Database, Museum of Fine Arts, Boston. www.mfa.org/artemis/fullrecord.asp?oid=33665.

Mill, John Stuart. *The Subjection of Women.* 1869. In *Victorian Prose: An Anthology,* edited by Rosemary J. Mundhenk and LuAnn McCracken Fletcher, 121–31. New York: Columbia University Press, 1999.

"Mimili" [engraving]. Drawn by F. F. Burney and engraved by W. I. Fry. In *Forget Me Not: A Christmas and New Year's Present for 1824,* edited by Frederic Shoberl. London: R. Ackermann, 1824.

The Mirror of Literature, Amusement and Instruction. Vol. 10, no. 288, supp. (December 1827). Project Gutenberg, February 2004. www.gutenberg.org/etext/11326.

———. Vol. 14, no. 402, supp. (1829). Project Gutenberg, March 2004. http://www.gutenberg.org/files/11457/11457-h/11457-h.htm.

———. Vol. 16, no. 474, supp. (January 1831). Project Gutenberg, June 2004. http://www.gutenberg.net/dirs/1/2/6/8/12685/12685-h/12685-h.htm

Montgomery, James. "Epitaph on a Gnat." In *Forget Me Not: A Christmas and New Year's Present for MDCCCXXIX,* edited by Frederic Shoberl, 67. London: R. Ackermann, 1829.

"Mother and Child" [engraving]. In *The Literary Souvenir; or, Cabinet of Poetry and Romance,* edited by Alaric A. Watts, 64. London: Hurst Robinson, 1825.

Neele, Henry. "Forget Me Not." In *Forget Me Not: A Christmas and New Year's Present for 1825,* edited by Frederic Shoberl, 4–5. London: R. Ackermann, 1825.

The New Comic Annual for 1831 [Falstaff's Annual]. Preface, v–viii. London: Hurst, Chance, 1831.

The New Forget-Me-Not: A Calendar. Illustrated by Rex Whistler. London: Cobden-Sanderson, 1930.

The New Keepsake. Illustrated by Rex Whistler. London: Cobden-Sanderson, 1931.

Norton, Caroline. Notice to Readers. In *Fisher's Drawing Room Scrap-Book,* 2. London: Fisher, Son, and Jackson, 1847.

Old Poor Robin: An Almanack. London: Company of Stationers, 1800.

P., B. E. Preface to *Friendship's Offering: A Literary Album,* edited by B.E.P., iii–vii. London: Lupton Relfe, 1827.

Patmore, Coventry. "The Angel in the House." 1854–62. In *The Norton Anthology of English Literature,* edited by M. H. Abrams, 2:1599–1601. 6th ed. New York: W. W. Norton, 1993.

Pinnock, W. *Iconology; or, Emblematic Figures Explained, in Original Essays on Moral and Instructive Subjects.* London: John Harris, 1830.

Pocock, I. "The Parting." In *The Musical Bijou: An Album of Music, Poetry, and Prose, for MDCCCXXX,* edited by F. H. Burney, 123. London: Goulding and D'Almaine, 1830.

"Poetical Address." In *Forget Me Not: A Christmas and New Year's Present for 1823,* edited by Frederic Shoberl, 3–4. London: R. Ackermann, 1823.

The Poetical Register and Repository of Fugitive Poetry for 1802. 2nd ed. London: F. and C. Rivington, 1803.

Polwhele, Richard. "To a Young Lady Playing at Chess." In *Forget Me Not: A Christmas, New Year's and Birthday Present,* edited by Frederic Shoberl, 325–26. London: Ackerman [*sic*] and Co., 1834.

————. *The Unsex'd Females* [facsimile and introduction]. 1798. Electronic Text Center, University of Virginia Library, 1994. http://etext.lib.virginia.edu/britpo/unsex/unsex.html.

Pope, Alexander. "The First Epistle of the Second Book of Horace." In *The Complete Poetical Works of Alexander Pope*, edited by Henry Walcott Boynton, n.p. Boston: Houghton, Mifflin & Co., 1903.

"Préface aux dames." In *Hommage aux Dames,* edited by Charles Malo. Paris: Chez Janet, 1815. Translated by Christophe Pouchot, 2004.

Pringle, Thomas. Preface to *Friendship's Offering: A Literary Album and Christmas and New Year's Present for 1831,* edited by Thomas Pringle, v-vi. London: Smith Elder, 1831.

————. Preface to *Friendship's Offering: A Literary Album and Christmas and New Year's Present for 1832,* edited by Thomas Pringle, v-vii. London: Smith Elder, 1832.

————. Preface to *Friendship's Offering, and Winter's Wreath: A Christmas and New Year's Present, for MDCCCXXXIII,* edited by Thomas Pringle, v–vii. London: Smith Elder, 1833.

Quarles, Francis. *Emblems, divine and moral, together with Hieroglyphicks of the life of man.* London, 1635. http://emblem.libraries.psu.edu/quarltoc.htm.

"Reading the News" [engraving]. In *Friendship's Offering: A Literary Album, and Christmas and New Year's Present, for MDCCCXXX,* edited by Thomas Pringle. London: Smith Elder, 1830.

Reynolds, Frederic Mansel. Preface to *The Keepsake for 1828,* v–viii. London: Hurst, Chance, 1828.

————. Preface to *The Keepsake for 1829,* iii–v. London: Hurst, Chance, 1829.

Robberds, John W., ed. *A Memoir of the Life and Writings of the Late William Taylor,* vol. 1. London: John Murray, 1843.

Rosa. "Hope and Memory." In *Friendship's Offering: A Literary Album,* edited by B.E.P., 68. London: Lupton Relfe, 1827.

Roscoe, Thomas, ed. *The Landscape Annual: The Tourist in Switzerland and Italy.* London: Robert Jennings and William Chaplin, 1830.

Roscoe, William. "Lines." In *The Keepsake for 1829,* edited by Frederic Mansel Reynolds, 312. London: Hurst, Chance, 1829.

Rowton, Frederic. Preface to *The Female Poets of Great Britain.* 1853. Reprint, Detroit: Wayne State University Press, 1981.

"Rushbrook Hall, Suffolk" [engraving]. In *The Country and Town Ladies' Memorandum Book, or Polite Pocket Museum.* London: Otridge and Rackham, 1822.

Ruskin, John. "Of Queen's Garden." 1864. In *Victorian Prose: An Anthology,* edited by Rosemary J. Mundhenk and LuAnn McCracken Fletcher, 259–65. New York: Columbia University Press, 1999.

Sackville-West, Vita. Introduction to *The Annual: Being a Selection from the* Forget-Me-Nots, Keepsakes *and Other Annuals of the Nineteenth Century,* edited by Dorothy Wellesley, i–x. London: Cobden-Sanderson, 1930.

"Sacontala" [engraving]. In *Forget Me Not: A Christmas and New Year's Present for 1825,* edited by Frederic Shoberl. London: R. Ackermann, 1825.

Schloss's English Bijou Almanac for 1841. London: A. Schloss, 1841.

Scott, Sir Walter. "I have song of war for knight." Title page of *Literary Souvenir,* edited by Alaric A. Watts. London: Hurst Robinson, 1826.

———. *The Waverley Album.* London: Charles Heath, [c. 1838].

Senefelder, Alois. *A Complete Course of Lithography.* London: Ackermann, 1819.

"The Seventh Plague" [engraving]. In *Forget Me Not; A Christmas and New Year's Present for MDCCCXXVIII,* edited by Frederic Shoberl. London: R. Ackermann, 1828.

Shelley, Mary. *Frankenstein; or, The Modern Prometheus.* 1818. Edited by J. Paul Hunter. London: W. W. Norton, 1996.

Shelley, Percy Bysshe. "A Defense of Poetry." 1822. In *Shelley's Poetry and Prose.* Edited by Donald H. Reiman and Sharon B. Powers, 480-508. New York: Norton, 1977.

Sheridan, Richard. *School for Scandal.* London, 1777.

"She Walks in Beauty, Like the Night" [engraving]. In *The Comic Annual [The Anniversary of the Literary Fun],* edited by Thomas Hood. 2nd ed. London: Charles Tilt, 1830.

Shoberl, Frederic. Editor's note in *Forget Me Not: A Christmas and New Year's Present for MDCCCXXIX,* 161. London: R. Ackermann, 1829.

———. Editor's note in *Forget Me Not: A Christmas and New Year's Present for MDCCCXLIV,* 353. London: R. Ackermann, 1844.

———. Letter to T. J. Serle, February 28, 1835. British Library, 1835 Add. 52477 f. 156.

———. *Narrative of the Most Remarkable Events Which Occurred in and near Leipzig . . . 1813.* 7th ed. London: R. Ackermann, 1814.

———. *Parables by D. F. A. Krummacher: Translated from the German by Frederic Shoberl.* London: R. Ackermann, 1824.

———. Preface/"Advertisement" to *Forget Me Not: A Christmas and New Year's Present for 1823,* v–viii. London: R. Ackermann, 1823.

———. Preface to *Forget Me Not: A Christmas and New Year's Present for 1824,* iii–iv. London: R. Ackermann, 1824.

———. Preface to *Forget Me Not: A Christmas and New Year's Present for 1825,* i–iv. London: R. Ackermann, 1825.

———. Preface to *Forget Me Not: A Christmas and New Year's Present for 1826,* i–iii. London: R. Ackermann, 1826.

———. Preface to *Forget Me Not: A Christmas and New Year's Present for 1827,* iii–vi. London: R. Ackermann, 1827.

———. Preface to *Forget Me Not: A Christmas and New Year's Present for 1828,* iii–iv. London: R. Ackermann, 1828.

———. Preface to *Forget Me Not: A Christmas and New Year's Present for MDCCCXXIX,* iii–v. London: R. Ackermann, 1829.

———. Preface and editor's note to *Forget Me Not: A Christmas and New Year's Present for MDCCCXXX,* iii–vi, 38. London: R. Ackermann, 1830.

———. Preface to *Forget Me Not: A Christmas, New Year's and Birthday Present,* 5–6. London: Ackerman [*sic*] and Co., 1834.

———. Preface to *Forget Me Not: A Christmas and New Year's Present for MDCCCXXXV,* 3–6. London: Ackermann and Co., 1835.

———. Preface to *Forget Me Not: A Christmas and New Year's Present for MDCCCXLIV,* 3–6. London: R. Ackermann, 1844.

———. *A Short Account of Successful Exertions in Behalf of the Fatherless and Widows after the War in 1814.* Oxford, UK: Printed for private circulation, 1871.

Simpson, Stephen. *Simpson's Gentleman's Almanack and Pocket Journal.* London: J. Sharpe, 1816.

"Single Blessedness" [engraving]. In *The Comic Annual; The Anniversary of the Literary Fun,* edited by Thomas Hood. 2nd ed. London: Charles Tilt, 1830.

Smith, George Murray. *Recollections of a Long and Busy Life.* 1896. Edited by Bill Bell. Unpublished manuscript, University of Edinburgh.

"Sonnet." In *Vergissmeinnicht ein Taschenbüch,* edited by H. Clauren [Karl Heun]. Leipzig, 1821. Translated by Gerhard Joseph and Scott Westrem, 2004.

Southey, Robert. *The Annual Anthology.* London: Longman and O. Rees, 1800.

———. *Selections from the Letters of Robert Southey,* vol. 1. London, 1856.

"A Spill Case" [engraving]. In *The Comic Annual; The Anniversary of the Literary Fun,* edited by Thomas Hood. 2nd ed. London: Charles Tilt, 1830.

Stephanoff, P. "Constancy" [engraving]. In *Forget Me Not: A Christmas and New Year's Present for MDCCCXXIX,* edited by Frederic Shoberl. London: R. Ackermann, 1829.

Swain, Charles. "Constancy." In *Forget Me Not: A Christmas and New Year's Present for MDCCCXXIX,* edited by Frederic Shoberl, 162. London: R. Ackermann, 1829.

Swift, Jonathan. "The Lady's Dressing Room." 1732. In *The Longman Anthology of British Literature,* vol. 1C, edited by David Damrosch and Stuart Sherman, 2445–48. 2nd ed. New York: Longman, 2003.

Taylor, William. *Historic Survey of German Poetry, Interspersed with Various Translations,* vol. 2. London: Treuttel and Würtz 1830.

———. *A Memoir of the Life and Writings of the Late William Taylor,* vol. 1. London, 1843.

Thackeray, William. *Vanity Fair: A Novel without a Hero,* vols. 5 and 6. Harvard Classics Shelf of Fiction. New York: P. F. Collier and Son, 1917. Reprint, Bartleby.com, 2000. www.bartleby.com/305/.

[———]. "A Word on the Annuals" (taken from *Fraser's Magazine*). *London Times,* December 26, 1837.

Thompson, Mr. "This is affection's tribute." Title page for *Friendship's Offering.* London: Smith Elder, 1829–44.

Thurston, J., and J. Thomas. *Religious Emblems, Being a Series of Engravings on Wood, Executed by the First Artists in That Line, from Designs Drawn on the Blocks Themselves by J. Thurston, Esq.; The Descriptions Written by the Rev. J. Thomas, A.M.* London: T. Bensley and R. Ackermann, 1809. Facsimile, www.archive.org/stream/religiousemblemsoothur#page/n5/mode/1up.

Twain, Mark. *Adventures of Huckleberry Finn.* New York: Penguin Group, 1959.

Vergissmeinnicht ein Taschenbüch. Edited by H. Clauren [Karl Heun]. Leipzig, 1818 and 1821.

Vox Stellarum, or a Loyal Almanack. Edited by Francis Moore. London: Company of

Stationers, 1800.

Watts, Alaric A., ed. *Cabinet of Modern Art and Literary Souvenir.* 2nd series. London: Whittaker, 1836.

———. "The Conversazione: A Fragment." In *The Literary Souvenir,* edited by Alaric A. Watts, 222–51. London: Longman, Rees, Orme, Brown and Green, 1832.

———. Preface to *The Literary Souvenir, or Cabinet of Poetry and Romance,* edited by Alaric A. Watts, iii–viii. London: Hurst Robinson, 1825.

———. Preface and Postscript to *The Literary Souvenir, or Cabinet of Poetry and Romance,* edited by Alaric A. Watts, v–xi, 412. London: Hurst Robinson, 1826.

———. Preface to *The Literary Souvenir; or Cabinet of Poetry and Romance,* edited by Alaric A. Watts, v–xvi. London: Longman, 1827.

———. Preface to *The Literary Souvenir; or Cabinet of Poetry and Romance,* edited by Alaric A. Watts, v–xvi. London: Longman, Rees, Orme, Brown and Green, 1828.

———. Preface and Postscript to *The Literary Souvenir,* edited by Alaric A. Watts, v–xii, 364–65. London: Longman, Rees, Orme, Brown and Green, 1830.

———. Preface to *Literary Souvenir,* edited by Alaric A. Watts, v–x. London: Longman, Rees, Orme, Brown and Green, 1832.

———. Preface to *Literary Souvenir and Cabinet of Modern Art,* edited by Alaric A. Watts, v–viii. New series. London: Whittaker and Co., 1835.

Watts, Alaric Alfred. *Alaric Watts: A Narrative of His Life, by His Son, Alaric Alfred Watts.* 2 vols. London: R. Bentley and Son, 1884.

Wellesley, Dorothy, ed. *The Annual Being a Selection from the Forget-Me-Nots, Keepsakes, and other Annuals of the Nineteenth Century*. London: Cobden-Sanderson, 1929.

[Wilde, Jane F.] "The Countess of Blessington." *Dublin University Magazine* 45 (1855): 333–53.

Wilson, John. "Monologue, or Soliloquy on the Annuals." *Blackwood's Edinburgh Magazine* 26 (December 1829): 948–76. Available in *The Poetess Archive*, 2004.

Wither, George. *A collection of Emblemes, Ancient and Moderne, Quickened withe metricall illustrations, both Morall and divine: And Disposed into lotteries, that instruction, and good counsell, may bee furthered by an honest and pleasant recreation.* 4 vols. London, 1635. http://emblem.libraries.psu.edu/withetoc.htm.

Wollstonecraft, Mary. "Letter V." In *Letters Written during a Short Residence in Sweden, Norway, and Denmark,* 37–52. Edited by Carol H. Poston. Lincoln: University of Nebraska Press, 1976.

——— [Mr. Creswick]. *The Female Reader.* London: Joseph Johnson, 1789. In *The Works of Mary Wollstonecraft,* vol. 4, edited by Janet Todd and Marilyn Butler. New York: New York University Press, 1989.

———. "Professions for Women." In *The Norton Anthology of English Literature,* vol. 2, 2006–10. Gen. ed. M. H. Abrams. 5th ed. New York: W. W. Norton, 1986.

———. *A Vindication of the Rights of Woman.* 1792. In *A Wollstonecraft Anthology,* edited by Janet Todd, 84–114. New York: Columbia University Press, 1989.

Wordsworth, William. "Lines Written a Few Miles above Tintern Abbey." In *The Longman Anthology of British Literature,* vol. 2A, edited by Susan Wolfson and Peter Manning, 352–56. New York: Longman, 2003.

SECONDARY TEXTS

366 "Ackermann." In *Dictionary of National Biography (DNB),* 1:58–59. Oxford: Oxford University Press, 1917.

Adas, Michael. *Machines as the Measure of Men.* Ithaca, NY: Cornell University Press, 1989.

Adburgham, Alison. *Women in Print: Writing Women and Women's Magazines from the Restoration to the Accession of Victoria.* London: George Allen and Unwin, 1972.

———. *Silver Fork Society: Fashionable Life and Literature from 1814–1840.* London: Constable, 1983.

Albree, Joe, and Scott H. Brown. "'A Valuable Monument of Mathematical Genius': *The Ladies' Diary,* 1704–1840." *Historia Mathematica* 36 (2009): 10–47.

Alexander, Christine. "'That Kingdom of Gloom': Charlotte Brontë, the Annuals, and the Gothic." *Nineteenth-Century Literature* 47, no. 4 (March 1993): 409–36.

Alexander, Meena. *Women in Romanticism.* Totowa, NJ: Barnes and Noble Press, 1989.

"Almanac." In *Oxford English Dictionary Online.* 2nd ed., 1989. Oxford: Oxford University Press, 2004.

Almeida, Joselyn. "Blanco White and the Making of Anglo-Hispanic Romanticism." *European Romantic Review* 17, no. 4 (October 2006): 437–56.

Althusser, Louis. "Ideology and Ideological State Apparatuses." 1969. In *Essays on Ideology,* 1–60. London: Verso, 1984.

Altick, Richard D. *The English Common Reader: A Social History of the Mass Reading Public, 1800–1900.* Chicago: University of Chicago Press, 1957.

Ames, Carol. "Nature and Aristocracy in V. Sackville-West." In *British Novelists since 1900,* edited by Jack I. Biles, 117–33. New York: AMS, 1987.

Ammon, Theodore G. "A Note on a Note in 'The Library of Babel.'" *Romantic Notes* 33, no. 3 (Spring 1993): 265–69.

Anderson, Benedict. *Imagined Communities: Reflections on the Origin and Spread of Nationalism.* Rev. ed. New York: Verso, 1991.

Anderson, Donovan. "Franco-German Conversations: Rahel Levin and Sopie von Grotthu in Dialogue with Germaine de Staël." *German Studies Review* 29, no. 3 (2006): 559–77.

Anderson, Katherine. "Almanacs and the Profits of Natural Knowledge." In *Culture and Science in the Nineteenth-Century Media,* edited by Louise Henson, Geoffrey Cantor, Gowan Dawson, Richard Noakes, Sally Shuttleworth, and Jonathan R. Topham, 91–111. Aldershot, UK: Ashgate, 2004.

Annals of English Literature, 1475–1950, edited by Robert William Chapman, 134–35. 2nd ed. Oxford: Clarendon Press, 1961.

"Anthology." In *Oxford English Dictionary Online.* 2nd ed., 1989. Oxford: Oxford University Press, 2004.

"Archive." In *Oxford English Dictionary.* CD-ROM. Oxford: Oxford University Press, 1999.

Armstrong, Isobel. "The Gush of the Feminine: How Can We Read Women's Poetry of the Romantic Period?" In *Romantic Women Writers: Voices and Countervoices,* edited by Paula R. Feldman and Theresa M. Kelley, 13–32. Hanover, NH: University Press of New England, 1995.

———. "A Music of Thine Own: Women's Poetry—an Expressive Tradition?" In *Victorian Women Poets: A Critical Reader,* edited by Angela Leighton, 245–76. Cambridge, UK: Blackwell Publishers, 1996.

Armstrong, Isobel, Joseph Bristow, and Cath Sharrock, eds. *Nineteenth-Century Women Poets.* Oxford: Clarendon Press, 1996.

Armstrong, Nancy. *Desire and Domestic Fiction: A Political History of the Novel.* New York: Oxford University Press, 1989.

Ashfield, Andrew, ed. *Romantic Women Poets, 1770–1838: An Anthology.* Manchester: Manchester University Press, 1995.

Atheneum Index of Reviews and Reviewers, 1830–1870. Online. Updated by Susan Jones, Ph.D. candidate, December 1998. http://web.soi.city.ac.uk/~asp/v2/home.html.

Austern, Linda Phyllis. "The Siren, the Muse, and the God of Love: Music and Gender in Seventeenth Century English Emblem Books." *Journal of Musicology Research* 18, no. 2 (1998): 95–138.

Bain, Ian. "Gift Book and Annual Illustrations." 1912. In *Literary Annuals and Gift Books: A Bibliography, 1823–1903,* edited by Eleanore Jamieson and Ian Bain, 19–25. Middlesex, UK: Private Libraries Association, 1973.

Baker, John P. "Rescuing the Record: A Centennial History of Preservation at the New York Public Library, Part I: 1895–1945." *Biblion: The Bulletin of the New York Public Library* 4, no. 1 (Fall 1995): 36–63.

Barthes, Roland. "Death of the Author." 1968. In *Image Music Text,* 142–48. Translated by Stephen Heath. New York: Hill and Wang, 1977.

———. "From Work to Text." In *Image Music Text,* 154–64. Translated by Stephen Heath. New York: Hill and Wang, 1977.

Beal, Peter. "Notions in Garrison: The Seventeenth-Century Commonplace Book." In *New Ways of Looking at Old Texts,* edited by W. Speed Hill, 131–47. Binghamton, NY: Medieval and Renaissance Texts and Studies, 1993.

Beall, Karen F. "The Interdependence of Printer and Printmaker in Early 19th-Century Lithography." *Art Journal* 39, no. 3 (Spring 1980): 195–201.

Beauvais, Jennifer. "Domesticity and the Female Demon in Charlotte Dacre's *Zofloya* and Emily Brontë's *Wuthering Heights.*" *Romanticism on the Net* 44 (2006): 1–10.

Beetham, Margaret. *A Magazine of Her Own: Domesticity and Desire in the Woman's Magazine, 1800–1914.* London: Routledge, 1996.

Beetham, Margaret, and K. Boardman, eds. *Victorian Women's Magazines: An Anthology.* Manchester: Manchester University Press, 2001.

Behrendt, Stephen C. "The Gap That Is Not a Gap: British Poetry by Women, 1802–1812." In *Romanticism and Woman Poets: Opening the Doors of Reception,* edited by Harriet Kramer Linkin and Stephen C. Behrendt, 25–45. Lexington: University Press of Kentucky, 1999.

Bell, Bill. "The Secret History of Smith and Elder: 'The Publisher's Circular' as a Source for Publishing History." In *A Genius for Letters: Booksellers and Bookselling from the 16th to the 20th Century,* edited by Robin Myers and Michael Harris, 167–79. New Castle, DE: Oak Knoll Press, 1995.

Benjamin, Walter. "The Work of Art in the Age of Mechanical Reproduction." In *Illuminations,* 217–51. Translated by Harry Zohn. New York: Harcourt Brace, 1968.

Bennett, Betty T. "Feminism and Editing Mary Wollstonecraft Shelley: The Editor and?/or? the Text." In *Palimpsest: Editorial Theory in the Humanities,* edited by George Bornstein and Ralph G. Williams, 67–96. Ann Arbor: University of Michigan Press, 1993.

———. *Mary Diana Dods: A Gentleman and a Scholar.* Baltimore, MD: Johns Hopkins University Press, 1994.

Bermingham, Ann. *Learning to Draw: Studies in the Cultural History of a Polite and Useful Art.* New Haven, CT: Yale University Press, 2000.

———. "Urbanity and the Spectacle of Art." In *Romantic Metropolis: The Urban Scene of British Culture, 1780–1840,* edited by James Chandler and Kevin Gilmartin, 151–76. Cambridge: Cambridge University Press, 2005.

"Biedermeier." In *Encyclopedia of the Romantic Era,* edited by Christopher John Murray, 1:88–89. London: Fitzroy Dearborn, 2004.

Blain, Virginia. "Letitia Elizabeth Landon, Eliza Mary Hamilton, and the Genealogy of the Victorian Poetess." *Victorian Poetry* 33, no. 1 (Spring 1995): 31–52.

Bleich, David. "Gender Interests in Reading and Language." In *Gender and Reading: Essays on Readers, Texts and Contexts,* edited by Elizabeth A. Flynn and Patrocinio P. Schweickart, 234–66. Baltimore, MD: Johns Hopkins University Press, 1986.

Bock, Carol. "'Our Plays': The Brontë Juvenilia." In *The Cambridge Companion to the Brontës,* edited by Heather Glen, 34–52. Cambridge: Cambridge University Press, 2002.

Boisset-Astier Claude. "A French Bookbinder in London: Auguste Marie de Caumont." *Book Collector* (Summer 1981): 182–215.

Booth, Bradford Allen. Preface and introduction to *A Cabinet of Gems: Short Stories from the English Annuals,* ix, 1–19. Berkeley: University of California Press, 1938.

———. "Taste in the Annuals." *American Literature* 14, no. 3 (November 1942): 299–305.

Borges, Jorge Luis. "The Library of Babel." 1941. In *Ficciones*. Edited by Anthony Kerrigan, 79–88. New York: Grove Press, 1994.

Bornstein, George. "How to Read a Page: Modernism and Material Textuality." *Studies in the Literary Imagination* 32, no. 1 (Spring 1999): 29–58.

Bose, A. "The Verse of the English 'Annuals.'" *Review of English Studies* 4, no. 13 (January 1953): 38–51.

Bossche, Chris R. Vanden. "The Value of Literature: Representations of Print Culture in the Copyright Debate of 1837–1842." *Victorian Studies* 38, no. 1 (Autumn 1994): 41–68.

Boyle, Andrew. Preface to *An Index to the Annuals (1820–1850).* Vol. 1, *The Authors,* iii–vi. Worcester, UK: Andrew Boyle, 1967.

Boyle, Catherine, and Zachary Leader. Introduction to "Literary Institutions." In *Romantic Period Writings, 1798–1832: An Anthology,* edited by Zachary Leader and Ian Haywood, 182–87. London: Routledge, 1998.

Brander, Laurence. *Thomas Hood.* London: Longmans, Green, 1963.

Brandt, Bruce. "Teaching Spenser: The Three Graces." In *Proceedings of the Eighth Annual Northern Plains Conference on Earlier British Literature*, edited by Robert J. DeSmith, 63–70. Sioux Center: Dordt College, 2000.

Breisach, Ernst. *On the Future of History: The Postmodernist Challenge and Its Aftermath.* Chicago: University of Chicago Press, 2003.

Burke, William Jeremiah. *Rudolf Ackermann: Promoter of the Arts and Sciences.* New York: New York Public Library, 1935.

Burrows, Toby. "Toward a Typology of the Electronic Text." Unpublished paper, October 1997.

Burwick, Frederick. Foreword to "William Taylor of Norwich: A Study of the Influence of Modern German Literature in England" [1897], by Georg Herzfeld, 2–4. Translated by Astrid Wind. *A Romantic Circles Scholarly Resource.* 2007. www.rc.umd.edu/sites/default/files/chandler_herzfeld.pdf.

Calè, Luisa. *Henry Fuseli's Milton Gallery: "Turning Readers into Spectators."* Oxford: Oxford University Press, 2006.

Caplan, Cora. "Mary Wollstonecraft's Reception and Legacies." In *Cambridge Companion to Mary Wollstonecraft,* edited by Claudia L. Johnson, 246–70. Cambridge: Cambridge University Press, 2002.

Capp, Bernard. "The Potter Almanacs." *Electronic British Library Journal* 4, Article 4, 2004.

Carter, John. *ABC for Book Collectors.* 7th ed. Revised by Nicolas Barker. New Castle, DE: Oak Knoll Press, 1995.

CEIR Project Report 5. "British Fiction, 1800–1829: A Database of Production and Reception, Phase II: *The Flowers of Literature.*" *Cardiff Corvey: Reading the Romantic Text* 7 (December 2001): online.

Chandler, David. "William Taylor's Pluralist Project: The Major Translations, 1789–91." *European Romantic Review* 11, no. 3 (2000): 259–76.

"Charles Heath, the Engraver." www.jjhc.info/heathcharles1848.htm.

Chartier, Roger. "Readers and Readings in the Electronic Age." *Text-e.org.* http://text-e.org/conf/index.cfm?fa=printable&ConfText_ID=5.

Chartier, Roger, Lydia Cochrane, and Guglielmo Cavallo. *A History of Reading in the West.* Amherst: University of Massachusetts Press, 2003.

Charvat, William. *The Profession of Authorship in America, 1800–1870.* New York: Columbia University Press, 1992.

Clubbe, John. Introduction to *Selected Poems of Thomas Hood.* Cambridge, MA: Harvard University Press, 1970.

———. Introduction to *Victorian Forerunner: The Later Career of Thomas Hood.* Durham, NC: Duke University Press, 1968.

Colclough, Stephen. "Clare and the Annuals: A Previously Unpublished Letter from John Clare to L.T. Ventouillac, Editor of *The Iris.*" *Notes and Queries* 244, no. 4 (December 1999): 468–70.

Copeland, Edward. *Women Writing about Money: Women's Fiction in England, 1790–1820.* Cambridge: Cambridge University Press, 1995.

Costa, Shelley. "The *Ladies' Diary:* Gender, Mathematics, and Civil Society in Early-Eighteenth-Century England." *Osiris,* 2nd ser., 17 (2002): 49–73.

Crook, Nora, ed. *Mary Shelley's Literary Lives and Other Writings.* London: Pickering and Chatto, 2002.

———. "Sleuthing towards a Mary Shelley Canon." *Women's Writing* 6, no. 3 (October 1999): 413–24.

Cruse, Amy. *The Englishman and His Books in the Early Nineteenth Century.* New York: Thomas Y. Crowell, 1930.

Culler, Jonathan. "Reading as a Woman." In *On Deconstruction: Theory and Criticism after Structuralism,* 43–64. Ithaca, NY: Cornell University Press, 1982.

Curran, Stuart. "The I Altered." In *Romanticism and Feminism,* edited by Anne K. Mellor, 185–207. Bloomington: Indiana University Press, 1988.

Currie, Janette. "Two Early Versions of Tales from Literary Annuals." *Studies in Hogg and His World* 11 (2000): 87–121.

Darnton, Robert. "What Is the History of Books?" *Daedalus* 111, no. 3 (1982): 65–83.

Davies, J. Q. "Julia's Gift: The Social Life of Scores, c. 1830." *Journal of the Royal Musical Association* (2006): 1–23.

Dawes, Kathryn. "Anonymity and the Pressures of Publication in the Early Nineteenth Century." In *Cardiff Corvey: Reading the Romantic Text* 4, no. 3 (May 2000): online.

Day, Aidan. *Romanticism.* New York: Routledge, 1996.

Derrida, Jacques. *Archive Fever: A Freudian Impression.* Translated by Eric Prenowitz. Chicago: University of Chicago Press, 1996.

Di Bello, Patrizia. "Mrs. Birkbeck's Album: The Hand-Written and the Printed in Early Nineteenth-Century Print Culture." *19: Interdisciplinary Studies in the Long Nineteenth Century* 1 (2005). www.19.bbk.ac.uk/index.php/19/article/view/435.

Dibert-Himes, Glenn T. "Sight, Sound, and Sense: LEL's Multimedia Productions." In *Approaches to Teaching British Women Poets of the Romantic Period,* edited by Stephen C. Behrendt and Harriet Kramer Linkin, 170–74. New York: Modern Language Association of America, 1997.

Dickinson, Cindy. "Creating a World of Books, Friends, and Flowers: Gift Books and Inscriptions, 1825–60." *Winterthur Portfolio: A Journal of American Material Culture* 31, no. 1 (Spring 1996): 53–66.

Dock, Julie Bates. *The Press of Ideas: Readings for Writers on Print Culture and the Information Age.* Boston: Bedford Books / St. Martin's Press, 1996.

Dooley, Allan C. *Author and Printer in Victorian England.* Charlottesville: University Press of Virginia, 1992.

Douglas, Wallace W. "Wordsworth as Businessman." *PMLA* 63, no. 2 (June 1948): 638–40.

Douglass, Paul. "Lord Byron's Feminist Canon: Notes toward Its Construction." *Romanticism on the Net* 43 (August 2006): 1–18.

Easley, Alexis. *First-Person Anonymous: Women Writers and Victorian Print Media, 1830–1870.* Burlington, VT: Ashgate, 2004.

Edgecombe, Rodney Stenning. "Emblems and Ecphrases." *Dickens Quarterly* 27, no. 2 (June 2010): 105.

"Edward F. Burney." Tate Collection. December 1997. www.tate.org.uk.

Eilenberg, Susan. "Nothing's Namelessness: Mary Shelley's *Frankenstein.*" In *The Faces of Anonymity: Anonymous and Pseudonymous Publications from the Sixteenth to the Twentieth Century,* edited by Robert J. Griffin, 167–92. New York: Palgrave Macmillan, 2003.

Eisenstein, Elizabeth. *Divine Art, Infernal Machine: The Reception of Printing in the West from First Impressions to the Sense of an Ending*. Philadelphia: University of Pennsylvania Press, 2012.

"Emblem." In *Oxford English Dictionary Online.* 2nd ed., 1989. Oxford: Oxford University Press, 2004.

"Ephemera." In *Webster's New Universal Unabridged Dictionary.* 2nd ed. New York: Simon and Schuster, 1979.

Erickson, Lee. *The Economy of Literary Form: English Literature and the Industrialization of Publishing, 1800–1850.* Baltimore, MD: Johns Hopkins University Press, 1996.

Ess, Charles. "The Political Computer: Hypertext, Democracy, and Habermas." In *Hyper/Text/Theory,* edited by George Landow, 225–67. Baltimore, MD: Johns Hopkins University Press, 1994.

Ezell, Margaret. *Writing Women's Literary History.* Baltimore, MD: Johns Hopkins University Press, 1996.

Faxon, Frederick W. *Literary Annuals and Gift Books: A Bibliography, 1823–1903.* Reprint, Surrey, UK: Gresham Press, 1973. Originally published 1912.

Feldman, Paula R. "Endurance and Forgetting: What the Evidence Suggests." In *Romanticism and Women Poets: Opening the Doors of Reception,* edited by Harriet Kramer Linkin and Stephen C. Behrendt, 15–21. Lexington: University Press of Kentucky, 1999.

———. Introduction to *The Keepsake for 1829,* 7–25. Peterborough, ON: Broadview, 2006.

———. "The Poet and the Profits: Felicia Hemans and the Literary Marketplace." *Keats-Shelley Journal: Keats, Shelley, Byron, Hunt, and Their Circles* 46 (1997): 148–76. Reprinted in *Women's Poetry, Late Romantic to Late Victorian: Gender and Genre, 1830–1900,* edited by Isobel Armstrong and Virginia Blain, 71–101. New York: Macmillan–St. Martin's, 1999.

———. "Woman Poets and Anonymity in the Romantic Era." *New Literary History* 33 (2002): 279–89.

———. "Women, Literary Annuals, and the Evidence of Inscription." *Keats-Shelley Journal* 55 (2006): 54–62.

Feldman, Paula R., and Theresa M. Kelley, eds. *Romantic Women Writers: Voices and Countervoices.* Hanover, NH: University Press of New England, 1995.

Feldman, Paula R., and Daniel Robinson, eds. *A Century of Sonnets: The Romantic-Era Revival.* New York: Oxford University Press, 1999.

Felman, Shoshana. *Writing and Madness.* Translated by Martha Noel Evans and Brian Massumi. Ithaca, NY: Cornell University Press, 1987.

Fergus, Jan, and Janice Farrar Thaddeus. "Women, Publishing, and Money, 1790–1820." *Studies in Eighteenth Century Culture* 17 (1987): 191–208.

Ferris, Ina. "Antiquarian Authorship: D'Israeli's Miscellany of Literary Curiosity and the Question of Secondary Genres." *Studies in Romanticism* 45 (Winter 2006): 523–42.

Ferry, Anne. *Tradition and the Individual Poem: An Inquiry into Anthologies.* Stanford: Stanford University Press, 2001.

"Finden, William." In *LoveToKnow 1911 Online Encyclopedia.* November 2004.

Finke, Laurie A. "Afterword: From Text to Work." In *Feminist Theory, Women's Writing,* 191–96. Ithaca, NY: Cornell University Press, 1992.

Flint, Kate. *The Woman Reader, 1837–1914.* Oxford, UK: Clarendon Press, 1995.

Flynn, Elizabeth A. "Gender and Reading." In *Gender and Reading: Essays on Readers, Texts and Contexts,* edited by Elizabeth A. Flynn and Patrocinio P. Schweickart, 267–88. Baltimore, MD: Johns Hopkins University Press, 1986.

Ford, John. *Ackermann 1783–1983: The Business of Art.* London: Ackermann, 1983.

———. "Ackermann Imprints and Publications." In *Maps and Prints: Aspects of the English Booktrade,* edited by Robin Myers and Michael Harris, 109–24. Oxford: Oxford Polytechnic, 1984.

Ford, John, and Ted Fraser. *George Ackermann (1803–1891): Brave New Worlds.* Charlottetown, PEI: Confederation Centre Art Gallery and Museum, 1999.

Foucault, Michel. "What Is an Author?" 1979. In *The Foucault Reader; Language, Counter-Memory, Practice: Selected Essays and Interviews,* edited by Paul Rabinow, 101–20. New York: Random House, 1984.

Francis, Emma. "Letitia Landon: Public Fantasy and the Private Sphere." *Essays and Studies* 51 (1998): 93–115.

Franklin, Colin. "The Prison Manuscripts of William Combe." *Essays and Studies* 26 (1973): 53–65.

Freedman, Estelle. "Two Case Studies of Hysteria." In *Victorian Women: A Documentary Account of Women's Lives in Nineteenth-Century England, France and the United States,* edited by Erna Olafson Hellerstein, Leslie Parker Hume, and Karen M. Offen, 110–13. Stanford: Stanford University Press, 1995.

Freud, Sigmund. "A Note upon the 'Mystic Writing Pad.'" In *Collected Papers,* 175–80. Translated by Joan Riviere. London: Hogarth Press, 1925.

Furr, Derek. "Sentimental Confrontations: Hemans, Landon, and Elizabeth Barrett." *English Language Notes* 40, no. 2 (December 2002): 29–47.

Fuss, Diana. *Essentially Speaking: Feminine, Nature and Difference.* New York: Routledge, 1989.

Gallagher, Catherine. *Nobody's Story: The Vanishing Acts of Women Writers in the Marketplace, 1670–1820.* Los Angeles: University of California Press, 1995.

Galloway, Alexander R. *Protocol: How Control Exists after Decentralization.* Cambridge, MA: MIT Press, 2004.

Garvey, Ellen Gruber. "Anonymity, Authorship, and Recirculation: A Civil War Episode." *Book History* 9 (2006): 159–78.

———. "Scissorizing and Scrapbooks: Nineteenth-Century Reading, Remaking, and Recirculating." In *New Media: 1740–1915,* edited by Lisa Gitelman and Geoffrey B. Pingree, 207–27. Cambridge, MA: MIT Press, 2003.

Gaskell, Philip. *A New Introduction to Bibliography.* New York: Oxford University Press, 1972.

Gassan, Richard H. "Carey and Lea: Printer and Publisher." *From Revolution to Reconstruction* (November 20, 2002). http://odur.let.rug.nl/~usa/E/carey_lea/carey03.htm.

———. "First American Tourist Guidebooks: Authorship and Print Culture in the 1820s." *Book History* 8 (2005): 51–74.

Gaull, Marilyn. *English Romanticism: The Human Context.* 6th ed. New York: W. W. Norton, 1988.

Gellrich, Jesse. *The Idea of the Book in the Middle Ages: Language Theory, Mythology and Fiction.* Ithaca, NY: Cornell University Press, 1985.

Genette, Gerard. *Paratexts: Thresholds of Interpretation.* Translated by Jane E. Lewin. Cambridge: Cambridge University Press, 1997.

Gernes, Todd S. "Recasting the Culture of Ephemera." In *Popular Literacy: Studies in Cultural Practices and Poetics,* edited by John Trimbur, 107–27. Pittsburgh: University of Pittsburgh Press, 2001.

Gezari, Janet. "Fathoming 'Remembrance': Emily Bronte in Context." *ELH* 66, no. 4 (1999): 965–84.

"Gift Books and Annuals." *American Memory.* Library of Congress. http://memory.loc.gov/ammem/awhhtml/awgc1/gift.html.

"Gift Books and Annuals." Harris Collection, Brown University. February 2003. www.brown.edu/Facilities/University_Library/collections/harris/Harris.GiftB.html.

Gigante, Denise. *Taste: A Literary History.* New Haven, CT: Yale University Press, 2005.

Gilbert, Sandra M., and Susan Gubar. *The Madwoman in the Attic: The Woman Writer and the Nineteenth-Century Literary Imagination.* New Haven, CT: Yale University Press, 1984.

Glynn, Jennifer. *Prince of Publishers: A Biography of George Smith.* London: Allison and Busby, 1986.

Godburn, Mark. "The Earliest Dust Jackets—Lost and Found." *Script and Print* 32, no. 4 (2008): 233–39.

———. "A Short History of Sealed Wrappings." October 2010. www.finebooksmagazine.com/fine_books_blog/2009/04/earliest-known-dust-jacket-found-at-oxford.phtml.

Golden, Catherine J. *Images of the Woman Reader in Victorian British and American Fiction.* Gainesville: University Press of Florida, 2003.

Gorsky, Susan Rubinow. *Femininity to Feminism: Women and Literature in the Nineteenth Century.* New York: Twayne Publishers, 1992.

Green, David Bonnell. "William Wordsworth and Lydia Huntley Sigourney." *New England Quarterly* 37, no. 4 (December 1964): 527–31.

Greetham, David. *Textual Scholarship: An Introduction.* New York: Garland, 1994.

———. *Textual Transgressions: Essays toward the Construction of a Biobibliography.* New York: Garland, 1998.

———. *Theories of the Text.* New York: Oxford University Press, 1999.

Greg, W. W. "The Rationale of Copy-Text." *Studies in Bibliography* 3 (1950–51): 19–36.

Griest, Guinevere. *Mudie's Circulating Library and the Victorian Novel.* Bloomington: Indiana University Press, 1970.

Griffin, Robert J., ed. *The Faces of Anonymity: Anonymous and Pseudonymous Publications from the Sixteenth to the Twentieth Century.* New York: Palgrave Macmillan, 2003.

Grigely, Joseph. *Textualterity: Art, Theory and Textual Criticism.* Ann Arbor: University of Michigan Press, 1995.

Hall, Martin. "Gender and Reading in the Late Eighteenth Century: The *Bibliothèque Universelle des Romans.*" *Eighteenth-Century Fiction* 14, nos. 3–4 (April–July 2002): 771–89.

Haller, William. *The Early Life of Robert Southey, 1774–1803.* New York: Columbia University Press, 1917.

Harris, Jocelyn. "Does Anybody Own This Text? Eighteenth-Century Readers as Consumers and Producers." *Age of Johnson* 13 (2002): 457–71.

Harris, Katherine D. "Borrowing, Altering and Perfecting the Literary Annual Form—or What It Is Not: Emblems, Almanacs, Pocket-Books, Albums, Scrapbooks and Gifts Books." *Poetess Archive Journal* 1, no. 1 (2007). https://journals.tdl.org/paj/index.php/paj/article/view/23.

———. "Feminizing the Textual Body: Women and Their Literary Annuals in Nineteenth-Century Britain." *Publications of the Bibliographical Society of America* 99, no. 4 (December 2005): 573–622.

———. *The Forget Me Not: A Hypertextual Archive of Ackermann's Nineteenth-Century Literary Annual; An Edition from the Poetess Archive.* www.orgs.miamioh.edu/anthologies/fmn/.

———. *The Forgotten Gothic: Short Stories from British Literary Annuals, 1823–1831.* Crestline, CA: Zittaw Press, 2012.

———. "Literary Annual." In *The Encyclopedia of Romantic Literature,* edited by Frederick Burwick, Nancy M. Goslee, and Diane Long Hoeveler, 791–803. Oxford, UK: Blackwell Publishing, 2012.

———. "Rudolph Ackermann." In *The Encyclopedia of Romantic Literature,* edited by Frederick Burwick, Nancy M. Goslee, and Diane Long Hoeveler, 15–19. Oxford, UK: Blackwell Publishing, 2012.

Harris, Susan K. Review of *Before Victoria: Extraordinary Women of the British Romantic Era,* by Elizabeth Campbell Denlinger. *Nineteenth-Century Contexts* 27, no. 4 (December 2005): 383–403.

Hasler, Johann. "Performative and Multimedia Aspects of Late-Renaissance Meditative Alchemy: The Case of Michael Maier's *Atalanta Fugiens* (1617)." *Revista* 39 (2011): 135–44.

Havelock, Eric A. *The Muse Learns to Write.* New Haven, CT: Yale University Press, 1986.

Hawkins, Ann R. "'Delectable' Books for 'Delicate' Readers: The 1830s Giftbook Market, Ackermann and Co., and the Countess of Blessington." *Kentucky Philological Review* 16 (2002): 20–26.

———. "'Formed with Curious Skill': Blessington's Negotiation of the 'Poetess' in *Flowers of Loveliness.*" *Romanticism on the Net* 29–30 (February–May 2003). www.erudit.org.

———. "Marguerite, Countess of Blessington, and L.E.L.: Evidence of a Friendship." *ANQ: A Quarterly Journal of Short Articles, Notes, and Reviews* 16, no. 2 (2003 Spring): 27–32.

———. "Marketing Gender and Nationalism: Blessington's *Gems of Beauty/L'Écrin* and the Mid-Century Book Trade." *Women's Writing* 12, no. 2 (November 2005): 225–31.

Herzfeld, Georg. "William Taylor of Norwich: A Study of the Influence of Modern German Literature in England." 1897. Translated by Astrid Wind, with an introduction by David Chandler and foreword by Frederick Burwick. *A Romantic Circles Scholarly Resource.* 2007. www.rc.umd.edu/ sites/default/files/chandler_herzfeld.pdf.

Hewitt, Martin. Review of *Women and the People: Authority, Authorship and the Radical Tradition in Nineteenth-Century England,* by Helen Rogers. *Nineteenth-Century Contexts* 27, no. 4 (December 2005): 400–403.

Hewitt, Regina. *Possibilities of Society: Wordsworth, Coleridge and the Sociological Viewpoint of English Romanticism.* Albany, NY: SUNY Press, 1997.

Hickock, Kathleen. *Representations of Women: Nineteenth-Century British Women's Poetry.* Westport, CT: Greenwood Press, 1984.

Hill, Richard. "Scott, Hogg, and the Gift-Book Editors." *Romantic Textualities: Literature and Print Culture, 1780–1840* 19 (Winter 2009). http://www.romtext.org.uk/articles/rt19_n01/.

Hill, Rosemary. "A. C. Pugin." *Burlington Magazine* 138, no. 1114 (January 1996): 11–19.

———. "Reformation to Millennium: Pugin's Contrasts in the History of English Thought." *Journal of the Society of Architectural Historians* 58, no. 1 (March 1999): 26–41.

Hoagwood, Terence. *Politics, Philosophy and the Production of Romantic Texts.* DeKalb: Northern Illinois University Press, 1996.

Hoagwood, Terence Allan, and Kathryn Ledbetter. *"Colour'd Shadows": Contexts in Publishing, Printing, and Reading Nineteenth-Century British Women Writers.* New York: Palgrave Macmillan, 2005.

Hofkosh, Sonia. *Sexual Politics and the Romantic Author.* Cambridge: Cambridge University Press, 1998.

———. "The Writer's Ravishment: Women and the Romantic Author—The Example of Byron." In *Romanticism and Feminism,* edited by Anne K. Mellor, 93–113. Bloomington: Indiana University Press, 1988.

Hogg, James. *Contributions to Annuals and Gift-Books.* Edinburgh: Edinburgh University Press, 2006.

Holland, Jeane. "Scraps, Stamps and Cutouts: Emily Dickinson's Domestic Technologies of Publication." In *Cultural Artifacts and the Production of Meaning: The Page, the Image, and the Body,* edited by Margaret J. M. Ezell and Katherine O'Brien O'Keeffe, 139–81. Ann Arbor: University of Michigan Press, 1994.

Homans, Margaret. "Keats Reading Women, Women Reading Keats." *Studies in Romanticism* 29 (Fall 1990): 341–70.

Hootman, Harry. "British Literary Annuals and Giftbooks, 1823–1861." University of South Carolina, 2004. *Dissertation Abstract* 65, no. 4 (October 2004): 1379.

Horwitz, Barbara J. *British Women Writers, 1700–1850: An Annotated Bibliography of Their Works and Works about Them.* Lanham, MD: Scarecrow Press, 1997.

Howe, Ellic. *A List of London Bookbinders, 1648–1815.* London: Bibliographical Society, 1950. MacDonnell Press, 2011.

Hunnisett, Basil. *Steel-Engraved Book Illustration in England.* Boston: David R. Godine, 1980.

Hunt, Leigh. *Leigh Hunt's Literary Criticism.* Edited by Lawrence Huston Houtchens and Carolyn Washburn Houtchens. New York: Octagon, 1976.

Hutchison, Earl R. "Giftbooks and Literary Annuals: Mass Communication Ornaments." *Journalism Quarterly* 44 (1967): 470–74.

Huxley, Leonard. *The House of Smith Elder.* London: privately printed, 1923.

Introduction to Richard Polwhele's *The Unsex'd Female.* 1798. University of Virginia E-Text Center, 1994. http://etext.lib.virginia.edu/britpo/unsex/unsex.html.

Irigaray, Luce. *This Sex Which Is Not One.* Translated by Catherine Porter. Ithaca, NY: Cornell University Press, 1985.

Jack, Ian. *English Literature, 1815–1832.* Oxford, UK: Clarendon Press, 1963.

Jackson, J. R. de J. *Romantic Poetry by Women: A Bibliography, 1770–1835.* Oxford, UK: Clarendon Press, 1993.

Jacobs, Edward. "Eighteenth-Century British Circulating Libraries and Cultural Book History." *Book History* 6 (2003): 1–22.

Jacobus, Mary. *Reading Woman.* New York: Columbia University Press, 1986.

Jervis, Simon. "Rudolph Ackermann." In *London: World City, 1800–1840,* edited by Celina Fox, 97–109. New Haven, CT: Yale University Press, 1992.

Jordan, John O., and Carol T. Christ, eds. *Victorian Literature and Victorian Visual Imagination.* Berkeley: University of California Press, 1995.

Jump, Harriet Devine. "'The False Prudery of Public Taste': Scandalous Women and the Annuals, 1820–1850." In *Feminist Readings of Victorian Popular Culture: Divergent Femininities,* edited by Emma Liggins and Daniel Duffy, 1–17. Aldershot, UK: Ashgate, 2001.

Kaplan, Nancy. "Literacy beyond Books: Reading When All the World's a Web." In *The World Wide Web and Contemporary Cultural Theory: Magic, Metaphor, Power,* edited by Andrew Herman and Thomas Swiss, 207–34. New York: Routledge, 2000.

Keane, Angela. *Women Writers and the English Nation in the 1790s: Romantic Belonging.* Cambridge: Cambridge University Press, 2001.

Keep, Christopher. "Blinded by the Type: Gender and Information Technology at the Turn of the Century." *Nineteenth Century Contexts: An Interdisciplinary Journal* 23, no. 1 (2001): 149–73.

Kennedy, Deborah. Review of *Gothic Feminism: The Professionalization of Gender from Charlotte Smith to the Brontës,* by Diane Long Hoeveler. *Romantic Circles* (May 1999): n.p.

Keynes, G. L. *William Pickering, Publisher: A Memoir and a Check-List of His Publications.* Rev. ed. New York: B. Franklin, 1969.

Kilgour, Frederick. *The Evolution of the Book.* New York: Oxford University Press, 1998.

Kirkham, E. Bruce, John W. Fink, and Ralph Thompson. *Indices to American Literary Annuals and Gift Books, 1825–1865.* New Haven, CT: Research Publications, 1975.

Kontje, Todd. "Male Fantasies, Female Readers: Fictions of the Nation in the Early Restoration." *German Quarterly* 68, no. 2 (Spring 1995): 131–46.

Kooistra, Lorraine Janzen. *Poetry, Pictures, and Popular Publishing: The Illustrated Gift Book and Victorian Visual Culture, 1855–1875.* Athens: Ohio University Press, 2011.

Kooy, Michael John. *Coleridge, Schiller, and Aesthetic Education.* New York: Palgrave, 2002.

Korsmeyer, Carolyn. "Tastes and Pleasures." In *Romantic Gastronomies,* edited by Denise Gigante. *Romantic Circles* (January 2007): n.p.

Kutcher, Matthew. "Flowers of Friendship: Gift Books and Polite Culture in Early Nineteenth-Century Britain." Ph.D. diss., University of Michigan, 1999. *Dissertation Abstract* 59, no. 10 (April 1999): 3830–31.

Lachèvre, Frédéric. *Bibliographie sommaire des keepsakes et autres recueils collectifs de la période romantique, 1823–1848.* Paris: L. Giraud-Badin, 1929.

Lambourne, Lionel. *Victorian Painting.* London: Phaidon Press, 1999.

Lawford, Cynthia. "Bijoux beyond Possession: The Prima Donnas of L.E.L.'s Album Poems." In *Women's Poetry, Late Romantic to Late Victorian: Gender and Genre, 1830–1900,* edited by Isobel Armstrong and Virginia Blain, 102–14. New York: Macmillan–St. Martin's, 1999.

———. "'Thou Shalt Bid Thy Fair Hands Rove': L.E.L.'s Wooing of Sex, Pain, Death and the Editor." *Romanticism on the Net* 29–30 (February–May 2003). www.erudit.org.

Leader, Zachary, and Ian Haywood, eds. *Romantic Period Writings, 1798–1832: An Anthology.* London: Routledge, 1998.

Ledbetter, Kathryn. "'BeGemmed and beAmuletted': Tennyson and Those 'Vapid' Gift Books." *Victorian Poetry* 34, no. 2 (Summer 1996): 235–45.

———. "'The Copper and Steel Manufactory' of Charles Heath." *Victorian Review* 28, no. 2 (2002): 21–30.

———. "Domesticity Betrayed: *The Keepsake* Literary Annual." *Victorian Newsletter* 99 (Spring 2001): 16–24.

———. "Lucrative Requests: British Authors and Gift Book Editors." *Papers of the Bibliographic Society of America* 88, no. 2 (June 1994): 207–16.

———. "Protesting Success: Tennyson's 'Indecent Exposure' in the Periodicals." *Victorian Poetry* 43, no. 1 (2005): 53–73.

———. "'White Vellum and Gilt Edges': Imaging *The Keepsake*." *Studies in the Literary Imagination* 30, no. 1 (Spring 1997): 35–47.

Ledbetter, Kathryn, and Terence Hoagwood. "Introduction to *The Keepsake*." In *L.E.L.'s Verses and "The Keepsake" for 1829: A Hypertext Edition*. Edited by Terence Hoagwood and Kathryn Ledbetter. *Romantic Circles, Electronic Editions* (April 2002). www.rc.umd.edu/editions/contemps/lel/keepsake.htm.

Lee, Debbie. "*The Wild Wreath:* Cultivating a Poetic Circle for Mary Robinson." *Studies in the Literary Imagination* 30, no. 1 (Spring 1997): 23–33.

Lehuu, Isabelle. *Carnival on the Page: Popular Print Media in Antebellum America*. Chapel Hill: University of North Carolina Press, 2000.

Leighton, Angela. "'Because Men Made the Laws': The Fallen Woman and the Woman Poet." In *Victorian Women Poets: A Critical Reader,* edited by Angela Leighton, 215–34. Cambridge, UK: Blackwell Publishers, 1996.

Leighton, Angela, and Margaret Reynolds. Introductions I and II in *Victorian Women Poets: An Anthology,* edited by Angela Leighton and Margaret Reynolds, xxv–xl. Cambridge, UK: Blackwell Publishers, 1995.

Levy, Valery. "Lydia Maria Child and the Abolitionist Gift-Book Market." In *Popular Nineteenth-Century American Women Writers and the Literary Marketplace,* edited by Earl Yarington and Mary De Jong, 137–52. Newcastle upon Tyne, UK: Cambridge Scholars Publishing, 2007.

Lieberman, Michael. "Earliest Known Dust Jacket Found at Oxford." *Book Patrol: A Haven for Book Culture,* April 19, 2009. http://bookpatrol.net/earliest-known-dust-jacket-found-at-oxford/.

Linkin, Harriet K. "Romantic Aesthetics in Mary Tighe and Letitia Landon: How Women Poets Recuperate the Gaze." *European Romantic Review* 7, no. 2 (Winter 1997): 159–88.

Linkon, Sherry Lee. "Reading Lind Mania: Print Culture and the Construction of Nineteenth-Century Audiences." *Book History* 1 (1998): 94–106.

Linley, Margaret. "A Centre That Would Not Hold: Annuals and Cultural Democracy." In *Nineteenth-Century Media and the Construction of Identities,* edited by Laurel Brake, Bill Bell, and David Finkelstein, 54–74. New York: Palgrave, 2000.

———. "The Early Victorian Annual (1822–1857)." *Victorian Review* 35, no. 1 (Spring 2009): 13–19.

———. "Sappho's Conversations in Felicia Hemans, Letitia Landon, and Christina Rossetti." *Prism(s): Essays in Romanticism* 4 (1996): 15–42.

"Literary Annuals." American Antiquarian Society. September 2004. www.americanantiquarian.org/annuals.htm.

"Literary Annuals." Special Collections and Archive, University of Liverpool. April 2004. http://www.liv.ac.uk/library/sca/colldescs/litann.html.

Lodge, Sara. "Romantic Reliquaries: Memory and Irony in the Literary Annuals." *Romanticism: The Journal of Romantic Culture and Criticism* 10, no. 1 (2004): 23–40.

Lokke, Kari. "Poetry as Self-Consumption: Women Writers and Their Audiences in British and German Romanticism." In *Romantic Poetry: Comparative History of Literatures in European Languages,* edited by Angela Esterhammer, 91–111. Amsterdam: Benjamins, 2002.

Lootens, Tricia. "Hemans and Her American Heirs: Nineteenth-Century Women's Poetry and National Identity." In *Women's Poetry, Late Romantic to Late Victorian: Gender and Genre, 1830–1900,* edited by Isobel Armstrong and Virginia Blain, 243–60. New York: Macmillan–St. Martin's, 1999.

———. "Hemans and Home: Victorianism, Feminine 'Internal Enemies,' and the Domestication of National Identity." *PMLA* 109, no. 2 (March 1994): 238–53.

———. "Receiving the Legend, Rethinking the Writer: Letitia Landon and the Poetess Tradition." In *Romanticism and Women Poets: Opening the Doors of Reception,* edited by Harriet Kramer Linkin and Stephen C. Behrendt, 242–59. Lexington: University Press of Kentucky, 1999.

Louis, Margot K. "Enlarging the Heart: LEL's 'The Improvisatrice,' Heman's 'Properzia Rossi,' and Barrett Browning's Aurora Leigh." *Victorian Literature and Culture* 26, no. 1 (1998): 1–17.

Löwenthal, Leo. *Literature and Mass Culture.* New Brunswick, NJ: Transaction Publishers, 1984.

Mack, Anne, and J. J. Rome. "Marxism, Romanticism and Postmodernism." *South Atlantic Quarterly* 88, no. 3 (1989): 605–32.

Maidment, Brian. "'Penny' Wise, 'Penny' Foolish? Popular Periodicals and the 'March of Intellect' in the 1820s and 1830s." In *Nineteenth-Century Media and the Construction of Identities,* edited by Laurel Brake, Bill Bell, and David Finkelstein, 104–21. New York: Palgrave, 2000.

———. "Re-arranging the Year: The Almanac, the Day Book and the Year Book as Popular Literary Forms, 1789–1860." *Rethinking Victorian Culture* (2000): 91–113.

Malcomson, Robert W. *Popular Recreations in English Society, 1700–1850.* London: Cambridge University Press, 1973.

Mandell, Laura. "Hemans and the Gift-Book Aesthetic." *Cardiff Corvey: Reading the Romantic Text* 6 (June 2001). www.cf.ac.uk/encap/corvey/update/index.html.

———. "Introduction: The Poetess Tradition." *Romanticism on the Net* 29–30 (February–May 2003). www.erudit.org.

———. "Putting Contents on the Table: The Disciplinary Anthology and the Field of Literary Criticism." *Poetess Archive Journal* 1, no. 1 (2007): 1–34. https://journals.tdl.org/paj/index.php/paj/article/view/29/31.

Manning, Peter J. "Wordsworth in the *Keepsake,* 1829." In *Literature in the Marketplace,* edited by John O. Jordan and Robert L. Patten, 44–73. Cambridge: Cambridge University Press, 1995.

Marchand, Leslie A., ed. *Letters of Thomas Hood from the Dilke Papers in the British Museum.* New York: Octagon, 1972.

Maxted, Ian. "The London Book Trades, 1775–1800: A Preliminary Checklist of Members." Folkstone, 1977. *Exeter Working Papers in British Book Trade History.* 2007. http://bookhistory.blogspot.com/2007/01/london-1775-1800-introduction.html.

Mayo, Robert. "Gothic Romance in the Magazines." *PMLA* 65, no. 5 (September 1950): 762–89.

———. "The Gothic Short Story in the Magazines." *Modern Language Review* 37 (1942): 448–54.

McClintock, Anne. *Imperial Leather: Race, Gender and Sexuality in the Colonial Contest.* New York: Routledge, 1995.

McGann, Jerome J. *A Critique of Modern Textual Criticism.* Charlottesville: University of Virginia Press, 1992. Originally published 1983.

———. *The Poetics of Sensibility: A Revolution in Literary Style.* Oxford: Clarendon Press, 1996.

———. *The Romantic Ideology: A Critical Investigation.* Chicago: University of Chicago Press, 1983.

———. "The Rossetti Archive and Image-Based Electronic Editing." *Journal of Pre-Raphaelite Studies* 6 (Spring 1997): 5–21.

———. *The Textual Condition.* Princeton: Princeton University Press, 1991.

McGill, Meredith. Introduction to *American Literature and the Culture of Re-printing, 1834–1853.* Philadelphia: University of Pennsylvania Press, 2007.

McKenzie, D. F. *Bibliography and the Sociology of Texts.* New York: Cambridge University Press, 1999.

McKeon, Michael. *The Origins of the English Novel, 1600–1740.* Baltimore, MD: Johns Hopkins University Press, 1988.

McMullen, B. J. "Precursors of the Dustwrapper." *Bulletin* 24, no. 4 (2000): 257–66.

Mellor, Anne. *Romanticism and Gender.* New York: Routledge, 1992.

Mitch, David F. *The Rise of Popular Literacy in Victorian England: The Influence of Private Choice and Public Policy.* Philadelphia: University of Pennsylvania Press, 1992.

Mitchell, W. J. T. *Iconology: Image, Text, Ideology.* Chicago: University of Chicago Press, 1987.

Monthly Review, The. Waterloo Directory of English Newspapers and Periodicals: 1800–1900 Series 2, edited by John S. North. http://www.victorianperiodicals.com/series2/.

Moring, Meg M. "George Eliot's Scrupulous Research: The Facts Behind Eliot's Use of the *Keepsake* in *Middlemarch.*" *Victorian Periodicals Review* 26, no. 1 (Spring 1993): 19–23.

Moser, Kay. "The Victorian Critics' Dilemma: What To Do with a Talented Poetess?" *Victorians Institute Journal* 13 (1985): 59–66.

Mueller-Vollmer, Kurt. "On Germany: Germaine de Staël and the Internationalization of Romanticism." In *The Spirit of Poesy: Essays on Jewish and German Literature and Thought in Honor of Ge'za von Molnar,* edited by Richard Block and Peter Fenves, 150–66. Evanston: Northwestern University Press, 2000.

Mussell, James, and Suzanne Paylor. "Mapping the 'Mighty Maze': The Nineteenth-Century Serials Edition." *Interdisciplinary Studies in the Long Nineteenth Century* 19, no. 1 (2005). www.19.bbk.ac.uk.

Nestor, Pauline A. "A New Departure in Women's Publishing: The English Woman's Journal and the Victoria Magazine." *Victorian Periodicals Review* 15, no. 3 (Fall 1982): 93–106.

Newlyn, Lucy. *Reading, Writing and Romanticism: The Anxiety of Reception.* Oxford: Oxford University Press, 2003.

"Nineteenth-Century British and American Literary Annuals." Rare Books and Special Collections, University of South Carolina, Columbia. www.sc.edu/library/spcoll/britlit/litann.html

Nissenbaum, Stephen. *The Battle for Christmas.* New York: Vintage, 1997.

Nunberg, Geoffrey, ed. *The Future of the Book.* Berkeley: University of California Press, 1996.

P., W. "Rudolph Ackermann of the Strand, Publisher." *Notes and Queries,* 4th series, vol. 4 (August 7, 1869): 109–12.

———. "Rudolph Ackermann of the Strand, Publisher." *Notes and Queries* 4th series, vol. 4 (August 14, 1869): 129–31.

Paley, Morton D. "Coleridge and the Annuals." *Huntington Library Quarterly* 57, no. 1 (Winter 1994): 1–24.

Pasco, Allan H. "Literature as Historical Archive." *New Literary History* 35, no. 3 (Summer 2004): 373–94.

Pascoe, Judith. "Mary Robinson and the Literary Marketplace." In *Romantic Women Writers: Voices and Countervoices,* edited by Paula R. Feldman and Theresa M. Kelley, 252–68. Hanover, NH: University Press of New England, 1995.

———. "Poetry as Souvenir: Mary Shelley in the Annuals." In *Mary Shelley in Her Times,* edited by Betty T. Bennett and Stuart Curran, 173–84. Baltimore, MD: Johns Hopkins University Press, 2000.

Past Masters, 2004–2005. InteLex. www.nlx.com.

Pearl, Matthew. *The Dante Club.* New York: Random House, 2004.

Pearson, Jacqueline. "Women Reading, Reading Women." In *Women and Literature in Britain, 1500–1700,* edited by Helen Wilcox, 80–99. Cambridge: Cambridge University Press, 1996.

———. *Women's Reading in Britain, 1750–1835: A Dangerous Recreation.* Cambridge: Cambridge University Press, 1999.

Peers, E. Allison. "The Literary Activities of the Spanish 'Emigrados' in England (1814–1834)." *Modern Language Review* 19, no. 3 (July 1924): 315–24.

"Periodicals Indexed" and "Choice of Periodicals." *Science in the Nineteenth-Century Periodical.* www.sciper.org/coverage.html.

Perkins, Maureen. *Visions of the Future: Almanacs, Time, and Cultural Change, 1775–1870.* Oxford: Oxford University Press, 1996.

Peterson, Linda H. "Rewriting a History of the Lyre: Letitia Landon, Elizabeth Barrett Browning and the (Re)Construction of the Nineteenth-Century Woman Poet." In *Women's Poetry, Late Romantic to Late Victorian: Gender and Genre, 1830–1900,* edited by Isobel Armstrong and Virginia Blain, 115–32. New York: Macmillan–St. Martin's, 1999.

Phegley, Jennifer. *Educating the Proper Woman Reader: Victorian Family Literary Magazines and the Cultural Health of the Nation.* Columbus: Ohio State University Press, 2004.

Phelps, C. Deirdre. "Where's the Book? The Text in the Development of Literary Sociology." *TEXT* 9 (1996): 63–92.

Pike, Judith. "Resurrection of the Fetish in *Gradiva, Frankenstein,* and *Wuthering Heights.*" In *Romantic Women Writers: Voices and Countervoices,* edited by Paula Feldman and Theresa M. Kelley, 150–58. Hanover, NH: University Press of New England, 1995.

Piper, Andrew. *Dreaming in Books: The Making of the Bibliographic Imagination in the Romantic Age.* Chicago: University of Chicago Press, 2009.

"Pocket-book." In *Oxford English Dictionary Online.* 2nd ed., 1989. Oxford: Oxford University Press, 2004.

Poovey, Mary. *The Proper Lady and the Woman Writer: Ideology as Style in the Works of Mary Wollstonecraft, Mary Shelley, and Jane Austen.* Chicago: University of Chicago Press, 1985.

Potter, Franz. *The History of Gothic Publishing, 1800–1835: Exhuming the Trade.* New York: Palgrave Macmillan, 2005.

Price, Leah. *The Anthology and the Rise of the Novel.* Cambridge: Cambridge University Press, 2003.

Pulham, Patricia. "'Jewels–Delights–Perfect Loves': Victorian Women Poets and the Annuals." In *Victorian Women Poets: Essays and Studies,* edited by Alison Chapman, 9–31. Woodbridge, UK: Brewer, 2003.

Quarles, Francis. *Emblems, divine and moral, together with Hieroglyphicks of the life of man / written by Francis Quarles,* London, 1635. http://emblem.libraries.psu.edu/quarltoc.htm.

Rajan, Tilottama. "Framing the Corpus: Godwin's 'Editing' of Wollstonecraft in 1798." *Studies in Romanticism* 39, no. 4 (Winter 2000): 511.

———. "Mary Shelley's 'Mathilda': Melancholy and the Political Economy of Romanticism." *Studies in the Novel* 26, no. 2 (Summer 1994): 43–69.

———, ed. *Romanticism, History and the Possibilities of Genre: Re-forming Literature, 1789–1837.* Cambridge: Cambridge University Press, 1998.

Rappoport, Jill. "Buyer Beware: The Gift Poetics of Letitia Elizabeth Landon." *Nineteenth-Century Literature* 58, no. 4 (March 2004): 441–73.

Raven, James. *The Business of Books: Booksellers and the English Book Trade, 1450–1850.* New Haven, CT: Yale University Press, 2007.

Reilly, Susan. Review of *The Economy of Character: Novels, Market Culture, and the Business of Inner Meaning,* by Deidre Lynch. *Romanticism on the Net* 13 (February 1999): 1–5.

Renier, Anne. *Friendship's Offering: An Essay on the Annuals and Gift Books of the 19th Century.* London: Private Libraries Association, 1964.

Rhodes, Jacqueline. "Copyright, Authorship and the Professional Writer: The Case of William Wordsworth." *Cardiff Corvey: Reading the Romantic Text* 8 (June 2002). www.cf.ac.uk/encap/corvey/update/index.html.

"Richard Westall." In *LoveToKnow 1911 Online Encyclopedia.* November 2004.

Riess, Daniel. "Laetitia Landon and the Dawn of English Post-Romanticism." *Studies in English Literature* 36, no. 4 (Autumn 1996): 807–27.

Robinson, Charles. *Mary Shelley: Collected Tales and Stories with Original Engravings.* Baltimore, MD: Johns Hopkins University Press, 1990.

Robinson, Eric. "John Clare and Weather Lore." *John Clare Society Journal* 14 (1995): 61–79.

Robinson, Jeffrey C. "The Poetics of Expiration: Felicia Hemans." *Romanticism on the Net* 29–30 (February–May 2003). www.erudit.org.

Robson, Catherine. "Standing on the Burning Deck: Poetry, Performance, History." *PMLA* 120, no. 1 (January 2005): 148–62.

Rogers, Katherine. *Feminisms in Eighteenth Century England.* Champaign: University of Illinois Press, 1982.

Rose, Mark. *Authors and Owners: The Invention of Copyright.* Cambridge, MA: Harvard University Press, 1993.

Ross, Marlon B. "The Configurations of Feminine Reform: The Woman Writer and the Tradition of Dissent." In *Re-visioning Romanticism: British Women Writers, 1776–1837,* edited by Carol Shiner Wilson and Joel Haefner, 91–110. Philadelphia: University of Pennsylvania Press, 1994.

———. *The Contours of Masculine Desire: Romanticism and the Rise of Women's Poetry.* New York: Oxford University Press, 1989.

———. "Romantic Quest and Conquest: Troping Masculine Power in the Crisis of Poetic Identity." In *Romanticism and Feminism,* edited by Anne K. Mellor, 26–51. Bloomington: Indiana University Press, 1988.

Rowton, Frederic. Introduction to *The Female Poets of Great Britain.* 1853. Reprint, Detroit: Wayne State University Press, 1981.

Ruwe, Donelle. Introduction. *Nineteenth-Century Contexts* 27, no. 4 (December 2005): 311–14.

Ryan, Marie-Laure. *Narrative as Virtual Reality: Immersion and Interactivity in Literature and Electronic Media.* Baltimore, MD: Johns Hopkins University Press, 2001.

Samuels, Allen M. "Publishing the Picturesque: Ackermann, Rowlandson, and the Art Scene." *Trivium* 29–30 (1997): 239–56.

———."Rudolph Ackermann and *The English Dance of Death.*" *Book Collector* 23, no. 3 (Autumn 1974): 371–80.

Sanders, Valerie. "'Meteor Wreaths': Harriet Martineau, 'L.E.L.', Fame and *Fraser's Magazine.*" *Critical Survey* 13, no. 2 (2001): 42–60.

Saul, Nicholas. "Aesthetic Humanism (1790–1830)". In *The Cambridge History of German Literature*, edited by Helen Watanabe-O'Kelly, 202–71. Cambridge: Cambridge University Press, 1997.

Scholz, Bernhard F. "From Illustrated Epigram to Emblem: The Canonization of a Typographical Arrangement." In *New Ways of Looking at Old Texts,* edited by W. Speed Hill, 149–57. Binghamton, NY: Medieval and Renaissance Texts and Studies, 1993.

———. "Re-editing the Book of Nature: Observations on a Nineteenth-Century Attempt at Modernizing a Seventeenth-Century Book of Emblems." In *Signs of Change: Transformations of Christian Traditions and Their Representation in the Arts, 1000–2000,* edited by Nils Holger Peterson, Claus Clüver, and Nicolas Bell, 191–215. New York: Rodopi, 2004.

Schweickart, Patrocinio P. "Reading Ourselves: Toward a Feminist Theory of Reading." In *Gender and Reading: Essays on Readers, Texts, and Contexts,* edited by Elizabeth A. Flynn and Patrocinio P. Schweickart, 31–62. Baltimore, MD: Johns Hopkins University Press, 1986.

Scott, Matthew. "The Circulation of Romantic Creativity: Coleridge, Drama, and the Question of Translation." *Romanticism on the Net* 2 (1996). www.erudit.org.

Secord, James A. *Victorian Sensation: The Extraordinary Publication, Reception, and Secret Authorship of* Vestiges of the Natural History of Creation. Chicago: University of Chicago Press, 2000.

Sha, Richard C. "'Keeping Them Out of Harm's Way': Sketching, Female Accomplishments, and the Shaping of Gender in Britain." In *The Visual and Verbal Sketch in British Romanticism,* 73–104. Philadelphia: University of Pennsylvania Press, 1998.

———. *Perverse Romanticism: Aesthetics and Sexuality in Britain, 1750–1832.* Baltimore, MD: Johns Hopkins University Press, 2009.

———. *The Visual and Verbal Sketch in British Romanticism.* Philadelphia: University of Pennsylvania Press, 1998.

Shaw, Margaret L. "Constructing the 'Literate Woman': Nineteenth-Century Reviews and Emerging Literacies." *Dickens Studies Annual: Essays on Victorian Fiction* 21 (1992): 195–212.

Showalter, Elaine. *The Female Malady: Women, Madness and English Culture, 1830–1980.* New York: Penguin, 1987.

———. *A Literature of Their Own: British Women Novelists from Brontë to Lessing.* Princeton: Princeton University Press, 1977.

———. "Towards a Feminist Poetics." In *Women Writing and Writing about Women,* edited by Mary Jacobus, 22–41. London: Croom Helm, 1979.

Siegel, Robert. "Gutenberg Bible Goes Digital: High-Tech Photos of Library of Congress Copy Allow Web Scrutiny." *All Things Considered.* NPR, February 19, 2002. www.npr.org/programs/atc/features/2002/feb/gutenberg/020219.gutenberg.html.

Silver, Brenda. "Whose Room of Orlando's Own? The Politics of Adaptation." In *Margins of the Text,* edited by D. C. Greetham, 57–81. Ann Arbor: University of Michigan Press, 1997.

Simpson, Ethel C. "Band of Duodecimos." *Arkansas Quarterly: A Journal of Criticism* 2, no. 3 (Summer 1993): 250–57.

Smith, Andrew, and Diana Wallace. "The Female Gothic: Then and Now." *Gothic Studies* 6, no. 1 (May 2004): 1–7.

Smith, Helen. "'Printing Your Royal Father Off': Early Modern Female Stationers and the Gendering of the British Book Trades." In *TEXT: An Interdisciplinary Annual of Textual Studies,* vol. 15, edited by W. Speed Hill and Peter L. Shillingsburg, 163–86. Ann Arbor: University of Michigan Press, 2002.

Sonoda, Akiko. "Coleridge's Later Poetry and the Rise of Literary Annuals." *Coleridge Bulletin* 26 (Winter 2005): 58–74.

Spencer, Jane. *The Rise of the Woman Novelist: From Aphra Behn to Jane Austen.* New York: Blackwell, 1987.

———. "Romantic Heroines: The Tradition of Escape." In *The Rise of the Woman Novelist: From Aphra Behn to Jane Austen,* 181–212. Oxford: Basil Blackwell, 1986.

Spender, Dale. Introduction: A Vindication of the Writing Woman. In *Living by the Pen: Early British Women Writers,* 1–34. New York: Teachers College Press, 1992.

Stallybrass, Peter. "The Library and Material Texts." *PMLA 119:5* (2004): 1347–52.

St. Clair, William. *The Reading Nation in the Romantic Period.* Cambridge: Cambridge University Press, 2004.

———. *The John Coffin Memorial Lecture in the History of the Book: The Political Economy of Reading.* Pamphlet, Institute of English Studies, 2005.

Steig, Michael. "Dickens and Browne: Illustration, Collaboration, and Iconography." In *Dickens and Phiz,* 1–23. Bloomington: Indiana University Press, 1978.

Stephenson, Glennis. "'For Women of Taste and Refinement': The Use and Abuse of the Drawing Room Annual." In *Letitia Landon: The Woman Behind L.E.L.* Manchester: Manchester University Press, 1995.

———. "Letitia Landon and the Victorian Improvisatrice: The Construction of LEL." *Victorian Poetry* 30, no. 1 (Spring 1992): 1–17.

Stevens, Joan. "'Woodcuts Dropped into the Text': The Illustrations in *The Old Curiosity Shop* and *Barnaby Rudge*." *Studies in Bibliography* 20 (1997): 114–34.

Stevenson, Randall. "A Golden Age? Readers, Authors, and the Book Trade." In *The Oxford English Literary History,* vol. 12, *1960–2000: The Last of England?* 125–61. Oxford: Oxford University Press, 2004.

Stiles, Anne. "Gypsy Scholarship: Regenia Gagnier on the Perils and Opportunities of Interdisciplinary Study." *Interdisciplinary Studies on the Long Nineteenth Century* 1 (2005). www.19.bbk.ac.uk.

Strom, Linda J. "Vita Sackville-West (9 March 1892–2 June 1962)." In *Dictionary of Literary Biography,* vol. 195, *British Travel Writers, 1910–1939,* edited by Barbara Brothers and Julia M. Gergits, 289–95. Detroit, MI: Gale Research, 1998.

Sussman, Charlotte. "Stories for the *Keepsake*." In *The Cambridge Companion to Mary Shelley,* edited by Esther Schor, 163–79. Cambridge, Cambridge University Press, 2003.

Sussman, Herbert. "Cyberpunk Meets Charles Babbage: *The Difference Engine* as Alternative Victorian History." *Victorian Studies* (Autumn 1994): 1–24.

Swann, Karen. "Harassing the Muse." In *Romanticism and Feminism,* edited by Anne K. Mellor, 81–92. Bloomington: Indiana University Press, 1988.

Tallent-Bateman, Chas. T. "The 'Forget-Me-Not.'" *Papers of the Manchester Literary Club* 28 (1902): 78–98.

Tanselle, Thomas G. "Book-Jackets, Blurbs, and Bibliographers." *Library,* 5th ser., vol. 26 (1971): 91–134.

———. *A Rationale of Textual Criticism.* Philadelphia: University of Pennsylvania Press, 1992. Based on 1987 lecture.

Taylor, Beverly. "Elizabeth Barrett Browning's Subversion of the Gift Book Model." *Studies in Brown and His Circle* 20 (1992): 62–69.

Thompson, Ann. "Feminist Theory and the Editing of Shakespeare: *The Taming of the Shrew* Revisited." In *Margins of the Text,* edited by D. C. Greetham, 83–103. Ann Arbor: University of Michigan Press, 1997.

Thompson, E. P. *The Making of the English Working Class.* New York: Vintage, 1966.

Thompson, Judith. "From Forum to Repository: A Case Study in Romantic Cultural Geography." *European Romantic Review* 15, no. 2 (June 2004): 177–91.

Thompson, Ralph. *American Literary Annuals and Gift Books, 1825–1865.* New York: H. W. Wilson, 1936.

———. "Emerson and *The Offering* for 1829." *American Literature* 6, no. 2 (May 1934): 151–57.

———. "The Liberty Bell and Other Anti-slavery Gift-Books." *New England Quarterly: A Historical Review of New England Life and Letters* 7, no. 1 (March 1934): 154–68.

Thomson, Douglass H. Review of *Romanticism and the Gothic: Genre, Reception, and Canon Formation,* by Michael Gamer. *Romanticism on the Net* 22 (May 2001): 1–4.

Todd, Janet. *The Sign of Angellica: Women, Writing and Fiction, 1660–1800.* New York: Columbia University Press, 1989.

Tomlinson, William. *Bookcloth, 1823–1980.* Stockport, UK: Dorothy Tomlinson, 1996.

Topham, Jonathan. "John Limbard, Thomas Byerley, and the Production of Cheap Periodicals in the 1820s." *Book History* 8 (2005): 75–106.

Trott, Nicola. "Sexing the Critic: Mary Wollstonecraft at the Turn of the Century." In *1798: The Year of the Lyrical Ballads,* edited by Richard Cronin, 32–67. New York: Macmillan–St. Martin's, 1998.

Tucker, Herbert F. "House Arrest: The Domestication of English Poetry in the 1820s." *New Literary History* 25, no. 3 (Summer 1994): 521–48.

Turner, Cheryl. *Living by the Pen: Women Writers in the Eighteenth Century.* New York: Routledge, 1992.

Vargo, Lisa, ed. "The *Anna Letitia Barbauld Web Page:* 1773 meets 2000." *Romanticism on the Net* 19 (August 2000). www.erudit.org.

Vera, Eugenia Roldán. *The British Book Trade and Spanish American Independence: Education and Knowledge Transmission in Transcontinental Perspective.* Aldershot, UK: Ashgate, 2003.

Vincent, Patrick Henri. "Elegiac Muses: Corinne and the Engendering of the Romantic Poetess, 1820–1840." PhD dissertation, University of California, Davis, 2000. *Dissertation Abstract* 61, no. 9 (March 2001): 3553.

———. *The Romantic Poetess: European Culture, Politics and Gender, 1820–1840.* Hanover, NH: University Press of New England, 2004.

Voss, Paul J., and Marta L. Werner. "Toward a Poetics of the Archive: Introduction." *Studies in the Literary Imagination* 32, no. 1 (Spring 1999): i–vii.

Wagner, Tamara S. "The Silver Fork Novel." *The Victorian Web: Literature, History and Culture in the Age of Victoria.* www.victorianweb.org/genre/silverfork.html.

Warne, Vanessa K. "'Purport and Design': Print Culture and Gender Politics in Early Victorian Literary Annuals." PhD dissertation, Queen's University (Canada), 2001. *Dissertation Abstracts* 62, no. 10 (April 2002): 3407.

Warrington, Bernard. "The Bankruptcy of William Pickering in 1853: The Hazards of Publishing and Bookselling in the First Half of the Nineteenth Century." *Publishing History* 27 (1990): 5–25.

Waterloo Directory of English Newspapers and Periodicals: 1800–1900. Edited by Michael Wolff. Research Society for Victorian Periodicals, n.d. www.victorianperiodicals.com/series2/TourOverview.asp.

Watt, Ian. *The Rise of the Novel: Studies in Defoe, Richardson and Fielding.* Berkeley: University of California Press, 1957.

The Wellesley Index to Victorian Periodicals, 1824–1900. Edited by Walter Edwards Houghton. Toronto: University of Toronto Press, 1966.

Wilkes, Joanne. "'Only the Broken Music'? The Critical Writings of Maria Jane Jewsbury." *Women's Writing* 7, no. 1 (2000): 105–17.

The William Blake Archive. Edited by Morris Eaves, Robert N. Essick, and Joseph Viscomi. www.blakearchive.org/.

Williams, Raymond. *Problems in Materialism and Culture.* London: Verso, 1980.

Williamson, Marilyn L. Introduction to Frederic Rowton, *The Female Poets of Great Britain,* xi–xxxii. Detroit, MI: Wayne State University Press, 1981.

Wither, George. *A collection of Emblemes, Ancient and Moderne, Quickened witheh metricall illustrations, Both Morall and divine: And Disposed into lotteries, that instruction, and good counsell, may bee furthered by an honest and pleasant recreation.* 4 vols. London, 1635. http://emblem.libraries.psu.edu/withetoc.htm.

Wolfson, Susan J. "'Domestic Affections' and 'the Spear of Minerva': Felicia Hemans and the Dilemma of Gender." In *Re-visioning Romanticism,* edited by Carol Shiner Wilson and Joel Haefner, 128–66. Philadelphia: University of Pennsylvania Press, 1994.

———. "Editing Felicia Hemans for the Twenty-First Century." *Romanticism on the Net* 19 (August 2000). http://www.erudit.org.

———. "Empson's Pregnancy." *Literary Imagination: The Review of the Association of Literary Scholars and Critics* 6, no. 2 (2004): 282–303.

———, ed. *Felicia Hemans: Selected Poems, Letters, Reception Materials.* Princeton: Princeton University Press, 2000.

———. *Formal Charges: The Shaping of Poetry in British Romanticism.* Stanford: Stanford University Press, 1997.

———. "Gendering the Soul." In *Romantic Women Writers: Voices and Countervoices,* edited by Paula R. Feldman and Theresa M. Kelley, 33–68. Hanover, NH: University Press of New England, 1995.

———. "Keats and the Manhood of the Poet." *European Romantic Review* 6, no. 1 (Summer 1995): 1–37.

———. "A Lesson in Romanticism: Gendering the Soul." In *Lessons of Romanticism: A Critical Companion,* edited by Thomas Pfau and Robert F. Gleckner, 349–75. Durham, NC: Duke University Press, 1998.

———. "Mary Wollstonecraft and the Poets." In *The Cambridge Companion to Mary Wollstonecraft,* edited by Claudia L. Johnson, 160–88. Cambridge: Cambridge University Press, 2002.

———. "'A Problem Few Dare Imitate': *Sardanapalus* and 'Effeminate Character.'" *ELH* 58 (1991): 867–901.

———. "Representing Some Late Romantic-Era, Non-canonical Male Poets: T. Hood . . ." *Romanticism on the Net* 19 (August 2000).

———. "'Their She Condition': Cross-Dressing and the Politics of Gender in *Don Juan.*" *ELH* 54, no. 3 (Fall 1987): 585–617.

Wu, Duncan. *Romantic Women Poets: An Anthology.* 2nd ed. Oxford: Blackwell, 1998.

Zimmerman, Sarah M. *Romanticism, Lyricism and History.* Albany, NY: SUNY Press, 1999.

Index

The letter *n* following a page number refers to a note; the letter *f* following a page number refers to a figure; the letter *t* following a page number refers to a table.

www.ingramcontent.com/pod-product-compliance
Lightning Source LLC
Chambersburg PA
CBHW060632310726
48982CB00003B/748